Focused Issues in Family Therapy

Series Editor

D. Russell Crane, Brigham Young University, Provo, UT, USA

More information about this series at http://www.springer.com/series/13372

Arlene Vetere • Jim Sheehan
Editors

Supervision of Family Therapy and Systemic Practice

Springer

Editors
Arlene Vetere
VID Specialized University
Oslo, Norway

Jim Sheehan
VID Specialized University
Oslo, Norway

ISSN 2520-1190 ISSN 2520-1204 (electronic)
Focused Issues in Family Therapy
ISBN 978-3-319-68590-8 ISBN 978-3-319-68591-5 (eBook)
https://doi.org/10.1007/978-3-319-68591-5

Library of Congress Control Number: 2017960807

Printed on acid-free paper

This Springer imprint is published by Springer Nature
The registered company is Springer International Publishing AG
The registered company address is: Gewerbestrasse 11, 6330 Cham, Switzerland

Preface

We want to say a few words about why we wanted to edit this book on systemic approaches to supervision and why we all wanted to write this book.

Overall, there are too few books written on supervision processes and practice. This is surprising given the crucial importance of supervision in looking after both the therapist and the client and thus the therapy. Although this book is written mainly for the supervision of family therapy and systemic practice, it contains much material that is relevant to other mental health and social care practitioners and psychotherapists, such as supervision processes and the learning and development of both the supervisor and the supervisee.

We are a group of systemic trainers, supervisors and practitioners, working in Oslo, Norway, and connected to each other over the years through shared interests, work and close relationships. All of us are dual qualified—both systemically trained and trained in other disciplines, such as education, social work, nursing and clinical psychology.

This book is about the family therapy supervision process and supervision practice. It is written for novice supervisors who are learning their craft, and for experienced supervisors who are reflecting on their learning and development in their various supervisory roles. The book covers the supervision of trainee and novice family therapists/systemic practitioners, post-qualification practice, and the supervision of experienced supervisors, both as supervisors and therapists in their own right. A central concern of the book is how, in supervision, we look after ourselves and each other and maintain our enthusiasm, wellbeing and vitality in the triangular relationships of supervisor and supervisee and therapy client/s. We explore the contexts that support effective supervision practice, for example, personal, relational and material resources, and also the special, and challenging work contexts that supervision is delivered within, such as working with substance misuse and violence in the family. The theory and evidence base for effective supervision informs each chapter.

We hope our book contributes to updating theory and practice in supervision by incorporating the recent developments in systemic reflecting processes, mentalisation and self-reflexivity, non-conscious relational responding and theories of trauma and affect regulation. We have tried, in turn, to pay attention to the supervisory needs of training, novice and experienced practitioners, and to the supervisory needs of the supervisors themselves. While there are many areas of family therapy supervision practice not specifically referred to in this book, we believe that supervisors will find here a rich pool of supervisory perspectives applicable in their own unique areas of supervision practice.

Oslo, Norway

Arlene Vetere
Jim Sheehan

Contents

Contributor Biographies

Randi Frieda Bagge has two master's degrees: a Master's in Special Needs (1990) and a Master's in Family Therapy and Systemic Practice (2000). She has been working with Roma families for 10 years (1980–1990) and has been working in family therapy with families in an institution for families in the child protection system for 15 years (1990–2005). Currently, she is leader of the family therapy master's programme at VID Specialized University, Oslo (2005–2017). She has published four articles in the Nordic Family Therapy Journal *Fokus på Familien.*

Halvor de Flon trained as a nurse in 1986 and in 2007 completed his master's training in systemic psychotherapy. He has a long experience of working therapeutically with individuals, couples and families where addiction is of concern. He has worked as a team leader in child and adolescent psychiatry services in Norway. Now he is associate professor at VID Scientific University, Oslo.

Gudmund Fossli trained as a Clinical Social Worker with an Advanced Degree in Family Therapy and Supervision education. His work experience has included social services, child protection services, psychiatric institutions and public and private family therapy services. Gudmund Fossli has practised as a supervisor, teacher, trainer, manager and as a family and couples therapist for 30 years. For 20 years he worked in private practice as a consultant in training and supervision for public services in various contexts. From 2011 he has been engaged in Modum Bad psychiatric hospital's unit for family treatment as a therapist, leader and supervisor. His publications include "*Bruk av ulike veiledningsmetoder i sosialtjenesten*" by Fossli, K. and Olsen, L.E.: ch. 8 in "Faglig veiledning i sosialt arbeid" Ed. By Strømfors. G. og Vindegg. J. Kommuneforlaget Oslo 2001; and "*Utprøving av systematisk tilbakemelding i par- og familieterapi - Barrierer og utfordringer*" by Terje Tilden, Åshild Tellefsen Håland, Knut Hunnes, Gudmund Fossli, and Camilla Jensen Oanes in Fokus på Familien, 04/2015.

Tone Grøver is an educated sociologist (mag.art), holds a master's degree in family therapy and systemic practice and has further education in narrative psychotherapy.

She teaches family therapy at VID University of Science, Oslo, in addition to being a therapist, supervisor and researcher. She has also published fiction.

Per Jensen is professor at the Master's Programme in Family Therapy and Systemic Practice at VID Specialized University, Oslo, Norway. There, he has been teaching and supervising the family therapy programme for 26 years. He has written several textbooks and articles in the field of family therapy, psychotherapy and mental health. His latest textbook is *Between the Words: Communication in Professional Practice*, with Inger Ulleberg (2011). He has also written a chapter called: *Mind the Map: Circular processes between the therapist, the client, and the therapist's personal life*, in Peter Stratton and Arlene Vetere's edited book: *Interacting Selves: Systemic solutions for personal and professional development in counselling and psychotherapy,* published by Routledge in 2016.

Hans Christian Michaelsen has a Master of Arts (Literature, Languages, Psychology, Medicine) and a Master's in Family Therapy and Systemic Practice. At present, he is assistant professor at VID Specialized University, Oslo. Previously he worked in a Psychiatric Institution for Adolescents and Families and was director for the LEON Federation for Addictive Behaviour and Family Therapy. Hans Christian Michaelsen has practised as a supervisor, teacher, trainer, manager and as a family and couples therapist for 30 years. He has worked in contexts such as child protection services, hospitals, human relations and in areas of intercultural communication. He is a Board Member of EFTA (European Family Therapy Association). He was editor of the Nordic Family Therapy Journal *Fokus på Familien*, 2011–2014.

Siv Merete Myra is assistant professor at VID Specialized University, Oslo, and a Ph.D. candidate at the Norwegian Centre for Addiction Research, University of Oslo. She teaches at the Faculty of social work in systemic practice and family therapy and has been working for 25 years in the addiction field. She supervises therapists in the field of addiction and family therapy. Her primary interest is children and families living with substance abuse disorder and the prevention of intergenerational transference. Her research is related to pregnant substance abusing women in compulsory and voluntary treatment settings in Norway.

Anne Kyong Sook Øfsti has been an associate professor at VID Specialized University, Oslo, Norway, since 2000. She completed her dissertation in 2008 with the Tavistock Centre, London, and University of East London: "Some Call it Love. Exploring Norwegian Therapists Discourses about Love and Intimacy". Anne Øfsti practises at a Family Therapy Guidance Centre in Oslo. She has edited the Scandinavian Journal: *Fokus på familien.* She published her first novel in 2014. Anne Øfsti has a long and varied experience of writing, training, supervision and therapy.

Jim Sheehan is professor of family therapy and systemic practice at the VID Specialist University, Oslo, Norway. He was Director of Family Therapy Training for University College Dublin at the Mater Misericordiae Hospital from 1987 to

2012. He is a social worker, family therapist, trainer, consultant and supervisor. In his Dublin-based private practice, he works with families, couples and children as well as supervising family therapists and counsellors.

Inger Ulleberg is associate professor at Oslo and Akershus University College of Applied Sciences, teaching pedagogy and supervision. She has been editor of the leading Nordic journal of systemic thinking and practice: *Focus on the Family. Nordic Journal for Family and Relational Work* (*Fokus på familien. Nordisk tidsskrift for familie- og relasjonsarbeid*). She is the author of the book *Communication and Supervision (Kommunikasjon og veiledning, 2014),* an introduction to Gregory Bateson's communication theory with stories from supervision practice. With Per Jensen she has written *Between the Words: Communication in Professional Practice* (Mellom ordene. Kommunikasjon i profesjonell praksis, 2011).

Anne Hedvig Vedeler is an assistant professor at VID Specialized College in Oslo, Norway, where she is the director of its ICCP. The ICCP is a Certificate Programme in Collaborative and Dialogical Practices, run in collaboration with Harlene Anderson and the Houston Galveston Institute. Anne Hedvig has her own private practice called *Dialogical Practice*, offering therapy, consultation, coaching, supervision and teaching. Her doctoral thesis "Diving into the Poetic Movements" explored how a belief in fluidity and complexity enables professionals to contribute to a space in different contexts which welcomes the freedom of a kind of *orientation* which is open towards situated, novel, emerging and provisional understanding.

Arlene Vetere is professor of family therapy and systemic practice at VID Specialized University, Oslo; visiting professor of clinical psychology at Universita degli Studi di Bergamo, Italy; and associate professor of family studies at Malta University. Arlene is a registered systemic psychotherapist and supervisor and a clinical psychologist and supervisor in the United Kingdom where she lives and practises. Arlene has published extensively on the topics of safe therapeutic work with violence in the family and on attachment narrative work in systemic practice.

Part I
Starting off in Supervision

Chapter 1
Beginning the Supervisory Relationship Within Family Therapy Training: Engaging Individuals, Groups and Settings

Jim Sheehan

This chapter highlights the importance of making a 'good enough' beginning between supervisor and supervisee within family therapy training practice modules. In suggesting that this beginning needs to be 'good enough', there is an acknowledgement that beginnings, while carrying their own excitement and promise, can present challenges and hazards for both supervisor and supervisee. When a good enough beginning is made, the platform is set for what will be, in all likelihood, a positive learning and development experience for the supervisee as well as a constructive and satisfying professional development experience for the supervisor. When the beginning does not prove to be good enough, this can lead to an early cessation of the supervisory relationship. While such early suspension of the relationship can often be a very constructive training decision, usually taken in the context of close collaboration between a training director, a supervisor and a trainee, the costs of having to make such a decision can be multiple and are usually paid for by a number of other individuals in the training system beyond the immediate supervisory dyad. Where the beginning is not good enough but does not require the suspension of the supervisory relationship the remainder of that particular practice module, with all its tasks and demands, can feel to both supervisor and supervisee as though it is being performed with a weight on their backs. Hence, there is a lot at stake in the effort to make a good enough beginning to the supervisory relationship within family therapy training.

The chapter will be an exploration of some factors that must be attended to by the supervisor in the process of commencement. While many of these factors will be immediately recognisable to the supervisor-reader of this chapter, not all of them will be relevant to all readers. Although family therapy training contexts share a great many similar features, they are also unique systems in unique contexts which give

J. Sheehan (✉)
Family Therapy Section, Faculty of Social Studies, VID Specialized University, Oslo, Norway
e-mail: jimssheehan@outlook.com

A. Vetere, J. Sheehan (eds.), *Supervision of Family Therapy and Systemic Practice*, Focused Issues in Family Therapy, https://doi.org/10.1007/978-3-319-68591-5_1

rise to their own unique challenges. What follows, therefore, reflects a limited set of factors and concerns arising out of one such unique context. The writer often thinks of the supervisory attention to such factors as akin to the planting of different kinds of seeds in a garden. The planting holds the hope of future blossoming on condition that the process of growth is well tended. From the beginning the supervisory relationship can be thought about as a site of learning (Stratton & Hanks, 2016) and, more particularly, as a site of adult learning (Knowles, 1984). It is also a site which carries potential for the personal and professional transformation (Mezirow, 1991; Mezirow & Taylor, 2009) of both supervisor and supervisee (Sheehan, 2016). All of the factors within the supervisory relationship are oriented from the beginning towards what is the central goal of family therapy training—namely, the progression of the trainee along the path towards the capacity for independent practice as a family therapist in which self-supervision (Todd, 2014) plays an increasingly important role.

Many factors influence the manner in which practice modules are delivered within the context of postgraduate training in family therapy. Local and national criteria for programme accreditation as well as the specific philosophies of training underpinning the academic or institutional base within which the training takes place all play a part in determining the shape of the modules in which family therapy supervision takes place. A key aspect of practice modules within postgraduate family therapy training concerns the extent to which the supervision of trainee's practice occurs within a group context which incorporates live supervision and whether or not such group-based supervised practice modules are accompanied elsewhere in the training by modules dedicated to individual supervision. The central focus of this chapter will be concerned with addressing the challenges of beginning the supervisory relationship within the context of group-based supervised practice modules that incorporate a high level of live supervision. In my experience, the numbers in such groups normally fall somewhere from three to six members but this number can vary greatly depending upon the unique set of circumstances in which supervisors and supervisees find themselves.

The chapter divides naturally into two parts. The first part concerns those factors that the supervisor must attend to in the process of their own preparations for making a 'good enough beginning' while the second part relates to a complex of other factors that require attention in the beginning phase of the group supervision process. While the developmental stage of trainees within the training and qualification journey has a critical impact upon the kind of supervisory relationships that are formed within the group-based supervised practice modules (see, for example, de Flon, Chap. 7), this developmental theme has been bracketed in the pages ahead in order to focus on the common set of factors that need to be addressed in the commencement of the group-based supervisory relationship across all stages of family therapy training.

Who Are the Members of the Supervision Group?

An important aspect of making a good enough beginning to the supervisory relationships within a family therapy training group is being well prepared for the beginning. One element of this preparation for the supervisor is being appropriately informed about who the members of the supervision group will be. It is not good enough for a faculty supervisor to turn up for the first meeting of their practice module supervision group armed only with the names of the group members and their current places of practice. Adequate coordination between a training director (who will normally have final responsibility for allocating trainees to specific supervision groups and supervisors) and the faculty or institute supervisor will insure that 'blind' beginnings do not take place. Postgraduate students of whatever level have usually spent several hours preparing their curriculum vitae as part of an application process prior to programme entry. While reading this application material is not the same as hearing directly from the trainee the story of their unique professional development pathway, it is an essential prerequisite for being able to convey to trainees, when the supervisor finally meets them, an attitude of care and appreciation for the unique professional journeys they have undertaken.

This reading of application material by supervisors has a number of purposes beyond simply acquiring a broad knowledge of who the group members will be. One of these other purposes is that it comprises a first level assessment by the supervisor of the resources that are likely to be available within the supervision group as it undertakes its clinical practice functions. If, in the context of the therapeutic challenges the group may face, the supervisor is to later model the use of existing resources in the form of available specialist knowledge and expertise, they must be aware of what the nature and range of this knowledge and expertise might be. Another side of this first level assessment of resources is that it can highlight for the supervisor the possible resource deficits that might arise within the whole group (supervisor and supervisees) in the face of certain clinical/therapeutic challenges. Such awareness of possible resource deficit might alert the supervisor to the need for making a short-term alliance with another supervisor whose expertise the group might draw upon should the need arise.

A second purpose of this reading is that it gives the supervisor a good picture of the range of therapeutic experience held by the different members of the group. As a family therapy training director and supervisor for many years, one of the challenges I have heard my supervisor colleagues note as among the most difficult is the management of varying levels of experience and expertise within the training group. For example, how does the supervisor speak with an experienced trainee at a level that does justice to their already acquired knowledge, expertise and experience at the same time as making enough sense for those others in the group with far less of the same ingredients? While there are undoubtedly supervisory challenges associated with widely varying experience levels between individuals within a training group, there are also likely to be supervisory opportunities arising from the same context. A prior awareness of this variation can set in motion within the supervisor a thinking process about what these opportunities might be.

A third purpose in reading application material is that it can alert supervisors to places where there might have been an overlapping in the prior personal or professional histories of some members in the group. For example, two of the members of the group may have worked together in the same agency over a number of years. Or we may observe that two members of the group grew up in the same small town or village and may even have gone to the same schools at the same time. In one particular training group this writer supervised many years ago two of the members had had a prior relationship 30 years previously where one supervisee had been a pupil in a primary school where the other supervisee had been her school principal. Why are these observations important? They are important because such shared histories may become the basis for either alliance formation or relational avoidance within the training group in a way that might be either facilitative of, or restraining upon, processes of individual and/or group learning. The anxieties associated with the commencement of a supervision group often predispose trainees to cling a little to those with whom they have had some prior connection. The supervisor needs to be alert from the beginning to the possible bases of these expectable alliance formations and to see that certain individuals are not excluded in the processes of support giving and receiving in the beginning phase of the training group.

A final purpose in reading the application material of the supervisee group is that it alerts the supervisor to the gender balance in the group. In some parts of the world of family therapy training, the ratio of males to females within training cohorts is very low while in other places this ratio approaches equity. The supervisor will have to consider whether the gender balance/imbalance in the group to be supervised might have particular consequences for both the therapeutic and supervisory relationships in the period ahead. This consideration will, of course, not simply be a private reflection in the mind of the supervisor but a theme for dialogue within the group in the context of a larger reflection on the meaning of differences of many kinds.

Appreciating the Pathway of Each Supervisee's Practice Development

Where the training group in a supervised practice module is in the second or third year of practice modules and the supervisor is commencing with a new group, part of the preparation must also include a careful review of each group member's evaluation data/feedback from their prior supervisor/s. The incoming supervisor must check to see if there is any aspect of the evaluation information on a student/trainee that needs further clarification before the commencement of the forthcoming supervised practice module. If the supervisor feels the need for clarification, they will have to decide how they should approach such clarifying task. More specifically, and depending upon the nature of the clarification being sought, the supervisor must decide whether they need to meet with a trainee's previous supervisor, whether this should be with or without the trainee's involvement, whether a meeting solely with the director of training would suffice, and with whom they should consult about the degree of transparency with which the clarification process should be conducted. The academic and professional systems within which a family therapy training supervision group is embedded are complex systems that, with the exception of newly emerging programmes, have evolved over time and it is likely that such established programmes will have their own set of protocols relating to the kind of clarification challenges just mentioned.

The Number of Supervisees in the Group

The final characteristic of the group that must be attended to by the incoming supervisor is the number of trainees who comprise it. The supervisor will be aware of the programme's different requirements for trainees within the practice module—for example, how many live-supervised sessions they must undertake, how many DVD reviews must be done, how many different couples and families must be seen, etc.—and the supervisor must make an initial plan for how these criteria can be met for each student within the fixed amount of meetings and training hours allotted to the module. Such a plan for the meeting of programme criteria will of course be worked out collaboratively with the trainees in the beginning phase of the group but it is the supervisor's job to have done the initial arithmetic around this dimension of the group's activity.

While supervisors normally experience greater challenges associated with managing the needs of a relatively large supervision group of five or six supervisees, smaller groups of three or four trainees can face uniquely different challenges. Anxieties for supervisors in large groups typically relate to making sure each supervisee reaches their targets for specific supervision practice tasks (number of live family consultations, number of DVD reviews, etc.). It is a case of managing a heavy task-load within limited time periods while continuing to address the group's central learning and development functions. The supervisor with a small number in the group faces the task of managing a relative abundance of time in which a limited number of tasks need to be met. If managed creatively, this apparent abundance of time may lead to a highly enriched supervisory experience for the small number of supervisees in the group. The time abundance may allow the supervisor to consider more aspects of a supervisee's practice experience and may facilitate a level of patient reflection with the supervisee that really enhances their learning opportunities. However, a group of this size can also lead to a level of intensity, both between supervisees themselves and between supervisor and supervisees, which provokes discomfort and a type of anxiety that inhibits rather than promotes learning. If the group meets weekly, for example, for a 5-h period, just imagine what an episode of influenza in the local area might do to the look and shape of the supervision group! Should two members of the group suffer this illness at the same time and be out of action for 2 weeks in a row the supervisor and a single supervisee will suddenly find themselves in a context neither of them had anticipated. Supervisors and client family members can also become ill, thus adding to the range of unanticipated factors that can face supervisors and their supervision groups. These unusual contexts require creative responses from the supervisor or replacement supervisor which utilise the unexpected opportunities arising at the same time as protecting the trainee from too much exposure to a supervisory eye.

Preparing the Physical Setting of the Group

Clinical supervision groups within a postgraduate training setting typically meet for a defined number of hours (for example, 4, 5 or 6 h) on a particular day (for example, on a Tuesday) at defined levels of frequency (for example, every week or every 2 weeks) across a defined duration (for example, a 1- or 2-year period). All told these groups spend a considerable amount of time together and they spend it in a particular physical setting at a particular location. An important part of beginning is the supervisor's preparation of this physical setting. Just as students can be either new or experienced with regard to the context of training, settings can also be either novice or experienced with regard to their reception of postgraduate family therapy supervision groups. Where the setting is 'experienced', it may be already well prepared to meet most, if not all, of the physical requirements of a typical supervision group. However, each group is a unique complex of individuals and no matter how experienced the setting it is the supervisor's job to become familiar with the physical setting the group will occupy and to consider how the possibilities of the setting can be maximised and its limitations managed in the interests of a positive training experience for individuals and the group. The setting also needs to be prepared for whatever adaptations might need to be made in light of the anticipated special needs of particular students or families.

The importance of this aspect of preparation is twofold. Firstly, it will communicate an attitude of care and concern on the part of the supervisor for the supervision group and its members. This attitude of care and concern is a vital building block within the supervisory relationship. Secondly, it will pave the way for the group to devote most of its energies to the learning tasks at the heart of the supervised practice module. It is very difficult, for example, to focus on observing certain interactional patterns within a therapist-family system from behind a one-way screen/mirror if you are sitting on a chair that is too small for you or if the observation room you share with some supervisee colleagues is so poorly ventilated that half your energy is devoted to working out how best you can get to the end of the session without feeling feint or falling asleep. Of course, it will be the job of administration to put these critical environmental factors in place in the light of anticipated student needs but the supervisor will need, at the very least, to acquaint themselves with the setting in advance of the moment when supervisees gather at the location for the first group meeting.

While experienced administration staff behind a postgraduate family therapy training programme will probably take responsibility for letting supervisees know in advance about the availability of car parking and related charges as well as about the availability and extent of kitchen facilities, it is important for the supervisor to be aware if this information has already been given to supervisees new to the setting or if they need to be informed directly by the supervisor. Practices will vary from programme to programme on these matters and it is never wrong for supervisors to check up on all these matters and to take appropriate initiatives where necessary. In my experience, there is often enough anxiety associated with supervisee performance and learning within a supervision group without such anxiety being displaced on to aspects of the physical setting that provide too many challenges.

Every supervisee needs to be informed of the following:

(a) Car parking facilities available to them or adjacent to the training setting
(b) Modes of public transport that will take them to the training centre
(c) How to gain access to, and exit, the building in which the training takes place
(d) The location of rest room facilities in the building
(e) The availability and location of kitchen and/or restaurant facilities in the building/area and their associated costs
(f) Information relevant to their unique special needs

Attending to different requirements for the physical setting often has the additional function of bringing the supervisor into contact with the administrative staff who will be supporting the clinical work of the training group in the period ahead. No training group can function well without a positive and respectful relationship between the group's supervisor and key administrative and support staff. Even though the supervisor may know these individuals really well, there needs to be a new joining of this team (supervisor and administrative/support staff) around the unique group about to commence their supervised practice module. Having a conversation with the administration professionals about who will be in the group and about any particular plans you may have (or they may have) for the first meeting of the group can be an important step in this relationship building. It can be critical also to have a conversation about the special needs any particular student may have and to assess together the extent to which these needs can be catered for within the resources available in the physical setting. Will there be a need to plan for an additional 'disability' space in the car park? Is the lift in the building sufficiently big to accommodate the wheelchair of one of the incoming students? What adaptations might need to be made to the layout of the clinical supervision space to accommodate the sight challenges of another student?

A number of years ago this writer was supervising a group where one of the supervisees had a severe visual impairment and required to be accompanied by her guide dog at all times. One of the other members of the group seemed to experience the presence of the dog in the group as somewhat troubling to her. She managed to express very tentatively some of her concerns about the way she experienced the presence of this additional 'group member' and wondered whether other students should not have been notified about this in advance. This led to a very creative and open discussion about our different reactions to different kinds of differences we meet in other people and what impacts our responses to these differences. We all noted the different dilemmas associated with the possibility of providing a 'heads up' about the dog in advance of the commencement of the training year and accepted that there were no easy answers to these dilemmas. The whole conversation contributed greatly to the development of a sensitivity within the group to the differences brought by client families throughout the year. At the same time it was acknowledged that if another supervisee had suffered from a dog phobia some other decisions would have had to be made!

The supervisor's engagement with administrative staff around any such matters relating to student special needs is all part of the setting itself beginning to become engaged around the unique group who will be arriving for training. If the supervisor themselves is new to the setting, they need to be sure that they introduce themselves, or have been introduced, to all the relevant administration and mental health professionals working in the same building or on the same floor. Some of these professionals may be sources of therapy referrals for the training group and may be part of the group's professional liaison network in the months ahead.

A final and critical task in the supervisor's preparation of the physical setting is checking to see that all the recording equipment necessary for the performance of training tasks within live supervision is in working order and that they know how this equipment works and can communicate this knowledge to the members of the supervision group. Experienced family therapy supervisors will attest to the amount of training time within a supervision group that can be lost because of problems with the functioning of equipment or because of a lack of readily available flip-charts, markers and blank DVDs. The supervisor must also be aware of where and how to access technical support should it be needed during the course of a training period. The sufficiently prepared supervisor is also someone who knows that the world rarely 'works' as planned even when the best of preparations are made. This supervisor will always have contingency plans available 'in their back pocket' when even the most up-to-date technology lets us all down.

Meeting Supervisees Individually in Advance of the First Group Meeting

When trainees are in the more advanced stages of their training, it is unlikely that they will need to meet the clinical supervisor alone in advance of the first meeting of the group. They are already well acquainted with each other and with most faculty supervisors. Such requests for meetings alone are more usual in the early phase of training and, in this writer's view, such requests should always be met. Indeed, some clinical supervisors may want to meet each of the supervisees joining the group on their own in advance of the formal start of the supervision group. Anxiety is not the preserve of supervisees alone and it may assist the comfort level of novice or experienced supervisors just to have a short one-to-one introduction to each of the supervisees before the group meets for the first time. For some supervisees it may be that they only know of a particular supervisor by reputation and have never met them in the context of other training modules. For these trainees, one function of such meetings can simply be to reduce the strangeness attaching to the supervisor in advance of the start. More importantly, however, such meetings are a first opportunity for engagement in the supervisory relationship where the supervisor 'receives' the supervisee as a member of the group and attempts to convey a sense of welcome to the supervisee as well as an appreciation of all the work needed along the path of their training journey.

More complex matters can arise from these meetings when supervisees try to use them to secure agreements from the supervisor outside of the context of the group's own process and emerging structure or outside of the context of the training as a whole. Both of the following examples demonstrate an early 'test' for the supervisory relationship. The first example is concerned with the management of a supervisee's anxiety about being observed in live supervision while the second example addresses the question of a supervisee's relationship to the boundaries of the practice module.

Alice was a 33-year-old social worker who asked to meet with her relatively novice supervisor, 42-year-old Diane, prior to the first meeting of the group. Having introduced herself as both a child protection social worker and mother of two young children, Alice came right to the point of why she had asked for the meeting. She explained that while she had a lot of experience of meeting with and interviewing families she had never been observed doing a 'live' session and she felt extremely nervous about it. She felt so nervous about it that she was now making a request to be the last person in the group to be observed 'live'. She felt that if she could go last with this dimension of the training she would get courage from being able to see the others 'go through this' first and 'come out the other side'. Diane responded to her by saying how glad she was that she had the courage to come and let her know what a big challenge she anticipated this dimension of the training would be for her and she tried to reassure her that she would be there to give her as much support as she might need whenever she had to take the step of doing her fist 'live' session with a family. She told Alice that she did not know how many of the other trainees might feel themselves to be in the same position and that it could be a very helpful contribution to the group if she was to share her worries about being observed in live supervision during the first meeting of the group a week later. She explained that she could not give her a commitment in advance to be the last in the group to see a 'live' family as there were a host of different variables that might have a bearing on when she or any other member of the group might have to commence live supervision. Alice agreed to share this part of her anxiety with the group when it met and was glad to think that she might not be the only one who felt anxious about the live supervision aspect of the module to come.

In the above example the supervisor, Diane, used the individual meeting to develop a supportive stance with the supervisee at the same time that she withstood the temptation to respond to the supervisee's anxiety by making a commitment that would have positioned her unhelpfully both in relation to this trainee and to the group as a whole before the formal beginning of the module. In the following example, the supervisor faced a different kind of challenge.

Four days before a group supervision practice module commenced Gwen, a 38-year-old psychologist, asked to meet urgently with her third year practice module supervisor, 52-year-old Peter. Gwen wanted to meet to make a request of Peter. Her request was that she be allowed to leave the supervision group, which was due to meet every Wednesday from 1 p.m. to 6 p.m., at 5.45 p.m. each week to enable her to catch a 6.10 p.m. train from the local station which would allow her collect her 8-year-old twin boys from their childminder by 6.40 p.m. The childminder had to be relieved of her care of the boys by 6.45 p.m. in order to make the start of her English Language classes by 7 p.m. When Peter asked her if she had a partner or someone else in her life who might help her out with child collection on that evening during the week, Gwen told her that she had a husband but that he was rarely able to leave work on any evening before 6.30 p.m. Peter sympathised with her dilemma and acknowledged the series of challenges she must have faced since the commencement of her training in order to turn the jigsaw of her training, her work and the afterschool care of her children into a workable system. He stressed, however, that he had no authority to deal with her request and suggested she talk it over without delay with the Programme Director who had responsibility for addressing questions relating to supervisee attendance at training modules. She agreed that she would do that and Peter heard nothing more about it until the day of the first meeting of the supervision group. During a break on that day, Peter quietly inquired from Gwen how her meeting with the Programme Director had gone. She told him that there had been no need to set up the meeting because her husband, once he heard how difficult it would be for her to leave the training early on a weekly basis, found a way to finish his work a little earlier on Wednesdays in order to pick up the children from the childminder. Later she commented within the group that her husband's adjustment showed her that he really understood how important this postgraduate training was for her ongoing professional development.

In this example, the supervisor turned what was essentially a very problematic request (a request for special arrangements for one supervisee which, if conceded, could have had a series of problematic knock-on effects for both the individual supervisee and the group process) into an opportunity to acknowledge the context giving rise to the request at the same time as pointing to an important boundary between the sphere of his own decision-making and that belonging to the Programme Director as the guardian of the rules relating to supervisee attendance at different program modules.

The First Three Meetings of the Clinical Supervision Group Within Family Therapy Training

Beginning a supervision group within family therapy training is a process that happens over time. In the first section of this chapter, we have followed some of the tasks the supervisor typically undertakes as part of his/her own commencement of the process of supervising a group. As we can see from the paragraphs above, some of these tasks bring the supervisor into contact with supervisees thereby informally setting the supervisory relationship in motion. Other tasks are more oriented towards the establishment of an immediate context for the training to come and do not involve any contact with supervisees. Supervisees will also make their own preparations for commencement and these will vary from individual to individual depending upon the unique mix of personal and professional responsibilities that make up their lives. While we will not be going into this matter in any great detail here, the supervisor needs to be aware that each supervisee will probably have had to make adjustments to their work schedules and personal lives in order to give themselves the opportunity of successfully completing the training. These adjustments usually mean that other people have made adjustments to facilitate the supervisee's professional training goals. These adjustments often add up to a great many sacrifices of different kinds on the part of many individuals who the supervisor may never meet. That network of people comprises the 'hidden' context of the training without which the demands of training would be unrealisable for most supervisees. If, as the Chinese proverb tells us, it takes a village to raise a child, it certainly takes a network of many individuals from different parts of the professional's life to train a family therapist. The supervisor will do well to communicate to supervisees their awareness and appreciation of the multiple adjustments and adaptations made by several people in their personal and professional networks.

In this second part of the chapter, the focus will be on the range of tasks the supervisor must undertake as the clinical supervision group gets underway and makes its own 'real' beginning. In my experience, these supervisory tasks have usually taken root over the first three meetings of the group even though they require ongoing attention and performance by the supervisor until the work of the supervision group is complete.

These tasks can be thought of as falling under five headings as follows:

1. Building the group as a cohesive working group
2. Stating the module goals and requirements.
3. Proposing learning structures and commencing them
4. Pointing towards evaluation of supervisee performance, learning structures and the group's own process
5. The self-care of the supervisor and the supervision of supervision

While these tasks are clearly intertwined with each other, we will separate them from each other here for the purposes of description and analysis.

Building the Group as a Cohesive Working Group

Much of the excitement and potential for learning attaching to participation in a family therapy supervision group within a training context is closely associated with its greatest challenge. For many groups, this challenge can be stated as follows: how can the supervisor and supervisees together transform a group of individuals of different ages, genders, sexual orientations, beliefs and capacities, professional backgrounds and experience, and from different cultures into a cohesive working group capable of delivering a competent therapeutic service to families and couples at the same time as evolving into a learning community capable of facilitating the ongoing development of therapeutic capacities in its supervisee members? The supervisor must plan for a beginning of the group that allows all of these differences to be seen, heard about and appreciated in so far as they can be. This is the *first* level of 'building' that must be attended to as the supervision group commences its own life. It is the level of recognition of who we all are with respect to our differences and our apparent sameness. The *second* level of 'building' relates to sharing of how each member came to be interested in undertaking this particular training in family therapy within 'this' programme at 'this' particular point in time. This is the level that allows for the meaning of participation in the training by each member in the group to be understood by the other group members. It is at this level of building that supervisees are enabled to see the different ways that participation in family therapy training fits into the whole trajectory of each supervisee's personal and professional life journey as they understand it. The *third* level of 'building' relates to the introduction of members of the group to each other as 'learners' with respect to family and couple therapy skills and expertise. This level of building involves the making of opportunities for each supervisee to share with the group where they are at with respect to their own learning of skills and expertise relevant to family and couple therapy practice. It means making a space for each person to share with others their own unique and specific 'learning agenda' with respect to these skills and associated expertise. The importance of this level of building lies in the supervisor's awareness that if the group is to become a 'learning community' it must become a place that is more than a venue wherein each individual member sequentially goes on a 'solo learning run' accompanied by the supervisor. It must become a place where each supervisee develops an 'investment' not only in their own learning agenda but also in the learning agendas of each of the other members in the group. For this writer the communication by the supervisor to supervisees of this message—that we are a learning community present to each other in the hours we spend together and responsible and accountable to each other for giving and receiving support and assistance to and from each other in our learning and development endeavours—situates the supervisor within the core of a *systemic philosophy of family therapy supervision.*

But how should the supervisor go about these three levels/stages of building the group as a cohesive working group? Each supervisor will initiate the accomplishment of this goal in their own unique way and with different degrees of structure. This writer's bias is to have a considerable amount of structure built in to the group process in the beginning meetings of the group as this will probably have the function of containing anxiety levels in both supervisees and supervisors at the same time as insuring that a certain amount of necessary work is completed. It is important to note, however, that such structure should in no way inhibit the supervisor from commencing the development of a real and personal bond with each of the supervisees. Watkins (2011a, 2011b), albeit commenting from a psychoanalytic perspective on supervision, underlines the importance of attending to this real and personal bond between supervisor and supervisee as the very basis and foundation of the supervisory relationship itself. This bond functions in just the same way when the supervisor is working within a systemic framework where this personal bond becomes the base on which all aspects of the supervisory relationship are built.

Here are two exercises which commence the cohesion-building process within a supervision group in the context of family therapy training. The first of these exercises addresses the first two levels of this building process while the second exercise relates to building the third level. They can be performed over the first two meetings of the clinical training group.

Exercise 1: Telling the Story of Our Professional and Personal Development

The purpose of this exercise is to allow the members of the supervision group to make a beginning connection with each other through listening to a reasonably short account of each person's personal and professional history. This can be accomplished through having each person interviewed/facilitated in their telling of this story for a specified and limited amount of time (about 25 min) by another person in the group with the rest of the group being invited to listen carefully before being offered the opportunity in turn to make any brief observation or ask any clarifying question about what they have just heard. The group can be given the exercise in advance of the first meeting thus giving each person an opportunity to consider what they would like the group to know about them, personally and professionally, at their first meeting. The supervisor should also do the exercise and invite some member of the group to facilitate them in the moderately brief telling of their personal/professional story. The person being interviewed should be asked to 'tell' the parts of their story they wish to tell directly to their interviewer/facilitator rather than reading a set of prepared notes. The letter going out to the clinical supervision group members a week in advance of the first meeting might announce the exercise in the following way:

Dear Rachel,

I look forward to having you as a supervisee in my clinical supervision group over the next X months. By now the Program Director will have let you know who the other members of our group will be. You may know some of them a little and there may be others who you do not know at all. The nature of the training work we will be doing together necessitates that we all get to know each other fairly well over the course of the time we spend together. As a way of beginning this process there will be an exercise during our first meeting next week which will take about two and a half hours to complete. The format of the exercise will be as follows: each person will be interviewed by another person in the group for 25 minutes about the personal and professional pathways they have been on in their life and, in particular, about the way they see this current training in couple and family therapy fitting into their life and all its contexts at this moment. Everyone else in the group will listen attentively to these dialogues. I will also invite a member of the group to interview me about my own personal and professional pathways. At the end of each interview there will be a five minute period during which the remaining members in the group may make a brief comment if they wish about what they have heard or ask some clarifying question about what has been told. Following this we will review the exercise together as a whole group by considering what the conversations have meant to each one of us. Each person will be invited to share as much or as little as they like during the exercise and no pressure will be put on any one of us to share aspects of our experience we might not wish to share. I look forward to meeting with you and the other group members next week.

Sincerely,
Jim Sheehan (Family and Couple Therapy Supervisor)

This exercise usually creates a strong beginning through which the group members have the opportunity to introduce themselves to each other along many different dimensions as well as alerting the group to important aspects of the meaning of participation in training for each member of the group at this point in time. The second exercise which might happen during the second meeting of the supervision group will be described in the next section of this chapter given that it reflects a kind of dovetailing of two supervisory objectives in the beginning phase, namely, developing a supervisory alliance with each supervisee at the same time as a further building of the cohesion of the group as a working group around key learning objectives.

Stating the Module Goals in the Context of Building the Supervisory Alliance

Accredited family therapy training programmes, whether institute or university-based, will normally set out in the formal programme literature the broad learning objectives attaching to each module as well as the specific competencies students are required to demonstrate in order to complete the module successfully. This is the case for supervised practice modules just as it is for all other modules and it is the supervisor's job to find a space in the beginning phase to articulate these objectives and competencies for the group and each of its members. This is more difficult than it sounds and requires more than just a verbal repetition by the supervisor of what supervisees have already read in the programme literature. In undertaking the task, the supervisor faces something of a paradox. This paradox emerges from the fact that the language of objectives and competencies is a production arrived at by consensus among key leaders/practitioners in the education and training field while those to whom the language is addressed within training are often novice therapists and comparatively inexperienced mental health professionals. This means that the articulation of objectives and competencies by the supervisor must be the start of a *dialogue* between the supervisor, the group and each of its members. The supervisor must try to facilitate each supervisee to achieve a good enough personal understanding of the competencies required in order to feel the kind of safety that will allow them to take necessary risks in the learning journey to come. In this dialogue, the supervisees must feel that the supervisor is listening carefully to all of their comments and questions and not just wanting to tell them things from a pre-existing set of rules.

This dialogue with the group is the first of two different kinds of dialogue in the beginning phase that are oriented towards the building of *the supervisory alliance.* The supervisory alliance is nothing more than the mutual engagement between supervisor and the group around the learning tasks at hand. Several authors (Bordin, 1983; Calvert, Crowe, & Grenyer, 2016; Efstation, Patton, & Kardash, 1990; Ladany, Ellis, & Friedlander, 1999) have emphasised the *work* character of this alliance while others (Reiner, 2014) place emphasis on the *learning* nature of the alliance or on the nature of the alliance as *collaborative partnership* (Fleming & Bendek, 1983). All of these aspects are integral to the manner in which the family therapy supervisor in training-based supervision groups attempts to build the supervisory alliance both with the group and with each individual supervisee.

If the dialogue mentioned above about module learning objectives and required competencies is a key building block in *the supervisory alliance with the group* in the beginning phase, a corresponding dialogue happens between the supervisor and each of the supervisees which aims at building *the supervisory alliance with the individual supervisee*. The supervisor needs to attend to how they individualise each of these dialogues within the physical space occupied by the group. This can be done by either placing their chairs somewhat apart from the rest of the group members while the dialogue takes place or it can be done with the remaining group members observing/listening from behind a one-way screen should the space allow. Whatever the spatial arrangements it is imperative that the supervisee has maximum supervisor attention during this one-to-one dialogue. While the supervisor will invite the rest of the group to *listen* very carefully to their supervisee colleague in dialogue with them (the supervisor), nothing is likely to be more facilitative of this careful listening than the supervisor's modelling of their own attentive listening to the supervisee.

What are these individual dialogues about? First and foremost they are a space in which the supervisee is facilitated to articulate for the supervisor his own understanding of where his/her practice is at with respect to the competencies required and to say something *in their own words* about either challenges to their understanding of concrete client situations they face in the therapy room or challenges to their relational skill levels in the same contexts. Together they will try to find agreement on the relational competencies and other systemic skills that will give future direction both to supervisee learning effort and to supervisory focus. This is the heart of the individual supervisory alliance in the beginning phase and the particular shape of these alliance-building dialogues will naturally be influenced by the stage of training and the stage of a particular supervisee's development. While the primary objective of this dialogue is the building of the individual supervisory alliance between a unique supervisor and a unique supervisee, the dialogue also facilitates the development of that real interpersonal relationship (Watkins, 2011a, 2011b) between the two. In their exchanges, the supervisor will demonstrate a commitment to give support and encouragement to the supervisee along their learning journey and will convey an interest in, and commitment to, their unique practitioner development.

Exercise 2: Setting the Learning Agenda for Each Supervisee

The supervisor may organise the second exercise towards the end of the first meeting of the group but it may not be performed until the second meeting as it involves each supervisee doing some preparatory written reflection on their own learning agenda for the practicum. The exercise is commenced and set up by the supervisor asking each supervisee to make a one-page written statement about their own assessment of where their systemic understanding and practice is at. The supervisor will note that although this assessment will be influenced by previous supervisor evaluations the statement they write should be very much their own. The statement should include a list of the three most important learning objectives for them in the practicum to come. The supervisor should indicate that as part of the next meeting they will have a focussed dialogue with each supervisee about their statement and learning objectives during which they will plan together ways that their joint work on these objectives can begin. During these individual supervisor–supervisee dialogues, the other supervisees will be invited to listen carefully at a small physical distance from the dyad in dialogue and will be invited to make a short brief comment at the end of each dialogue should they wish to do so. The supervisees might be asked to send the statement to the supervisor a couple of days in advance of the dialogue.

This exercise marks the real beginning of an individualised supervisory working alliance. The dialogues are about how they will approach the specific learning objectives of each supervisee. They are a message to the group that within the group context of working and learning together there are a series of individual working/learning contracts taking place that are of the utmost importance to the supervisor. But it is also a time for the supervisor to mark that the supervisee group is not simply a sympathetic audience for the work being undertaken in each of these working/learning contracts but has an important function within the learning process through the manner in which its members give attention and feedback to each other along the path of each individual's concrete learning journey. The supervisor will point out certain parallels between the skills they will develop in order to be meaningful participants in each other's learning and the skills they are developing in the assistance of client learning in the therapeutic context.

Developing and Commencing Learning Structures

By the end of the second meeting, the supervisor will be beginning to put learning structures in place with the supervisee group. There are a predictable number of core learning structures that emerge in the context of the group-based supervised practicum. These core structures include: the live supervision of family or couple sessions; the tape/DVD review of recorded therapy sessions; case discussions and planning; consultations around supervisee work-based therapy; role-play; group dialogue with supervisor about therapy-related themes; and observation of experienced practitioners at work with couples and families. Each of these seven learning opportunities has their own unique character and requires that the supervisor clarify the structure of roles and responsibilities of supervisees and supervisor around each of these group 'events'. For example, in advance of the first live-supervised session the supervisee needs to have some idea from the supervisor about the reasons why a supervisory call might be made to the therapist mid-session and about whether there will be a planned break after a certain amount of the session time for a supervisor–supervisee dialogue. Likewise, the supervisees who are not directly involved in the therapy need to know how they might engage with their own learning agenda beyond simply following the live therapy session. For a successful group learning event to take place, the supervisor needs enough time to plan with the group and its individual members a series of structures that will facilitate the meaningful engagement of each supervisee with some aspects of their own learning agenda. While each supervisee is an adult learner and will have their own *learning style* which needs to be respected by the supervisor, it is still the supervisor's responsibility to engage with supervisees about suitable ways for them to engage with the learning opportunities emanating from each learning event. These brief dialogues about engagement underline a key feature of the group process the supervisor will try to promote—namely, *the processes of mutual accountability* that mark the relationship of each supervisee with self, other supervisees and the supervisor (Boston, 2010).

While a close examination of possible supervisory structures surrounding each of these seven group-based learning events within the supervised practicum goes beyond the scope of this chapter, a description of a possible structure surrounding one of these learning events—the DVD review with a supervisee of a prior live-supervised family/couple therapeutic meeting—will illustrate the process of structure building that must occur in the beginning phase of the group-based supervision practicum.

The setting up of a structure surrounding a DVD review commences as part of the completion of the structure surrounding the live-supervised session. Towards the end of this learning structure, the supervisor will be initiating a small dialogue with the supervisee about their ‘homework’ arising from the live-supervised and recorded session. The supervisee may have expressed a view in the post-session discussion that one of their focuses within the session had been on asking circular questions but they were uncertain about the extent to which they had used relevant opportunities within the session for this and were also uncertain as to how the family had responded to these efforts. While the supervisor will probably have given the supervisee some preliminary feedback about this question as part of the post-session review, the setting of focussed homework for the supervisee about this matter will be the *first* part of the learning structure for the DVD review. In the case of this example, the supervisor and supervisee might agree that the supervisee will just examine closely an agreed 20-min segment of the session DVD with the task of selecting three places within the segment where they noticed opportunities to ask a circular question and making an evaluative/observation of their response to these opportunities as well as of the families subsequent responses to these therapeutic responses. The *second* part of the structure around the DVD review group-based learning event will be accomplished at the time of the review itself when the supervisor will briefly engage with each of the other supervisees about how they will engage with the review process in the interests of their own learning as well as the learning of their fellow supervisee. This planned engagement within the learning structure will sometimes have two elements to it. One of these will be an invitation to observe closely the selected pieces of DVD from the perspective of the therapist/supervisee who is showing the recording—that is, examining how the supervisee noticed opportunities to ask circular questions as well as the subsequent therapist and family responses. This element of their engagement will be directed towards giving their supervisee colleague some feedback when the appropriate moment for this arises within the learning structure. The second element of their engagement within the DVD review exercise concerns relating the opportunities arising from this particular review to their own individual learning agenda. For example, if one of the elements that a supervisee is trying to learn concerns the way a therapist maintains balance and fairness in their therapeutic dialogue with parents or members of a couple, they may be invited to notice the manner in which this particular supervisee therapist maintains such balance and fairness within the context of the DVD segments chosen for examination. Hence, the invitation to such dual focus by the non-central supervisee should maximise the possibilities to contribute to both their own learning and the learning of their fellow supervisee. The *third* part of the structure concerns the clarification of roles in the first stage of the actual DVD review process. For example, the supervisor might decide that the first 30 min of the review period will be an individualised two-person dialogue between the supervisor and supervisee with the other supervisees making written notes and private reflections from their observation during this period without making any direct verbal contributions at this stage. The *fourth* part of the structure concerns the making clear to the supervisee reporting on their homework exercise the manner in which the supervisor will engage with their homework report—for example, will the supervisor wait until the supervisee has shared one particular segment of the session along with their focussed observations on the issues at stake before initiating a dialogue in which some of their feedback is embedded or will they indicate that they might ask the supervisee to 'stop the tape' in the middle of the segment being shown in order to have a supervisory dialogue in the context of just seen micro elements of the therapeutic dialogue. The supervisee and their colleagues need to know as much as possible about supervisor intentions in this regard in order to be able to settle in as assuredly as possible to their own learning processes in the context. The *fifth* part of the structure concerns information about how the supervisor will invite feedback from other supervisees about their own learning in the context of the DVD review and whether this should happen in the form of an 'open dialogue' between all members of the group or whether supervisees will be invited sequentially to offer feedback on their own learning processes to the supervisor and the group. The *sixth* and final part of this possible structure might be an invitation to supervisees to make a small written entry on the spot in their learning journal concerning their reflections at the end of the whole group learning event. Family therapy supervisors will have a myriad of ways in which they might co-ordinate a structure around such a learning event and it must be emphasised that what has just been described is simply one possible structure among many that might be deployed in the context of this very typical learning event within the supervised practice module.

Pointing Towards Evaluation: Supervisee Performance, Learning Structures and Group Process

For supervisees in a family therapy training group, the very word 'evaluation' may fill them with a degree of apprehension and anxiety. Neither are supervisors automatically immune from such emotions which can surround the processes of evaluation of different kinds. Yet each supervisee and supervisor know that it is the event and process of evaluation that defines their shared participation as a *training* which may lead for supervisees to *qualification* and/or *registration* or *licensing* as a family therapist. In the commencement phase of a supervision group within a family therapy training context, the supervisor must attend to three levels of evaluation. The first level concerns the evaluation of individual supervisee performance in the context of a predefined set of practice competencies relevant to the particular training level involved; the second concerns the supervisor's joint evaluation with supervisees of the functionality of learning structures in relation to the learning and development goals of each supervisee; the third concerns the evaluation of the group's own process as a context of learning for all involved.

In the beginning phase of the supervision group, the supervisor will be 'pointing towards' evaluation and its related structures rather than engaged directly in evaluation. The supervisee will need to know that while evaluation will be taking place throughout the whole time period of the group in the form of specific supervisor feedback to supervisees upon their performance and participation there will also be more focussed and formal evaluation of their performance at both the mid-point and end-point of the time period of the supervision group. The supervisee will need to know that there will be some aspects of their evaluation conducted with fellow supervisees present and other aspects that will happen with just themselves and the supervisor present. If there are particular programme-designated forms that will be used by both supervisor and supervisees in this evaluation process, it is critical that supervisees are given copies of these from the beginning along with some information about how they will be used. For example, if there are both self-evaluation and supervisor evaluation forms in use the supervisee needs to know if these provisionally completed forms are going to provide a starting point for a supervisor–supervisee evaluation dialogue which will inform their own respective and subsequent completion of the forms for the Programme Director or Course Coordinator. The supervisor needs to remind themselves and supervisees that evaluation is part of both the supervisory relationship and the learning processes in the group and not an event that stands outside of both. If there is a grading structure to be used which will supplement documented processes of feedback, the meaning of these differential grades needs to be clear from the outset for supervisees. Boston (2010) reminds us of the immense significance evaluation can have even for extremely experienced mental health professionals who enjoy live supervision in the context of family therapy training. Positive feedback and evaluation from live supervision has the capacity to confer on the supervisee an enhancement of their professional identity arising from the credibility attaching to evaluations received on the basis of a direct observation of their practice by the supervisor. Evaluation events can also be the vehicle for the transformation or refinement of individual learning goals for supervisees.

The supervisor will also highlight for supervisees in the beginning phase that although they will be 'imposing' certain learning structures and exercises on the group as it proceeds with its work there will be opportunities to review the functioning of these structures with respect to their functionality in assisting with the achievement of specific supervisee learning objectives as these may be evolving. Indeed, the review and revision of these structures is part of the individualising of the supervisory process and forms a key element in the ongoing development of the supervisory alliance with both group and individuals. Such supervisee participation in structure review and revision is also in keeping with well-established principles of adult learning (Knowles, 1984).

The final aspect of evaluation that the supervisor points towards in the beginning phase of the supervision group concerns the group's own evolving process. Burck and Daniel (2010, XX1V) note with some surprise the lack of theorising of group processes within the systemic supervision literature. This is all the more surprising given the apparently strong preference for delivering family therapy training supervised practice modules within a group context. This lack of specifically systemic theorising of group process may be accounted for somewhat by the strong contribution that other frameworks have already made to this area of our understanding. Clarke and Rowan (2009), while arguing for the importance of attending to group processes within team-based delivery of systemic psychotherapy, consider the theories relating to groups arising from systemic theory and group analytic theory as more complementary than oppositional. In a similar vein, Granville (2010) suggests a significant continuity between a range of concepts from psychoanalytic and group analytic literature and systemic thinking. An example of this continuity is Bion's concept of the 'work group' (Bion, 1961) which can add to the systemic supervisor's understanding of group process as the matrix through which the training goal is fulfilled. For Bion the idea of the work group relates to 'mental activity by the group members that relates to the task that is the agreed purpose of the group' (Granville, 2010, 129). The supervisor will know that when the group is working well together and its members are engaged positively in their own and each other's learning agendas this is a sign that the group is in work group mode. However, when people come together in groups of any kind and for whatever purposes, a variety of psychological and relational processes can take place that can interfere with the ongoing functioning of the group within a work group mode. When this happens, these matters will need to be addressed within the group no matter what stage of the training period has been reached. However, the supervisor does not need to wait until something appears to be going wrong to address the group process. By pointing in the beginning to spaces of time in the future when the group and supervisor together will be invited to evaluate the quality of functioning of the group with respect to its learning tasks, the supervisor is signalling to supervisees the importance of the group process within this overall task. It should be noted here that when things are moving reasonably satisfactorily it is probable that only a small amount of group time will need to be spent on this evaluative process and it is likely that supervisees will express a desire to return to the central tasks. Notwithstanding this impetus the supervisor needs to be sure that the group, including themselves, are not running away from something difficult in their midst. Making sure that each supervisee has an opportunity to speak about the way they are experiencing this process is probably the safest way to ensure that there is no avoidance going on. The last thing the supervisor wants to do in the beginning phase is to somehow convey to supervisees an expectation that things might go very wrong in the supervision group and that the group may have to go in to something like group work mode in order to sort matters out. That said, it is often wise for a supervisor to have a backup plan for another supervisor to come in to the group for a group consultation about its own process should this evolving process seem to be seriously interfering with the central function of the group. Of course, the supervisor will already have attempted to address these processes with the group in advance of any such decision to involve someone from the outside. If the position taken by this writer is that an external consultant to the group should only be engaged when the group is in difficulty, Parry and Doan (1994, 205), working from within a narrative framework, describe a position where the periodic entrance of an external consultant into the group takes place in the service of hearing stories from each supervisee about their experience of the group's contribution to their developing journey as a family therapist.

The Self-Care of the Supervisor and the Supervision of Supervision

The final dimension that the supervisor must pay attention to is the putting in place of a support and supervisory structure for their own supervision. No matter how experienced a practitioner/supervisor may be, the supervisor, like their supervisees, is continuously exposed to a range of challenging clinical contexts. Domestic violence (Hanks & Vetere, 2016), child abuse (see Bagge, Chap. 8, this volume), depression, suicide, gender-based discrimination, unanticipated death, addiction (see Myra, Chap. 7, this volume), and chronic illness are among the many themes that the supervision group as a whole may experience in the course of their client work. It is the supervisor's task to support supervisees as they endeavour to remain in a reflexive position in relation to these themes in the context of practice. In this supervisory task, it is the supervisees' experiences and responses rather than those of the supervisor that will be to the forefront of exploration. The supervisor facilitates such exploration in the interests of both supervisee development and enhanced client outcomes. This can be an extremely challenging task for the supervisor as they bear responsibility for the containment of a diverse range of emotional responses of supervisees to client themes and positions. But who will facilitate the containment, management and exploration of the emotional responses of the supervisor and how can this be achieved? While there is no doubt that much of this task is managed alone by experienced supervisors, it may be that this 'self-management' occurs because of the lack of available resources and structures for 'the supervision of supervision' (see Sheehan, Chapter 16, this volume). Novice supervisors will certainly require a structure of care and supervision around them as they undertake this further stage of development in their professional lives and an ethics of supervisory practice should clearly draw the links between having such structures in place and the training institution's responsibilities to clients, supervisees and supervisors.

Four different kinds of structures can support the self-care and 'supervision of supervision' requirements of supervisors, novice or experienced. The first structure is a peer supervision group in which supervisors of relatively similar experience levels come together at agreed intervals to offer each other a 'supervision of supervision' experience. A second structure is where a group of supervisors come together for supervision of their supervision with an experienced supervisor in the role of supervisor of supervision. A third structure is where a supervisor engages another supervisor on a one-to-one basis to supervise them in relation to their supervision practice. Skype creates many possibilities for accessing 'supervision of supervision' through the engagement of a supervisor who may be far removed both geographically and institutionally from the site of the supervisor's practice. This one-to-one structure may be the most relevant and feasible structure for many family therapy training organisations and typically involves a relatively inexperienced supervisor entering a supervisory relationship with a relatively experienced supervisor for the duration of their supervision group. A fourth structure is a self-supervision structure in which a supervisor, through the medium of a reflective diary or journal, monitors and explores their own responses, relationships, and positions within the supervision group they are currently working with. This fourth structure can extend to the examination, with the permission of supervisees, of recordings of the supervision group in motion. Such recordings can be the basis for supervision also in the first three structures mentioned.

While the reader may be able to add a number of variations to the four structures mentioned above, the key point being made here is that in the beginning phase of the supervision group responsible supervision practice requires that the supervisor put in place some structures for the supervision of their own supervisory practice. Such structures need to be seen as part of the way we care for ourselves and for each other in the context of very complex service and training providing institutions and agencies.

Conclusion

This chapter has underlined the importance of making a 'good enough' beginning to the set of supervisory relationships at stake where a supervisor works with a group of supervisees as part of their supervised practice modules within the context of postgraduate family therapy training. Such training-based supervision groups normally include some live supervision of trainees' practice. Emphasis has been placed not simply on the engagement of both individuals and the group within a series of interconnected supervisory relationships but also on the engagement of 'the setting' into the training endeavour. The process of beginning has been thought about as comprising two stages. The first of these involves a series of 'preparations' undertaken by the supervisor before the initial meetings of the supervision group. In this initial stage of 'preparation', the supervisor needs to attend to the likely implications for the group of such factors as the professional histories and experience of the supervisee group members, the numbers and gender balance in the group to be supervised, the physical context and resources available to the group as it relates to its members ordinary and unique needs, and the information arising from individual meetings/communications with supervisees before the actual commencement of the supervision group.

The second half of the chapter examined the range of factors that need the attention of the supervisor over the course of the first three meetings of the supervision group. The five key factors noted included the building of the supervision group as a cohesive working group, the articulation of module goals and competencies within the context of developing the supervisory alliance with individuals and the group, the development and commencement of learning structures, the pointing towards the evaluation of individual supervisees, learning structures and the group process itself, and the self-care of the supervisor in the context of the supervision of their own supervision.

In conclusion, it is worth noting again what was said earlier in the chapter. The set of concerns described above emerge from the unique experience of a unique supervisor in a unique context. The supervisor-reader will bring their own unique experience and context to the reading of the chapter and are invited to reflect on the meaning of these differences and similarities for their own supervisory practice.

References

Bion, W. (1961). *Experiences in groups*. New York: Basic Books.
Bordin, E. S. (1983). A working alliance model of supervision. *The Counselling Psychologist, 11*, 35–42.
Boston, P. (2010). The three faces of supervision: Individual learning, group learning and supervisor accountability. In C. Burck & G. Daniel (Eds.), *Mirrors and reflections: Processes of systemic supervision*. London: Karnac.
Burck, C., & Daniel, G. (Eds.). (2010). *Mirrors and reflections: Processes of systemic supervision*. London: Karnac.
Calvert, F. L., Crowe, T. P., & Grenyer, B. F. S. (2016). Dialogical reflexivity in supervision: An experiential learning process for enhancing reflective and relational competencies. *The Clinical Supervisor, 35*, 1–21.
Clarke, G., & Rowan, A. (2009). Looking again at the team dimension in systemic psychotherapy: Is attending to group process a critical context for practice? *Journal of Family Therapy, 31*(1), 85–87.
Efstation, J. F., Patton, M. J., & Kardash, C. M. (1990). Measuring the working alliance in counsellor supervision. *Journal of Counselling Psychology, 37*, 322–329.
Fleming, J., & Bendek, T. (1983). *Psychoanalytic supervision: A method of clinical teaching*. New York: International Universities Press.
Granville, J. (2010). Minding the group: Group process, group analytic ideas, and systemic supervision—Companionable or uneasy bedfellows? In C. Burck & G. Daniel (Eds.), *Mirrors and reflections: Processes of systemic supervision* (pp. 123–140). London: Karnac.
Hanks, H., & Vetere, A. (2016). Working at the extremes: The impact on US of doing the work. In A. Vetere & P. Stratton (Eds.), *Interacting selves* (pp. 65–84). London: Routledge.
Knowles, M. (1984). *Andragogy in action*. San Francisco: Jossey-Bass.
Ladany, N., Ellis, M. V., & Friedlander, M. L. (1999). The supervisory working alliance, trainee self-efficacy, and satisfaction. *Journal of Counseling and Development, 77*, 447–455.
Mezirow, J. (1991). *Transformative Dimensions of Adult Learning*. San Francisco: Jossey-Bass.
Mezirow, J., & Taylor, E. (2009). *Transformative Learning in Practice: Insights from Community; Workplace and Higher Education*. San Francisco: Jossey-Bass.
Parry, A., & Doan, R. E. (1994). *Story re-visions: Narrative therapy in the postmodern world*. New York: Guilford.
Reiner, P. A. (2014). Systemic psychodynamic supervision. In T. C. Todd & C. L. Storm (Eds.), *The complete systemic supervisor: Context, philosophy and pragmatics* (pp. 166–185). Oxford: Wiley.
Sheehan, J. (2016). Self and world: Narrating experience in the supervisor/supervisee relationship. In A. Vetere & P. Stratton (Eds.), *Interacting selves: Systemic solutions for personal and professional development in counselling and psychotherapy* (pp. 109–129). London: Routledge.
Stratton, P., & Hanks, H. (2016). PPD as processes of learning that enable the practitioner to create a self that is equipped for higher levels of professional mastery. In A. Vetere & P. Stratton (Eds.), *Interacting Selves: Systemic solutions for personal and professional development in counselling and psychotherapy* (pp. 7–32). London: Routledge.
Todd, T. (2014). Pursuing the universal goal of self-supervision. In T. Todd & C. L. Storm (Eds.), *The complete systemic supervisor: Context, philosophy, and pragmatics* (2nd ed., pp. 151–165). London: Wiley.
Watkins, C. E., Jr. (2011a). Toward a tripartite vision of supervision for psychoanalysis and psychoanalytic therapies: Alliance, transference-countertransference configuration and real relationship. *Psychoanalytic Review, 98*, 557–590.
Watkins, C. E., Jr. (2011b). The real relationship in psychotherapy supervision. *American Journal of Psychotherapy, 65*, 99–116.

Chapter 2
Starting Supervision

Inger Ulleberg and Per Jensen

Introduction

Starting up supervision can take a little time and clarification, or it can take a somewhat longer time before the actual supervisory work begins. This is dependent on who participates and what the goal of the supervision is. In this chapter, we will consider several themes, most of which are relevant at the start of both individual supervision and group supervision. The work of clarification before the start of a supervision group or individual supervision demands that an array of conditions are explored and considered (Ulleberg, 2014; Vråle, 2015), and we will look more closely at some of these conditions. In the following, we will use the term "group" for the most part about the unit seeking supervision, but as a rule what we say can be read in approximately the same way for the individual, a team, or a staff group. This chapter will build on the authors' extensive experience as supervisors and supervisees with fewer references to literature. When we look into the supervision literature, it's not much to find about starting a supervision group.

A group composed of therapists with lengthy experience from both family therapy and supervision has, as a rule, a different starting point than beginners who have little previous experience with supervision. Also, some supervisory work is part of an educational program, development work, a project, or a course, and this context will provide different frames. It is always necessary to use some time to explore to which extent the supervisor and supervisee have shared ideas about what they

I. Ulleberg (✉)
Faculty of Education and International Studies, Department of Primary and Secondary Teacher Education, Oslo and Akershus University College of Applied Sciences, Oslo, Norway
e-mail: inger.ulleberg@hioa.no

P. Jensen
Family Therapy Section, Faculty of Social Studies, VID Specialized University, Oslo, Norway
e-mail: per.kri.jensen@gmail.com

A. Vetere, J. Sheehan (eds.), *Supervision of Family Therapy and Systemic Practice*, Focused Issues in Family Therapy, https://doi.org/10.1007/978-3-319-68591-5_2

should pursue and how to do it. How much time is necessary for these clarifications is dependent on many conditions. There is, as we have said, a difference between having experienced and beginning therapists in supervision. There are great differences between supervision conducted within an established frame, for example a workplace or an educational course, and supervision without such a connection. There can be great differences between beginning supervision with therapists with experience of being in supervision and starting with therapists that do not have such experience.

By having a communication perspective as a point of departure in the request for supervision, in the clarification and the start of supervision it becomes clear that there can be many questions to explore on several levels and in different areas. Taking the time at the beginning to explore these relevant areas for clarification will often be time well spent. In supervision, we are dependent on sharing a common understanding about what we are doing, the frames we are working within, and how often and how long we are going to meet. We must agree on common rules and share an understanding of how we will relate to the stories we will share through participation in the supervision process.

In the following, we will look more closely at some aspects that can be useful to consider in the process of starting a supervision group. Sometimes, the supervisor is an employee in the organization with supervision tasks as most of or parts of their job. This can entail some opportunities and some challenges that are different from those encountered when you invite an external supervisor. In any case, there can be several shared distinctive features, and we will also look at themes that can be of interest for the start of supervision more generally.

We will first consider the request the supervisor receives, and then look more closely at the different questions that can be explored at a "clarification meeting" or in the clarification process. The first supervision meeting will be given attention because we there often establish ways of working and relations that can dominate the supervision. Questions about beginners and experienced therapists in supervision will also be touched upon. Finally, we will look at voluntary or mandatory participation in supervision, and dilemmas that can arise in connection to this issue.

The Request

The request or the invitation to supervision can go in two directions. It can be an invitation *from* a supervisor offering supervision to employees at the workplace, to students, or to therapists within a specific work area. Such invitations or offers can be part of the working methods at a workplace; supervisees can find offers through educational institutions, via colleagues, the Internet and from other sources.

Secondly, the request for supervision can come *to* a supervisor from a working community, from managers at different levels in the organizations, institutions, schools, from individuals, or from groups. This request is, as a rule, the first opportunity to consider whether this is a task the supervisor wants or can take on.

Now and then, it is clear already in the initial request that someone is asking for something the supervisor cannot or will not offer. For example, this might concern conflict resolution in a staff that has struggled with internal conflicts over a longer period, or a situation in which those asking for supervision are working with tasks of which the supervisor has no knowledge or does not wish to get involved with. Some supervisors can then refer to other supervisors who work with conflict resolution in organizations and between employees, or to supervisors with special competence or interest in the area for which supervision is requested. The next issue the supervisor must consider is whether she has the time, capacity, and opportunity to take on the work, regardless of whether this concerns external or internal supervision. Receiving and answering the request is the first step on the way to a clarification process. The supervisor should also take the initiative to hold a clarification meeting with the supervisees and possible managers to establish as sound and clear a frame as possible before the work of supervision can begin.

The Clarification Meeting

Even when the request sounds both relevant and appropriate, it can be sensible to plan a first, noncommittal clarification meeting. This meeting can be constructed to give both parties the opportunity to think about and assess whether they can find a shared point of departure before they decide the further course of the supervision. As a rule, this will contribute clarification and transparency through the articulation and discussion of implicit and explicit terms of the supervision. Sometimes, the work of clarification can be comprehensive, especially when there is a great degree of confusion at the start, or when the participants have little experience with receiving supervision. In such cases, the work of clarification can take place over longer time in parallel with the supervisory work, and one can arrange to have supervision for a limited period. By working with examples of what the group will use the supervision for from the point of view of the supervisees, one can begin the supervision itself while clarifying the terms. Together the supervisor and the group can explore whether they can find a shared platform for continuing the cooperation.

An Internal or External Supervisor

Sometimes we have an *internal supervisor* where the supervision is a required part of the work tasks the supervisees have, and where the supervisor must take on the tasks of supervision as these are already defined. This may for example be related to new employees who shall have a specified form of follow-up, to professional supervision in a group of therapists, or to supervision of specific projects. In any case, it will be important to clarify the form and content of the supervision and find a shared platform; however, if the supervision is mandatory for the supervisees, this will pose special challenges for the supervisor. The same applies if the supervisor is an internal employee, as this can create lack of clarity in the shaping of the role and pose special challenges for both the supervisor and supervisee. It can be challenging to create adequate space for reflection and exploration of challenging situations and vulnerable and uncertain aspects of professional practice if the supervisor also has the role of manager or colleague, or risks encountering the supervisees in staff meetings or union meetings.

Having a manager as supervisor can pose special challenges for both the supervisor and supervisee. A young therapist had received a temporary position at a family office, and the manager offered her regular supervision to discuss the challenges she encountered in the job. The manager was an experienced family therapist and had much to offer, and the supervision functioned well as help for the routine work and as academic support, and was a good introduction to the culture and working methods of the office. The supervision was characterized by training and by the manager having the desire to help the newly hired therapist function as well as possible in the job by offering concrete advice, tips, and suggestions for solutions to the challenges she would encounter as a new employee. This was in many ways a support for the young therapist, but she had the perpetual awareness that the position was temporary and that the manager had the power to either allow her to continue or to end the working relationship when the year was up. This dominated the types of problems the therapist chose to discuss in the supervision, as she wanted to appear as competent and reflective as possible in her meetings with the manager.

How the supervision finds its place in the organization is well worth investigating, and if the manager is the supervisor, one must consider what advantages and possible challenges this can involve. The same will be the case if a manager wants to participate in a supervision group with the employees; this must be clarified with the manager and the group in relation to the opportunities and limitations this can involve. When the supervisor is internally employed, it must also be decided what relationship the supervisor should have with the supervisee's manager, and whether, to what extent and in which ways themes from the supervision are to be shared at the management level in the organization. Supervisors can discover problems and challenges in different areas through the work of supervision that can be natural to report on further in the organization, and this must be clarified with the supervisees both initially and during the process. If the supervision is part of a development of systemic competence in an organization, they can decide how experiences and themes from the supervision can be passed on and shared in the organization.

At other times, the supervisor is an *external, independent person* who performs supervision in their own firm or who takes on supervisory work alongside their regular job. Such a supervisor should have an active and lively relationship with the content of the supervision and carefully assess their own capacity and ability to do a good job, and here a clarification meeting will be central to establishment of a shared foundation for the supervision. Aspects such as content of supervision, extent, and time frame must be considered by an external supervisor when he or she decides whether the answer to an request is to be "yes" or "no," or "not yet, but come back to me later." An external supervisor can have the advantage of not meeting the supervisees in other contexts and can develop an unambiguous supervisory role in meetings with the supervisees. Not having inside knowledge of the organization or workplace in which one supervises, on the one hand, can sharpen the eye and increase curiosity, while on the other hand, one can miss aspects by not having organizational knowledge. There can be advantages and drawbacks to being both internal and external supervisor, and therefore it can be well worth thinking through what the aim and content of the supervision should be and whether this can be covered best by an internal or external supervisor. The relation of the supervisor to the supervisees should also be investigated from several angles and at many levels both initially and during the supervisory process. We will continue to look closely at whether participation in supervision is a voluntary choice for supervisees or whether it is mandatory, and what this can have to say about the work of supervision.

Mandatory or Voluntary Supervision?

Unlike several other countries, Norway has a long tradition of regarding supervision as a sanctuary where ideas and stories from practice can be shared without managers or specialists having the authority to influence or control the participants' professional activity and work. This model is not the only one we find. At some workplaces, supervision is a required part of the work. Mandatory supervision is also often connected to therapy education.

Sometimes, managers may instruct individual therapists to receive supervision so that they can improve their practice. The therapist is then usually in a situation in which they feel pressured to attend supervision and where the work situation and relationship to the closest manager are pressured and stressed. A supervisor who takes on such tasks should be especially aware of what tasks he/she is taking on and which obligations appear to be most important. In our opinion, it is always the client's best interests that must determine the practice of supervision.

Supervision from an external person can also be *more or less voluntary* for those participating. This will be one of the questions it will be fruitful to clarify initially: whether the supervisees have applied for supervision in accordance with their own wishes, if the whole team or work group have applied and some are reluctantly participating, or if the manager has made it a requirement for the team or the individuals to receive supervision. Also, when the supervisor is an external person, the relationship between the supervisor and management must be clarified. Questions one can ask are whether the supervisor should report on the supervision to management, and what should then be shared with the management. What the supervisor should observe confidentiality about and not share with the management must also be clarified.

In the beginning of all supervision relationships, it will be well worth spending time on clarification of whether the supervision is required for some or for all, whether the supervisor has an internal or an external position, and what the relation between the supervisor and management is.

The Manager as Part of the Group?

What do you do if a manager or someone who is a superior to the other participants wishes to participate in the group? There is no simple answer to this. It is a normal prerequisite that all who participate in a supervision group have cases they wish to work with in supervision. The first question the supervisor could ask is whether the manager can present cases from professional work relevant for supervision, as some managers do not work only as managers but participate in professional work on the same level as their colleagues. In such situations, there can be room for the manager to participate in a supervision group. If the manager does not have cases to bring into the group, participation will normally not be possible.

A manager contacted a supervisor with a request to start a supervision group for the personnel staff managed. The supervisor said she was interested, and at the first meeting, she asked the group about the manager's participation in the group. Some participants expressed that he had a natural place there, but some said that his participation would possibly limit what cases they presented and how they presented their cases. When the supervisor asked the manager if he could give some examples of the cases he wanted to present for the group, there was a longer pause. And he concluded that his cases were so different from the others' that the group perhaps would work best without his participation.

The manager's participation in the group could influence some of the group participants in terms of how they would present their cases and which cases they would choose to bring into supervision. It is important that all such questions are addressed openly at the start of supervision if there is a question of whether the manager should participate or not in a supervision process.

Other Conditions and Frames

In every request for supervision, there lie several explicit and some implicit conditions that can be objects for clarification. It is not always the case that these conditions are fixed once and for all, and some of the supervisees have not thought of these issues prior to the request. It is therefore central that the supervisor contributes to the clarification of many aspects of the supervision work before the supervision begins. In the following, we will look at a number of these conditions.

Who Request Supervision?

The wish or requirement for supervision can originate from different sides. There is not necessarily a contradiction between a wish and a requirement. In most therapeutic educational programs, supervision is a requirement connected to practice and is a part of the educational program itself. Within clinical specialization programs and training in different therapy directions, supervision is an obligatory part of the specializations. In some workplaces, supervision is a required aspect of the work, and for many professionals in institutions, family offices, and educational programs, supervision is an attractive community of practice that contributes to recruitment both to education and clinical work.

The duality in requirement and wish can make the question of who is asking for supervision less important. This question becomes important when a person feels that the manager "send" them to supervision or when someone attends supervision without getting anything out of it.

Sometimes managers will use supervision to develop an overview over what their employees are doing and are concerned with, and they want to participate in the supervision as observers. Others want report from the supervisor concerning issues explored in the supervision. In such cases, the supervisor must take time to clarify these questions with all parties and find solutions that supervisor, supervisees, and managers agree on.

As supervisor, therefore, you should consider: who has invited you to take on the job? Who has required supervision? Who is to decide the themes you are to work with or the content of the supervision? Is it the participants, the manager, the institution, the education program, or others? Is the supervision part of an education, a project, developmental work, or an innovation in the workplace? Are there any predefined goals or requirements to relate the supervision to? What do different partners expect from your work? What do they think the benefit of the supervision should be? Is anyone to receive a report from you? In which case, what should it contain?

As a supervisor, one can encounter several dilemmas and challenges that are worth clarifying and finding good solutions to in cooperation with the supervisees. It is important and sensible that such questions be clarified at the start and preferably before the supervision begins.

The Frames of Supervision

The frames of a supervision job can also have different sources, and before you begin a supervision process, the supervisor should clarify the frames that exist for the supervision. Is this part of a project or a new practice is the supervision part of the strategic plan of the workplace? Is the supervision part of a qualification process for the participants? The answers to these questions can be part of deciding the goals and content of supervision.

Many educations, specialist training and unions have their own requirements both for the content of the supervision and for the supervisor's professional background and competence. For example, it is common for unions to have a minimum requirement that the part of the supervision connected to the union's own qualification routines should be with a member of the union in question. This is the case for social workers, nurses, and psychologists and it is also a special requirement when the supervision is part of processes of certification of clinical competence. There may also be requirements regarding the number of hours with the same supervisor, and the extent to which the supervision should occur individually or in a group.

Some organizations and institutions expect their values and goals to be maintained and respected through the supervision process. The supervisor can therefore often benefit from becoming acquainted with the ethical guidelines, the institution's values, and the project goals when such concerns are relevant.

Who Should Participate in the Supervision?

When staff in a department or an office ask for supervision, it should be important to find out and consider who should be invited to participate. Who participates actively in the work? What do the different roles involve in terms of client contact? Should, for example, cleaning staff, assistants, secretaries, substitute staff, and students be invited to participate? Should this be a cross-disciplinary supervision group or should the supervision be specific with relation to professional orientation? Should it be connected to professions or to disciplinary approaches? Must everyone in the department, the team, or the professional group participate, or can each person decide if they wish to participate?

There are no standard answers to these questions, but the supervisor should make time to explore these questions in the start-up phase of a supervision process.

The Frequency of Supervision

Supervision is a place for creativity and a space in which new ideas about practice can arise and be reflected on. Supervision is concerned with the processes between the participants, their professional practice, and the supervisor, and this is relevant for both the frequency and the structure of the supervision. Supervision is dependent on there being spaces of time between supervisions for practice. A supervision process is dependent on participants having time to try out new ideas and new understandings that have developed during the supervision sessions.

How often one should meet for supervision can vary. Some supervision relations are intensive and characterized by closeness in both time and intensity. Other supervisory relationships last for a long time and the sessions occur only a few times each half year.

At the start of supervision, the supervisor and the group should agree on how often they are to meet and it is recommended that they make plans for the first period of supervision. This planning should be very concrete with days and times identified for the meetings, and as far as possible to locate times when everyone can meet. The supervisor should investigate whether the participants who have other commitments have the possibility of moving them making room for supervision, so that all can meet. This can take time, but is time well spent.

Confidentiality

Confidentiality is part of a reciprocal commitment in a supervision group. Confidentiality means that the participants only have ownership over their own stories. All the stories of others from the supervision conversations are not to be shared outside the supervision meetings. Everyone who participates in group supervision has the right to be able to trust the principle of confidentiality to be respected. Sometimes situations in supervision conversations occur where information is presented that demands that confidentiality must be broken. This is quite rare and must be handled with discretion. It is both the supervisor's and the supervisee's duty to ensure that "the relevant persons" are given the information necessary to ensure that life and health are preserved, and that an ethically responsible practice is carried out. Whether the supervisor has a confidentiality agreement in relation to management is another question that must be clarified in each individual case, and toward which there must be openness. In any case, such agreements become important frames around the supervision conversations. It is sometimes the case that assessment of professional practice is a part of a supervision process, and the supervisor is supposed to report the result of the assessment. In such cases, the supervisor and the supervisee must clarify these premises at the start of the supervision. When the supervision begins, these different requirements must be clear and both parties must know from whom the job is coming and to whom it must be reported.

Confidentiality is not there to protect the supervisor. The participants can usually talk about the supervisor and her or his forms of work also outside of the group.

Expert Supervisor or Process Supervisor?

The forms of supervision described in this book are all process oriented; that is to say, we are speaking about the forms of supervision that last over time and with stability of frequency and participation. We distinguish between expert supervision and process supervision as different expectations connected to the request (Westmark, Nissen, Offenberg, & Lund-Jacobsen, 2012). An expert supervisor has a focus on the professional content of the supervision, while a process supervisor places the main emphasis on the processes in the supervision or the supervision group. In expert supervision, training can be a central element in the supervision, while in process supervision, the focus is on development of the supervisees' own reflections, critical thinking, judgement, and independence in the performance of professional practice.

When the request asks explicitly for supervision connected to professional content (for example, couples therapy, families with children, violence in the family, drug problems), it is expected that the supervisor have expert competence connected to this professional practice. We want to claim that the process element is central in all supervision work, in the sense that an expert supervisor must always have an eye on the process aspects of the supervision. One of the aims of supervision work as opposed to courses and lectures is exactly the opportunity to integrate new knowledge with one's own thinking and understanding and to look more closely at the supervisee's own clinical practice.

Who or What Determines the Content of the Supervision?

Supervisees are usually active in negotiating which content the supervision could comprise. The participants in supervision are often members of contexts that are part of determining the content of the supervision; if one works in a psychiatric outpatient clinic or in an institution for treatment of drug addiction, these backgrounds will be part of determining the content of the supervision. When the supervision is part of an educational or introductory program or a development project, this can also place conditions on what the content of the supervision should include.

On the other hand, the competence, experience, and professional interests of the supervisor will be apparent in the supervision. If the supervisor is professionally oriented toward reflection or dialogue, these orientations will be a part of the answer to the question of who determines the content of the supervision. Then a dialogue about the content can occur through a process that is part of the supervision, and in which content themes can be negotiated and renegotiated throughout the supervision course. There are reasons to initially place some limitations on themes that clearly will fall outside the supervision conversations. In clinical supervision, themes such as conflicts in the workplace or personal and private problems fall outside the supervision, and it can be wise to make such boundaries clear from the start. In any case, it can be worthwhile to investigate such aspects in connection to the professional challenges that are addressed. Both conflicts in the workplace and personal and private problems can be relevant contextual understanding or central aspects of professional challenges in therapeutic work with couples, families, or individuals.

As we see, there are no simple answers to who it is who decides the content of the supervision. This occurs in interaction with the ordering body, the supervisees, and the supervisor, and sometimes the ordering body and the supervisees are one and the same.

The First Meeting

Now we will look more closely at the start of the supervision work. The necessary clarifications and arrangements are in place. The task is defined; it has been decided who is to participate; frequency, content, and frames of the meetings are decided; and the supervision itself can begin.

Who Wants What from the Supervision?

Clarification of content and working methods is never accomplished once and for all, but continues throughout the practical work of supervision. What the supervisees wish from the supervision and what the supervisor can offer are two important questions to find a common answer to during the start-up phase of a supervisory relationship. This should however not present a limitation on the work, but can form a platform for a shared start with common ideas among participants about the outcome of the supervision.

Two questions that can expand the conversation in the introductory phase of the start-up of supervision are:

> *If supervision is the answer, what is the question?*
>
> *If supervision is the solution, what is the problem?*
>
> (Holmgren & Holmgren, 2015, p. 81)

When supervisees explore how these questions can be answered, they can discover a multitude of answers. Through this exploration, the supervision can open opportunities for group processes that offer both creativity and variety. The answers to these questions can also provide insight into how the supervisees think and how they understand their own work situation. This can also say something about the work culture they come from. Is supervision the answer?

Being Among Friends

Supervision is a place for critical thinking, creativity, and reflection. At its essence, supervision is an encounter of professionals who want the best for one another. Sometimes one thinks that a friendly environment leads to toothless and irresolute conversations. This is a misunderstanding. There is no place with greater space for ideas and nuances than between people who like and support one another. The main purpose of a supervision group is to help one another with professional development and reflection. In an environment in which you can be certain that all participants want the best for each another, there is room for critical thinking and challenging conversations. With a great degree of security, follows the opportunity for an equal degree of creativity and daring. In an insecure environment, such possibilities are reduced. The certainty that we are among friends creates the best starting place for a supervision process.

In the first supervision meeting, the supervisor, through her choices of working methods and attitudes, contributes to establishing a culture of listening to one another, asking explorative questions and creating a reflective conversation about professional practice. The introductory moves the supervisor uses in the first meeting should not be underestimated.

Taking the Role of Supervisor

Both relatively inexperienced supervisors and experienced supervisors must work to take on the role of supervisor in meeting with a new group. Every meeting with a new group brings new experiences and no group is the same.

Taking on the role of supervisor concerns everything from placing oneself centrally in the room in relation to the supervision group, to taking leadership and structuring the first meeting with the group. By placing herself centrally and taking leadership, a supervisor must be able to move in and out from these positions. The supervisor should offer the group several forms of work to choose from and use time to find a form or a structure all can agree upon. It is often sensible to use the form one finds (for example, the reflecting team) for a set period. Beginners in supervision especially have the need to learn to attend supervision.

There is often a paradoxical connection between a fixed structure and freedom. A fixed structure offers greater freedom when everyone has learned the structure and no longer needs to think of how it is built up and how it should proceed. In the period in which participants are uncertain of the structure and how they should understand their tasks within it, creativity and curiosity can be blocked. The structure stands in the center of attention and the freedom to reflect recedes. When the way in which the supervision is performed is predictable and well known, the space to concentrate on the content of the supervision becomes greater.

Establishment of Relations in Supervision

When people meet, they want to establish relationships. In the first meeting, as a rule, there is the opportunity for a first presentation of oneself as professionals and for a conversation about what one wishes to get out of the supervision. When the members of the supervision group are to present themselves to one another, this can offer opportunities to introduce some ways of working and relevant themes for the supervision group. During the presentation round, it can be fruitful to encourage participants not only to tell their professional stories of education and practice, but also small personal stories that do not have any special relation to professional life. The supervisor can advantageously introduce working methods in this first meeting that include creative and personal aspects, and methods that are related to the reflection aspect and which create cooperation and make the participants responsible.

Beginners in Supervision

Beginners in supervision are to learn to attend supervision. When we start a group for therapists or students in therapy educational programs who have not received much supervision, it is important to include this perspective. To make use of supervision as part of work or education is something that must be learned. Many will derive benefit from several rounds in the start-up phase to find examples from participants' stories, experiences, situations, and cases that they consider are relevant for supervision. The supervisor can also make small demonstrations of how they can work with some of these in a supervision session. By bringing in such a meta-perspective from the beginning, the supervisor can create space for a conversation about the requirements the supervision should observe at the same time, as everyone is a part of sharing these requirements.

One of the supervisees in a supervision group had not taken a single initiative or shared a single story for the first half year of supervision. At the last meeting of the half year, the supervisor asked everyone if they could tell some stories that connected the work the supervision group had done with what they had done in their professional practice. For the first time, the one who had not brought her own stories came forward. She told how several of the stories she had heard had inspired her to new practice in several areas. In this way, she showed that she had absolutely been a participant in the group to the greatest extent in spite of her few words and stories.

It can be sensible to allow the supervisees to develop their active participation in supervision in their own pace. Some are full of stories and often ready to tell new stories at every meeting. Others are more restrained and need more time to get started. One piece of advice is to give different people different amounts of time in the supervision work.

In a supervision group of six inexperienced therapists, the supervisees presented at each meeting what they wanted to talk about, and then took turns in presenting their challenge from practice. One of the supervisees said "pass" each time, but at last her turn had arrived. She seemed insecure and did not have anything she wanted to present this time either. The supervisor decided that in this supervision meeting, they were to work to find current cases from her practice, and they began exploring different situations she had been in, tasks she had had, and relations she was involved with. When the supervision meeting was at the end, they had identified four or five relevant issues. The supervisee was asked: "If we were now to start the supervision session, which of these cases would you have presented?" Through this conversation, the supervisee experienced what issues from her practice that could be relevant to look at more closely in supervision, and in the further work of the group she was never short of cases to present.

Experienced Supervisees

The start-up of a group of experienced supervisees also has some aspects that should be explored and talked about. Exploring which forms of supervision or methods the supervisees have experienced can be a way of promoting a variety of forms of supervision. The supervisor can ask how the supervisees consider and evaluate different experiences with different forms or methods used in supervision. This is also an opportunity for the supervisor to offer the group new ways of working that can be a new experience for all the group participants. If a group wants to work with well-known supervision methods they have experience with, the group can instead expand their repertoire by reading literature they can bring into the supervision conversations. The supervisor must also present her repertoire as supervisor. This can be an opportunity for the supervisor to profile herself and present her own experience as supervisor.

Groups with Both Beginners and Experienced Supervisees

It can be challenging to work with supervision groups that have both experienced members and beginners. Especially if these do not share a common field or cooperate in everyday practice, the gap in the group can become so great that the experienced participants find their benefits from participation become extremely limited. This is a problem that should be addressed right from the start, and possibilities for starting several groups or ensuring that the work is organized in a way that all the supervisees are ensured as great an advantage as possible should be explored.

A possibility is letting the experienced group participants have the roles of supervisor in relation to those less experienced. By trying out the role of supervisor, they are offered the opportunity to expand their own repertoire. Within such a structure, the supervisor can herself take on the role of supervisor of the supervisor and introduce some simple metaconversations between her and the one who has the supervisor role while the rest of the supervisees listen. In this way, one can also demonstrate how reflection and open dialogue can be used as working methods in supervision.

Some Dilemmas in Starting supervision

In the following, we will look at dilemmas or difficulties that we encounter now and then during the start-up phase or during work with a supervision group. It is difficult to provide standard answers to most of these dilemmas. They are highlighted here to include them in the reflections around the start-up of and work in a supervision group. They can bring many answers and each individual dilemma in the actual situation in a group should find its own local solution.

Acquaintances and/or Friends

What do you do if acquaintances or friends want to participate in a supervision group that you are to lead? Many supervisors would rather avoid encountering friends or privately known individuals in a supervision group one is leading. On the other hand, acquaintances and colleagues from work are often participants in supervision groups. What are private conversations and what should we understand as part of the work? There can be extremely fine lines dividing conversations that belong between friends from professional conversations. One of the best pieces of advice for avoiding too much mixing of roles and conversations is to obtain a supervisor from outside for group supervision that lasts over time. This is not always possible in smaller places or when one is working within the same field, but it is important that the supervisor is careful to distinguish between roles, themes, and what belongs where.

Investigating the relations between participants at the start of a supervision group will also be able to bring out the stories they have with one another. The supervisor's relationship to the participants should also be open for all the participants at the introduction to the course of supervision.

One with Greater "Ownership" of the Supervision

Now and then, there are one or two participants who have taken the initiative for the supervision and who are especially interested in getting such activity started. This can be someone who feels a special responsibility that this be begun and who takes much responsibility for the productivity and success of the sessions. At other times, one or several participants will be more than usually active and others may feel that they are both domineering and authoritarian. Some participants are more active than others and take up more space than others. The great challenge in such situations is to both take care of the enthusiastic engagement of the one or several of these supervisees and at the same time ensure that the group remains an open space for all.

It will often be sensible to take this situation up with the group early in the process. As supervisor, you can say that you notice that there is a difference in how active the members are when it comes to expressing themselves in the group. All participants should then express something about this condition and one can further ask if someone has a suggestion for what can be done differently. The supervisor should be careful with establishing solutions that concern a tight structure in which the conversation can begin to seem like a meeting in a union chapter or a committee meeting. In supervision, there must be room for spontaneity, eagerness, and impulsive suggestions and ideas.

Often, such problems will be resolved or regulated after they have been discussed in the group. If this does not help, it is then important not to wait too long to take concrete measures in relation to such a dynamic. In some cases, a supervisor can take on the role of moderator for a time, but it is important that this not be viewed as the solution. The supervisor can also use work methods that involve structures that regulate the participation in the supervision, such as rounds, reflecting team, or witnessing team.

When the Supervisor Has Information That the Supervisees Do Not Have

The supervisor has now and then information of different sorts about different factors connected both to the location of the supervision, the clients the participants work with and knowledge about the individual participants in the supervision. At the start of a supervision group, the group has a presentation round. This is an opportunity in which also the supervisor can tell what she or he knows about and that is relevant to mention. The supervisors should, for example, mention previous contacts with the participants in the group and about prior and current contacts with managers and colleagues outside the supervision group.

The supervisor should strive for the greatest possible openness and avoid having conversations with managers or participants outside the supervision. Information that supervisors receive in such conversations should to the greatest possible extent be shared with the supervisees so that the prerequisites for participation in the conversation and creation of meaning in what is told is to the greatest extent shared and open. In the cases in which the supervisor cannot be open about information she has, she must herself actively work to sort through, limit and exclude what she knows that can influence the supervision.

Conclusion

In this chapter, we have given you some of our experiences from starting up supervision groups. The importance of clarifying the request and using enough time in meetings with the supervisees is necessary. We need to share some ideas about what this supervision is about, how we can use it, and which frames we shall work within.

In the first meeting, it is important to take on the role of supervisor and to establish this role in the supervision group. There are differences between working with a group of experienced professionels and a group of beginners in supervision. A thorough and creative start of a supervision group is the best premise for a good and lasting working process.

References

Holmgren, A., & Holmgren, A. (2015). *Narrativ supervision og vejledning*. Snekkersten: DISPUKs Forlag.

Ulleberg, I. (2014). *Kommunikasjon og veiledning : en innføring i Gregory Batesons kommunikasjonsteori - med historier fra veiledningspraksis* (2. utg. ed.). Oslo: Universitetsforlaget.

Vråle, G. B. (2015). *Veiledning når det røyner på*. Oslo: Gyldendal akademisk.

Westmark, T., Nissen, D., Offenberg, L., & Lund-Jacobsen, D. (2012). *Konsulent - men hvordan? Narrativt konsulentarbejde i praksis*. København: Akademisk Forlag.

Part II
The Supervision Process: Listening, Action and Reflection

Chapter 3
Asking Questions in Supervision

Inger Ulleberg and Per Jensen

As you ask, you will be answered

Norwegian saying

Introduction

Questions are asked in most conversations, and a question is a type of sentence that appears in all languages. An example can be the first question in the Bible where the snake is posing a question to Eve, saying: "Has God truly said that you may not take of the fruit of any tree in the garden?" (Bible, 2000, Gen.3.1.). It lies in the question's nature, that it demands an answer. The question opens up to different answers, and in the myth of the fall of man from divine grace, a question is what releases all the misery (Lauritzen, 2015). A seemingly innocent question can have unforeseen consequences and can actually be the beginning of the end of man's life in the Garden of Eden.

Questions are also a central element in many professional conversations, and in this chapter we will take a closer look at questions in supervision. We start by taking a general look at the phenomena, before we explore more closely which position and function questions can have in supervision.

We relate to ourselves and our surroundings in a questioning/inquiring way, and all human actions can be understood as questioning. To ask questions defines us as human beings, and the idea that the road from ignorance to knowledge is found through asking questions is an idea stemming from antiquity. To ask questions is therefore the basic ingredient in pedagogy, education, therapy, supervision—and in research precise questions are asked to become wiser, and to explore and develop knowledge in a field.

I. Ulleberg (✉)
Faculty of Education and International Studies, Department of Primary and Secondary Teacher Education, Oslo and Akershus University College of Applied Sciences, Oslo, Norway
e-mail: inger.ulleberg@hioa.no

P. Jensen
Family Therapy Section, Faculty of Social Studies, VID Specialized University, Oslo, Norway
e-mail: per.kri.jensen@gmail.com

A. Vetere, J. Sheehan (eds.), *Supervision of Family Therapy and Systemic Practice*, Focused Issues in Family Therapy, https://doi.org/10.1007/978-3-319-68591-5_3

At the same time, opinions, interpretations, and choices lie implicitly within what we do or do not ask, and how we ask: "The questions we do and do not ask define our understanding of and our relationship with our environment" (Lauritzen, 2015, p. 14). A question can open up to new perceptions and perspectives, but at the same time it creates a framework and thereby limits our understanding. Which questions we ask, say something about how we perceive the world. How we socialize and use questions is related to our culture.

Before we take a closer look at how questions can be asked and which questions can be asked in supervision, we want to emphasize that it is possible to be inquiring and curious without asking questions. To be questioning can be understood as mannerism, and it is a matter of meeting others with a genuinely curious attitude and taking on a not-knowing position. It is not necessarily whether the question is well formulated which decides if it will spark reflection and consideration, but that a relationship has developed, and an ambiance of openness and curiosity. It is necessary to develop not only a broad repertoire of good questions as a supervisor, but also wisdom and sensitivity in the meeting with the individuals and the group. Good questions at the right time can drive the conversation in helpful and fertile directions. To practise asking questions in a one-sided way, as a technical skill, is not sufficient to be able to become a good supervisor. We would like to present a few fundamental ideas of how we as supervisors can understand the asking of questions:

- Our questions contribute to a process of "shared shaping" of the conversation.
- Our questions can be possible interventions, and be a contribution towards creating movement, expansion of the framework of understanding and change.
- Different questions create opportunities to think and answer on different levels, domains, or fields.
- How questions are perceived is determined by the person hearing it.

Interactional Perspective on Questions

We maintain that questions always have to be understood as *one* part of a conversation, and that studying questions in an isolated manner might relate more to the rhetorical content of the question, as detached from the context and the relation it is asked in. Nevertheless, we choose to take a closer look at the asking of questions, and hope that this can contribute to an understanding of how they can work in conversations with other people, in relationships and interactions. It is important to understand and interpret the questions' contribution to conversations in an interactional way (McGee, Vento, & Bavelas, 2005). McGee, del Vento, and Bavelas present in the paper "An Interactional Model of Questions as Therapeutic Interventions" the following ideas about questions:

1. Questions need answers—they invite a reply.
2. The respondent has to give meaning to the question, interpret the wording, and understand what is being asked.

3. The question limits and directs the respondent towards a specific aspect of her experience. The reply's content is decided by the question. How a question is asked opens up for different ways of replying, but at the same time creates a framework and limits possible replies.
4. To be able to reply, the respondent has to go through an extensive "here-and-now" effort, assess personal experiences and knowledge, opinions and conclusions, stories and details which might be relevant and related to the question which has been asked.
5. The respondent usually does not explicitly take into consideration prerequisites or presumptions which the question is based on.
6. A built-in prerequisite is malleable and can be changed or negotiated through the conversation. This might be facts, frameworks, interpretation of emotional expression, which direction seems interesting, etc. Through these "negotiations", it is possible to establish a shared understanding; for example, if the supervisor asks: "What do you do when you get annoyed?", and the supervisee replies: "I don't get annoyed!", then this might change the direction of the conversation.
7. The answer can thereby create a new, shared starting point for further exploration.
8. The answer is "owned" by the respondent. It is the respondent who gives the answer meaning and owns the interpretation of his or her own answers.
9. After the answer is given, it should be the asker's initiative to comment, paraphrase, etc., to ask a new question or bring the others from the group in.

McGee et al. maintain that "… all questions are constructive because they offer a perspective that the client (or supervisee, our addition) is very likely to join in with and contribute to. Asking about success can create a conversational space for an account filled with positive and helpful details, while asking about failings will probably lead to a very different perspective of the same life" (McGee et al., 2005, p. 382). In addition to having a look at different categories of questions, it is possible to analyse one's own supervision, and having a look at how the questions arise from what is said and how they are perceived and received.

At the same time as we are awake and attentive when it comes to which questions we ask, we need to be aware of and sensitive to how the question is perceived and answered by the other. How our questions work and how they are perceived depends on how it is heard by the other person. This is closely related to the person's utilization of words and language, how they understand reality, and their understanding of the current relation and situation.

Questions can be compared to a spotlight which enlightens some aspects or sides to the situation or problem in focus, while other parts remain in the darkness (Hornstrup, Tomm, & Johansen, 2009). As supervisors, we cannot and we should not decide in which direction the shared creation of the conversation should go; however, we need to explore an unknown landscape where the participants are co-creators of which areas to be examined more closely. The aim is to create better social worlds—both in the supervision group and as an inspiration to the other social worlds the participants partake in (Pearce, 1994).

Questions are thus based on different basic ways of understanding and are asked with different motives. We need to underline that there can be a discrepancy in the connection between the supervisor's motive for asking a question and the question's actual influence on the supervisee, between what the supervisor is asking and what the supervisee hears. How the supervisee hears and interprets a question depends on, among other things, the context in which the supervisee hears the question and the relationship between the supervisor and the supervisee. The supervisor can develop a sensitivity towards a question's likely, possible, unlikely, and unthinkable ways of being understood (Tomm, 1989, p. 165).

In some traditions it is common to use the metaphor "interviewer" about the supervisor, and the interview format is used as a part of the supervision work (Westmark, Nissen, Offenberg, & Lund-Jacobsen, 2012). This includes both the supervisor interviewing the supervisee and the participants interviewing each other, usually using interview guides made by the supervisor. The interview stands out from other conversational formats because the focus is on the supervisee's experiences, ideas, and thoughts, while the others' input is restricted. The questions asked are central in an interview, and the roles in the conversation are clear—one person is asking and another is replying. Certain sequences in supervision can consequently be directed and shaped as an interview, where the focus on which questions are being asked becomes very clear.

The Context of the Questions

A central element in supervision is asking the supervisee questions. Questions can be asked both by the supervisor and by the other participants in the group. Questions used to be considered a tool to collect relevant information, while in newer years questions are also understood as powerful interventions or as invitations to the co-creation of meaning (Tomm, 1988). In the following, we will have a closer look at different questions a supervisor can ask, but keep in mind that

- The meta-learning is of importance in supervision.
- The supervisor can act as a model for the participants.
- Different rounds of questions can be included as a part of supervision methods.
- The participants can transfer ways of asking to their professional practice.
- It is possible to have an inquiring, wondering attitude without asking questions.

The context a question is understood within varies from person to person, and depends on what kind of relationship which exists with the person asking the question, and in which context it is asked. For instance, in school many have been thoroughly taught that if you are asked a question, the aim is to find the right answer. It can be argued that one ritual in the classroom goes like this: question, hand-up, right or wrong answer, the answer is evaluated, new question. This kind of conversation follows what is called an IRE-structure in pedagogical literature: initiative (from the teacher), response (from the student), evaluation of the answer (from the teacher) (Mehan, 1979). Many will have learned this so thoroughly that they automatically think that it is important to have the right answer in other contexts as well, and it can take some time to establish another understanding of which purpose questions should serve. When you ask a question, it is not done without assumptions: you choose to ask about something based on how you have understood the problem, what you think is related to the problem, and what you think can contribute to solving it. All in all: you ask based on your framework of understanding. There can also lie camouflaged advice about what people should do in the questions. For example, if you ask: Have you tried to…? or Could it be sensible to try to…?

Different models and lists for productive and useful questions have been developed for the supervision field. Some operate with simple binaries such as open/closed or authentic/rhetoric questions, while others have more complex models or lists (Langslet, 1999a; Tomm, 1989).

First, we will take a look at meta-questions which invite to a conversation about conversation. This deals with both process-oriented and process-disruptive questions, which are asked to create involvement and to clarify and create a framework for supervision in different ways. Subsequently, we will take a closer look at four different kinds of questions which are asked about the issue, the situation, or the story being told, and will keep a particular focus on with which motives the questions are asked. We will draw questions especially from four sources, and place different question categories in four overarching categories:

1. To map out, get informed, clarify, or explore the situation
2. To influence, challenge, or move the supervisee's understanding
3. To complicate, thicken, or expand the supervisee's understanding
4. To explore what works and to find solutions

The sources we get the questions from are firstly from the Canadian family therapist Karl Tomm, who developed a model for questioning which he called "interventive interviewing". He claimed that to ask questions could involve interventions and contribute to movement and change (Tomm, 1988). He draws a model based on the therapists' position connected to the questions asked, with one vertical line and one horizontal line crossing each other at the middle. The vertical line illustrates the dimension from therapists' linear assumptions on the top to circular assumptions at the bottom. The horizontal line is concerned with the therapists' purpose of posing the questions from informative to more influential questions. In the model we then find four different areas for questions, linear (linear assumptions, informative purpose), circular (circular assumptions, informative purpose), strategic (linear assumptions, influential purpose), and reflective (circular assumptions, influential purpose). The ideas and the model are used both in therapeutic practice and clinical work, and in supervision, consultation, and organizational development, and has been further developed the last few years (Hornstrup et al., 2009; Solem & Ulleberg, 2013). The second source we get questions from is the Norwegian professor Tom Andersen, who developed the reflective team (Andersen). The third source is questions developed within a solution-focused approach, where we in particular use Norwegian and Swedish authors (Korman, 2002a, 2002b; Langslet, 1999a). The fourth source we draw questions from is the narrative tradition in general, and a Danish book about consultancy work in particular (Westmark et al., 2012). But first we will take a closer look at meta-questions which can be asked in supervision.

Meta-Questions

Meta is a Greek prefix meaning "between, after, or over", and in this context meta-questions will invite a conversation about the conversation. By meta-questions we refer to questions concerning the way of framing how to speak or listen, or the content in what we are going to talk about. It concerns viewing communication on several levels and from different angles: which relationship do we have and should we have to each other, which relationship do we have or can we have to the content of what we are talking about, and how should we talk to each other. In other words, it can be a question of what we should talk about, how we should talk about it, which methods we should use, and which questions to ask. In establishing a supervision group, meta-questions are of importance to clarify the shape and content of the supervision. We will take a closer look at meta-questions which can be asked in the beginning, underway, and in conclusion of supervision.

At the Beginning of the Conversation

At the beginning of each supervision meeting it can be beneficial to use meta-questions, as a way of mapping out the road ahead and they can contribute to creating an openness and a reflection about the work. We can ask questions such as "Has anyone thought about what we talked about last time, which you want to address?" The input can be about the content of the conversation and how the content was angled and explored. It can also deal with which models and conversational structures were used and how they were perceived, or reflections made about general professional or supervision questions can be shared.

Subsequently, questions can be asked to start the day's supervision, for example: What do you want to talk about today? Which problem for discussion should we have a look at? Which challenge should we explore? The supervisor can also encourage participation in the choice of methods in supervision, and can for example ask: Do you have any ideas about how we should organize the conversation? Should we use a specific method? Do you want the others in the group to listen for something in particular when we are talking? Should they angle their listening in a specific way? (father's perspective, client's, leader's, etc.)

Underway in the Conversation

Meta-questions can be process-disruptive underway in supervision and can contribute to lowering the tempo. We can for example ask: "Are we talking about what you find most relevant to talk about now?" The questions can invite a meta-conversation where the supervisor, the supervisee, and the participants get the chance to deliberate and explore if what is talked about is experienced as important and useful.

Through asking process-disruptive questions at crossroads, it is possible to increase participation and engagement in the conversation (Westmark et al., 2012). One such question can be: "I am seeing at least three directions we can explore further, and maybe you are seeing even more. Where should the conversation go from here?" In this way it is possible to have a meta-conversation about which possible directions we can see together for the further conversation, and through this the participants are explicitly co-responsible for the benefits of the supervision.

Process-disruptive questions can deal with the content in the conversation: "Are we talking about what you prefer to talk about? Are there other sides to this problem you would rather explore? Are there any questions you want me to ask you?" The supervisor can also introduce parts of the story which interests her in particular, and for example ask: "I am so interested in your feelings in this situation, can we have a closer look at that?", or she can ask: "Which question would you like for me to ask you now?" The questions can also deal with the way we speak: "Would it be helpful to have the participants share their ideas for possible solutions? Should we ask the participants to create a reflective team now? Which listening assignments would you like for the different participants in the team to have?"

In Conclusion: About the Issue

As a conclusion or review of the supervision, the supervisor can ask meta-questions about the content of the supervision. The supervisee can be challenged to think through: "What do you think about your problem now—your challenge—your situation? If you could articulate it in one sentence, what would it sound like?" Other questions which could help the supervisee in taking on a meta-perspective to his/her situation could for example be:

- What will you keep doing about the problem?
- What will you do more of—less of?
- Is there anything you will stop doing?
- Is there anything new you want to try?
- Is there any more information you would like to obtain, any sides to the problem you would like to have a closer look at?
- Are there any important sides to the problems which we have not addressed?

In Conclusion: About the Conversation

The whole group can be asked questions about the conversation, for example: "How did you experience talking to each other in this way? What was challenging? What was helpful? Which questions were opening? What affected you?" The supervisee can also be asked questions, like "Was anything of what you have heard difficult, challenging, or uncomfortable to listen to? Were any certain contributions or angles especially helpful?" By concluding with a conversation about the supervision in this way, the participants get the opportunity to adjust and improve the direction of the cooperation in the group. This is also of importance to the supervisor's further work. Such a concluding conversation, based on meta-questions, can also give the participants the idea of doing this in other conversations they partake in.

Different Questions Asked About the Issue

In quite a bit of literature about supervision and counselling, it is underlined that the conversations should follow a certain composition, where you move from exploring the issue, to problematizing the issue, and then finding possibilities or solutions (Egan, 2013). We believe these ideas of following a template, a structure, or a certain order might be limiting to the development of the conversation, and would like to underline that every conversation is created by those participating. The challenge for the supervisor is to be alert to the possibilities she sees, and pay attention to which directions the conversation takes. Nevertheless, we often start by asking explorative or mapping questions about the situation presented by the supervisee. From there, however, the way the conversation moves can vary from conversation to conversation. A conversation can move from exploring to challenging and back to exploring further, to finding solutions or being emboldening, and further to creating "thicker descriptions" or thicker stories (Geertz, 1994). There does not exist a certain direction for the conversation to follow or a certain sequence the different elements should be in. The conversation can move in unexpected ways, and in the middle of the challenge we see that we need to explore more or focus more on resources or solutions. Nevertheless, it can be useful to the supervisor to stay alert to the different kinds of questions, and keep an extra eye on when meta-questions can be productive. Now we will delve into different questions which can be asked about the situation, the story, or the issue, which is presented by the supervisee as the content in supervision.

1: Questions to Map Out, Get Informed, Clarify, or Explore the Situation

When we have agreed upon what is going to be the subject, the case, or the issue that the supervision will centre around, the supervisor starts to get informed about the different sides to the situation. This mapping out or exploration is often done through asking question and forms the backdrop to the further conversation.

A part of the conversation in supervision is hence to *map out or explore* the problem which is presented. The supervisor asks questions and the supervisee answers, and the questions can contribute to clarifying a situation, they can be explanatory, and they can act expanding. However, questions can also be revealing and exposing, and the supervisee can experience the conversation as an uncomfortable interrogation, where they might feel trapped or exposed.

These explorative questions have to be asked from a basis of genuine curiosity or interest, and with an intersubjective participation from both supervisor and the other participants. Intersubjective participation refers to an active and inclusive subject–subject communication. We can talk of three different types of intersubjectivity which can appear at the same time: primary, secondary, and tertiary intersubjectivity (Braten, 1998; Moen, 2016; Sjøberg, 2009). Primary intersubjectivity deals with tuning into each other's physical-emotional conditions and expressions, while secondary intersubjectivity involves having a shared attentiveness towards an object. Tertiary intersubjectivity entails a communication where we share something through symbols and language (Matusov, 2009; Moen, 2016). An intersubjective participation means then that we communicate on different levels at the same time, and that the subject–subject relationship is developed in many ways (Bateson, 1972). Intersubjective participation presupposes an altercentric participation, which means being able to take a part of, feel, and mirror, for example another's movements (Braten, 1998). "Alter" is a designation of "the other", and an example of altercentric participation is when an adult is feeding a small child with a spoon, and does the same motions with his/her mouth which is expected from the child. By way of asking explorative or mapping questions, the wish is to tune into how the other understands the situation, to have a common attentiveness towards this, and as far as possible see the issue the way the supervisee sees it. We will now take a closer look at which types of question can be used to map out and explore. We will start with the informative questions from Karl Tomm's model, the linear and the circular, in this part. We will get back to the influential questions from the model, the strategic and reflexive, in the next part of the chapter. The categories of questions we will take a closer look at here are thus linear questions, circular questions, scale-questions, and questions which display well-established stories.

Linear Questions

We can/might be searching for how people understand and explain the situation or the problem within a linear understanding. This is a part of a predominant everyday understanding within Western culture. The aim with the questions is to give an account of how the supervisee thinks about and understands the situation. Linear questions derive from Karl Tomm's model, and a linear question invites a linear description (Tomm, 1989, p. 157). The basic questions are: "Who did what? Where? When? Why?" Within the cause-effect paradigm, it is traditionally common to search for the cause of a problem. The main idea is that it is necessary to find the cause to be able to solve a problem. In a systemic context, we think differently. When someone answers a why-question, they usually also say something important about how they think. And it is how the supervisee thinks which is most interesting to the supervisor.

Supervision is often opened with a few linear questions, and we can also call it problem-explanatory or problem-defining questions (Tomm, 1989). If we want to explore how a person thinks around a problem or a conflict, questions such as "Why do you think that…" or "What do you think the reason for…" can be good questions to take part in someone else's understanding of reality. Linear questions do not aim to create change; however, they can contribute to an important exploration of how the supervisee experiences the problem or the situation. To explore thoroughly how people think and understand a problem or a situation can be a good starting point for asking more challenging questions. If the supervision is predominantly dominated by linear, mapping questions, then we risk that there will not be "a difference which makes a difference" (Bateson, 1972). The questions become too usual, as Andersen says (Andersen, 2005), and are not fit to create an expansion or change in the understanding of the problem, but can nevertheless be a good starting point to build on.

The questions which are normal, well known, and which the person has heard many times before and knows well how to answer, can be a good place to start the conversation. These questions are not meant to create movement, challenges or change in the supervisee's understanding or framing of the situation or problem. If the conversation only circles around these kinds of questions, it can contribute to a social world or a culture where exploration and curiosity are not central elements in the conversation, but where the conversations follow conventional courses. The risk with this pattern is that the supervision might contribute to the strengthening of unfortunate established practices, rather than being an element in a professional development of the supervisee.

Circular Questions

Through asking *circular* questions, you get information about differences and similarities between ideas, values, experiences, and situations. This is a question of having a curiosity towards how incidents and problems can be understood and interconnected. With reference to Bateson, Tomm claims that we can have two general types of circular questions: "difference-questions" and "context-questions" (Tomm, 1989, p. 160), and he has developed a list of possible categories of circular questions, for example:

Difference-questions:

- Between people
- Between relationships
- Between experiences and ideas
- Between past and present

An example of a difference-question to a young boy in a family where the parents feel that they no longer have control can be: Who reacts the most when you don't follow the family's rules, mom or dad?

Context-questions:

- How to frame and interpret a behaviour
- How to frame and interpret a relationship
- How to frame and interpret an episode

An example of a context-question can be: How would you explain that your daughter does not listen to you, but does what she wants?

By asking circular question you wish to clarify the context and the connections which the problem or situation can be understood within. The aim is to develop a contextual and relational understanding for the supervisor and for the participants of the group. In family therapy, circular questions can be used to explore the relationships between the members of a family, while in supervision the relationship between the supervisee and her co-workers, clients, or patients is explored.

Scale-Questions

With the solution-focused approach, a line of categories of questions has been developed, and one of them is scale-questions (Korman, 2002a; Langslet, 1999a). When asking a scale-question, a scale is established from for examples 1 to 10 to express how the supervisee judges the current situation or problem. This can be formulated in this way: "On a scale from 1 to 10, where 10 means that you are very pleased with your effort and 1 means that you are very displeased and that you could have performed much better, where would you place yourself now?". "On a scale from 1 to 10, where 10 means you have a strong confidence in being able to help this person and 1 means you have given up hope, where would you place yourself now?" (Korman, 2002a).

In the continuation of the conversation we can explore why the person did not place himself another place on the scale, where on the scale he thinks it is okay to be, what he thinks is needed to move up the scale, where it would be realistic to expect to get in the following weeks, etc. Questions such as "what else?" and "which other things?" are central follow-up questions throughout the conversation. They contribute to thoroughly exploring what the core elements of people's solutions and smart moves are (Langslet, 1999a). By using scale-questions it is possible to concretize the current situation compared to the preferred one, and with this as a starting point it is possible to look for ways of creating changes to the situation.

Displaying Well-Established Stories

Other ways of exploring the current situation can be to ask questions to display well-established stories, derived from a narrative tradition (Westmark et al., 2012). This is not a question of developing a limited, coherent story, rather to give people the chance to take a pause and relate to aspects they might have overlooked. This can be done by for example asking a number of questions about details, which more or less can provoke an inner movie in the supervisee's mind. When asking questions to display well-established stories, the aim is to increase the richness of detail and reveal concrete descriptions which can come before the conclusions. If a person says about a client "She is so difficult", by interviewing the person it is possible to move away from this general statement to getting concrete and detailed descriptions. It does not deal with challenging the supervisee's perceptions, but to explore the creation of meaning which exists before conclusions are reached. "At times even the supervisor does not understand how a result has been reached" (Westmark et al., 2012, p. 73).

Questions such as "What happened? Where were you? Who did what? What happened then? What did you say? What did she say then?" can contribute to revealing nuances and can give the supervisee the opportunity to bring some of the complex, living life into the conversation. Through displaying the story in this manner, it is possible to avoid understanding too quickly. Anderson and Goolishian (1988) underlined that it is not wise to believe that you understand how things look to the other person, but that through the questions we ask it is possible to develop possible approaches and to be a part of process of trying to understand oneself and the other.

The questions asked also need to be closely tied to what *the supervisee is actually saying*, and have a starting point in the language, the metaphors, and the central words which the supervisee uses. If a supervisee shares a story about a conflict, then the supervisor can explore the supervisee's feelings connected to conflicts, different experiences the supervisee has with conflicts, whether conflict is seen as something good or bad, which other words the person could use about the situation, etc. Other examples of words and expressions which can be explored are "I was *on thin ice* then", "I was *scared* then", "she was so *angry*", "she was going to *fix it*", "I was *bored*", "it was like *being on the decline*". In these situations, the supervisor can ask the supervisee if she can share a story about being in similar situations before, or if this reminds her of something she has previously experienced. In this way the supervisee might be able to tie together stories from her own life and own experience.

2: Questions to Influence, Challenge, or Move the Supervisee's Understanding

As a part of the influential or challenging questions, we will present externalizing questions, fairly unusual questions, strategic questions, reflexive questions, and miracle questions. These types of questions are in many ways found in the core of the supervision work. The aim of supervision is to contribute to the supervisee finding new possibilities to understand and to take action, and through supervision the wish is to disturb, to move, and to challenge. It deals with the expansion of understanding through creating new meaning together. When we have examined a story or the situation, there can be a gliding transition to the more challenging or influential questions. If the supervisor asks a circular question about relations to get informed, it might seem influential to a supervisee who has not thought in those terms before. A scale-question which is asked to explore how the supervisee thinks about a problem can seem expanding by introducing the idea of a scale, and it is possible to move up and down this scale. As a supervisor, the aim is to create movement, influence the supervisee to reflect and take a look at their practice, challenge the supervisee on certain issues, or expand the framework of understanding of the problem presented. This can be done in many different ways, and we will take a closer look at some basic ideas and some categories of questions.

Externalizing Questions

Within the narrative tradition, a central idea is to use *an externalizing language* when referring to problems and challenges, and this might be challenging and expanding to the supervisee. This is a specific way of thinking and talking about problems where you move different inner qualities and problems we usually attribute to people (she is so anxious, he is so controlling, she has a bad temper, I become so discouraged) to rather talking about the problem as something outside of the person. "This anxiety, this control, this temper, this discouragement"—What does it do to you? How can you handle it? Where did the idea of this being a problem come from? What does it make you do? Do you have episodes when it's not there? This can be linked to the idea of moving the focus from people's inner qualities to understanding behaviour as relationships between people, and underline that all descriptions of characteristics can be understood in light of relationships between people (Bateson, 1972).

Further, in the discussion about phenomena introduce a three-linked relationship, where a common topic is the object of exploration between two subjects (Skjervheim, 1957, p. 52). If this topic is that the supervisee feels discouraged, gets angry, feels inadequate, or the like, these phenomena can be "put on the table" for collective examination using externalizing language. Here we can also mention communication as a triadic model, and we maintain that in any conversation there are at least three elements present: me, you, and the case or topic (Ongstad, 2004) (Fig. 3.1).

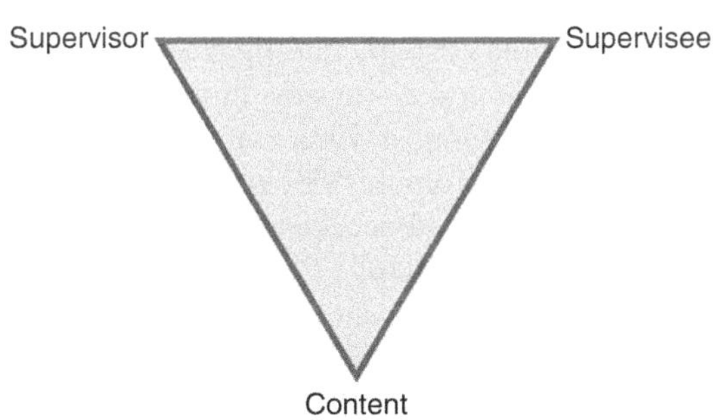

Fig. 3.1 Three-linked relationship

This is how the idea of the three-linked relationship and a triadic model can support the externalizing questioning. By way of this thought-model we can avoid questions which might seem psychologizing and limiting as in a three-linked relation where an equality sign between the person and the case (you are anxious—you + anxiety), and it can increase curiosity on all parts.

Fairly Unusual Questions

Another angle to challenging questions is Tom Andersen's idea that there are three types of differences: too small, too large, and suitable, but that only one of them *makes* a difference or creates movement and change, and that is the one which is *suitably* different (Andersen, 2005). He says: "The reaction from those being asked the question is the only thing which can tell us whether our questions are too usual, suitably unusual, or too unusual" (Andersen, 2005, p. 63). Andersen thus claims that the third type of question, the suitably unusual ones, can create movement and contribute to people being able to "move a bit", to see the situation from new positions, or open up to examining the situation in new ways. He calls it "questions which create more, and hopefully new, openings". By being attentive of how people respond to our questions, we can discover the suitably unusual questions. If we find these questions, they can open up to movement, change, wonder, and reflection.

On the other hand, it is possible to ask questions which are *too* unusual, too provoking, and too distant from the participants' or the supervisee's understanding and framing of the situation. This can lead to the supervisee defending his/her views, not understanding the question, or rejecting the suggestion completely. In this way, too unusual questions can also contribute to fortifying an unreflected practice, and make people not question their way of reasoning and understanding.

Strategic Questions

One of the categories of questions which Tomm presents is the strategic questions. In everyday speech we know the strategic questions as "leading questions". These questions aim to affect people in a specific way, in the "right" direction. "The aim with these questions is first and foremost corrective. It is presumed that it is possible to interact in an instructive way" (Tomm, 1989, p. 160). By way of this, the wish is to limit possibilities and give expert advice, and considering the expert's advice and recommendations as important and useful.

On the other hand, it is possible to ask useful strategic questions in an expert supervision, and through this direct the participants' attention towards values, research, theories, and syllabus, which is relevant to the particular problem. These leading questions might be for example "How can you get feedback from your clients about your therapy?" or "How can you give the mother's voice more space?" "How can you bring up this problem with your boss? How can you influence the next of kin to come visit more often? How can you set clearer limits for him?" Using these questions, we are giving indirect advice about actions to take, and want to affect the supervisee in a certain direction in our professional practice. There are good and legitimate reasons to ask strategic questions in supervision, not least when the supervision is a part of education. Not all practice has the same quality, and the supervisor might want to challenge the supervisee in directions which are in line with the content in the educational programme's objectives.

A supervision course attached to for example a family therapy education can legitimize strategic questions as a part of the training. When considering a case, and you are going to do a narrative or structural analysis, the supervisor can help by asking for example: How do you understand the boundaries between parents and children in this case? Or: Is it possible that there are special alliances in this family, which might help us understand this dynamic?

Strategic questions are originally based on a traditional linear way of thinking and can be a framework for a cause-effect-understanding for both the supervisor and the participant. By asking these strategic questions throughout the conversation, it is possible to establish an expert-position which will affect the conversation and the relationship. In this way, the possibilities for thinking and understanding in new ways are diminished, and through this increase possible new alternatives of taking action. This is connected to Tom Andersen's idea about too normal questions, which do not create change.

Reflexive Questions

Karl Tomm speaks of *reflexive* questions as well, which invites an open exploration of possible ways of understanding the complexity of a problem or situation (Tomm, 1989). The purpose is to influence or challenge the supervisee, but there are no built-in answers or directions in the way the questions are asked. The supervisee is seen as someone who can find a direction or path on his own, and together it is possible to examine a situation where everyone can contribute with new understanding and constructive input. This can be linked to an acknowledging attitude (Schibbye, 2009) and a not-knowing position (Anderson & Goolishian, 1992).

The purpose of the reflexive questions is to open the conversation up to possible ways of understanding and acting related to the specific problem or dilemma, which can contribute to acting wisely when at a crossroads (Pearce, 1994). New meaning can be created through conversation. At the same time, a desired outcome is that through using reflexive questions those in supervision will trust in their own judgment when going forward and finding one's own path.

The reflexive questions have their starting point in a systemic and social-constructivist understanding where the wish is to keep focus on relations and context-understanding, and where the aim is to explore alternative ways of understanding and thinking (Hornstrup, Tomm, & Johansen, 2008). Tomm presents a string of different reflexive questions (Tomm, 1989), and we will take a closer look at some of his suggestions. By looking at the problem in different contexts and from different angles, together it is possible to create a more complex, nuanced, and composite understanding of the situation. Tomm speaks of "future-oriented questions" where he examined hypothetical possibilities such as "What do you think would happen if you talked to him about it/if you didn't comment on it/if you got angry and harsh/if you started to laugh?" In this case, there are no hidden advice in the contribution, just a playful attitude towards the exploration of possibilities.

With "observer-perspective questions" it is possible to reflect around how the client might perceive and interpret the situation: "If I were to talk to your client, what do you think she would say?" Tomm also focuses on that we can ask questions which contain an unexpected change of context, for example: "If we change focus from seeing the problem as a problem, to looking for how the problem can be a solution to something—what can this problem be a solution to?" We can also ask "In which other ways is it possible to frame the problem?" Questions can also be asked which involve a challenge and a comparison of norms and culture, for example: "How could this situation be understood in another time, in another culture, with different norms?" or "Which cultural norms or ways of understanding can be relevant to this situation?"

In supervision of students you can switch between an expert and process position, and switch between more or less strategic and more or less reflexive questions as a supervisor, because the aims of the study specify some directions and frames as more professionally desirable than others to develop (Westmark et al., 2012). If you only ask reflexive questions without a direction, you risk that the student is not introduced to central ideas from the profession's knowledge base. If you on the other hand only ask strategic questions, the supervision will not contribute to growth, to critical and independent attitudes, and to a development of judgment and personal knowledge.

The strategic questions can also have a place in supervision of family therapists in practice. The supervision can be framed by goals for a project at a workplace, or it can be agreed upon to explore topics in supervision such as "the clients' contribution" or "professional-ethical norms' significance to practice". In these cases, there has been established an agreement of within which frameworks and in relation to which values the professional practice should develop. The supervisor can act as a "watchdog" who brings this up by way of strategic questions. There can be gliding transitions between categories of questions, and what is important about operating with many different categories of questions is not to decide where the questions belong, but to inspire to analysis of and reflection about practice (Ulleberg, 2014).

There can be gliding transitions between the strategic and the reflexive questions, and also between the circular and the reflexive questions. There might be a continuum between getting informed about other people's way of understanding and the wish to influence and challenge this understanding, and a circular question asked with the intent of getting informed can be perceived and act influencing by a client in a certain situation, who has never thought that way before.

Miracle Questions

Miracle questions are described within the solution-oriented approach (Korman, 2002a). The aim of these questions is to move the supervisee so that he can discover new sides to the situation he is in. A miracle question might sound like this: "*When you wake up tomorrow morning and a miracle has happened so that your problem has gone away, how would you experience this? What is the first thing you would notice?*" This is an example of a hypothetical question where you explore what a future where the situation is radically changed looks like, where the challenge or problem in focus in the supervision has been solved. Follow-up questions can be asked, such as "*What is different? What are people around you doing differently?*"

Through this it is possible to explore both own and others' desired actions, and they might even start doing some of this? We can link this question to Tomm's reflexive questions, and these questions can demand that the person who gets the question has enough time to reflect the different possibilities which the question opens up to. Harry Korman gives the following advice when you have asked a client or supervisee a miracle question:

> "Count to six without batting an eyelid, and especially important, not nodding. This is good practice for self-discipline and leads to the majority of clients starting to develop an answer. Especially if you lift your pen to a notepad and act as if you are waiting for something to write. To those who have not answered after six seconds, you can say: "This is a difficult question", and then wait six more seconds … When the client has answered this (the miracle question in this case), we ask "what else?" at least 3–4 times" (Korman, 2002a, p. 2).

In our opinion, we need to be careful with following this type of advice. It does not have a specific effect or function. It will vary from supervisor to supervisor. On the other hand, it's possible to try and fail, and think of it as an inspiration to practice.

3: Questions to Complicate, Thicken, or Expand the Supervisee's Understanding

Within this category of questions, we will take a closer look at exception questions and questions which are asked about the landscape of the story and meaning, but first we will say something general about asking questions to expand the supervisee's understanding. In addition to asking questions to examine and explore the issue, and to challenge or influence the supervisee to see it from new angles, we can ask questions to create "thicker" stories. These are questions which are borderline exploring and challenging. The purpose of these questions is to increase the complexity of the story being told. Gerald Caplan, who among other things developed the "consultee based case consultation", once said that many believe that when things become more complex, they become more difficult to bear, but that is not the case. Greater complexity increases the possibility of understanding and thereby to act (Caplan, 2013). To avoid generalized descriptions of phenomena or problems, we can develop hermeneutical circular movements where we shift between examining parts of wholes and how the whole gives meaning to the parts (Krogh, 2009). This circular movement can also exist between the questions asked, the answers given, and new questions which grow out of the answers in the exploration of what we are talking about, and here we can allude to an interactional understanding of questions in the conversation (McGee et al., 2005). By way of these movements in the conversation, we can see which connections and relations in a story are parts of developing together a more nuanced and rich understanding of the situation or problem. While a "thin" description can lead to simplifications and stereotypies and can limit our understanding, the thick descriptions can contribute to a nuanced picture and increasing the different ways of understanding, and thus alternative courses of action.

Exception Questions

Within a solution-focused approach, exception questions are described as constructive questions to ask (Langslet, 1999b). In this case, we are examining the exceptions from the rule, experiences, or episodes when the problem *did not* dominate: "Can you remember a time it worked well? A situation when the problem wasn't so big?" With exception questions the wish is to explore the situations where the problem was smaller or gone completely, and what was different then. Through this it is possible to get a more nuanced picture of the story, and with this, new possibilities for understanding and action. When an exception is conjured up, it is possible to ask supplementary questions to get a richer or "thicker" description of which actions the person took then. "How did you manage that? Where did you get the idea that it was wise to do?" These questions can also be tied to exploring the speech acts the person has carried out (Cronen, Chen, & Pearce, 1988).

When expanding the field of other possible stories, listening is central to finding traces of something to pursue. We will stick to which questions might be helpful in this work. We can ask for fragments, stories, and voices which are otherwise overheard, but which can increase the complexity and pull the story in another direction. This can be done by asking for unique incidents, exceptions, and cracks in the dominating storyline. A story can thus always be told in many ways, with different nuances, from different perspectives, and by exploring other possible parallel stories, we can expand ways of understanding the problem. We can also tie this to exception questions from the solution-focused approach. It is also possible to ask about what is absent, what is not happening, when was it not like this, what could have happened, but didn't.

Through this kind of questioning it is possible to find traces of small stories which can be worked on to thicken them (Geertz, 1994). This deals with creating more ample and detailed descriptions, and through this, make the stories more viable as real alternatives and possibilities. In this way it is possible to develop a series of parallel stories which can be in different areas, different levels, and which creates nuances in the understanding of the situation.

The Landscape of Action and the Landscape of Meaning

From a narrative tradition we get the idea that stories develop both in the actions that happen, but also in the meaning which is ascribed to these actions. Stories can thereby be made thicker and more complex by asking questions on two different levels: to the landscape of action and to the landscape of meaning. "The landscape of action" deals with the part of the story consisting of descriptions of actions and the course of events, and here we can explore what it looks like now and how it can look in the future. "The landscape of meaning" comprises the parts of the story which belongs to the person's thoughts, values, expectations, and considerations (Westmark et al., 2012).

The landscape of meaning on the top of the figure

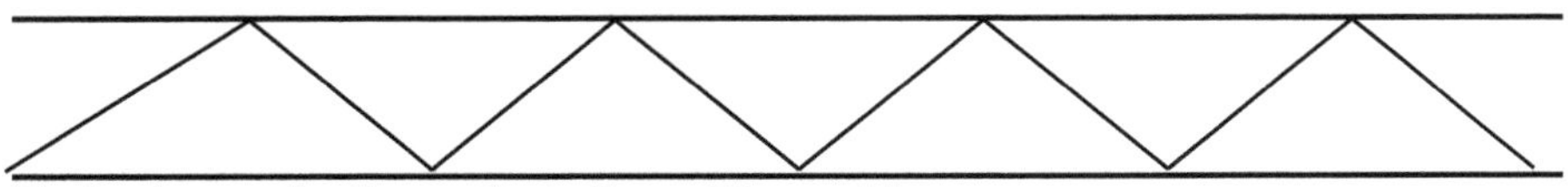

The landscape of action on the bottom of the model

In supervision or an interview, we can switch between these two positions, and first ask questions about the landscape of action. Here we can ask for examples of specific actions and episodes, both about what has happened and what might happen in the future. This can also be linked to future-questions (Tomm, 1989). Once we move over to the landscape of meaning, we explore the considerations, understandings, and justifications the supervisee can develop in connection with his/her actions. Which thought might be behind it, which values and attitudes can be revealed in this action, why is it a good idea to do it this way? A conversation can move between these two landscapes, where it is possible to explore which actions can be linked to a meaning, attitude, or idea—and again explore which thoughts and justifications might be tied to an action.

Working with developing stories and thickening and creating parallel stories, we can keep our attention directed at using a fumbling jargon. We find ourselves in an explorative mode or a landscape of exploration, where we are not looking for the right or wrong answers or the well formed and clear descriptions, but on the other hand we want to experiment, try out, and be curious. The way we ask questions can lead the conversation so that the curiosity about the problem, each other, and oneself can increase. The supervisor can contribute to establishing this framework for the conversation in different ways. She can ask for temporary answers, such as "Your thoughts about this are probably fluctuating, but if you are to emphasize something which stands out as clear nowadays, what might that be?" A hypothetical jargon can support the complexity and temporality in understanding.

4: Questions to Explore What Works and to Find Solutions

Within this category, we will present coping questions and questions about progress. In supervision the focus is often on a problem, a challenge, an issue where the person is stuck, and the conversations can often deal with what the supervisee does not master or where he is stuck. Using the aforementioned questions, we can explore, challenge, and thicken the descriptions, and through this create new opportunities for understanding and for action. The supervisor can also introduce other and new perspectives and a new energy to the conversation, by focusing on what works, where we succeed, and what we actually master. We will take a closer look at which questions can introduce this to the conversation.

A solution-focused approach is a strategy to develop and create solutions, not to solve problems. The strategy is based on the "Solution focused therapy" (De Shazer, 1988), who drew inspiration from systemic family therapy and Bateson's theoretical ideas. The approach is also inspired by social-constructionism and narrative therapy, and is used within different professional fields, such as organizational development, in conversations with children and youth, in family therapy, and in supervision. The overarching aim of the solution-focused approach is to promote growth and development, to in this way strengthen people's distinctive solution skills, their qualities, and clever moves (Langslet, 1999b). Within the solution-focused approach there has been developed a line of categories of questions which can be productive, and which can contribute in supervision. We have had a look at some of them previously (scale-questions and exception questions). These questions can contribute to the concretizing of people's wishes and their strategies for solutions, and what they have done which has actually worked. Through the questions it is also possible to explore the supervisees' resources, qualities, and skills (Korman, 2002a; Langslet, 1999b).

Coping Questions

Sometimes questions about a time when coping well in a situation can be helpful. This deals with searching for resources and good solutions one has found, for example: "When the situation is that hopeless, how do you get through the day? What makes you not give up?" By asking about this, it is possible to expose other or more preferable stories. Through exploring these stories, it is possible to create a greater hope for change. It is also possible to focus on what these people actually master or bear in a desperate situation: There will always be something a person manages or succeeds doing, and by asking for these things it is possible to strengthen the constructive contributions. By exploring this, people get the chance to concretize the solution strategies they use and which succeed, and to think about own qualities as resources.

Questions About Progress

"What has improved?" is a central question to ask, and through this one's wish is to turn attention towards what actually works well. In a solution-focused approach, the main idea is that we should explore the progress made, explore the solutions which are tried out, and analyse the improvements. When improvements are illuminated, this might contribute to a concretization and recognition of the individual's contribution. Through this it is also possible to identify new branch point and explore possible alternative courses of action.

Jocelyn Korman maintains that:

> "Solution focus in supervision is a co-creation of stories about the supervisee and those who the supervisee works with, where the focus is on what the supervisee wants to be different in his/her work and successful experiences in that direction" (Korman, 2002b, p. 4).

At times we are supervising professionals about their execution of practice based on a solution-focused approach, and *at the same time* they want to learn how they themselves can apply solution-focus in their work. The training in the approach becomes a part of supervision, and it makes it possible to have productive meta-conversations about the questions which are asked. Other times, questions from a solution-focused approach can be included as a part of the supervisor's repertoire and can be combined with questions derived from other traditions. In supervision, the questions asked are linked to work-related challenges and situations.

Conclusion

When we now have had a look at different ways of asking questions, it is important to emphasize that all types of questions can be relevant, depending on when, where, and how they are asked. It is often natural to start by asking questions to get informed about the situation and follow up with questions to develop a more complex understanding. Through this work it is possible to create a foundation to be able to ask good, challenging questions to further the conversation. The aim of supervision is to contribute to a personal and professional development, and to increase the possibility of understanding challenges we meet and to act wisely. If we only stick to the informative questions, we might miss out on challenging the supervisee to think further. If we only stick to the influential questions, they might be poorly adjusted to the context-understanding of the people we are talking to. In supervision of experienced practitioners, we can see a movement in supervision in the direction of reflexive questions, while certain strategic questions might be more appropriate in supervision with students.

As a preparation to supervision, the supervisor might articulate a few open, reflexive questions, which can be used in many contexts, such as "After our conversation, which opportunities do you see?" or "If you are to try something completely new in relation to the problem, what might that be?" If the supervision is to happen within a certain framework, the supervisor can make a draft with questions beforehand, which can lead the conversation in certain directions, such as client participation.

The supervisor can switch between being in an exploratory, informative mode, or having a more influential, expanding, and challenging attitude. The categories presented above can be used in an analysis of completed supervision. We can work on raising consciousness about which questions supervisors actually ask in supervision. This can be done both as a part of an education and in post-qualifying education and in supervision. The conversation can be taped and analysed, and we can categorize and discuss critically which questions worked well, which could have been revised, and which additional question could have been asked. It is also interesting to examine how the questions follow up on the answers which are given, and how the interaction in sequences in the conversation develops. "More broadly, we are proposing an empirical approach to social construction in which the process of construction is examined in the details of the interaction" (McGee et al., 2005, p. 382). We can thereby examine the movement in the conversation and take a look at the relationship between the individual categories.

Exercises Linked to Questions

- Plan a few introductory meta-questions, a few process-disruptive questions, and a few terminating questions you can use at the next supervision.
- Take a break in supervision where you plan some questions you would like to ask, and write them down.
- Record a supervision session, see if you can identify bifurcation points, write down which questions you ask there. See which other possible questions you could have asked.
- Choose a sequence and analyse the interactional connection between questions and answers.
- Choose a line of questions you have asked and see which presumptions you have built into your questions. How could they have been revised?

References

Andersen, T. (2005). *Reflekterende processer-Samtaler og samtaler om samtalerne* (3rd ed.). København: Dansk Psykologisk Forlag.

Anderson, H., & Goolishian, H. A. (1988). Human systems as linguistic systems: Preliminary and evolving ideas about the implications for clinical theory. *Family Process, 27*(4), 371–393.

Anderson, H., & Goolishian, H. (1992). The client is the expert: A not-knowing approach to therapy. In S. McNamee & K. J. Gergen (Eds.), *Therapy as social construction* (pp. 25–39). London: Sage.

Bateson, G. (1972). *Steps to an ecology of mind*. New York: Ballantine Books.

Bible, H. (2000). *King James version*. Richmond, TX: National Publishing Company.

Braten, S. (1998). Infant learning by altercentric participation: The reverse of egocentric observation in autism. *Intersubjective Communication and Emotion in Early Ontogeny*, 105–124.

Caplan, G. (2013). *An approach to community mental health* (Vol. 3). London: Routledge.

Cronen, V. E., Chen, V., & Pearce, W. B. (1988). Coordinated management of meaning: A critical theory. *Theories in Intercultural Communication*, 66–98.

De Shazer, S. (1988). *Clues: Investigating solutions in brief therapy*. New York: WW Norton & Company.

Egan, G. (2013). *The skilled helper: A problem-management and opportunity-development approach to helping*. Brooks/Cole: Cengage Learning.

Geertz, C. (1994). Thick description: Toward an interpretive theory of culture. *Readings in the Philosophy of Social Science*, 213–231.

Hornstrup, C., Tomm, K., & Johansen, T. (2008). *Interventive interviewing revisited and expanded*. Unpublished manuscript.

Hornstrup, C., Tomm, K., & Johansen, T. (2009). *Kunsten at stille de mest effektfulde spørgsmål i rette tid*. s: MacMann Berg, Erhvervspsykologi.

Korman, H. (2002a). *Mirakelfrågan och mirakelskalan*. Retrieved from http://www.sikt.nu/wp-content/uploads/2015/06/Mirakelfragan-och-Mirakelskalan.pdf

Korman, J. (2002b). Lösningsfokuserad handledning. In M. Søderquist (Ed.), *Möjligheter: Handledning och konsultation i systemteoretiskt perspektiv*. Stockholm: Studentlitteratur AB.

Krogh, T. (2009). *Hermeneutikk. Om å forstå og fortolke*. Oslo: Gyldendal Akademisk.

Langslet, G. J. (1999a). *LØFT: løsningsfokusert tilnærming til organisasjonsutvikling, ledelsesutvikling og konfliktløsning*. Oslo: Ad notam Gyldendal.

Langslet, G. J. (1999b). *LØFT: løsningsfokusert tilnærming til organisasjonsutvikling, ledelsesutvikling og konfliktløsning*. Oslo: Gyldendal Akademisk.

Lauritzen, P. (2015). *Spørgsmål*. Aarhus: Aarhus Universitetsforlag.

Matusov, E. (2009). *Journey into dialogic pedagogy*. New York: Nova Science Publishers.

McGee, D., Vento, A. D., & Bavelas, J. B. (2005). An interactional model of questions as therapeutic interventions 1. *Journal of Marital and Family Therapy, 31*(4), 371–384. https://doi.org/10.1111/j.1752-0606.2005.tb01577.x.

Mehan, H. (1979). "What time is it, Denise?": Asking known information questions in classroom discourse. *Theory Into Practice, 18*(4), 285–294.

Moen, T. (2016). *Positive lærer-elev-relasjoner: En fortelling fra klasserommet*. Oslo: Gyldendal akademisk.

Ongstad, S. (2004). *Språk, kommunikasjon og didaktikk: Norsk som flerfaglig og fagdidaktisk resurs*. Bergen: Fagbokforlaget.

Pearce, W. B. (1994). *Interpersonal communication: Making social worlds*. New York: Harper Collins College.

Schibbye, A.-L. L. (2009). *Relasjoner: Et dialektisk perspektiv på eksistensiell og psykodynamisk psykoterapi*. Oslo: Universitetsforlaget.

Sjøberg, J. (2009). *Kan deltakelse i kroppsorienterte og gruppedynamiske oppvarmingsøvelser påvirke intersubjektiv deltakelse i etterfølgende smågruppesamhandling?* Master thesis, Oslo University Oslo.

Skjervheim, H. (1957). *Deltakar og tilskodar [Participant and observer]. Deltakar og tilskodar og andre essays*. Oslo: Tanum-Norli.

Solem, I. H., & Ulleberg, I. (2013). Hva spør lærere om? In H. Christensen & I. Ulleberg (Eds.), *Klasseledelse, fag og danning*. Oslo: Gyldendal Akademisk.

Tomm, K. (1988). Interventive interviewing: Part III. Intending to ask lineal, circular, strategic, or reflexive questions? *Family Process, 27*(1), 1–15.

Tomm, K. (1989). *Systemisk intervjumetodik: En utveckling av det terapeutiska samtalet*. Stockholm: Mareld.

Ulleberg, I. (2014). *Kommunikasjon og veiledning: En innføring i Gregory Batesons kommunikasjonsteori—Med historier fra veiledningspraksis* (2nd ed.). Oslo: Universitetsforlaget.

Westmark, T., Nissen, D., Offenberg, L., & Lund-Jacobsen, D. (2012). *Konsulent—Men hvordan? Narrativt konsulentarbejde i praksis*. København: Akademisk Forlag.

Chapter 4
Listening and Silence in Supervision

Inger Ulleberg and Per Jensen

Life by its very nature is dialogic.
To live means to participate in dialogue:
To ask questions, to heed, to respond,
to agree... In this dialogue a person
participates wholly and throughout his
whole life: with his eyes, lips, hands, soul,
spirit, with his whole body and deeds.

(Bakhtin, 1984, p. 293)

Introduction

All conversations are transactions between the persons who participate, and all contribute with their bare presence, with their glances and smiles, their listening, their questions and their understanding. They contribute with their experiences and their stories, their knowledge and values. Everything that is said is basically said against a background of something else and as an answer to something (Dysthe, 2001). The dynamic in a conversation is between asking, listening and bringing new contributions into the conversation. When someone speaks, the others listen. When someone asks a question one or more of the others answer, out loud or silently to themselves.

Analytically, we can distinguish participation in conversations in terms of three different activities; listening, asking questions and answering, commenting, or contributing. In this chapter, we will look more closely at one of the three different elements, the listening. When treating one of the elements separately, we break up the living flow that

I. Ulleberg (✉)
Faculty of Education and International Studies, Department of Primary and Secondary Teacher Education, Oslo and Akershus University College of Applied Sciences, Oslo, Norway
e-mail: inger.ulleberg@hioa.no

P. Jensen
Family Therapy Section, Faculty of Social Studies, VID Specialized University, Oslo, Norway
e-mail: per.kri.jensen@gmail.com

A. Vetere, J. Sheehan (eds.), *Supervision of Family Therapy and Systemic Practice*, Focused Issues in Family Therapy, https://doi.org/10.1007/978-3-319-68591-5_4

characterizes conversations between people. If we compare a conversation with a football game or a tennis match, we can isolate the different elements from a purely analytical standpoint: to centre, to shoot, head, dribble (or to serve, backhand, forehand, smash and so on). The elements can be studied by looking at videos of games, and they can be learned through different exercises in training. However, when one plays a game, the skills, experience and knowledge is in continual interplay with other people.

During supervision, we can also include, to a certain extent, the practice of specific elements as part of the supervision; we can focus on questions, listening and answers and other types of contributions through our working methods (in structures such as rounds, reflecting teams, witnessing teams and so on), but the different elements are here practised primarily through education and coursework. The supervisor should develop and expand his or her repertoire within all these positions and include this as a central and fundamental part of their supervisory competence. The supervisor should contribute so that the participants, through the supervision, can develop their own repertoires in these areas. It will be of importance for participants in all professional conversations to know when one can pose which questions (see Chap. 3), how one can listen in different ways and what new contributions might be helpful and appropriate at different points and in different settings.

In the following, we want primarily to direct attention toward the supervisor's positions and tasks, but also to have in mind that meta-learning through supervision is of great importance and that it can be made explicit now and then.

The participants can also shift between these positions in how they participate in the conversation, and this can be made the object of meta-conversations about the supervisory conversation. To receive sufficient benefit from supervision, it is important that also the participants develop their competence in these three areas. In addition, as we have mentioned these elements will be present in all types of professional conversations with colleagues, clients, patients, relatives or guardians, or with students or children. Knowledge and skills developed through participation in supervision can be transferred to the practice of the profession in other contexts.

Now that has been said, let us look more closely at the contribution from the communication theory, CMM, Coordinated Management of Meaning (Cronen, Chen, & Pearce, 1988; Jensen & Ulleberg, 2011) before we explore the concept of listening and some sides of silence in supervision.

Social Worlds, Bifurcation Points and Co-creation

In every conversation—and in all supervisory conversations—there is co-creation of the conversation in which all participants make their own contributions. Conversations involve creative and creating processes in which content, focus and direction will always be dependent on those who are present. When a participant leaves or a new participant enters the group, the conversation will play out differently. Every conversation is essentially new and every meeting between people is unique and unpredictable. This specific encounter has never happened before. "Every person expresses him or herself differently in every new situation, which makes this openness a demanding task" (Buber, 1988, p. 39). Both what a person says and what he is silent about, how he says something, how he listens, how he is oriented in a bodily way and where and how his gaze goes contribute to the development of the conversation. In all meetings between people social worlds are created that are unpredictable, unfinished and ambiguous (Pearce, 2007). We all contribute to the development and change of the social world and we will try to coordinate our actions with those of others in accordance with how we understand and give meaning to what happens. All persons are actors in the sense that they are co-creators of social worlds in which their actions have meaning for the further development of communication.

In all supervisory conversations, there are moments in which further communication can take many different directions. We make choices as supervisor, we choose whether we should give a contribution attention, whether we should pose an exploratory or a challenging question, whether we should invite the others in the group to comment or whether we should contribute our own associations. There will always be untold possibilities, and it will always be possible to act differently. The choices we make and the speech acts we perform contribute to the further co-creation of the social world.

There will arise bifurcation points in the conversation at which one can choose between different directions, levels or ways to move forward (Pearce, 2007). In all situations or conversations, there are moments in which it is possible to act differently. The bifurcation point is a term for those points or moments in the communication where we can change direction. Social worlds are created, among other ways, from how we act at the bifurcation points. The choices we make and the actions we perform contribute to the further co-creation of the communication.

It can be difficult to find central bifurcation points in the middle of a communication sequence. With reflection and afterthought, alone or with others, you can analyse the communication you have been part of. This can prepare you to act in a wiser manner at the next supervision meeting or similar situation. The idea of bifurcation points can contribute to increase our repertoire and opportunities for choice so that together we can create better social worlds. In supervision the supervisor can also stop now and then, and together with the supervisees explore which direction you will take, which perspective you wish to explore further.

We begin by looking more closely at listening, which can be viewed as a fundamental, continual activity in all conversations. Listening runs as an undercurrent whether one is talking to oneself, others are speaking or it is quiet. At the end of the chapter, we will reflect on some of the other central phenomena in supervision as in other conversations. These are silence, tempo, time and pauses.

About Listening

"To be a good listener requires the ability to remain silent." (Cooper, 2012, p. 54)

In a supervisory conversation, listening is an important element. Through listening to one another, we can understand something of how the other sees the world. This will be a prerequisite to being able to pose good questions, for the co-creation of meaning and for taking the conversation further. It is important that both the supervisor and participants listen to one another.

In Michael Ende's book about the little girl "Momo", the following is said about listening:

> No, what Momo was better at than anyone else was listening.
>
> Anyone can listen, you may say—what's so special about that?—but you'd be wrong. Very few people know how to listen properly, and Momo's way of listening was quite unique.
>
> She listened in a way that made slow-witted people have flashes of inspiration. It wasn't that she actually said anything or asked questions that put such ideas into their heads. She simply sat there and listened with the utmost attention and sympathy, fixing them with her big, dark eyes, and they suddenly became aware of ideas whose existence they had never suspected.
>
> Momo could listen in such a way that worried and indecisive people knew their own minds from one moment to the next, or shy people felt suddenly confident and at ease, or downhearted people felt happy and hopeful. And if someone felt that his life had been an utter failure, and that he himself was only one among millions of wholly unimportant people who could be replaced as easily as broken windowpanes, he would go and pour out his heart to Momo. And, even as he spoke, he would come to realize by some mysterious means that he was absolutely wrong: that there was only one person like himself in the whole world, and that, consequently, he mattered to the world in his own particular way.
>
> Such was Momo's talent for listening. (Ende, 1990, p. 17)

Ende points out that Momo had all her attention and feeling directed toward what was being said. At the same time, she looked at the one speaking. These are central elements in how one acts as a listener. The listener becomes a co-creator in what is told by communicating concentration and attentiveness with small signs and signals. "Being able to listen in this sense is absolutely the most basic and important form of being and skill in supervision and other professional helping conversations" (Løw, 2009, p. 76). Momo is a good example of this kind of listening.

Hearing can indicate a physiological process of perceiving and decoding sounds, while listening indicates the complex process in which we create meaning in what we hear. We listen with more than our ears, and we listen with all of ourselves on several levels at the same time. Therefore, we use the term "listen" about a comprehensive activity in which ears, eyes, feelings, thoughts and experiences are involved. Observation is thus included in the term, "listen". It concerns both attitudes and skills, and it is about being directed and having an attentive sensitivity. We can listen for the words that are said and we can listen and look for what is communicated between, over or under the words. We can listen for what creates resonance in us of associations, stories, thoughts and feelings. To listen is also an active action, and by speaking out loud while someone listens you allow your version of reality to be known and to be made public. In this way you open also for possible change and expansion of your version and you open to the possibility for it to be discussed, interpreted and recreated.

In this chapter, we will, as we have said, look more closely at listening. The three positions, actions or activities in a conversation are all seamlessly connected so that the supervisor must listen for a time before she poses a question, listens further and makes a comment or a summary. There will also always be someone listening, and we will in the following look more closely at the different aspects of the character of listening from different positions. The central focus will be on the supervisor, but we will also comment on how the participants take part in the listening. Here, meta-learning is also of great importance, because listening to others will be central in all professional practice. "Training and professional development of therapists benefits from a deeper understanding of the role listening behaviors in dialogue" (Bavelas & Gerwing, 2011, p. 195), and this will also concern supervisors and other professional practitioners.

Two Positions

We can distinguish between two different listening positions in a supervision conversation: one is the face-to-face position in which we can define the role of the listener as an addressee, a conversation partner or interviewer. The other position is as overhearer or observer in which one listens to the story as developed in the encounter between two (or more) who participate in the conversation (Schober & Clark, 1989). In the supervision, one can have conversations in which there are more than two conversation partners and in which the complexity of the co-creation and listening is increased. We can also structure the conversation so that it is clear what fundamental listening position one is in in relation to the supervisee. Both positions can be important in a supervisory conversation and can have different contributions in terms of exploring and unfolding stories and developing new meaning and potential new ways of understanding.

The Addressee

First, we will investigate the listening position one has as an addressee. We will look more closely at microanalyses of conversations between two persons, with special focus on listening, and transfer knowledge from this to supervision (Bavelas & Gerwing, 2011; Schober & Clark, 1989). In one study, two people sat together who did not know one another, and where one was to tell a story and the other was to listen to the story as an addressee, face-to-face. When the focus was on the one who was to listen to the story it was found that, without interrupting, she made small responses with facial expression, gaze, smiles, head and hand movements and small sounds. At the beginning, these small signs were general and consisted mainly of nods, smiles and small sounds of the type "Mmmm". After a while, as the story unfolded, the responses became more specific such as opening of the eyes, raising eyebrows, stopping smiling and showing shock and in this way adapting the responses to the story being told (Bavelas & Gerwing, 2011). "Each specific addressee response appeared to be shaped for the particular point in the speaker's narrative where it occurred" (Bavelas & Gerwing, 2011, p. 188). These specific responses were carefully adapted and synchronized with regard both to timing and meaning. Even without saying anything, the addressee is a co-creator in the story being told. We can also connect this to an understanding of the position of the reciprocal interaction partner within a systemic, circular understanding where the expression of one is an answer to the expressions of the other, as Bakhtin understands dialogue (Shotter, 2009). Listening is part of a dialogical encounter.

As part of this study, the researchers gave the addressee the task of listening for something in particular such as counting how many words beginning with t the person used in their story. The addressee then became a poorer co-creator, she gave general nods and smiles but these were not especially connected to meaningful points in the story. "Distracted listeners made virtually no specific responses" (Bavelas & Gerwing, 2011, p. 188). The specific, well-adjusted responses were also gone. This led to the story becoming weaker, less nuanced and significantly less well-told. Distracted or less attentive addressees did not contribute to the co-creation of the story and functioned more as overhearers or observers.

The Overhearer

Schober and Clark created a study in which three persons sat with a screen between them so that they could not see one another. They were each given their own card pack with illustrations. The first person laid all the cards out in a special pattern and was to communicate this pattern to the other person only through conversation. They could not see one another, but could speak together, ask questions and answer. The third person was only an overhearer of the conversation between these two; he did not see them and was to solve the task of laying the cards in this specific pattern only by listening to what they said.

What they found was that the addressees or conversation partners developed several metaphors and ways of speaking that made the solving of the task easier, while the overhearers missed some of these internal codes: "Overhearers clearly realized they did not understand some references" (Schober & Clark, 1989, p. 221). In the resolution of a concrete, objective task in which there was one correct solution this was a drawback. In the development of meaning and understanding in a field that is concerned with complex contexts, interpretation and meaning creation and in which there are no stock answers we can see this as an advantage, a resource.

Through a conversation or an interview, a more or less shared understanding is developed, and co-creation and development of themes may emerge in the conversation between participants. The addressees listen from the foundation of their understanding of reality and contribute through this to the directions the conversation takes, and follow the supervisee carefully. The overhearer can find himself or herself on the outside of this shared understanding and can view it externally. She can be aware of what she does not understand; listen for what is being taken for granted; and can contribute to new perspectives, other questions and other frames for the problem. The overhearer can capture lost opportunities, thicken stories and produce other and fresh perspectives.

The foundation for understanding can thus be different for an addressee and an overhearer, and the clarification of different listening positions can contribute to the supervision conversation becoming an exploratory meta-conversation. Everyone participates in their own way in a co-creation process with the goal of developing many different angles, relations and contexts to understand the theme. Everyone must participate in this process during the supervision meeting. The conversation can be organized so that the individual shifts between being in an addressee or a conversation partner position (either as interviewer or as supervisee) or in an overhearer position in the conversation that is underway. In a narrative tradition, structures have been developed with groups of overhearers that initially take a pure listener position so that they can retell the stories being told and the knowledge and skills that have been expressed (Lundby, 2006). In a similar way, on-hold listening is described within a linguistic systemic tradition (Anderson, 2007, p. 38), in which groups are put into a listener position with a particular task to which to direct their listening.

Different Ways of Listening

As preparation for supervision, we can benefit by determining how we are to listen and what we should listen for. We can listen in different ways, some of which are more helpful than others in the attempt to establish an inclusive and supportive conversation, and to create opportunities and develop new meaning. There is a big difference between listening to find fault and to correct, and listening to attempt to understand the experience of the other.

> "One must fix oneself in the shifts and nuances of the client and in the whole multiplicity of the interaction. To be able to do this we must put our needs, feelings and thoughts to one side to 'clear' our consciousness. This is about a radical openness" (Schibbye, 2009, p. 268).

Schibbye compares such listening to listening to music. We must capture the melodic lines, heights of tone, acoustic colours and keys (Schibbye, 2009).

We will look more closely now at the different ways in which to listen, different positions from which to listen, different sides upon which to focus in the listening. Through making what it is we are listening for and how we are listening explicit, both the supervisor and the group can become qualified in being progressively better and more helpful listeners.

What we say in the following about listening applies to all who participate in supervision: the supervisor, the supervisee and the other participants in the group. Sometimes we will nevertheless have our focus directed more toward the role of the supervisor, but all participants will shift between being the interviewer or conversation partner and being the overhearer of others' conversations. This will vary in accordance with how one structures the conversation and which methods one uses. Listening is also a continual activity or attitude that remains uninterrupted in a conversation—whether we listen to one another, to ourselves, to the resonance from what is being said or to silence.

Listening to What the Other Says

The fundamental and general listening position in supervision is to listen to what the other says because one wishes to understand, because one is curious and interested in what the other says and because one is open to being told something one does not already know. We will never completely understand the other, but will continually strive to try to understand. To understand means to construct meaning while one listens (Penne & Hertzberg, 2015). We listen to the supervisee to understand, we listen for particularly important points and central information. When something is presented, we can note it down and check whether we have understood it correctly, explore it further with questions and investigate whether there are other points that are important for us to know. We can connect this to linear and circular questions in which getting to know how others have framed the problem is central.

It is important to listen to what people actually say, the words and expressions they use and how they tell about and describe the problem or situation (Anderson & Goolishian, 1988). Our project is not to find out what people really mean, what lies under or behind what they say, but pay attention to what they actually say. With what they actually say as a point of departure, the conversation can become a shared exploration of the relevant theme.

For her part, the supervisee listens to her own description and presentation (more about that later), listens to the questions she is asked and the contributions the supervisor (addressee/conversation partner/interviewer) offers. The supervisee can also be placed in an overhearer position in which she can listen attentively for new contributions that can unfold the story further and nuance and complicate it.

Listening on Several Levels

> We are made to be conductors of multiple perception and meaning making processes in relation to all that is around us, now, in the past and in the future. (Nora N. Bateson, 2011)

Another listening position can be listening with one's whole self, with a holistic, sensitive attention and being aware of the analogue aspects of communication.

> "The listener does not just listen to every word said, but sees also how the one speaking takes in his own words. The listener will notice that some of the spoken words are not merely heard by, but also move the speaker himself. Now and then there might be a movement of the facial expression, hands can be clenched or opened, there might be a cough or tears or a sigh, or there might be a pause and so forth" (Andersen, 2006, p. 42).

This can apply to the addressees, but also to the overhearers. One can open for everything that is communicated in parallel with the words spoken, how they are said, how the body language underscores what is said and what mood one perceives the other is in when he speaks about the different relations the user has to the topic one is speaking about and the feelings that are aroused.

At the same time as we always communicate on several levels, we can also listen and perceive on several levels in parallel and synchronically. We can, among other things,

- Hear the words that are spoken
- Assess and interpret them
- Associate to, and compare with other experiences and previous stories
- Note ways to move forward
- Become emotionally involved
- Plan a new question
- Note how the others react
- Look at the time

Most of us multi-task while we listen, and it is perhaps impossible for people to listen in a completely empty or totally receptive state. Another view of listening on several levels is the practice of double listening or multiple listening (Westmark, Nissen, Offenberg, & Lund-Jacobsen, 2012). As one listens to the problem descriptions to understand the supervisee's situation, one can have attention directed toward small elements that may provide other perspectives on the problem. These might be small initiatives or ideas that draw us in a different direction, and which can open for experiences that otherwise can be overlooked or unexplored. "In practice, we can 'have ears for' these entries to other stories by listening carefully for the details in what the person is saying" (Westmark et al., 2012, p. 79). The supervisor's listening can also move in several directions at the same time, and she can listen for possible openings or alternative ways to move forward at the same time as she explores the story being told.

Listening and Writing

In witnessing teams, one is asked to listen with pen in hand and to write down something of what is said, something of what awakens attention (Westmark et al., 2012). As supervisor/interviewer/conversation partner, one can also note or draw something as one listens. This can help to capture what is said, and one can go back to what one has noted down. This can communicate that what the speaker has said is so important that it is worth writing down. At the same time, the other can claim that such practices can disturb attention and the development of the conversation, and that it is best not to have anything between his or herself and the supervisee in the conversation. Here each person must try to find his or her preferred way of working.

In an overhearer position, it can be a help to note down something of what one hears and that one can bring into the conversation later. This can contribute to increasing variety and opportunities, and to counteract the danger of the conversation following one line or track exclusively.

Writing while one listens can consist of private writing of notes to support one's own reflection. It might also be public writing, for example on a board (whiteboard, flip-over) as a support for the continuing conversation. It can also be a support for attention when one has a special listening task to write notes.

Listening "As-If"

Those in an overhearer position can have the task of listening as if they were one of the persons important to the story being told. The interviewer can then, along with the supervisee, find central persons whose voices and perspectives can be desirable to include in the conversation. After this, the observers can be given the task of listening to the conversation about the problem or situation as if they were this person. They might be clients/patients, relatives, colleagues, bosses, and so forth.

A Story About "As-If-Listening"

Harlene Anderson tells the following story from a workshop in the Czech family therapy association in which she used "as-if" listening as part of the method (you can read the whole story in Anderson, 2007, pp. 40–45). The therapist Pavel wanted a consultation; he worked in a prison and told about the terrible behaviour of the prison guards. Anderson divided the participants in the workshop into three groups—the prison guards, the inmates and Pavel himself—and asked them to listen as though they were these people. When they had listened to Pavel's story from their perspective (in an overhearer position), the group had the opportunity to speak together to discuss what they had heard (in an addressee or participant position).

Thereafter, Anderson asked Pavel if he wanted to listen to what the groups had to say, and he answered that he did (in an overhearer position). He went to one group at a time and heard their conversations and reflections from their perspectives. She noticed that it was moving for Pavel to listen to them, and that some of the comments from the "prison guards" particularly were very emotional. Finally, she had a short conversation with Pavel in which they talked about his reaction to the voices. Pavel said that it had been a strong and useful experience to have a consultation in this way. One month later, Andersen received a mail from Pavel where he wrote:

> "Also, the "problem" has stopped to appear as a problem since our conversation even if I have not made any radical changes in my behaviour. I am able to see my relationships with prison guards from many different positions now, and the problem has somehow lost" (Anderson, 2007, p. 42).

In a later communication, he expands on this and says:

> "But it was very interesting to realize that they (the guards, the clients) may really have similar conversations to what I heard—and that there are so many different conversations" (Anderson, 2007, p. 43).

He continues his reflection by saying:

> "So, when I went to the prison the following days, something had changed. When the guards made some funny comments about med it did not hurt me; I just did not mind. I started to be more interested in the guards, in their view on some things and some clients. And now I do not perceive the situation to be a problem. I did not make big and radical changes, I just started to look at the situation and to think about it in a different way" (Anderson, 2007, p. 44).

To view a situation from several standpoints and listen to other perspectives can contribute to new understanding. Through using "as-if" listening in the consultation, Anderson introduced a curiosity for the others and curiosity can be infectious.

Anderson emphasizes the importance of facilitating inner and outer dialogues. The teller tells her story uninterrupted while the participants listen to what she calls an "on-hold position" in which they are not to interrupt or ask questions, but be in a situation with the possibility for inner dialogue. This will also be the case in an overhearer position. The next time, it is the teller who is in an overhearer position in which they can listen to many voices, many understandings and many versions of how the different participants have perceived the situation.

> "Through the 'as-if' exercise—a polyphonic plurality of the imagined, unspoken voices—therapists encounter the openness, invitation, and respect for, and of, the other as well as the closedness, prejudices, and judgment of the other. They encounter the feeling heard and understood as well as misheard and misunderstood. They experience the richness of different counter-voices, and they experience what is lost when only the expert's voice is heard and when voices are moved towards consensus or synthesis" (Anderson, 2007, p. 45).

This is a way of working that invites enthusiasm and openness and which can offer the participants new opportunities to understand and to practice.

Listening to Oneself Speak

"You don't know what you think until you say it" was one of Harry Goolishian's favourite sayings (Andersen, 2006, p. 40). Speaking is a creative process in which one can attempt to put words to unfinished ideas. One speaks to oneself just as much as to the other, perhaps one speaks mainly to oneself? (Løw, 2009).

> "It can be enough that the person one is speaking with has the chance to speak uninterrupted without me having to contribute more than listening. I must say to myself all the time that when the other is speaking, she is speaking primarily to herself. While she listens to her own description she can think about it in peace and perhaps change it" (Andersen, 2006, p. 41).

When we speak we also listen to ourselves, and through the development of a careful, exploratory use of language we can become curious about our own frames, associations and constructions. We can connect this to meta-cognition—knowledge and insight into our own thought processes—and be concerned in supervision with how we hear ourselves, whether we are surprised about something we say. Listening to oneself can also be connected to the expanded triadic model in which one can explore one's own relationship to the case.

Listening Introspectively

Tom Andersen emphasized the importance of creating space for both outer and inner dialogues in conversations (Andersen, 2005). In an overhearer position, we can focus sharply on the inner dialogue and listen introspectively while hearing the story that is being told and developed.

Being in an overhearer position provides one with the freedom to be able to listen at many levels at once, and can provide time and space also to listen for what is awakened in us when we listen with all that we carry with us in terms of values, knowledge, experiences, feelings and stories that arise in connection to the current story. We can listen for the resonance the story awakens in us, and listen introspectively for recognition and similar, parallel stories.

How one then uses what one finds out will be dependent on the relation and the situation. In some cases, one can choose to bring this explicitly into the conversation while at other times one keeps it as a background for further listening, or for the questions one poses in the continuing conversation. We can listen for the feelings that are awakened in us, whether we become moved, affected or shaken (Bang & Nilsen, 2003). We can listen for the professional perspectives, concepts or theories that arise connected to the story we hear.

Special Listening Tasks

We can also listen in a focused way, listen in particular for something. These different listening tasks can be part of a supervision education course or they can be used as listening tasks for participants in an overhearer position. We do not recommend having a special listening focus when one is in an addressee/interviewer position, as this can disturb the development of the conversation and the fine-tuned co-creation there and then. Through training, one can in any case develop a "nuanced" ear, and have practised listening in special ways that can inspire listening when in the position of conversation partner.

We can listen for the significant words, expressions and metaphors the supervisee uses. Examples of this might be that someone speaks about "responsibility" all the time, another might speak a great deal about "uncertainty", or that they become "angry" or that they are "bored". Some use pictures or metaphors concerning their problems, for example that they "lose their grip" or that they are "on thin ice". By noting down such words and expressions, one can explore them further together.

We can listen for meaningful stories the user tells, and we can listen for connections between stories. We can listen for different events, and we can listen for hesitancy and uncertainty (Westmark et al., 2012).

We can listen for the possible contextual understandings that it appears the supervisee has for the current problem.

A problem is seldom merely a problem. A problem can also be a solution to something. A headache is a problem, but the headache can also be a good reason not to go to a party you would rather not attend. In this way, the headache can also be viewed as a solution. We can listen for what the problem can be a solution for and how this problem as presented in fact can contribute to resolve a situation or be positive for the supervisee. Now and then it may be the case that our efforts to rid ourselves of a problem can serve as a solution to another and perhaps larger problem (Hårtveit & Jensen, 2004). It is therefore always important to investigate a problem to see what it might be a solution for. When a problem can also be understood as a solution, we can often understand that a problem often continues. It is demanding to lose solutions.

We can listen for the relation between personal elements and professional perspectives and hunt for how the supervisee brings in private experiences or personal stories in their professional efforts.

We can listen with attention directed toward possibilities and challenges connected to particular professional perspectives, and we can use the metaphor "guard dog" for this. This can be especially relevant when the supervision is connected to family therapeutic approaches or family therapeutic methods in which such perspectives are defined, or in which the supervision group wishes to have their attention directed toward particular professional approaches. An observer, for example, can be especially concerned with strategic family therapy and listen for examples of this. Another might have a focus directed toward narrative perspectives and on places in the story where one can listen for traces of this, while another looks for possibilities for or lack of "cooperation".

One can listen for everything she thinks can go well and is positive in the story with focus on solution-oriented approaches, while another can listen for all the stumbling blocks and everything that can really go wrong.

We can listen introspectively, for parallel stories that are awakened in me when I hear this story. These can be stories from the profession or from private life, or stories one has heard, books one has read, films one has seen, fairy tales one has heard and so on. We can listen for values, skills and knowledge at the same time and in parallel with the problem that is unfolded (Holmgren & Holmgren, 2015).

Suggestion for Listening Exercises

"Circle Training"

We have 3–5 listening stations in which the person has received listening in a special way as a task. The supervisee goes from table to table, spends 5–10 min at each table and tells their story to the different listeners, who make notes. The listening tasks might be, for example:

1. Listening without saying anything
2. Listening for what is said, taking hold of this and using it
3. Listening for what this awakens in me, using it
4. Listening for the exceptions, the small traces or trails, the derailments
5. Listening for the relations that are meaningful—asking about this
6. Listening for how the problem is framed—challenging the frame.

After some rounds, the listeners change tasks and are to listen in a different way. Summarize as a group.

Silence, Time, Pauses and Tempo in Supervision

> "It is in the silent interspaces that deep thought and reflection can arise" (Alerby, 2012, p. 67)

To develop listening as we have described it previously in the chapter, it is necessary to create a conversation with a different character than many of the other professional encounters a busy workday can be filled with. The working day of the family therapist contains many demands to perform, be effective and use time well, as we find that the pressure on the first-line service is increasing with, among other things, increased bureaucratization and reporting.

In this, often chaotic work, supervision can be a space for conversations of a different nature, with a different tempo and with time and space for silence. The supervisor can, through his or her attitude and with a repertoire of methods and ways of working, contribute to creating reflective conversations. Here we will take the perspective of the supervisor and ask: how to be attentive to the different sides of silence, timing, pauses and tempo? In ourselves and in the others? These topics can highlight an area, each gripping the different elements in something wordless and silent, while in interaction they can inspire us to direct our attention toward some of the analogue aspects of the supervisory reality.

About Silence

Silence is a mystical and mysterious phenomenon. Silence can have importance for the inner dialogue in the individual. What silence can mean for the individual person will differ. Silence can communicate something in and of itself and can have dialogical qualities in the sense that a space is created by it for reflection and afterthought. Andersen spoke about "listening to the reverberations or resonance of what is said"—in the silence that ensues. Silence can be experienced in different ways in different relations and settings, and can be filled with calm, rest and security, or be experienced as threatening and stressful. Silence will be the absence of sound that is intrusive or prominent, while hearing sounds from the environment such as a busy street or the ocean waves, or listening to music can be a part of silence (Cooper, 2012). In supervision, we can gather ourselves and calm ourselves by listening to music at the beginning of a supervision meeting. It can attune our mind to a listening position and mark that this encounter is of a different character than those of the busy, active practice.

Silence stands in opposition to something else, and by seeing these oppositions we can develop a richer concept about what stillness can involve and contain. Firstly, we can speak about silence as the absence of sound and where the inner dialogue, listening introspectively, can be given time. We can be quiet together, where all can direct their attention toward a question asked or something one has talked about. Such shared silence in groups can be experienced in different ways, as uncomfortable, difficult, boring, fruitful, reflective and so forth. It will be the supervisor's special responsibility to be aware of this and to act to develop a group culture and good atmosphere in the group. Silence can facilitate the individual in maintaining the space to develop their own thoughts, and as help in supervision we can use reflective writing during these sequences.

Secondly, we can speak about silence as the absence of words, an inner silence in which the inner dialogue is stilled, where we become quiet in ourselves, where we are at a point at which words are gone, but from which words again can flow (Van Manen, 1997). This type of silence can be found in important points in the supervision both for the supervisor and the supervisees. With openness and sensitivity toward ourselves and the other we can approach important, wordless experiences—or let them remain wordless, but still provide space for them.

Perhaps not everything should or can be put into words? Gregory Bateson often referred to the expression, "Fools rush in where angels fear to tread", and we can connect this to the analogue level in communication. He also cited the dancer Isadora Duncan, who once commented on her dance by saying, "if I could tell you what it meant, there would be no point in dancing it" (G. Bateson, 1972, p. 137).

The Canadian pedagogue Max van Manen (Van Manen, 1997, p. 112 and on) operates with three categories of silence: literal silence, epistemological silence and ontological silence. First, we have literal silence which refers to the absence of talk. Sometimes it is better to be silent than to ask new questions or comment. In a conversation, being silent can promote a more reflective response. This can also refer to what we choose not to speak about, with the thought that it is better left unsaid.

Secondly, we have epistemological silence. This is silence that arises when we are confronted with something we do not have words for. We know and have skills for more than we can express, and tacit knowledge becomes a background or a contextual understanding for what we can say. This tacit knowledge is in any case present, but in the form of an implicit language. We can have knowledge at one level that is not available for expression.

Ontological silence is the third category van Manen emphasizes, and it occurs when we become quiet after a meaningful experience or a moment of deep insight. Silence is necessary to complete the thought or to dwell in the experience (Alerby, 2012).

The silence we encounter in a person—or the silence we experience in ourselves—can belong to these different categories, and it can be important to sense what the silence creates in us in a conversation, what form of silence is involved. How we are to meet the supervisee who becomes silent, who does not say anything, who loses or cannot find the words will depend on the situation and the relation. In a story from supervision, the supervisor says: "speaking would only have a minimal effect in this situation. Silence, tempo and patience were the working tools we chose" (Becker, Carson, & Mansfield, 2002, p. 102). Or as Alerby says: "The quality of conversation improves if silent interspaces are permitted" (Alerby, 2012, p. 74).

How can we as supervisors create space for silence and afterthought for the participants and for ourselves as supervisors? Silence can absorb all the participants in a conversation, it can be spontaneous or choreographed, and it can be connected to pauses and the tempo of a conversation. Through our working methods, we can take action that creates space for silence in the conversations. One can be quiet together in a situation where all have several minutes to think again and to sense what they wish to take up, what a story awakens in them or what reflections arise. This can also be connected to creating space for an inner dialogue, and one can also use thought writing as a method.

Time

Time can be experienced differently by different people, and it is one aspect of our subjective experience. The experience of time will also depend on our understanding of the context and our experiences and intuitions in the situation. Five minutes can be experienced differently in the dentist's chair (will he never finish drilling?) in relation to a good conversation in which one feels that one has much to contribute (finally there is someone listening to me).

We can speak about two different perceptions of time, the monochromatic and the polychromatic. The monochromatic perception of time is that of the bureaucrat and of modern time perception, in which keywords are control, doing one thing at a time, low awareness of context, focus on procedures, deadlines and effectiveness. This perception of time is linear and can be said to characterize working life and western culture (Hargreaves, 1994). A barrier to listening to others is that one has an experience of not having enough time and continually running toward something else. The polychromatic perception of time on the other hand is circular, and keywords here are high context awareness, doing several things at once, a focus on people and relations and an attitude that work takes the time that it needs to take. This perception of time characterizes the private sphere, and perhaps it might also eventually characterize supervision meetings.

What we use time on in supervision can communicate what we place emphasis on. If all the time is spent talking about problems, we can overlook what we stand to learn from positive experiences. Who it is that gets to use the time can also communicate something to the group. It is the supervisor's responsibility to manage the time and distribute it. The supervisor must have an attentive gaze directed toward how time is used, that the group gets enough time to reflect, to summarize, to round off the current theme and to have a meta-conversation about supervision.

One can also make strict time structures for the conversation. In a supervision group connected to a course of education of family therapists, they had the task of being supervisees and speaking to the group in turns for 10 min about the theme "reflections around problem of understanding as a therapist". After this, the rest of the group was to speak together about what they had heard, while the supervisee sat with her back to them until finally they had a conversation together. The supervisor said to the first person: "I will time you, and you have ten minutes at your disposal. You do not need to fill the time completely, so if you don't have more to say we'll just sit quietly together. We have enough to think about". After about 5 min, the supervisee did not have more to say, and silence fell over the group. After a couple of minutes, several more thoughts and perspectives had arisen in the supervisee, and she spoke further for the remaining time. The others had received help to start through this and had more than enough to fill their own 10 min with.

In supervision education, we have also used exercises such as placing people together in couples and then having one interview the other about something from practice for 20–30 min. One of us experienced once in a seminar being interviewed by another person for 60 min. It was a unique experience to be able to develop a long string of thoughts about one's own practice with an interested observer.

Pauses

The pauses in the conversation contain silence. "The very pauses that occur in conversation are not empty but filled with reflection on what has been said and on what remains to be said" (Bollnow, 1982, pp. 45–46 in Alerby, 2012 , p. 77).

We will now look more closely at pauses that arise in the supervisee in the interview when she becomes quiet before she answers. These pauses can have different meaning and can be equally useful for the supervisor to notice. In a research project the meaning such pauses for the clients could involve or contain was examined (Levitt, 2001). The researchers videotaped the therapy session and identified the pauses in the conversation in which the client waited for more than 3 s before she said something.

The pauses followed a question from the therapist or they could occur in the middle of an answer or a flood of speech. Then these sequences were played for the client and he or she was asked, "Can you describe your experience during this moment?" Along with seven clients the researchers investigated 168 pauses and through an analysis of the answers, arrived at the conclusion that pauses are a heterogenous and complex phenomenon. Pauses can be active moments in which important things occur, both in the client's relation to the topic and in relation to the therapist. The researchers found that in general, there were three different types of pauses.

The first of these was the productive, helpful pauses in which the client was emotionally moved in a good way, or where she experienced a movement in ideas and thoughts. The second type was the neutral pauses that concerned locating and remembering episodes or stories, or associations to the topic in other ways. The third type they identified was the pauses that were connected to when something had stopped, when questions became too threatening or emotionally challenging. A therapy situation is different from supervision of course, but perhaps we can use these categories as a model to have in mind in our conversations. Perhaps we can also connect this to Andersen's ideas about the three types of question—too usual, adequately usual or too unusual (Andersen, 2005). By being aware of the pauses in the conversation, one can as a supervisor receive information about how the questions we ask function for the supervisee. Perhaps one can also speak about this, and investigate what the pauses mean?

We shall look more closely at some of the subcategories identified in this research project and see how they can be relevant for supervision conversations (Levitt, 2001). First, we have the emotional pauses, in which the client becomes quiet because she is overwhelmed by feelings such as fear, anger, sadness, melancholy or joy. Sometimes clients put words to this, other times not, but it is clear that the client is emotionally moved. In supervision, it can also be correct and important to explore feelings connected to a story, and such pauses can be markers that the supervisee feels something that can be worthwhile to explore further.

Expressive pauses were another category identified, and these include the points in the conversation where the client looks for a word to cover what they are trying to say. This can be connected to experiences and intuitions they have not put into words before, and where pauses are required for the client to search for and locate descriptions, connections and interpretations that might be appropriate expressions. We can also connect this to the epistemological silence, to the tacit knowledge in which, through conversation, one can attempt to articulate something one has not yet verbalized. The supervisor may be aware of this, and take ample time to explore the unarticulated together with the supervisee.

Another category identified in the study was that of reflexive pauses, in which the client explores questions, develops an awareness or understanding of the complexity in a theme or makes connections to their own experiences. This will occur often in supervision, where the supervisee, in connection to a problem or a story, wonders, analyses, judges, evaluates and creates connections. The emotional, expressive and reflexive pauses are judged as productive and helpful. In a more neutral variant, they identified pauses connected to memory, in which the client recalled details or events connected to the topic being discussed. We can connect this to the linear questions in which we ask for information to create a picture for ourselves of a situation.

In terms of more problematic pauses, they found two categories: the first was those pauses in which the client disconnected from the topic, where they wanted to distract, and get the conversation onto a different track because it was nearing themes that were too difficult, challenging or painful. After these pauses, the client could make summary or dismissive comments, or make a joke.

In supervision, we can be aware of when we are getting closer to something the supervisee is not ready to speak about, something that can be too private or too challenging, and pauses in the conversation can be signs of this. We can also investigate what the pauses might mean, and ask the supervisee: "I noticed that you hesitated, shall we go further and explore this or shall we choose a different path?" The second category included pauses in which the client's attention was directed toward the therapist or toward aspects of the interaction between them. This might be about episodes in which the client was confused and tried to understand where the therapist wanted to go. In supervision, examples of this might be if the supervisor poses cryptic, strategic questions to lead the supervisee in a special direction, and the supervisee does not understand where the therapist wants to go. This can result in an uncomfortable feeling of being wrong or answering incorrectly, and can also be connected to the development of a two-part relation in which the supervisee can feel that there is an equivalence made between the supervisee and the case.

This might also be the case in situations in which the therapist was critical or negative toward the therapist's contribution without taking it up, with the attention subsequently being directed more toward the relationship between them than toward the theme being explored. The relation between client and therapist is of greater importance than the relation between supervisor and supervisee, but we feel in any case that this category of pauses can be of interest for supervision.

The supervisor may also stop and take a break before she asks the next question or comments on a contribution in the supervision conversation. By doing this, she can communicate, for example, "now I don't really know what I should ask about"; "where should we go from here I wonder?"; "I have to think about this before I comment on it". By giving herself enough time to think, she can contribute to establishing a conversation characterized by delicacy, wonder and exploration. The supervisor can also put words to what the pause is filled with from her own side and say, for example, "Now I have to think a bit" or "I wonder what we should take hold of here?" Both the supervisee and the participants in the group can be invited to think again and contribute to the further direction of the supervision.

Tempo and Rhythm

> ".... we should probably ask ourselves all the time: is the conversation I am having with this person sufficiently slow so that the other and I have enough time for our 'inner' conversations?" (Andersen, 2005, p. 43)

How to have an appropriate tempo in supervision conversations? How can the supervisor create space for the different tempi of the participants? How can she adjust to their tempo in conversations and interviews? The tempo the individual has will vary from person to person and it can be a challenge for two with very different tempi and different needs for pauses to find a good rhythm. As supervisor, it is important to tune into the participants' tempo and need for thinking pauses in the conversation. It can be important to listen to the reverberations of what has been said, and now and then to take good time to formulate the next thing to say (Andersen, 2005). There can be good reason to meta-communicate about this in supervision, and to see parallels to other encounters family therapists have with colleagues and service users.

The tempo in a conversation can perhaps change in accordance with where one is in the conversation. How much time one needs to answer will also be associated with what kinds of questions one is asked. A simple question such as "How many were present?" can be answered more quickly than a circular question such as "What do you think the student believes you mean about his truancy?" One must ensure that the supervisee has sufficient time to rethink. How much time they will need will also depend on personal style, on the theme one is talking about and on how complicated the question one asks is. Now and then, the tempo can be faster in the beginning of a supervision session than toward the end, but this may also vary in accordance with the theme or the participants.

In a conversation or an interview, the tempo of the talking can be extremely quick, much information can emerge in a short time and the supervisor can experience almost being deluged by information. At these times, it can be difficult to listen well enough, and it can be good to slow the tempo down. One can do this by summarizing what has been said so far, by asking follow-up questions or simply by saying, "I have to think a bit more about how we should move forward now". The supervisor can develop a rich repertoire for creating sufficiently slow, adequately calm and reflective conversations with time and space for the individual. Questions about tempo, time and silence can also be taken up explicitly and made the object of evaluation in the supervision. In this way, the supervisor can gain knowledge of how this is experienced by the individual and can adjust his use of working and supervision methods and his work with the culture of the group. Different supervision structures and methods can be a help to create space for this.

References

Alerby, E. (2012). Silence within and beyond education. In H. F. Hägg & A. Kristiansen (Eds.), *Attending to silence*. Kristiansand: Portal Academic.

Andersen, T. (2005). *Reflekterende processer-Samtaler og samtaler om samtalerne* (3rd ed.). København: Dansk Psykologisk Forlag.

Andersen, T. (2006). Reflekterende samtaler; min versjon. In H. Eliassen & J. Seikkula (Eds.), *Reflekterende prosesser i praksis*. Oslo: Universitetsforlaget.

Anderson, H. (2007). Creating a space for a generative community. In H. Anderson & P. Jensen (Eds.), *Innovations in the reflecting process* (pp. 33–45). London: Karnac Books.

Anderson, H., & Goolishian, H. A. (1988). Human systems as linguistic systems: Preliminary and evolving ideas about the implications for clinical theory. *Family Process, 27*(4), 371–393.

Bakhtin, M. (1984). *Problems of Dostoevsky's poetics*. Minneapolis: University of Minnesota Press.

Bang, S., & Nilsen, L. (2003). *Rørt, rammet og rystet: Faglig vekst gjennom veiledning*. Oslo: Gyldendal Akademisk.

Bateson, G. (1972). *Steps to an ecology of mind*. New York: Ballantine Books.

Bateson, N. (Writer). (2011). *An ecology of mind: A daughter's portrait of Gregory Bateson*. Reading, PA: Bullfrog Films.
Bavelas, J. B., & Gerwing, J. (2011). The listener as addressee in face-to-face dialogue. *International Journal of Listening, 25*(3), 178–198.
Becker, K. W., Carson, D. K., & Mansfield, T. (2002). Creative moments in supervision: A case study in silence, pace, and patience. *Journal of Clinical Activities, Assignments & Handouts in Psychotherapy Practice, 2*(2), 95–103.
Buber, M. (1988). *The knowledge of man: Selected essays*. New York: Humanity Books.
Cooper, D. (2012). Silence, nature and education. In H. F. Hägg & A. Kristiansen (Eds.), *Attending to silence*. Kristiansand: Portal Academic.
Cronen, V. E., Chen, V., & Pearce, W. B. (1988). Coordinated management of meaning: A critical theory. *Theories in Intercultural Communication, 12*, 66–98.
Dysthe, O. (2001). Sosiokulturelle teoriperspektiv på kunnskap og læring. In O. Dysthe (Ed.), *Dialog, samspel og læring* (pp. 33–72). Oslo: Abstrakt Forlag.
Ende, M. (1990). *Momo* (J. Maxwell Brownjohn, Trans.). United Kingdom: Penguin Books Ltd.
Hargreaves, A. (1994). *Changing teachers, changing times: Teachers' work and culture in the postmodern age*. London: Cassell.
Hårtveit, H., & Jensen, P. (2004). *Familien—Pluss én: Innføring i familieterapi* (2. utg. ed.). Oslo: Universitetsforlaget.
Holmgren, A., & Holmgren, A. (2015). *Narrativ supervision og vejledning*. Snekkersten: DISPUKs Forlag.
Jensen, P., & Ulleberg, I. (2011). *Mellom ordene—Kommunikasjon i profesjonell praksis*. Oslo: Gyldendal Akademisk.
Levitt, H. M. (2001). Sounds of silence in psychotherapy: The categorization of clients' pauses. *Psychotherapy Research, 11*(3), 295–309.
Løw, O. (2009). *Pædagogisk vejledning: Facilitering af læring i pædagogiske kontekster*. København: Akademisk Forlag.
Lundby, G. (2006). Reflekterende team som hedrende seremoni. In H. Eliassen & J. Seikkula (Eds.), *Reflekterende prosesser i praksis*. Oslo: Universitetsforlaget.
Pearce, W. B. (2007). *Kommunikation og skabelsen af sociale verdener*. København: Dansk Psykologisk Forlag.
Penne, S., & Hertzberg, F. (2015). *Muntlige tekster i klasserommet*. Oslo: Universitetsforlaget.
Schibbye, A.-L. L. (2009). *Relasjoner: Et dialektisk perspektiv på eksistensiell og psykodynamisk psykoterapi*. Oslo: Universitetsforlaget.
Schober, M. F., & Clark, H. H. (1989). Understanding by addressees and overhearers. *Cognitive Psychology, 21*(2), 211–232.
Shotter, J. (2009). Listening in a way that recognizes/realizes the world of 'the other'. *The International Journal of Listening, 23*(1), 21–43.
Van Manen, M. (1997). *Researching lived experience: Human science for an action sensitive pedagogy* (2nd ed.). London, ON: Althouse Press.
Westmark, T., Nissen, D., Offenberg, L., & Lund-Jacobsen, D. (2012). *Konsulent—Men hvordan? Narrativt konsulentarbejde i praksis*. København: Akademisk Forlag.

Chapter 5
The Resonance from Personal Life in Family Therapy Supervision

Inger Ulleberg and Per Jensen

Introduction

As professionals, we are always present as complete human beings. Who we are as people, which family background we have, which culture we have grown up in, and which experiences we have, all affect how we shape and realize our practice. This is an especially important perspective to keep in mind in professions where our actions are directed towards other people, and where our execution of the profession largely encompasses personal assessments and judgements.

In this chapter, we will present an understanding of the relation between the therapist's private and personal experiences, and the encounters with different clients (Jensen, 2008). This is a perspective which we can bring with us into supervision conversations. The map which is drawn and the concepts presented are developed in relation to family therapists, yet can contribute to the analysis of the meeting between the supervisor and the supervisee as well, and can be a starting point for questions being asked and subjects being explored in supervision.

I. Ulleberg (✉)
Faculty of Education and International Studies, Department of Primary and Secondary Teacher Education, Oslo and Akershus University College of Applied Sciences, Oslo, Norway
e-mail: inger.ulleberg@hioa.no

P. Jensen
Family Therapy Section, Faculty of Social Studies, VID Specialized University, Oslo, Norway
e-mail: per.kri.jensen@gmail.com

A. Vetere, J. Sheehan (eds.), *Supervision of Family Therapy and Systemic Practice*, Focused Issues in Family Therapy, https://doi.org/10.1007/978-3-319-68591-5_5

The Resonance Concept

The map of resonance was originally made to develop a more reflective and nuanced language in the understanding of how family therapist's personal and private experiences from their own lives affect their therapeutic practice. The resonance concept derives from the world of music, and in this context concerns what in the clients that might resonate with the therapist. The encounter with the clients might remind the therapist of something from own experience or own history. Subsequently, this resonance can affect what the therapist chooses to emphasize, and what she does in the meeting with clients or families. The map of resonance can help us talk about these connections in supervision.

In the supervision context, we thus have the opportunity to work with and adapt to challenges and possibilities in family therapeutic practice. The map of resonance presents concepts such as "reciprocal resonance" and "therapeutic colonization", which can make it possible for us to talk about how personal and private experiences from our own lives can affect and reveal itself in our own clinical work. The map of resonance concerns the part of clinical practice which is understood and affected by the therapist's personal and private experience from his/her own life. These experiences can be resources for the therapist, but they can also contribute to non-therapeutic moves and can represent blind spots in the practice. Through supervision the link between private and personal experiences and professional practice can be explored and challenged.

Relational Resonance

The resonance concept entails that there is a resonance or a harmony between different sides of our perception of reality. The starting point for our understanding of the resonance concept is the idea that *context* is our mental, psychological framework for understanding our lives and our experience. The framework or understanding of context which is of interest here is when the resonance between the family therapist's private and personal life and the clinical practice appears as a meaningful whole. Resonance is thus the concept we use to give meaning to the circularity which can be revealed in the interaction and recognition in the therapist's personal and private experiences. This includes the challenges the clients or families represent, as well as the stories the clients present. This can also relate to the emergence of completely opposite personal experiences of the sort "it was never like that in my house" or "my father never spoke to my mother that way". This can be called *personal resonance*, and it affects the way you understand the situations and relations you are in, and how you carry out your clinical practice.

In a supervision meeting a relatively newly educated family therapist, who is going to one of her first at-home-therapy sessions, shares an unexpected experience. She has herself grown up in a home where order and cleanliness has been the norm. In addition to this, there was always a humoristic tone in her childhood home. When she thinks back, she thinks of her childhood as harmonious and happy. She is now going to visit a family's home to start a therapy, which has been initiated through an offer from the public health centre. It is a family with a young child, who according to the public health centre is struggling with the interaction in the family, and the division of labour at home. She rings the doorbell at the family's house and is received in a friendly and open manner by the mother who carries the child on her arm. When looking around it strikes her that the house reminds her of her own childhood home. Everything is clean, tidy, and well kept. The family therapist sits down, and starts an initial conversation with the couple, and after a while she also recognizes the humoristic tone from her own childhood. Her immediate impression is of a surplus, with humour, laughter and quick wit which makes the conversation flow.

How can the recognition of her own childhood home affect her evaluations in the encounter with this family? What can she avoid to talk to them about? These are the questions which the map of resonance can help us talk about.

The personal resonance can consequently make you see the world in a specific way, in which some elements will have ample significance because of recognition, while other elements might be overlooked. Subsequently the personal resonance will play out in the meeting between therapist and clients, and contribute to a relational resonance, where resonance or lack of resonance can influence the relationship. Relational resonance can contribute to the relations developing in different directions. Relational resonance can contribute to both good and stimulating relations, narrow and locked relations, and to conflicts and abuse of power. Resonance can exist both in the family therapist's consciousness and feelings in encountering a situation (personal resonance), and at the same time the resonance will take place in the relationship between the therapist and the clients. We thus need to keep two things clear: both how our contextual understanding develops in meetings with other people, situations, or phenomena, and on the other side how this understanding subsequently contributes to developing relations with other people. The resonance concept is designed to include both *personal resonance* and *relational resonance*, and the relationship between these two levels.

Psychotherapy research demonstrates that the therapeutic relation is of central significance as a contribution to change in psychotherapy. Thus, it is important to understand how this factor provides meaning to therapeutic practice (Lambert, Bergin, & Garfield, 2004; Norcross, 2010; Orlinsky & Rønnestad, 2005; Wampold, 2001). In the same way that the therapeutic relation is important in psychotherapy, it can be argued that this also holds true in supervision. How can we include therapists' private and personal life experience as an important factor in the understanding of the development of clinical practice? The relationship between the therapist and the client is in large part a deciding factor of the outcome of the collaboration between them. If the resonance from the therapist's own private and personal life affects the clinical practice, it would be meaningful to include these aspects in an understanding of this practice.

The resonance between private values and experiences, and what we experience in the meeting with clients, can take on different dimensions. In some situations, our entire way of thinking and our attitude towards the current situation or the client can be within a framework of specific personal presumptions or own local culture. This can for example reveal itself in relation to children's situation in connection to a divorce, where a therapist who her/himself has been through a divorce with children involved would have her/his own story as a central part of the resonance in the work with families who are going through similar processes. The whole interaction in the meeting with the client in question can be coloured by preconceptions or prejudices, and the relational resonance can be understood within this framework. In other instances, the relational resonance can be limited to a certain theme, and will not be the headline for the whole collaboration or affect all aspects of the relationship.

Parallel Contexts

The resonance concept also consists of what can be called parallel contexts, which entails that the family therapist at the present moment is in a situation which is parallel to that of the clients, in a way which makes the therapist recognize her/his current life situation in the clients' stories. This can pose a special challenge for the therapist, and the therapist might need help with limiting and clarifying the situation to be able to keep a professional role. If the therapist is working with families in child- and adolescent psychiatry, and is her/himself part of a family with a child who has a serious psychological problem, it might affect the work. At the same time, it might mean access to an understanding which can contribute positively to the clinical work. Other examples might be a therapist who works with clients with psychological problems, and who her/himself has grave psychological troubles, or working with addicts when the therapist her/himself is living in a family with someone with an addiction problem. It can also be to meet someone who is grieving, when the therapist her/himself recently has lost someone close to them. These parallel situations can be processed in supervision.

In peer support work in patient organizations and ideal/volunteering organizations it is common to make use of the potential in these parallel contexts in a systematic way, through for example people with chronic illnesses guiding new patients with the same diagnosis. The same is true for group therapy and other types of (conversation) groups, where these parallel contexts are made use of as an opportunity for change and growth. It can, however, be more problematic to mix the roles; when one appears to be professional, yet at the same time has current private experiences as pivotal in their understanding of the problem in question. In some cases, the therapist can choose to let a colleague take over the work with the specific problem, or choose to change work tasks for a period of time.

In Supervision

In supervision, the concepts personal and relational resonance can contribute to the conversation on several levels. Resonance tied to personal and private experiences can be a contributing factor in the continued development of the therapist, and it is therefore crucial that these connections are discovered and processed. The supervisor has a special responsibility to examine these connections through conversation, and both the supervisor and the participants in the supervision group can get associations to their own personal and private experiences.

Through supervision we get to partake in a long list of stories from other's clinical practice. Some of these stories might seem strange and unusual to some of the participants, while other stories might reconstruct memories from their own private and personal lives. The abundance in the different parallel stories which can be brought to life within the participants in supervision can contribute to the supervisees being able to critically examine their own experiences. A supervision group is thus a good place to work with these connections. Also, here we will have two views or two levels, where the supervisor can, on one level, ask for these connections in what the supervisees are presenting. This will be the main focus in this chapter. On another level the supervisor can keep in mind her/himself and her/his own practice as supervisor, and be on the lookout for her/himself experiencing resonance between a story which is being told, and her/his own private or personal experiences.

We will now present a map of different kinds of relational resonance which can appear in the meeting between therapist and client. This map can expand the supervisor's repertoire and be a starting point for ways to go, topics to examine, and questions to ask during supervision. The supervisor can also present the map for the participants in the group and use it as a shared reference frame in the supervision work. In addition to this, the map can give the supervisor insight into her practice as supervisor, and make her aware of relational resonance which can arise between herself and the participants in supervision.

The Relational Map of Resonance

The map of resonance is developed to contribute to the understanding of clinical practice when it comes to impact from the therapist's private and personal experiences from her/his own life, and can be a starting point for exploration in supervision. An overview of the structure and the concepts of the map of resonance looks like this (Fig. 5.1).

In the following we will take a closer look at some of the most important concepts, and highlight these with a few illustrative stories. It is important to underline that the following designations of relations between therapist and client might describe a short and limited sequence of interaction, or it might be a description of an ongoing and comprehensive process.

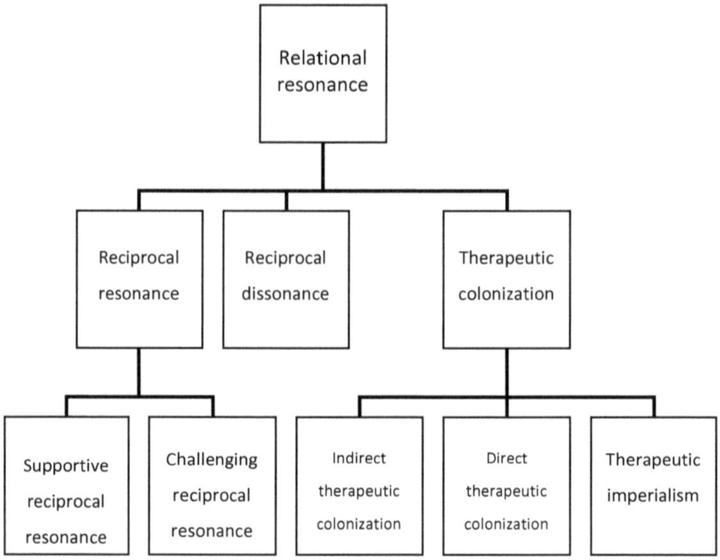

Fig. 5.1 The relational map of resonance

Reciprocal Resonance

Reciprocal resonance covers a sequence or an ongoing collaboration where the relationship between the family therapist and the clients is distinguished by a reciprocal understanding. This involves connecting and being on the same wavelength, and speaking the same language. Many studies show that what the therapist does and says to create a good alliance is the most important contribution towards change and a positive result from the treatment (McClure in Jennings, Goh, Skovholt, Hanson, & Banerjee-Stevens, 2003). Reciprocal resonance covers those meetings between therapist and client in which a client's story or situation evokes memories and feelings in the therapist, which connects them in a shared understanding. This connection of stories and feelings can be both unarticulated and articulated. These connections do not necessarily need to be talked about for them to be meaningful.

Reciprocal resonance is not *either* supportive or challenging, but can be punctuated as more or less supportive and as more or less challenging, both by the therapist and the client. Reciprocal resonance can spring from the therapist's current life situation and parallel problems the clients present. Some therapists find ways of dealing with these parallel situations, and some would even say that they can show a special support and empathy in these situations. The recognition can contribute to the therapist being able to understand the client's situation, and to being open and responsive to nuances to the problem which is being collaborated on, and that this strengthens the relationship between them. Others experience that they are not able to work with clients who are struggling with serious problems which they have in common with the clients.

Supportive Reciprocal Resonance

Supportive reciprocal resonance can be seen as a part of making a connection between the family therapist and the family (Jensen, 2009; Minuchin, 2012). In reciprocity there lies a process where all the participants substantiate this connection. Supportive reciprocal resonance does not describe the whole process, but the parts of it from which the therapist gets material from her own life to be able to substantiate the affiliation to the family. Supportive reciprocal resonance can act as a framework for a sequence or a few sequences where the resonance from the family's history, behaviour, habits, culture, and background adds meaning to or supports the therapist in being able to build a relationship with the clients, and provides a direction to the clinical work.

Supportive reciprocal resonance can in some instances contribute to a situation becoming even more deadlocked, or the problem's framework can be agreed upon to the degree that one no longer sees the framework—or change or solutions involving breaking with the frameworks. In the story we told initially, about the family therapist at a home visit, we can imagine that the relationship between the therapist and the family might develop towards a supportive reciprocal resonance. This could contribute to them having a sound collaborative relationship, but it could also make the therapist overlook problematic situations in the family, and result in not asking the parents challenging questions.

Ellen is an experienced couple's therapist. She has a long career as a therapist behind her. Before she got an education as a family therapist, she had worked as a nurse at a surgical department/clinic. As a young woman she had several relationships which had in common that when problems would arise, no one would listen to her. In several of these relationships they tried getting help by going to offices for family affairs and private therapists, but the same thing kept repeating itself; she felt that she wasn't heard.

When Ellen was 30 years old, she got married and had children. After a few years, problems arose in this relationship as well, and they decided (although with her being very doubtful) to seek help. They were assigned a young and recently graduated family therapist from the office for family affairs. She did not have much hope that it would be any different this time, but she thought "I will give him a chance". The beginning reminded her of earlier experiences, where her husband got to take up a lot of space and he told of a difficult relationship. She stayed calm, as usual, when hearing his stories from the relationship.

Then it was her turn to tell her story. She had hardly started before her husband interrupted her. As he was about to share his comments, he was politely stopped by the young therapist who said: "Now Ellen will tell her story, and you and I will listen to her without interrupting. Please, Ellen, continue". Ellen continued and after a few seconds her partner interrupted again. Again, the therapist reminded her husband that "now we are listening to Ellen's story and you will have time to comment afterwards". The therapist made sure to keep this structure throughout the conversation, and for the first time Ellen experienced being heard.

This turned out to be a pivotal moment for Ellen. Her experience as a client was so intense that it affected her career after this, both regarding the direction and content. She leaned towards psychological health work and conversation based practices, and got a job after a while in a family department and finished a family therapy education. Today she has worked in a family affairs office for 20 years and her principal idea in the meeting with all couples is that "everyone should be heard".

Ellen's own, good and important experiences from going to therapy herself constitute the principal norm for her own work. Ellen got this norm or ideal confirmed through her therapy education. The relational resonance which the therapist ties to own experience with her/himself going to therapy will be further brought into own practice. In this way, this represents *reciprocal resonance* (Jensen & Ulleberg, 2011). On the other hand, many therapists share this ideal.

Reflection: "Think about whether you have ever told a parallel, similar story from your own life to a client, a couple, or a family where you have thought that your story can lead to an increase in the chance of establishing a connection".

Challenging Reciprocal Resonance

Challenging reciprocal resonance can establish a framework for a sequence or a few sequences where the resonance from the client's history, behaviour, habits, culture, and background challenges the therapist's understanding, culture, and experiences. It represents a resonance which the therapist recognizes, but understands it in a different way, or which conflicts with her moral or understanding of right and wrong.

A family therapist who is interested and curious can in this type of meeting get new experiences and new knowledge of how some people live their lives, and how they understand the society they live in. If the challenges are too great, or if it becomes impossible to relate to the clients' experiences, the possibilities for a connection and conversation could be hindered. This can limit or threaten the relationship, but it can as mentioned also offer new possibilities in therapeutic practice. We can also imagine that the differences between the personal and private experiences are so great that the collaboration ends up suffering. A challenging reciprocal resonance can also be a starting point for new professional and personal understanding of a therapist's work.

A family therapist came to supervision and shared that she had encountered a challenge in her practice. A couple of young parents had come to her with some problems concerning their small child. The child was sleeping restlessly, waking often, and the couple wanted to discuss this with her. They had different views on parenting, and the woman in the couple said: "I want us to practice the whole family sleeping in one bed this first year, and I have many reasons for this. My husband thinks the child should sleep in her/his own room, but now it has ended up with him sleeping in his own room. This is completely untenable to me". The family therapist had her own, clear idea that children should sleep in their own bed from they are born, and preferably sleep in their own room from they are 6 to 12 months old. This is what her own children did, and she had given this advice innumerous times before when she had held a course for new parents.

The therapist was, on the whole, in agreement with the man in the couple, and wished to make the woman realize that what was in the best interest for everyone would be to not have everyone sleeping in one bed. Through supervision she was challenged about to what extent her view could be professionally validated, and how much it was based on her own private experiences. Because the therapist had her own personal and private standards challenged, it led to a necessary exploration of own prejudices, and she realized that her views were not necessarily professionally corroborated. Through this kind of challenging reciprocal resonance, the therapist had the opportunity to expand her repertoire for understanding children and sleeping, which was necessary to be able to establish a good collaboration with this couple.

Another example of a challenging reciprocal resonance can be a family therapist who worked with a noisy family at a psychiatric outpatient clinic for children and adolescents. He experienced the children as restless and noisy, and the parents as passive, recumbent, and on the whole completely unaffected by the noise and interruptions. This wasn't the reason why the family went to therapy; however, the therapist wanted to introduce and bring up this interaction in conversations with the family. He presented this challenge in supervision, with a request for input on how he could go forward.

Through supervision he was challenged on his own parenting style and family background, and how he could understand that the noisiness challenged him. He realized that this was closely related to his own strict childhood, and who he had become as a person. Attitudes towards adult–child relation and children's place in the family were deeply rooted within him, but did not necessarily rely on good, professional reasons for how one could live life in a family. By means of supervision, he discovered these connections and was motivated to keep expanding his repertoire in meetings with different families.

Reciprocal Dissonance

The dissonance concept is also derived from the world of music and describes a "sour note" or a discord in your ears. The American social psychologist Leon Festinger introduced the concept "cognitive dissonance" to describe situations where different thoughts conflict (Festinger, 1957). Cognitive dissonance represents a lack of agreement between values, attitudes, ideas, understanding, and experience in a person's life, or in a meeting between people. We strive to reduce the dissonance in our lives (Saugstad, 2009). Dissonance can create poor collaborative relations, but can also awaken us and inspire us to have a closer look at how our private and personal values and experiences affect our practice.

Reciprocal dissonance is revealed when clients present a story, challenges, or shows sides of themselves, which the therapist experiences as unfathomable, provoking, or uncomfortable, and which becomes a hindrance to curiosity and empathy. This can relate to personal dissonance, where one's own private experiences are completely opposite or are in stark contrast to what the clients are showing.

In this case, the therapist's understanding of context might not be helpful in understanding the client's challenges or problems. This can lead to the collaboration being reduced, or to the termination of the relationship. If it is not possible to move on from this situation, it is probable that the whole relation will appear to be barren and unsuccessful.

An example of reciprocal dissonance is if the family therapist in the example above is not in any way able to leave behind her idea about children sleeping in their own beds, and where these viewpoints dominate the conversations indirectly, and does something to the therapist's relationship with the mother in the family. Reciprocal dissonance can lead to cooperative relationships ceasing.

Sometimes, as mentioned, reciprocal dissonance can lead to therapists quietly discontinuing therapies by giving the clients appointments more rarely, or by the supervisors continuously having to cancel supervision meetings. On the other hand, the acknowledgement of dissonance can lead to new recognition and the discovering of new possibilities for the therapist. In this way experiences with dissonance can be the starting point for new understanding and new practices.

Therapeutic Colonization

Colonization is best known as a political concept and describes the process where a powerful country or state forces their language, their religion, their values, laws, and their societal norms upon another culture. In linguistics, the term "linguistic colonization" is used to describe how language can be a deciding factor in how we understand reality and how we see the world (Vedeler, 2007). An example of this is how dialects and ways of speaking is undermined or ridiculed by those who think they have the right to define the language.

In this context, we are using the term therapeutic colonization to describe a special type of unfortunate or oppressive resonance. It is distinguished by the absence of reciprocity, and the relation can develop into a kind of submission or subservience, or can also be characterized by struggle and conflict.

The concept "therapeutic colonization" does *not* mean that the colonization is therapeutically justified, but that the colonization is happening in a professional and occupational context. Therapeutic colonization is used to describe how the therapist's private and personal culture, experience, and moral values in different ways influence her or his clinical practice. Therapeutic colonization reduces the space where reciprocal communication can pan out and be revealed, and where the monologue thus becomes the ruling form of communication. This reduces the space for reciprocal communication, and the dialogue is shattered because the therapist uses her/his power to define and introduce topics of discussion and how the work should be done.

Ole is an experienced clinical social worker with many years' experience from child and adolescent psychiatry. However, he is a relatively newly educated family therapist and has his first job at a family affairs office. He meets a couple arriving for their first session. Because this is the first time he meets them, he has designated 2 h for this meeting.

The woman in the couple opens by saying that they are planning to divorce, but because they have children they need "help to communicate" when they are going to cooperate on taking care of the children. Ole asks about how their lives are at this time. In just 10 min they describe a life with many serious problems. She is exhausted and struggling with depression, which at times leaves her unable to work. Both children have troubles at school and problems with somatic illness. The husband is also chronically ill and has a serious alcohol problem. He is working, but is drinking large amounts of alcohol every day and every weekend.

The remainder of this first session, Ole is concentrating on trying to understand and intercept the husband's alcohol abuse and his social issues relating to this. The topic "alcohol" is discussed at length until the end of the session. Then the woman in the couple stands up and says: "This was strange. Alcohol was the only topic we had decided not to talk about, because I cannot stand it anymore".

In Ole's supervision the next week he shares that he was completely trapped by the topic "alcohol". He is himself struggling with the same problem at home, and Ole and his partner are going to therapy themselves because of an alcohol abuse problem.

This example illustrates how parallel processes in the therapist's and the couple's lives can end up dominating a meeting and a therapy session. This can also be an example that the resonance from the therapist's own life experience resonates in the therapist's practice, which can be seen as a *colonization* (Jensen, 2008; Jensen & Ulleberg, 2011) of the clients' wish for help to find a good way to handle a divorce. Instead of listening to the couple's asking for help, the therapist has his own life as a starting point and prioritizes own topics in the conversation.

When the therapist shows his power and reduces the space for dialogue, it is necessary to discuss ethical aspects to this type of practice. These are natural topics for professional conversations between colleagues and as topics for supervision. In the following, "therapeutic colonization" is divided into three: "indirect therapeutic colonization", "direct therapeutic colonization", and "therapeutic imperialism".

Indirect Therapeutic Colonization

Indirect therapeutic colonization is revealed when the family therapist's own personal and private experiences influence the therapeutic work in a non-planned and unarticulated way. The therapist is usually not even aware of how he or she brings his/her own good or bad experience into his/her therapeutic work. This can be unveiled through manners of working which the therapist her/himself is not aware of, and which he or she cannot give any professional justifications for. It appears to be a "natural" part of the therapist's way of working and understanding of reality. The power asymmetry can be hidden from both the therapist and the clients. The clients will rarely or never be able to see these connections and will think that this is defensible therapeutic practice.

The therapists' own ideas about what is determining for his or her practice are sometimes overruled by aspects which do not derive from the field and which do not belong to clinical practice. When a therapist claims that he or she is guided by own professional background and experience, and claims that it is theory, research, ethics, and other professional matters determining the practice, it can sometimes be more fruitful to look into the therapist's private and personal stories to find explanations for what is said and done.

Reflection: "Consider if you have ever given advice or recommendations in supervision which derives from your own experience in life, and where you cannot give any specific professional justification for the advice or recommendations".

Indirect therapeutic colonization might as well emerge for a very experienced family therapist as for a novice. The fact that it is unarticulated, and that it is usually a hidden practice, makes it especially hard to discover. It is often necessary with direct observation for this type of practice to be unveiled.

An example of this is if a therapist has an understanding from her family that conflicts always need to be solved, and that the way of solving them is through dialogue. Her absolute belief in this is actually one of the reasons she decided on therapy as a profession. The people in question should always talk, make up and solve disagreement and finally agree. She is not even aware of that there are other possibilities or other ways of solving conflicts, and thinks of other therapists as belligerent or irresponsible if they leave conflicts alone or do not pay enough attention to them. Her experiences have become as a reflex for her, and her practice is always determined by this, even when it contributes to her input creating further problems. She is indirectly forcing upon couples, families, and colleagues her personal views through her way of working.

When private and personal values shape clinical practice in this way, it can be argued that supervision should be a part of all therapists' work with people. This applies both to novices and to experienced practitioners. The therapist in the example above could hear other practitioners' opinions and experiences in supervision, and get to explore the connection between personal experiences and professional justifications.

Direct Therapeutic Colonization

Direct therapeutic colonization is revealed when the therapist uses her/his power to introduce and define what the problem is, and how it should be solved based on own private and personal experiences. In this way, the space for reciprocal dialogue is reduced and a power relation/asymmetry is established. This is where the therapist uses her/his definition power outside of the professional and theoretical frameworks to lead the client in the direction which the therapist thinks, is best for the family, the couple, or the client.

An example of this is a therapist who has a rule that openness about illness and problems is always a good thing. Her personal positive experience with openness around her own cancer diagnosis made her always recommend the same to families as a way of dealing with a new, serious challenge. She introduced openness as a topic and explored with relevant families who they should talk to and how they should do it. Objections were met with the reasoning that "openness is always the best policy"—for everyone. In a meeting with a family, she experienced being thoroughly contradicted. They had decided to keep a serious diagnosis a secret, even from the closest family and friends. The therapist brought this up as a problem in supervision and wanted input on how she could convince this family to reconsider openness. In supervision they explored the different ways of understanding this situation, and she heard other's stories of how it had been good for the family to wait with sharing the news, or only sharing the diagnosis or the problems only with very few people. She got the opportunity to explore her own practice, and to critically review the recommendations she used to give and the reasoning behind these. She thus expanded her understanding and her therapeutic repertoire.

Another example is of a family therapist who herself has experienced a lot of grief, and feels she has gotten through it by talking to family and friends about her grieving, and participating in grief counselling groups. In a meeting with a client she hears that the client has experienced a lot of grief in his life, and that the client has carried a lot of this with him alone and not talked about it. The therapist suggests straight away to the client that they can spend time talking about this in their sessions, and that he can get help to talk to his family and friends about it, and maybe participate in a grief counselling group.

The Swedish-Kurdish journalist Mustafa Can relates in his book *Tett inntil dagene* (2008) about his mother. She almost never talked about herself while living, and when she died, her son wanted to know more about her life. He found out, among other things, that she was carrying an enormous sorrow over having lost many children in Kurdistan before the family emigrated to Sweden in the 1970s. Can's aunt shared that they did not talk about it, because it would make the sorrow impossible to bear (Can, 2008). Life is experienced in different ways, and events are tackled in different ways, and as therapists we have a responsibility to have a dialogue with the people we are working with. This means exploring how they understand their lives and their relationships. If we lose this curiosity, then the monologue can end up dominating the relationship.

Therapeutic Imperialism

The concept imperialism is usually used to explain how power can be used to oppress a society, a culture, and a people. Imperialism is most commonly referred to as how a powerful culture conquers and changes another culture in order to make it more like own culture's ideas and values. The concept is therefore best used in describing a relationship where the power is unevenly distributed, and where the strong part is taking advantage of the power to fulfil own interests.

Therapeutic imperialism is different from therapeutic colonization in that power is exerted against the client's direct wishes. It is in this context defined as a situation or a sequence in professional work where the therapist is exerting power directly, against the family's will, to force views or measures which stem from the therapist's private and personal experience. The fact that this is happening against the family's direct and articulated wishes is what separates therapeutic imperialism and therapeutic colonization.

An example of what distinguishes therapeutic colonization from therapeutic imperialism is the story of two parents who go to family therapy to get help with their unruly youngest son. He is testing limits all over the place, and the parents are scared he might have started experimenting with drugs. In therapy they also share that he is not their biological son. The boy's mother was a childhood friend of theirs who had become addicted to drugs, and died of an overdose. At first they had him as a foster son, and when his biological mother died, they adopted him at 2 years old. The boy does not know any of this, nor do they wish for him to know. His mother's addiction to drugs makes them especially worried about him, and they are wondering whether this sort of addiction could be hereditary. The therapist is herself adopted; she has always known this, and she thinks that being open about this is something to be taken for granted, and that it is a human right to know your origin. She also thinks that the boy's opposition could stem from double and unclear signals which he is sent, and that the truth could be a support in the parent's problems with getting him under control. She decides, against the parent's wishes, to inform him of his origin. She invites the boy to a meeting and tells him of his biological mother and the adoption.

Ethical considerations when therapeutic imperialism is revealed in an ongoing clinical process can be a way out of the therapeutic imperialism's lack of respect for the clients' integrity. Therapists should essentially respect and support the clients' own values, choices, and culture. This is the starting point for all clinical practice. When ethical standards and conflicts arise between the therapist and the family, the therapist has to carefully bring up angles. In these situations, however, the therapist's exertion of power is direct and visible to everyone involved.

Conclusion

Relational resonance has to be understood as a process. It is never static, and every meeting with clients should be understood as a unique case. This means that the contextual understanding which in one meeting with a client develops into reciprocal resonance, can in the meeting with another client result in therapeutic colonization.

It is not possible to operate with standardized models which will be valid across different encounters. Something which starts out with reciprocal resonance can also develop into therapeutic colonization, and the other way around. This means that we need to be aware of simplifications, and make sure to share the "thick descriptions" when analysing the communication between therapists and clients (Geertz, 1994).

Therapeutic colonization is never good, but is it possible to avoid? If we identify and explore it, it can also lead to something positive. It can lead to an increased awareness of own clinical practice and become a contribution towards the empowerment of the clients.

A therapist who has clients who clearly and directly express their objections and disagreements with the therapist is very lucky. This, in turn, makes it possible to be open to input, which can stimulate curiosity. In this way, dialogue can once again be set in motion.

References

Can, M. (2008). *Tett inntil dagene: fortellingen om min mor*. Oslo: Cappelen.

Festinger, L. (1957). *A theory of cognitive dissonance*. Stanford, CA: Stanford University Press.

Geertz, C. (1994). Thick description: Toward an interpretive theory of culture. *Readings in the Philosophy of Social Science, 1*, 213–231.

Jennings, L., Goh, M., Skovholt, T. M., Hanson, M., & Banerjee-Stevens, D. (2003). Multiple factors in the development of the expert counselor and therapist. *Journal of Career Development, 30*(1), 59–72.

Jensen, P. (2008). *The narratives which connect*. Oslo: University of East London, Diakonhjemmet høgskole.

Jensen, P. (2009). *Ansikt til ansikt: kommunikasjons-og familieperspektivet i helse-og sosialarbeid*. Oslo: Gyldendal akademisk.

Jensen, P., & Ulleberg, I. (2011). *Mellom ordene—kommunikasjon i profesjonell praksis*. Oslo: Gyldendal Akademisk.

Lambert, M. J., Bergin, F. J., & Garfield, S. L. (2004). *Bergin and Garfield's handbook of psychotherapy and behavior change* (5th ed.). New York: Wiley.

Minuchin, S. (2012). *Families and family therapy*. London: Routledge.

Norcross, J. C. (2010). The therapeutic relationship. In B. L. Duncan, S. D. Miller, B. E. Wampold, & M. A. Hubble (Eds.), *The heart and soul of change: Delivering what works in therapy* (pp. 113–141). Washington, DC: American Psychological Association.

Orlinsky, D. E., & Rønnestad, M. H. (2005). *How psychotherapists develop: A study of therapeutic work and professional growth*. Washington, DC: American Psychological Association.

Saugstad, P. (2009). *Psykologiens historie* (2. utg. ed.). Oslo: Gyldendal akademisk.

Vedeler, A. (2007). Den bekymrede vandringsmannen—John Shotter om Tom Andersen i samtale med Anne Hedvig Vedeler. *Fokus på familien, 35*, 166–177.

Wampold, B. E. (2001). *The great psychotherapy debate: Models, methods, and findings*. Mahwah, NJ: L. Erlbaum Associates.

Chapter 6
The Reflecting Team Approach: Different Uses in Live Supervision and Group Supervision with both Family Therapy Trainees and Practitioners

Halvor de Flon

Introduction

Supervision is a major part of training in family therapy as well as in the development and maintenance of practice for qualified family therapists. Clinical discussions in working teams as a part of their routines and in the assurance of the quality of the work can also be looked at as an activity that has a supervision outcome. Such team-based discussions can be organized in ways similar to sessions of live therapy supervision. This chapter will mainly describe and focus on the supervision of therapeutic work. However, I hope it also will be seen as relevant for other arenas where the purposes for therapists are learning and development and the extension and development of ideas and possible ways to understand and meet the families with whom we cooperate.

Supervision in the context of family therapy training and in the development of qualified family therapists can be organized and structured in many ways, for example as live supervision where the supervisor is present in the therapy session or where the supervisor views recorded material from a session and/or as a presentation of clinical work presented by the supervisee after the session without the family present. Both types of supervision can be organized in groups or with an individual supervisee.

The reflecting team (Andersen, 1987) was originally described as a way to organize team discussions in family therapy sessions. The reflecting team is a way of working and thinking about practice that is well known by family therapists worldwide and often used in their daily practice. Reflecting processes is another name for the concept that is more descriptive of the way to work. The term reflecting

H. de Flon (✉)
Family Therapy Section, Faculty of Social Studies, VID Specialized University, Oslo, Norway
e-mail: halvor.de.flon@vid.no

A. Vetere, J. Sheehan (eds.), *Supervision of Family Therapy and Systemic Practice*, Focused Issues in Family Therapy, https://doi.org/10.1007/978-3-319-68591-5_6

team is associated with structure and organization, whereas reflective processes better describes what is going on in a reflecting team or between colleagues and family members. In this chapter, both terms will be used.

Initially reflecting teams were used by family therapy teams in the meetings with couples and families. The concept is now used in various settings and contexts for staff and supervision groups (Jensen & Hoffman, 2007). This chapter will offer a description of how the reflecting team can be used in different contexts of supervision of both pre- and post-qualification family therapists. These two groups usually have different goals within the supervision. The goals for supervision groups for students and trainees usually are to increase their theoretical and practical understanding of systemic work through their clinical work. Hopefully the supervision will contribute to improvement in the quality of the students work (Lowe, Hunt, & Simmons, 2008).

Post-qualification family therapists and family therapy teams will need to inform each other about their common work and to discuss how their resources can be used in the best way for the benefit of their clients. As a result of this, the participants hopefully will strengthen their theoretical understanding and develop their clinical capability (repertoire of action) (Jensen & Hoffman, 2007).

This chapter will seek to highlight how of the reflecting team may be used in these contexts. Although this is written in the context of family therapy practice, the ideas presented in this chapter hopefully will be useful for practice across a range of psychotherapeutic and counselling modalities. I shall present the central theoretical perspectives for practice and the research related to reflexivity and reflecting teams, and then I shall describe and discuss the different ways to apply reflecting team work.

The Reflecting Team Approach: Origins, Theory, and Practice

To work in teams is one of the most distinguished hallmarks of family therapy. The team can be placed both in the therapy room or behind a one-way mirror and can contribute in the therapeutic work in many ways. Papp (1980) describes the use of the team as a "Greek Chorus" where the members of the team have different voices in understanding the meanings of the different perspectives of the client group and in their different meanings and understandings as offered back to the clients. The voices are brought to the family or client by the therapist as messages and often as a result of discussions within the team. The content of the messages may be supportive, challenging, express surprise and confusion and all with the intention to help the system to change. The "Chorus" would often, just as in the Greek Theater, serve as an outsider panel of commentators to the drama of the system/family in therapy.

I have chosen to mention the "Greek Chorus" here because it has some similarities with the reflecting team approach although there are some important differences. The similarities are presented in the concept of bringing forward different perspectives. In the "greek chorus," the different perspectives are presented by different voices. In the reflecting team approach, different perspectives and voices are brought forward by the reflecting team in a wondering and open way (Andersen, 1987) while there in the "greek chorus" approach the team bring forward the different perspectives in a strategic and paradoxal way.

The origin of the reflecting team is first of all connected to the work done by the Norwegian psychiatrist Tom Andersen. He first described the concept in his article "Dialogues about dialogues in Family Process" (Andersen, 1987). The article describes the development of a practice where he and his team openly and in front of their clients had a conversation and reflection about what they had heard the clients say. This represented for trained therapists and counsellors something quite new and unusual in their practice. The most usual practice when teams worked together was that the team went by themselves into a separate room from the clients when there was a break in the session to talk about what they had heard and to discuss possible understandings and interventions. Andersen tells us that he developed an increasing sense of discomfort connected to the practice of talking about someone who is not present. The idea to make this discussion open to all concerned developed from the intersection of the therapist's ethical dilemmas and discomfort and their desire to develop another form of practice. The therapists did principally the same as they did before—they discussed their thoughts, assumptions and ideas about the clients and their described problems, sorrows, joys, resources, but now openly in front of the people that it concerned most. This movement from a discussion in a separate room to an open reflection probably affected the way the team discussed the family members' concerns and dilemmas. When you are talking in front of the people concerned and not behind their back, it is suggested that you will probably use other words to show respect and speak in an understandable and useful way for the clients.

The reflecting team was originally used in therapeutic conversations and later used in other contexts where highlighting different perspectives and different ways of understanding were in focus. In therapeutic conversations, teams of two or more are listening to the dialogue between the therapist and the client(s) and they might share their reflections and thoughts one or several times during the session. When the team has shared its reflections, the client(s) are given the opportunity to comment upon what is said. The client(s) are also in the position to not comment if they so wish and thus are free to leave something out and/or take into further consideration what they feel and think might be useful for them.

The reflecting team approach build on an assumption that in a conversation between two or more several conversations are taking place at the same time ie s the outer dialogue between the participants, the spoken word, and the inner conversations of the participants. The inner conversation of a person can be described as a polyphony of inner voices (Andersen, 1995; Bakhtin, 1981). In the context of supervision, we are talking about the outer and inner conversations of supervisors and supervisees. When using reflecting teams in therapy sessions or in supervision, the reflecting team is a way to create space for the inner conversation to be a part of the outer conversation. The inner conversations take part constantly both when we are in a listening position and when we are talking. When I am listening to what another person says there an inner conversation going on that contains many different things depending of my role and position in the conversation. Rober (2010) refers to his own research (Rober, 1999, 2005; Rober et al., 2008) and proposes a descriptive model of the therapist's inner conversations with four positions, which are: (1) attending to the clients' process; (2) processing the clients' stories; (3) focusing on the therapist's own experience; and (4) managing the therapeutic process. These four positions describe the complexity and richness of the inner conversations and could guide a supervisor in the process of exploration and for the reflecting team members, help organize their reflections by giving a place to different voices and perspectives and where the participants vary between speaking and listening.

When I am in the listening position, I hear what is being said by the other participants. What I hear affects my own thoughts and perhaps I might have some new ones. When I talk, how I position what I say will be influenced by what I have heard and my own original thoughts and feelings. By structuring the conversation in this way the ability to present more thoughts, multiple perspectives, and several alternative ways to understand and express will increase. When these expressions are given as open, nonjudgmental, and possible ways to understand, there is a possibility that new ideas can be developed.

The Reflecting Team Approach and Supervision

Supervision of both trainees and postgraduates can be organized as reflecting team processes (Reichelt & Skjerve, 2013; Lowe et al., 2008; Davis, 2012).

The structures can be varied, but will not be very different from the way the reflecting team is used in family and couple therapy and with individuals. The typical way to do this is to structure the session in an interview or conversation with one of the group members while the rest of the team builds a reflecting team. The interview or conversation will last about 30–45 min and during this time the team will be invited once or twice to share their reflections openly.

Reichelt and Skjerve (2013) describe how the reflecting team is used in an education program for postgraduate psychologists. Group supervision is one of the main activities in the program and the reflecting team is used in a structured way. Reichelt and Scherve are concerned about the quality of the reflections offered. Thus they describe how the participants are given a short introduction to the concept and principles such as that the reflections are given in a nonjudgmental and sort of wondering way. They also emphasize that it is important to sort out what should be in focus during the interview. In their research they found, among other things, that members of the supervision groups had a tendency in their reflections to focus on their own opinions and experiences more than on the needs and wishes of the supervisee in focus. Because of this it is important that the supervisor explains the concept and the principles in the early formation of the group and repeats this as and when it is needed.

Vetere and Dallos (2009) also raise critical points about this in connection to their work with family violence. They point out that the purpose of the reflections always has to be helpful to the family. They also point out that there should always be consideration of the timing of a reflection. An idea presented in a reflection could be very good, but if the timing is not right it will probably be less useful for the clients. Both Reichelt and Skjerve (2013) and Vetere and Dallos (2009) focus on the importance of how reflections that are given are based on what is useful and helpful for both the clients and the supervisees. In supervision it is the supervisor that is responsible for pointing this out for the group and who should seek to maintain this focus all through the supervision process.

Different Positions of the Supervisor in Live and Group Supervision

Both in group supervision and live supervision sessions, the supervisor can take different positions. In live supervision with clients present the supervisor can take the position of an observer, a co-therapist, a main therapist, and as a member of a reflecting team. In group supervision without the family present the supervisor can be in the interviewing position, or that of a reflecting team member to mention some examples. What decides which position will be chosen will be influenced by the needs and wishes of the supervisees, the group process, and the clinical implications. The clinical implications will predominate in live supervision with the family present. Issues for the supervisor to consider are connected to the clients' needs (individual, family, or couple), and to those of the supervisees. The supervisor is responsible for these considerations and the one who has the responsibility both for the clinical work and for the supervising process. This will decide how the session is organized.

Group Supervision

We shall now focus on ways to structure and organize supervision groups with the use of the basic principles of the reflecting team and reflecting processes. This can be done in different ways and in the following part of this chapter some of these will be described. Context and different aims of the supervision will influence how the supervision work will be organized. In some cases, it will be expedient to organize in a way to let in as many as possible ideas, thoughts, and perspectives to come through and to be expressed. In other cases though it might be more expedient to give room for more specific perspectives, themes, and issues applicable for the actual context of the supervision. This could be issues of interest for the actual clinical work in focus, issues connected to cooperation between students or therapists, or issues connected to techniques and approaches.

In the following part of this chapter, we shall describe three different models of supervision with the use of the concept of the reflecting team. The list of different models could be longer. The models chosen are to be seen as possible ways to work more than a complete list and it is the authors wish and intention that this might stimulate readers to develop other ways of using this approach in supervision and perhaps also in clinical practice even if that is not the topic in this chapter. Practical examples from the authors practice as a supervisor will be given.

Reflecting with Different Clinical Perspectives Connected to the Case in Focus and in Mind

When a clinical case is presented by the supervisee, there are several choices to be made by the supervisor, supervisee, and the group as a unit. We need to consider what will be most useful for the supervisee in focus and for the group. Often the supervisee comes to supervision with more or less clear thoughts about what he or she needs and what their wishes are.

The supervisor's first task is to explore what these needs and wishes of the supervisee are. This can be done in many ways. One way to do it is to have a small interview with the supervisee with the intention of sorting out and discussing possible ways to organize the supervision. The rest of the group will listen to this interview and be invited to comment and perhaps share ideas about how to go on.

The supervisee as a student will often bring cases to supervision from his or her work. Their need and wishes can be a mixture of wanting to learn more about family therapy approaches and how to use them in this particular case, to understand more of the client group they are working with and to have more ideas about how to move on. In the interview it is important to help the supervisee to sort out what will be most useful for him or her. I think it is also important that it is up to the supervisee to have the last word in this process of decision-making. If the supervisee decides to have focus on clinical perspectives and topics, it is also important as a supervisor to ask for the specifics about this to be as clear as possible about what the supervisees needs are. Clinical topics can be defined as topics connected to understanding of the problem(s) presented, understanding of the interaction within the family, and the interaction between the family and the therapeutic team. It can also be issues connected to concrete and practical choices of actions that the therapist and the therapeutic team have. Every therapist experiences from time to time that the numbers of choices of understanding and action are very limited or even none at all or alternately, there are too many to manage. Supervision can be, or should be, of help in such situations.

I will now present a constructed example in an attempt to clarify how this can be in practical supervision.

Example:

Carla who is a Masters level family therapy student participates in a group of five other students as a part of the training program. The students are told to bring clinical cases from their own work to supervision. After a round with all the students, the group decides to start with Carla and a case she is working with at the moment.

Carla works in a family unit within the child and adolescent psychiatry team as a family therapist. She gives a short introduction—telling the supervisor and the group about the family by drawing a genogram on a flip chart. The family consists of mother 35, father 39, Sam 9, and Elisabeth 14. It is Sam that is the referred patient diagnosed with ADHD. After this the supervisor interviews Carla about her thoughts in bringing this case to supervision. The supervisor tries to explore what Carla wants to get out of bringing the case to supervision and if there are specific issues she wants to focus on. In this short (5–7 min) interview, Carla says that her reason for bringing this case is because she is struggling to understand the interaction in the family and that she also struggles with how she and the team could organize the family sessions. Carla and the team have noticed that after a while Sam seems to get uneasy, struggling to sit on his chair and to concentrate and to answer when the therapist asks questions. This often leads to a situation where the parents starts yelling at Sam telling him to behave well in a way that Carla experiences as unnecessary and rough and not helpful for Sam. Sam has left the session several times and a lot of time has been needed to get him back which he usually does, but when he returns he is in a uneasy mood, showing with his body that he does not want to be in the session and refusing to answer questions from the therapist. Carla says in the short interview that she has tried "everything" to organize the session in a way that Sam can participate for him in a more helpful way.

The supervisor begins the interview by checking out with the supervisees that they have understood Carla's wishes and needs accurately. The supervisor's understanding is that Carla wishes to focus on (1) the interaction within the family and (2) ideas about organizing the family sessions. Carla confirms this. The supervisor then turns to the four other students that have been listening to the conversation between Carla and the supervisor. The supervisor suggests dividing the group in two such that one pair will focus on and reflect on the interaction in the family and the other on organizing the family sessions.

The supervisor then turns to Carla and starts interviewing her about the family's interaction and then about organizing the sessions. The interview lasts about 30 min and the supervisor tries to explore Carla's understanding and thoughts about the interaction in the family by asking questions about what the family are telling her, what she is observing and her thoughts and considerations about this. When you are working with families like Carla, you receive a lot of information on many levels. One of several challenges is to organize and to get an oversight of this information—not in the purpose of making categories in a diagnostic manner, but rather to achieve a kind of map to navigate a way forward. The supervisor's aim in this part of the interview is to help the supervisee to put words to her experiences in order to sort out all the information and perhaps to draw such a map and to clarify if there are (and there almost always are) issues that could be further explored by the supervisee/therapist. The supervisor also asks questions about Carla's experiences with the family in the sessions in order to achieve a picture of what is happening in the room. The supervisor asks quite concrete and detailed questions about how the family is placed in the room, who is usually starting to say something, how does Carla experience Sam when he is attending the sessions and at the beginning, and more questions about the interaction within the family and between Carla and the members of the family. An issue to explore is also whether there have been sessions when Sam has participated the whole time without running out or has been participating in a way the therapist thinks was OK and if this was the case—what did Carla do to achieve this? What was her contribution? The supervisor will try to draw a picture from what the supervisee is telling of what happens in the sessions.

After this brief interview the four other students are invited to reflect while the supervisor and Carla listen. The two students focusing on the interaction in the family start and share their thoughts and reflections and then the other two reflect on the topic of organizing the family sessions. This happens as two separate conversations with each pair of two.

After the reflections the supervisor asks Carla if she would like to comment on something that she has heard. In the following conversation with the supervisor she points out some ideas about the interaction in the family she has not thought about and some that she has thought about and that she thought was a kind of confirmation of her own ideas and ways to see things. The two students that reflected on ideas about organizing the sessions had among other things talked about concrete possible things to do in the sessions that Carla said she wanted to try out in the following sessions with the family. The things she wanted to try out were among others to start every session with explaining what was going to happen and for how long. She said that she also would like to try out some drawing exercises suggested by the team. The exercise she said applied to her most was one where the family members are asked to draw something from their family life they have done together and that they liked. After drawing the family members are asked to show their drawing and share their story about it. Carla said that she believed this exercise could be a contribution and an attempt to bring in a more hopeful and competent perspective and take away some of the negative focus on Sam. Hopefully this also could be an exercise and activity that was more adapted to Sam and his age.

Carla also said that she was pleased with the fact that as a result of the reflections she had achieved confirmation of some of her own thoughts and ideas about the interaction in the family and some new ones, and also some new concrete ideas about organizing the sessions that she wanted to try out later.

Hopefully as we read the example above we see how this approach to supervision contains possibilities about expanding perspectives on more than one level. In this case it was the level of understanding of the interaction in the family and the level of the therapist's possible actions in the sessions with the family. The supervisee has the opportunity to expand her perception of the family and to increase her bank of ideas and alternatives of action. For the students not in focus the session has the possibility to offer opportunities to train in focused listening, formulating reflections on the basis of their inner conversation during the interview with Carla. The students that form the reflecting teams are helped to stay focused on Carla's expressed wishes for the outcome of the supervision.

Reflecting with Different Theoretical Perspectives in Focus

The same model as described above can be transferred and used with other perspectives and angles in mind. In supervision of both students and qualified family therapists, theoretical perspectives will be of importance. For students supervision could be a good arena for learning and discussing theory connected to clinical work. For family therapists, supervision also has the potential to be an arena where different theories can be helpful to throw light on clinical dilemmas and questions. My experience is that most of us have a connection with our theoretical knowledge as a basis or background for our work and that these theories will have an impact on us in how we understand and interpret what we experience together with our clients and their families. Hopefully these theories can be one of the many factors that guide us in our professional activities. Also I often think that many of us have realized that the potential in our theoretical knowledge is not fully used. This probably is due to many and different reasons, but perhaps lack of time and space in a busy daily work routine is one. In supervision I think it is important to reflect on how our ideas and preferred theories both impact on us and influence what we think we see and know. Our theoretical knowledge is a source that could be more useful for us in our daily work.

Presentation of theory is usually presented in seminars or classes where the teacher more or less will use clinical examples. Supervision or clinical discussions could also be possible as arenas where theories are used to highlight different perspectives of clinical work and to increase both students' and qualified therapists' knowledge, understanding, and repertoire of action.

The amount of theories relevant for working with families and family therapy is almost endless, but in this chapter I will choose some examples that after my experience and in my own practice experience have been shown to be useful. The themes and issues presented in the clinical work will guide the supervisor and the supervision group in choosing theories to put into focus. To highlight one or more theories will be one of the questions that the supervisor and the supervision group have to discuss initially. As described above the initial interview with the student or therapist in focus will be of importance in this matter, for example, what will be the need and wishes for the group and the supervisee to be kept in focus? And what could enlighten the case discussed in the most fruitful way?

There are many theories that have the potential to enlighten systemic work with couples, families, and individuals. The issues connected to the case can be one of the factors that will guide the group and supervisor to choose the relevant theory. For supervision groups of students there can also be a wish for learning more about a specific theory and how this theory can be of help in the clinical work, for example, attachment theory (Bowlby, 1988), theories of Trauma (Coulter, 2011), theories about domestic violence (Cooper & Vetere, 2005), theories of family life like the family life cycle (Carter & McGoldrick, 1988), and many others. These are some examples of theories and research that could be relevant for supervision sessions. My own experience as a therapist and as a supervisor is that I often find it difficult to connect to theory when I am challenged to say something about what theory I use in this or that situation with a family or when I ask the questions to students or another therapist. I do not think this is due to a lack of theoretical knowledge, but I think that it is a matter of practice and training to have theory present in our minds when asked. And when I say present my intention is to say that theory could be a valuable source among other sources that we are guided by and inspired by in our work.

In order to use and to put in focus specific theories in supervision groups, the sessions can be organized in the same way as described in the example above with different clinical perspectives. The different members of the group can be given the task to listen to the conversation or interview with a specific theory in mind as a background. Again, this can be organized as pairs in the group that reflect together on the background and contribution of a theory and with another pair reflecting on the background and contribution of another theory. The supervisee in focus and the interviewer will listen as described above and have the opportunity to comment and summarize after the reflections. For the case presented above, reflections based on attachment theory and the family's attachment narratives could be of relevance. Examples are reflections containing questions about how the family members comfort each other and the supervisee's reflections about this. Another example could be questions about how the supervisees think about comfort and possible change (Dallos & Vetere, 2009).

Reflecting with Different Family Therapy Approaches in Mind

Reflecting on the basis of different kinds of family therapy approaches as we hold them in mind could be of specific interest for groups of family therapy trainees. This could be a good opportunity to learn more about the approaches and the differences and similarities between them.

In the Norwegian context, most family therapy training programs teach the students about different approaches or therapeutic schools of family therapy and systemic thinking. In the program I am connected to (VID scientific university) the students are offered teaching in the following approaches: Structural family therapy (Minuchin, Lee, & Simon, 2006); Strategic family therapy (Haley, 1980); Milan systemic family therapy (Hoffmann, 1981); Collaborative and dialogical approaches (Anderson, 1997; Bertrando, 2007); Reflecting processes (Andersen, 1987); Solution focused family therapy (de Shazer, 1991); and Narrative therapy (White, 2007). In addition to this, the program offers the students lessons in how to use discursive perspectives in family therapy and systemic practice.

The therapeutic approaches listed above are based on different theories and represent perspectives that could be seen as contradictory or even competing. Some of them can be defined as theories based in first- and second-order perspectives (Hoffmann, 1985; Lowe et al., 2008). Some approaches could be described as normative and some nonnormative, some inspired within a modernistic world view and some within a postmodern world view. To take these very different perspectives into the context of supervision gives the participants in the supervision group an opportunity to explore these different ways of thinking and doing in connection to practical therapeutic work. I think that in daily practical clinical work they (and us) seldom have the privilege of doing this in full scale. So, in addition to learning about the different approaches this also represents an opportunity to recognize these perspectives and discourses in action and to reflect upon the clinical implications of these approaches.

The way to do this is very much like as I described earlier in this chapter. The supervisees that are not presenting a case build a reflecting team. The team members are split up into pairs and then given the task to reflect on the basis of what they hear in the interview of the supervisee who is presenting a case within a chosen theoretical approach. After the interview with the supervisor about the case, the team then presents their reflections and the supervisor and supervisee summarize afterwards. The focus in this summary will be on the benefit for the supervisee, and for example, what will she or he will bring into the further work with the family and perhaps in what way.

In addition to this, the whole group has the opportunity to reflect and summarize together as a group about the different approaches and the perspectives they represent. A possible benefit from such a discussion could be that the group members achieve a deeper knowledge about the themes discussed. Such a discussion can also pin out dilemmas and ethical issues connected to the different approaches.

If we use the same clinical example as described above with Carla's work, we can imagine that two of the group members reflect with the ideas and concepts of structural family therapy in mind and the other with narrative therapy. The "structural" team is presenting thoughts and ideas on boundaries in the family—for example that the oldest child seems rather too much involved in what should be the responsibility of the parents. The "Narrative" team reflects upon how the problem is harassing the family and how the family is taking steps to minimize the power of the problem. These two approaches also raise questions about the position of the therapist. Some might see the structural therapist as an expert knowing how suitable boundaries in a family should look. A narrative therapist would probably take an opposite position in the sense of being an expert. The narrative therapist would not take a standpoint or even have a view on whether boundaries are healthy or not but put his or her attention to the family members' views and knowledge about being a family.

Reflecting with Different Perspectives Connected to Roles in the Family and the Professionals in Focus

In systemic supervision there will probably be a focus on persons and professionals involved, roles in the family and in the professional system and the relations within the family, within the professional system and between the family as a system and the professional system, and at last, between persons in the family and person within the professional system. The persons in the family and the professional system will have different roles, as a father, mother, daughter, grandparent, therapist, child protection worker, and so on. How the different person relates to each other and how they act and think will be influenced by which role they have and this matters a lot concerning how problems presented will be understood and worked with.

In supervision therefore it will be of interest to focus on the different perspectives that these different roles represent. This can be done in different ways and I think the most usual way is to interview the supervisee about this in an attempt to open up new thoughts and perspectives. Use of the reflecting team has the potential to add even more to this process and will be described below.

If we follow the model described above, an interview will be followed by reflections presented by the reflecting team members. In the initial interview the supervisor will ask questions to highlight the supervisee's thoughts, concerns, and questions about issues connected to this topic. As described above questions are asked about what the supervisee wants to focus on and if there are specific issues the team members should pay attention to. Another question to the supervisee is whether she or he has thoughts about how the reflections could be presented. The reflections might be presented from the perspectives of the different roles.

The way to do this in practice is to ask the members of the team to listen to the interview in the role of another person. If the team consists of four members, examples of roles could be mother, father, child, and therapist. The team members' task is to listen to the conversation between the supervisor and supervisee as if they actually were the different persons or more precisely, they listen as how they think the persons behind the different roles will feel and think about the issues discussed. When it is time to present the reflections and the members of the team have taken an "inside" position and actually reflect as if they were the person or in the role as a father, mother, daughter, or therapist, it can be quite powerful and the reflections can make a considerable impact on the people that are listening. I think this goes to the very heart of one of the most giving and challenging tasks of a (family) therapist—to listen to and take in as many perspectives as possible and make meaning of this enormous amount of information in order to help the people who seek our help in the best possible way. In this way of presenting the teams' reflections, the supervisee in focus has a valuable chance to listen in a structured way to the perspectives of the different roles and then the time and space to think and reflect about what impact this might have for the continuing work with the specific client or family and on developmental issues of personal and professional matters.

After the reflections the conversation will continue as usual between the supervisor and the supervisee. The task of the supervisor in this part of the supervision session is to help sort out what was valuable and useful for the supervisee. Questions concerning the roles in focus could be asked and/or questions about if, and perhaps how, the reflections were meaningful to the supervisee and if they gave some new thoughts and ideas to be used in their further work with the actual family or client.

Some Closing Comments

The aim of this chapter was to describe how the reflecting team and the ideas connected to reflecting processes (Andersen, 1987) could be useful in different kinds of supervision arrangements with family therapy students and qualified family therapists and also for other supervision groups in counselling and psychotherapy as well. The reflecting team and reflecting processes offer ways to structure and organize the supervision sessions that seeks to bring forward perspectives and ideas hopefully helpful for the participants and for the people that meet them in their work.

In all educational activities for therapists in all kinds of therapy models, I think and strongly believe that developing reflective practitioners is one of the main goals. Reflective processes and the different structures and ways to organize the reflective activity that the reflecting team models offer give supervisors many options to create contexts where development of both knowledge and essential therapeutic skills can take place.

References

Andersen, T. (1987). The reflecting team. Dialogue and meta-dialogue in clinical work. *Family Process, 26*, 415–428.

Andersen, T. (1995). Reflecting processes: Acts of informing and forming. You can borrow my eyes, but you must not take them away from me! In S. Friedman (Ed.), *The reflecting team in action: Collaborative practices in psychotherapy*. New York: Guilford Press.

Anderson, H. (1997). *Conversion, language and possibilities. A postmodern approach to therapy*. New York: HarperCollins.

Bakhtin, M. (1981). *The dialogical imagination*. Texas: Texas University Press.

Bertrando, P. (2007). *The dialogical therapist: Dialogue in systemic practice*. London: Karnac Books.

Bowlby, J. C. (1988). *A secure base: Clinical applications of attachment theory*. London: Routledge.

Carter, B., & McGoldrick, M. (Eds.). (1988). *The changing family life cycle. A framework for family therapy* (2nd ed.). New York: Gardner Press.

Cooper, J., & Vetere, A. (2005). *Domestic violence and family safety: A systemic approach to working with violence in families*. Chichester: Wiley.

Coulter, S. (2011). Systemic family therapy for families who have experienced trauma: A randomized controlled trial. *British Journal of Social Work, 41*(3), 502–519.

Dallos, R., & Vetere, A. (2009). *Systemic therapy and attachment narratives*. New York: Routledge.

Davis, J. (2012). The golden pig, reflections as ancestral blessings: The reflecting process in teaching famil therapy. *Family Process, 51*(3), 405–419.
de Shazer, S. (1991). *Putting difference to work*. New York: W.W. Norton.
Haley, J. (1980). *Leaving home. The therapy of disturbed young people* (2nd ed.). New York: McGraw-Hill.
Hoffmann, L. (1981). *Foundations of family therapy*. New York: Basic books.
Hoffmann, L. (1985). Beyond power and control. Towards an "second order" family systems therapy. *Family Systems Medicine, 3*(4), 381–396.
Jensen, P., & Hoffman, L. (2007). *Innovations in the reflecting process: The inspirations of Tom Andersen*. London: Karnac Books.
Lowe, R., Hunt, C., & Simmons, P. (2008). Towards multi-positioned live supervision in family therapy: Combining treatment and observations teams with first- and second-order perspective. *Contemporary Family Therapy, 30*, 3–14.
Minuchin, S., Lee, W.-Y., & Simon, G. M. (2006). *Mastering family therapy: Journeys and growth of transformation*. Wiley.
Papp, P. (1980). The Greek chorus and other techniques of paradoxical therapy. *Family Process, 19*, 45–57.
Reichelt, S., & Skjerve, J. (2013). The reflecting team model used for clinical group supervision without clients present. *Journal of Marital and Family Therapy, 39*(2), 244–255.
Rober, P. (1999). The therapist's inner conversation: Some ideas about the self of the therapist, therapeutic impasse and the process of reflection. *Family Process, 38*, 209–228.
Rober, P. (2005). The therapist's self in dialogical family therapy: Some ideas about not-knowing and the therapist's inner conversation. *Family Process, 44*, 477–495.
Rober, P., Elliott, R., Buysse, A., Loots, G., & De Corte, K. (2008). What's on the therapist's mind? A grounded theory analysis of family therapist reflections during individual therapy sessions. *Psychotherapy Research, 18*(1), 48–57.
Rober, P. (2010). The interacting–reflecting training exercise: Addressing the therapist's inner conversation in family therapy training. *Journal of Marital and Family Therapy, 36*(2), 158–117.
Vetere, A., & Dallos, R. (2009). Family mirrors: Reflective practice in systemic therapies. In J. Stedmon & R. Dallos (Eds.), *Reflective practice in psychotherapy and counselling*. Maidenhead: OU Press.
White, M. (2007). *Maps of narrative practice*. New York, NY: W. W. Norton.

Chapter 7
Creating a Dialogical Culture for Supervision

Anne Hedvig Vedeler

"Any standardized method of therapy,
no matter how effective with certain problems,
cannot deal successfully with the wide range
that is typically offered to a therapist.
Flexibility and spontaneity are necessary"

(Haley, 1987:8)

"Competent therapy requires that you
get outside of your comfort zone,
stretch, and learn how to interact with clients
in a way that works for them"

(Gehart, 2016:4)

Introduction

Professional supervision within the area of psychosocial services has traditionally been focused on the client, her[1] condition and her responses in therapy. This is in accordance with the view that problems are located within the individual, like any other medical condition. Later this view has been challenged and expanded to an interest also in the professional since it is realized that her relation to the client is of decisive importance. Both approaches are founded on the belief that therapy can be taught by speaking about the phenomena under scrutiny.

The approach I discuss in this chapter offers a different perspective. It is based on the idea that what goes on in the supervisory situation itself in terms of relationships between all involved, the climate and the culture created, serves as a model of

[1] In order to avoid the dominating gendered he/him/his, I am making a statement using the female she/her/hers, except when there is an explicit reference to a man. This statement is made in relation to an overarching tendency in the Modern Western society to "masculininize" humanity by the use of nouns. I have not found a "genderfree" noun that would free us from having to confront this dualism.

A.H. Vedeler (✉)
Family Therapy Section, Faculty of Social Studies, VID Specialized University,
Oslo, Norway
e-mail: annehedvigv@hotmail.com

A. Vetere, J. Sheehan (eds.), *Supervision of Family Therapy and Systemic Practice*,
Focused Issues in Family Therapy, https://doi.org/10.1007/978-3-319-68591-5_7

what can happen in the supervisee's own professional work. In other words: The logic behind this way of supervising rests on the transferability of a culture of supervision into the supervisee's professional work. Since the concept of culture implies the involvement of a plurality of people, it is natural that this kind of supervision takes the form of working in groups. That said, this does not mean that the ideas presented in this chapter are not useful in one-to-one supervision contexts as well.

The concept of dialogue is central. This term involves both verbal exchange and emotional and bodily levels of human communication, consciously and unconsciously. Experiences, over time, in a climate governed by dialogical principles, may create a dialogical group culture, which may profoundly affect the participants personally and professionally. The intention is to create a culture where movements, complexity, diversity, and surprises are dealt with as invitations to be flexible and improvised, in a benevolently open manner.

This chapter will offer detailed descriptions of supervision based on dialogue both through my own narrations; pieces of transcripts[2]; and stories shared by members of the supervision groups. I will share with you some stories of how attending ongoing dialogue groups helps professionals to maintain a dialogic awareness.

I have for many years now been engaged in supervisory work with professionals during and after their family therapy training. What I from now on will term dialogic work is about creating a dialogical culture, where all participants can experience dialogue from within, and develop a kind of sensitivity towards the interactive movements between people in their daily and professional life.

The terms supervision and supervisor do not fit in this context. The term *super* connotes a vertical relationship and does also imply an element of control. As the following text will show these characteristics of supervision are contrary to the values and practices we try to develop in our dialogical groups. Still, also this kind of group needs leadership as will be evident in the next paragraphs. I will therefore change the term supervisor with the term group leader and name the supervisees simply group members or participants.

[2] In October 2016, I invited members from five different dialogue groups to come together to reflect on our way of being together. Nine people came. I also invited a collegue, an experienced family therapist to *conduct* the reflecting session. I was a mere listener in the room. The reflecting session went on for 2hours. I voice recorded the conversation. The reflecting talks was a collaborative inquiry into these dialogue groups. I had asked "the conductor" to ask open questions about how the participants percieve the groups; what a dialogue group means to them, why they participate in them and if they feel being in the group makes a difference for them workwise. The reflecting sessions was led with very little structure, and I was amazed how easily they got into the mode of dialogue.

Another day, I asked one of the dialogue groups to have a reflection, while I was listening, about the same questions the people above had reflected on.

Later on I transcribed the recordings, and they serve as a background for part of this chapter. The quotes in the chapter are from these recordings. The participants are made anonymous, and they have all agreed to lend their voices to this chapter. So has Blossom, who wrote the story about her supervisory relationship with "Yngve."

Characteristics of Dialogue

In describing the concept of dialogue, it may be useful to compare it with monologue. In monologue, the speaker's aim is to express a view or a position without taking the listener into consideration. Evaluating a monologue will be about how accurate or clear the speech is in relation to the speaker's ideas and intentions. In dialogue, the utterances are shaped and adjusted relative to the listener who in turn forms her responses according to how the first speakers' utterance is perceived. Evaluation of dialogical communication is based on the partners' sense of being understood by the other.

Leaning on the Russian philosopher Mikhail Bakhtin (1981, 1984, 1986), language is in process of creating our world, and this is done through dialogue; we think, talk, and act dialogically and new meaning emerges on the threshold between voices in action. In dialogical conversations, the language is structured between the speaker and the listener (Bakhtin, 1981). The utterance is the decisive element in verbal communication; it has both an addressivity and receptivity. This means that everything said is said with a double voice, we have both ourselves and the others in mind when we speak. There is no vacuum from which we speak, nor a vacuum we speak in to. So, in addressing someone we will be conscious of whom we are addressing and how he or she might respond. This will affect the way we speak, which details to choose, and which values we appeal to. Voloshinov (1973) describes the word as a product of the mutual relationship between the speaker and the listener, a bridge between you and the other.

Bakhtin suggests the term unfinalizability as an all-purpose bearer of his conviction that the world is not only a messy place, but also an open place. Meaning is never a completed product. Bakhtin consistently opposes all ways of thinking that could reduce the present moment—each present moment—to a simple derivative of what went before. Time is open and each moment has multiple possibilities.

Dialogue is not only something that takes place between people like in an outer, observable conversation. Thinking can be understood as inner dialogues, and inner speech resembles the alternating lines of a dialogue (Voloshinov, 1973). Even when you are thinking by yourself, the way you speak to yourself is affected and determined by the ones you imagine you speak to. Michael Billig (1996) expands on this by claiming that thinking is a kind of inner argumentation modelled after the outer dialogue. In this way, our "inner attitudes" become rhetorical attitudes where we justify and criticize others and ourselves in a continuous inner rhetoric activity. According to Vygotsky (1986), there are still differences between inner and outer dialogues. In our inner dialogues, we take many things for granted. Many abbreviations and condensations take place in inner conversations. For example it is not necessary to explain the context in the same way as in an outer dialogue, we take it for granted that we understand ourselves. The sense of different words flow into one another and literally "influence" each other, so that earlier ones are contained in, and modify the later ones. "One word stands for a number of thoughts and feelings, and sometimes substitutes for a long and profound discourse" (Vygotsky, 1986: 248). A single word is so saturated with sense that to unfold it into outer speech, one would need a multitude of words.

When thoughts, inner dialogues, are to be externalized into outer utterances we have to make them sensible to others and we have to make many choices. Hence the outer conversation will almost never be the same as we imagined it would turn out in our inner conversation. This transformation between thought and word is not a thing but a process (Vedeler, 2004). It is a continuous movement back and forth, from thought to word and from word to thought. In the course of this process changes will occur both in thought and word, "thought is not merely expressed in words; it comes into existence through them" (Vygotsky, 1986: 218). Billig (1999) underlines that it would be wrong to assume that every utterance is an outer sign of thought processes. Sometimes the course of a conversation runs so fast that it is impossible to prepare for what to say next. "Often we hear ourselves saying something in response, only discovering what our thoughts are as we speak. The thinking is not hidden, but is happening out there in the conversation" (:48).

According to Bakhtin, the notions of the conscious and the unconscious hinge on a complex dialogue between multitudes of different voices, a polyphony of voices in our inner dialogues. "At any present moment of the dialogue there are great masses of forgotten meanings, but these will be recalled again at a given moment in the dialogue's later course when it will be given new life. For nothing is absolutely dead: every meaning will someday have its homecoming festival" (Bakhtin quoted in Holquist, 1990:39).

But out of all the meaning making processes we are involved in we find words for just a small bit. As Pascal Mercier (2008) writes in his novel, *Night Train to Lisbon:*

> "buried under all the mute experiences are those unseen ones that give our life its form, its colour, and its melody" (:17). These experiences are seen in our movements, our body's and facial gestures, in the tone of voice we use, and the pacing and pausing when we do find words.

Dialogical Processes in Supervision Groups; Formats, Values, and Principles

The creation of a dialogical group culture will depend on certain formats, values, and principles. These will now be listed in terms of some key elements: *Position of the group leader, invitation, format, insisting on a dialogical orientation, tuning in, responsiveness and musicality, improvisation, compassion, presence, pace and listening.*

The Group Leader

The group leader in dialogical groups could also be termed a host. This implies certain activities and attitudes on the part of the leader: The group leader invites the participants to be her guests. This means an effort on the part of the leader to make everyone feel welcome and equally included.

The leader has a special responsibility to realize the purpose of the meeting. In dialogical groups, her behavior and attitudes represent a model of what dialogue is about, not by teaching the concept but by showing in practice what it means in the here and now of the group life. The group leader conveys an attitude of a firm insistence on dialogue.

This responsibility implies the need to be aware of the minutiae of communications between all involved, not the least her own part. Dialogue entails exchanges on many levels and kinds of expression: words, intonation, facial expression, gestures, body expressions, all of which can be more or less conscious. All this mean an openness and a sensitivity which are directly relevant and transferable to any participant's own professional work.

The Invitation

The first encounter has the potential of creating a context for subsequent encounters. Therefore the invitation can be decisive for further developments in the group. The initial contact between me, and those who want to join a group or create a new group might be by email correspondence. From the very first contact, I want to welcome these people I might never have met before, in a way so they feel freed from presenting themselves as clever, smart, and bursting with knowledge. People usually want to be perceived as valid and valuable, sensible and intelligible. A self-imposed demand for coherence and consistency is naturally present in entering dialogical groups as it is in therapy. To counteract this I might write something like this in the initial email: "Come as you are, and let's see what happens. No need to prepare yourself in any special way. And you don't need to bring anything but yourself." My intention is to invite into a culture where we can experience from within the ongoing creation of relationships, how it is to be met as a person. In the following Amanda is recollecting her group's first encounter with me. We had arranged for a weekend with supervision and the four women from the north had been travelling for more than 15 h to meet me in a hotel.

> *"When we arrived at the hotel, way too late, running up the stairs dragging the suitcases behind us, I heard Eva panting 'I will need to shower before I feel human again'. She sounded torn. We were all feeling uneasy about being late for our first supervision session with you. And how you met Eva, when she needed to take a shower after her journey, so different from how we're usually greeted. There is usually lots of back- and-forth, but you said 'Go and shower, take a good long shower, as long as you need, don't feel you need to*

rush'. This has to do with respect for what is actually being expressed, not questioning it away in any way. It's just, 'of course, do it'." (Vedeler, 2011: 213–218)

My spontaneous reaction, meeting these women for our very first supervision session, emphasizes how I invite people into a dialogic space. It is about a way of being and moving with people, not a strategic action in order to create trust or alliance. It is based on an ethical stance, allowing us to enter into an inter-involvement with the others, and cease to set ourselves above them. I like to compare it with an inviting handshake, where the two holds each other's hands for a long time, to take in the other person's "situation"—"how things are for him" (Vedeler, 2011).

Preparing for dialogue is about reminding oneself to be present here and now, together with those present (not having your awareness anywhere else). I can do it by physically preparing the room, reminding myself of who is coming, their names and what we have "had" together from before. I might light candles, prepare tea and coffee, some snacks and arrange the chairs in a circle.

All these physical arrangements feel important, but more significant is my internal preparation. Sometimes I think of it as breathing them in, thereby opening myself towards the people I am going to meet. I believe this attentiveness can be seen in my bodily movements, in my facial expression, in the tone of voice, and in the pace and tempo I show.

This way of *preparing* is very different from *planning*. Planning is to me a way of orienting myself that makes me think many steps ahead. This often leads to being too self-occupied and less sensitive to what the others bring forth. Ideas that were useful in one context might not fit what emerges in new situations. Preparing is about being poised and present here and now, and responsive to newness.

Sometimes when I have not prepared myself like this, I feel uncomfortably non-present. I tend to forget people's names and what we have been talking about; then it might take some time before I feel we are ready to listen to each other and talk about our genuine concerns.

Format: Structure and Framework for Dialogue

One way of securing dialogical conversations to help them develop and keep them going is for the group leader to talk to each participant in turn, with the others in a reflecting position (Andersen, 1994). This arrangement we call "rounds." Such an arrangement should not be thought of as a technique but as a practical framework supporting dialogue. The point is that structure is there to protect freedom. I have often experienced that the usual way of talking, when there is not an attention to this, is that people talk and interrupt each other. Every one becomes more concerned with talking themselves, than being moved by the others' concerns.

The conversation initiated by the group leader is performed in a dialogical way so that any concern of the one who is talking is appreciated and her way of expression respected. The conversation should be allowed to last as long as it takes. When the group member starts to talk, I ask questions into what she is telling, thereby helping her to say what she wants to say and even has a chance to express more than she knew was important to her. The speaker is free to talk about whatever she wants. Participants might start with something from their professional work or from their private contexts. But already at this stage of the dialogical encounter, the host of the conversation is intensely poised towards how the speaker relates to what she is telling. The participants in the listening position are invited to do the same. From the very beginning, the group is encouraged to focus more on how the concerns are presented than the content. Already at this stage in our involvement with each other, I try to create possibilities for the group to experience from within how it is to be able to talk, listen and be listened to in an emotionally responsive manner.

After the talk between the host and the guest has come to an end, the other participants are invited to express whatever ideas and feelings they have of what they have seen and felt when listening to the talk. The purpose of the arrangement is to give everyone an opportunity to learn something about themselves and of the others, and about how such a context opens up a space for the unforeseen. Both speaker and listener become learners. One has to bear in mind that dialogue also means listening to oneself.

This procedure should be flexible: the host must keep a keen eye and have open ears to what is going on. The situation might require a much more in the moment responsiveness, and my position might change, and there may occasionally be more unstructured conversations. Insistening dialogue is more about frames, than content. And the frames need to be both firm and flexible in response to the ongoing reflexive context we are co-creating. We decide pauses, not only to relax but also for more considered reason, for example, if people need to think things over, or tensions are to be lowered.

Other structural elements influencing dialogical processes in groups involve fee, time span between meetings and the how long they last. This is something that we as a group initially negotiate and renegotiate as time goes on. I am aware of how people's professional and private lives change, and by that also the opportunities and needs they have in relation to participating in these groups. This also means that we time and again need to talk about taking in new group members. Groups that have created a sense of trust and safety might be reluctant to take in new members. I usually remind us that we should not be too comfortable with stability. The fact that we embrace the unknown, the newness, and the possible diversity helps to keep us open for what and whom we do not yet know. Tina, a group member reflects on this:

"We have invited some new people into the group, they came from somewhere else. Among others, a former colleague of me came, one of whom I had a whole different relationship with. And I was unsure if it would ruin things, that something strange would enter our nice group. But I think that it has only brought in a lot. It's gotten better, something I didn't think was possible. That's what I think is so strange. Now it seems like they are all "my people". I think this is about the dialogue and the flow of it."

Insistence

When we sit down, I try to be sensitive towards the actual and subjective context each one of us is in. I know that initially it might feel unusual and even uncomfortable to experience the openness I am inviting the group to be part of. I am also aware of the contextual paradox: I am insistently inviting them in to a dialogical culture, meaning that all voices and all meaning are welcome, and simultaneously saying that there is a way of being together that is preferred.

I do not explain or teach what that preference means. I rely on the power of experiencing it in practice. This can serve as an example: when our inner voices become vigilant, on alert and afraid of not being heard, they might wither away or become a monologue with a flow of words, going on and on ad nauseam. From daily experience we all know how embarrassing such situations can be. The speaker seems unable to stop her flow and the listeners do not know how to stop her. In such situations, when both the speaker and the listener seem stuck and helpless, I make an effort to invite in the one locked in her monologue, in all possible ways. It can be tempting to use my power as the group leader to stop her directly. Instead I may say: *"It is interesting what you are saying and there is no need to be exact, what is of significance will emerge."* In this way I indirectly demonstrate that a dialogical stance is possible even under pressure. One may call it a benevolent insistence.

Tuning in

My initial questions are about their hopes, their experiences from before, what makes them feel welcome, how would we/I know if they appreciate what we are doing. What would be the best way to proceed?

One day I said this:

> "Good to see you all. Are you all comfortable? Coffee, tea anyone? And remember this table is really a foot stool, but you may use it as a coffee table as well. (This is a joke, about me being in the habit of putting my feet on the table, and an invitation for a more informal setting. But it is just as much underlining that this is a space where nothing has a meaning outside the meaning we ascribe to something.) Should we just go around the circle, I would like to hear if there is something you want to share—something that you would like us to know—something from this morning, or from last time we were together? Maybe something from work, something any of you have read? Or about what you want us to do together today. Let us just start and see how it develops, what emerges during the round. It might be a short round, but as you know it might take the whole day. I will see to it, that all of you will have time to talk, if you want to, and listen."

I take my time, when saying this. The questions are not all meant to be answered; it is more a way of showing that anything may be talked about. It might be compared with the greeting *"how are you,"* which is a way too big question to be answered. It is more a way of showing that *I care,* and *welcome* you to talk. I believe the tempo and pacing is just as important as the words. My eyes wander around accompanying the words, as if telling each one present that I see them, and that they are welcome.

I am attentive to the vaguely sensed movements but not-yet-worded feelings, expressed in the room. By a willingness to become present in relation to the emerging actualities, I try to place myself "within" the relationship and make an effort to read the contexts I am involved with. And that is of course an impossible task, as the context is ever moving. But my point is to be mindful of the complex process, relate to it, and contribute to it. This attentiveness is also meant as an invitation to the others, so we can strive towards embracing each one present as unique individuals, while also being open to the group as a whole. It is a time for contemplation, not only to think and talk but also just as much to feel our bodies' presence.

Stumbling and Groping for Meaning

One of the premises I underline and encourage in our work in dialogical groups, both verbally and by my own presentation, is about appreciating stumbling. That means to recognize that our verbal expressions do not need to be clear and straightforward to deserve interest. Searching for words, hesitation, and pauses are after all the way people use to find out what they mean. This should be welcomed and appreciated in dialogical group work. And what is more: Striving for precise words is not only often in vain, it might be unnecessary. What is significant will emerge, where and when it is needed. I continuously stress: "There is no need to be exact; by stumbling around, groping for meaning, what is of significance will emerge." Liz appreciated this invitation:

> "I remember you used the word stumble, and how relieved I felt hearing that word. I am not in other contexts that value my stumbling. It was a new world to me, and I could hear that I talked differently when I was allowed to stumble. Yeah, it gave me a new opportunity to be me in a way I had never been before. It was soul-setting."

In Norwegian there is a saying about what happens in card games; if you first have thrown the cards you cannot take them back ("Done deal"). In a dialogical conversation, it is quite contrary; *"the table does not catch,"* the "deal" is newer done. The person who talks is encouraged to adjust, clarify, retreat, try again until she feels that she has expressed what she feels is in tune with her bodily feeling of "rightness." But this way of thinking does not come easily. It is difficult to oppose the powerful discourse so dominant in modern Western society that says there is one truth to be found and that words should have an exact meaning. This is the Western conception of *"the coolly, logical 'rational man', a man who is regarded as far more reliable than the much maligned woolly-minded, intuitive thinker"* (Devlin, 1997:182). The concept of control is immanent in this "accepted wisdom"; and it is connected to values of control over others as well as self-control, and a discouragement of not being in control. I can certainly recognize this from my encounters in supervision contexts as well as in everyday talk; sometimes revealed as embarrassment towards using too much time searching for meaning or a lack of agency (Anderson, 1997). It is also evident in the lack of trust in implicit knowing (Stern, 2004) or tacit knowledge (Polanyi, 1966). But what we refer to as logic simply cannot capture the real processes of human thought. Contextual improvisation, local, unique logic and living relationships are too complex, and as Devlin (1997) asserts, our minds are intimately intertwined with the world around us; even our social norms play crucial roles in the marvelously complex dance of human cognition.

I am concerned how this powerful and seductive force towards generalized logic, certainty, and consistency becomes a condition for being accepted and included. Being "outside" one might feel lost. Our society rewards those who claim certainty, show ability to categorize, and predict outcomes. The preference of logic and reason show itself in our everyday life. This conviction often creates an obligation to think and talk consistently and fluently, almost in the form of pre-rehearsed texts (Devlin, 1997; Dreyfus, 1979).

It might be hard to recognize that we move around in our lives according to a knowing that we are unable to verbally express. We might feel lost when we think that it should have been different, and we might become embarrassed when we stumble for words or hear our voice halt. Many people feel lonely when they do not feel understood, in spite of their attempts to make themselves intelligible. Some become silent and hesitate to talk out loud because they are vigilant they are the only ones who feel or relate in this or that way. Some lose their voice because they have not found anyone who would or could hear, and some feel at the margin of society because their truth is not that of the majority. Loneliness, embarrassment, and shame are words I often hear, and feelings I sense in others and can recognize in myself.

In the dialogue group we are creating a kind of counter culture. I believe the time we use; the pacing and the appreciation and embracement of tacit and provisional understanding would impress a visitor to a group session. How we welcome bodily movements, ambiguity, polyphony, and even anxiety into the room creates what some of us call a *safe haven*.

Responsivity, Musicality and Improvisation

In contradiction to a communication model that perceives communication as a process where there is a sender and a receiver, a dialogical perspective underlines the prerequisite interdependency between the speaker and the listener. There must be a willingness to be shaped and reshaped by the other. This is about lending your heart and ear to novelty, also to what is not so easily understood. I think of this as musicality.

Malloch and Trevarthen (2009) perceive dialogical musicality as a human capacity, which is acknowledged as vital to the interaction between a child and its caregivers.

In a dialogue group I relate in a way that takes for granted that we are all musical people. I choose to perceive that we just need to find our voices in tune with the other voices. There is no dissonance in itself; what we talk about as dissonance is always created in context, in relation to something. I am concerned with how I can show emotional interest and willingness to respond benevolently to the keynotes of everyone in the group (as to myself). Through this we are more able to create what I think of as musicality between us.

When a group member "misses out" and seems not to be tuned in, it is easy to feel discomfort. I might even be tempted to perceive her as an insensitive person. In such moments I am helped by thinking of her voice as being on another page than mine (the others) in the notebook. My challenge as the host (but the group members are often taking responsibility) is to stretch towards that voice and build the bridge that is needed to create a shared song. But choirs do not always need to be in perfect "harmony," much exciting music is created when different tones are allowed in a composition.

I am inspired by Ludwig Wittgenstein's suggestion: "Understanding a sentence is much more akin to understanding a theme in music than one might think (1953, no. 527). It serves as a reminder; to be sensitive to the emotional vibrations in the others voice and bodily expression, without always "getting to know the content of the whole story." This attentive position involves an approach to language as not decoding signs, but feeling one's way into the world of the other and listening to the uniqueness in what is expressed.

These ideas encourage me to welcome improvisation and to pay attention to the keynotes (expressions) of all present. If I compare our way of being together to a "jam-session," I will try to help all the voices to function together. This requires that one modulates reciprocally with the other group members so that the dynamic between us becomes a unique shared creation.

This way of being with people is hard to describe. Blossom, a group member, wrote the following as a metaphorical tale about her relationship with me (she called me Yngve):

> ""*Hold back your weight*", Yngve says, "*follow the snow. Feel it in your body, don't look and don't think, be sensitive and improvise*" he says. I can feel my anger: This was supposed to be an enjoyable day skiing. I usually stand aggressively. Changing weight from one ski to another, while sorting out which leg to maneuver feels like playing. My balance is good. It's a competition between me and the steel edge of my skis against the ground. When meeting Yngve I have to learn skiing all over again. The use of brute muscle power is of no use in the powdered snow, it's just damaging it. I can feel the snow under my skis, putting weight towards the back of the skis now. I am floating down the hill, yeah, I will improvise for sure. Yngve laughs and tells me to loosen up; "*follow the snow, let it show itself, don't be scared*". We carry on down the hill. I try to keep my body light and free; a dynamic body is what Yngve calls it. "*It will feel so much better if you manage to let the snow and the terrains guide you*", he says. "*You'll just feel exhausted if you plough your way, the snow will be spoiled and you'll miss out on the good feeling*". I went on many trips with Yngve that winter, improvising in powdered snow. My dynamic body would go off at full speed down the hill. Sensing my body's experiences, never letting it go on autopilot, the snow is never the same. The same steep hill is unique every time, I can never know what I will meet. I need to trust my body's abilities. I learn to improvise, be more creative. Me who used to

> calculate mathematically the force I needed to put down on the skis to get the optimal speed! I can't explain how it feels to go down an untouched snowy hillside, there are no words for it. Skiing in powdered snow is something else. I used to seek understanding and to control existence, as for now, I'm in the glide, I don't know where I am, who I will become or where I will end up…" (in Vedeler, 2011:141–142).

Blossom emphasizes the need for improvisation in contrast to calculation; powdered snow in a steep hill is compared with the uniqueness of every human encounter. She learned to trust that the genuine moving context would guide her if she lets go of seeking control. One to one, or in group settings, I have found it helpful to use any opportunity that shows up between us, to emphasize how we need to "meet" the other or otherness with benevolent curiosity. In this way differences are welcomed as nurturing an evolving context.

Relational Compassion

This term means to let the other person's emotional relation to what is talked about touch the listener's own emotional soundboard. It is an encouragement to be with the other person on her emotional journey, to let the other person explore and feel her way inside her landscape of experiences. Hence, such a stance is contrary to identify a "condition" or an assessment of what is being uttered.

In terms of listening, such a stance implies a willingness to listen with compassion—from a space of not knowing, accepting loss of control, loss of ideas and concepts. Compassionate listening means to be open towards the other, not shrinking what is expressed into already developed contextual forms. It means to let the uniqueness of the event touch the listener and change the listener as well as the speaker. The impact of creating such a space in a group is what I think of as a kind of synergy of relational compassion (Vedeler, 2011).

A story about lack of compassion may further shed light on this concept. Peter, a group participant, told me this:

> "I had a bad experience in a group some time ago, where I talked about my oldest daughter and her problems with alcohol. It was devastating. I could feel it right away, that they didn't carry my words and me. Even if it in the moment felt as a relief to express my concerns, I also felt bad, because the way they met me felt awkward. I could see it in their faces that they didn't understand how upset I was, and how touched I was by telling them about my daughter's binge drinking. As I was talking I know I felt that they thought I was a failure as a dad, because I hadn't been able to put my foot down. But it was impossible to stop talking, since it was as if I needed to get it out. I started to stammer, and then I laughed to get the edge off my concern. That feeling of being misunderstood, and then almost changing the story I was telling stayed with me long after I stopped meeting those people. Not only did I betray myself, it was also as if I let my daughter down."

Peter is giving a touching example of how his words were created on the border between himself and the other people present, and how his experience stayed with him long after they stopped meeting each other. Peter's words in their speaking were like deeds, and his utterances also showed values. Experiencing the group's response he felt he needed to change the way he was speaking to connect to the values of the others. Spontaneously he changed his tone of voice and emotional relationship with his own experience, from seriousness to humor. Intonation lies on the border of the verbal and the nonverbal, the said and the unsaid. Voloshinov (1987) explains, "...it is in intonation above all that the speaker comes into contact with listener or listeners—intonation is social par excellence. It is especially sensitive to all the vibrations in the social atmosphere surrounding the speaker" (p. 102). In this process Peter felt he betrayed both himself and his daughter.

The relational space where fluidity and complexity are cherished over definitions and explanations creates a space for what I sometimes call relational contemplation. I try to offer a space where the group listens to each other as unique persons, showing each other that we are interested in everything that is being expressed, that we want to hear more. We listen without interruptions, and with friendliness and acceptance. We try to follow the one who is talking, being sensitive whether there is more to come. We tune in on the other emotionally, and respond back with facial expressions, body language as well as with words.

As a therapist and group leader I am heartened to let myself become part of this space, where I myself am willing to lose control. I need to remind myself again and again of being curious, to search and be willing to redefine my position from expert to learner. It is often demanding because I feel there are always participants as well as my own competing discourses, craving to position me as "supervisor" in an expert position.

Pacing and Feeling Our Bodies

The tempo and the pacing in the groups appears to be significant. Moving slow is certainly not the only position I have in life, as I often think of myself as moving fast. I cook fast, drive fast and do my shopping in a high tempo. But when I sit down to talk in these groups, it has become easier to lower my tempo. This is not only an intellectual reasoning I dress up with. I have out of experience, been part of several such groups, seen people and relationships prosper from a low tempo. At the same time I have been struck by fascination taking in the complex processes that take place in and in between our bodies especially when we are silent. This is Linda's experience:

> "I feel that my group is a place where my tempo actually can lower. It has given me more time to think and feel. I need to calm down to be able to hear my inner dialogues. The same is the case, I think, for all members of the group. I do not know where I can spot this feeling of calm, but I can sense it in the whole of me."

I believe what Linda is talking about is responding to an invitation, an invitation to be in movement and feel that we are more than words, or word-seekers. To be able to live with what is not there as words, but as something emerging, sometimes into words, sometimes not.

Presence and Being Poised

Presence does not mean to be in tune as a stable position; presence means to seek being presence. In all human involvement there are ruptures, misunderstanding, gaps, lack of engagements, and disagreements. The presence and sensitivity towards the living I have tried to lay out here, means striving towards meeting every new situation open like a child, still with utmost sincerity. It is about abstaining from creating too much order or coherence, to listen without evaluation, judgment, or assessment but with a willingness to be touched and transformed by the other. To be able to do this, I feel like I need to "breathe the other in" the same way I take a newborn baby in and let it move me.

It is about being poised, to open us to the ever-changing newness in the moment of movements, and stretch towards the yet unknown.

Listening

Dialogue involves by definition that the partners listen to each other. The process of listening has been explicit or implicit as discussed in the text above. Still it deserves a special focus because it involves a challenge and is more complex than it seems. In situations like the ones we find ourselves in, such as dialogical groups, listening means not only hearing what people say but to take in, emotionally as well as cognitively, what it means for the speaker to say what she says. And not only that, listening to the other brings also our own concerns to mind. In other words, such listening involves an interest in the broad context in which the speaker and oneself are involved.

Such interest may be termed curiosity. The term curiosity can mean different things. It can mean to disclose or expose something that is hidden, like the work of a journalist or a detective. This would be a forceful act, opposite of what may be called a "benevolent curiosity" (Vedeler, 2011) with the aim of helping to bring forth things difficult to express. To be curious in that sense means to be open, putting oneself in a "not-knowing" position (Anderson & Goolishian, 1992), trying to consider and identify our prejudgments about what is heard.

Dialogical listening takes place both consciously and unconsciously, that is, it involves our thoughts, emotions, and bodies. To learn the art of listening means to learn to be sensitive to what goes on at many levels. This is not an ability to be acquired once and for all; it is to be rehearsed again and again in various contexts. I thank the dialogue groups for giving me an opportunity to be focused and to listen also when what I think I hear is something I do not want to hear.

Another aspect of listening in these groups is to be *allowed* to listen. Group members report that they feel privileged to be allowed to listen, without having to respond in the moment. They can sit and "take the other in," think about how they would have responded to questions that are asked, to let their thoughts wander off. This is how Kim sees it:

> "I can just sit there, for hours and listen to what is expressed. I feel so lucky, I can just sit there and listen and feel, and sometimes also think about my own stuff. And then, when I am invited to respond, I use the time I need to respond. Then I feel my response is much more sincere, and sensitive."

Further Reflections on Dialogical Processes

The reader may have noticed my frequent references to the work of the Russian scholar Mikhail Bakhtin (1981, 1984, 1986). Inspired by his work I comprehend dialogism as a philosophical stance, a continuously tension filled body of movements towards understanding. It is with quite some humility I plead the legacy of Bakhtin, in recognition to the complex and intricate volume of work he left behind. I will not take it upon myself to be an expert judge of his work; the very phrase expert judge is contradictory in relation to his legacy: one that invites openness, ambiguity, polyphony, and infinite understanding. Thus, it is also with boldness that I approach Bakhtin, and take the liberty of using his expressions and writings as a point of departure and as a haven to revisit. It would therefore be an obvious paradox if I treated Bakhtin's voice as canonized or exhaustive. I have rather related to his writing as an invitation to elaborate and as an opening stroke in a poly vocal chorus of voices.

Bakhtin claimed that language and communication are primarily constitutive of social reality. Language is in process of creating our world, and this is done through dialogue; we think, talk, and act dialogically and new meaning emerges on the threshold between voices in action. John Shotter agrees and asserts that language is not a device for picturing or mirroring an already existing language-independent reality (Shotter, 1993). The key assumption is that we are not knowable entities and we do not react in terms of predictable conditional responses (Bateson, 1972). In this perspective human beings are nature and culture (Moi, 2011); we are living, bodily, responsive, expressive and relational beings (Shotter, 2010). We are enmeshed in meaning making through language and in relational communities. As Bakhtin (1984) puts it:

> "to live means to participate in dialogue: to ask questions, to heed, to respond, to agree, and so forth. In this dialogue a person participates wholly and throughout his whole life, with his eyes, lips, hands, soul, spirit, with his whole body and deeds. He invests his entire self in discourse, and this discourse enters into the dialogic fabric of human life, into the world symposium. (…) Every thought and every life merges in the open-ended dialogue." (:293)

Morson and Emerson (1990) accentuate that what Bakhtin has in mind is "a conception of truth that allows every moment to be rich in potentials [and] arise from the experience of the 'open present' in each moment" (:236). It is in this landscape the dialogic sense of truth manifests its unfinalizability by existing on the threshold of several interacting consciousnesses, a plurality of unmerged voices, a polyphony of voices, all interacting. From this perspective language, knowledge, sense making, and understanding can be conceived as different words describing the process towards creating meaning.

Language is the movement, which can mediate meaning as an ongoing activity. The meaning in the language will be in motion, dependent upon the actual context in which it is used. The context is reciprocally created through language and creates language. Bakhtin (1981) termed this consistent infinite potentiality, heteroglossia. That is how there is potential for an indefinite "amount" of meaning immanent in every word we use, as well in all experiences and situations. Heteroglossia is a basic condition governing the operation of meaning in any expression. It is that which insures the primacy of context over text. Everything is understood as a part of a greater whole and there is a constant interaction between meanings. All of which have the potential of conditioning the others which will affect the other, how it will do so and to what degree what is actually settled at the moment of utterance.

Answerability and Ethics

To be answerable inside the unique situation is to throw us into the emergence of movements and be open towards what emerges. Rather than merely defining our ethics and letting our responsibility be governed by rule bound requirements or previously acquired meaning, acts are constituted as meaning by the locations in which they happen. I see our "*ought to do's*" not as connected to abstract law, generalized evidence, but as something being played out between real people in real situations, by the concrete ought conditioned by each person's *"unique place in the given context of the ongoing event"* (Bakhtin, 1993:30). The willingness to become present in relation to the emerging actualities, instead of being governed by fixed and generalized rules, and to become present "inside" the relationship, has made it decisive to learn to read the actual context we are involved in, to pay attention to the musicality of the present movements, sometimes to the expense of claims towards what is required of us, as for instance as professionals.

This ethical stance governs the dialogue groups. The tendency is often to look for rules and already decided models for interaction. I challenge group members to think and act in the moment, and to be sensitive towards what the context demands. We can never get outside this responsibility, and hide behind adopted rules without taking the current situation into consideration. Linda explains it like this:

> "To me, it is this openness about what we are going to do. It's not something that's set, something we have to plan, it's created here and now, co-created. In these groups we are with people who are willing to be here and now. Listening and wishing to move on together. I think that is important to me. It's some of the energy I have, after being in the group for eight years. It is so different from what is expected of me at work, even if it is therapy we are expected to do. Targets, preparation, planning and goals. My group is such an open space, comfortably open. It's a bit like a counterculture. Specially with pace. In the therapy center where I work it goes faster and faster, and there is more and more talk about production, and such things. The group is something completely different. In the beginning it was like, you know "I have to be prepared, have a pen and paper and so on. It's almost so that

one needs to re-learn a bit, because that's what we're used to: showing off that we are clever and exact. In my view, that doesn't necessarily make you an ethical working therapist."

The Concept of Self

The ideal standard of personhood in the West has been bound up with being a self-contained and coherent individual (de Peuter, 1998)—a healthy soul without ambivalence (Øfsti, 2010). In a culture based on a dialogical stance we assume that the stories we are able to tell about ourselves are created in contexts and dependent on the others gaze. The human being does not have an inner sovereign territory; it is always on the border, "looking inside himself, he looks into the eyes of another or with the eyes of another" (Bakhtin, 1984, p. 287). When telling the stories of our lives, Bakhtin says (Morson & Emerson, 1990) we do not mediate direct experience or memory but we tell stories through the imagined others' value and intonations. The self emerges through different stories dependent on the social context and the conversations that take place within these contexts.

How to Inquire into the Life of Dialogical Group Work

Dialogue, as accentuated in this chapter, is dependent on an ongoing awareness and willingness to pay attention to how it *is* for the other(s) and what is created in between us. I make it a habit of regularly asking for comments and reflections about our ongoing work together. Not so much to evaluate, as to calibrate—to make adjustments. In this way one can say that our work is continually researched. As for a more formal approach I invited members from across the different groups to come together, to make a collaborative inquiry into these dialogue groups (see the footnote). I wanted the group members to talk to a person from outside while I was a mere listener. They talked about how they perceive the groups; what a dialogue group means to them, what happens in the groups and why they participate in them and if they feel being in the group makes a difference for them workwise.

Some say they have experienced these group meetings as a "head spa," a place where they feel free to grope for meaning, live and talk about ambivalence and ambiguity. Some say they prioritize it above going to conferences because they feel the space is significant as a place for experience and as a reminder of how dialogue is prosperous. Some called it to calibrate, "to remember what it is all about."

Group members reported feeling more able to articulate and live with what has not yet been articulated but is there as part of their embodied being. They report that they feel freed to move more confidently around inside relationships that are not fixed but in the process of becoming. They feel more confident in relation to how this is of value because it is so different from much of what goes on it our society these days. I will share with you some quotes from the inquiry.

Peter said it like this:

> "I was really puzzled, to be honest, more than puzzled, I was annoyed. It was as if Anne Hedvig wasn't doing anything, just sitting there. It took me some time to understand, that there was much more going on *than just sitting there.* Today, I do this myself. But I know much more about what is going on in the client(s) and in me, or better said, between us. One day this man had a first appointment. He started to talk as soon as I entered the waiting room, and he continued for more than an hour. By the end of the session, he looked at me and said that it had been so helpful. I would not have been able to sit there and listen, if it hadn't been for my experiences in our group, and not least to know, with confidence, what was going on."

Kristina is also talking about how she is affected:

> "My experience is that I have become much more open after joining such a group. It has been challenging for me, both as a therapist and as myself. I have become more transparent about what I think and more openly responsive to what others say, and I am much more able to be open as a therapist in my job. Instead of thinking I should be like this and that, it's more about just being open and responding in the moment, and that has been a really big change for me. I'm much more responsive to those who come in and need to talk about what is the toughest thing they know about. My group has contributed to this. Maybe what surprises me the most, is that I can feel it in my body, it makes me more sensitive, especially at work. I am simply much more sensitive to those who come to me for therapy."

Mari underlined the significance of being allowed to listen:

> "I want to say something about listening. I've experienced it as being allowed to listen without having to answer. When someone else is talking, then you are allowed to just be present. Then I do not need to spend any energy on my own role, I may just sit and listen. I sometimes think that has been so luxurious. To be allowed to just listen."

Kim is talking about how listening has become important in relation to his work as a therapist:

> "What you said there I think is very true, because that's what the group offers. Too often it's like when you're listening, you're preparing for what to say and it's a must. But if you can only be allowed to listen like that and just accept what others say, then something else will come. You become more open, things doesn't strain me as much. It has been very useful to me, especially in meeting with clients."

Brit uses a clinical example to show the difference between mapping people's experiences, to listening in a way so her clients are able to express the unforeseen:

> "Most recently, I met a boy who was so astonished that it was possible to be met so nice and friendly. He appreciated that I didn't have an agenda on his behalf but was open to talking with him, in a completely different way. I think he was accustomed to psychiatry and many forms to map depression and anxiety and compulsion and everything. Then he came and was listened to without any particular goal in mind, everything could be addressed, and there was no direction. I think it's such a nice way to listen, experiencing how something new emerged; something even he didn't know was his concern. It was amazing how fascinated he was of it. I was curious and I went into small details of things he told. No one else had done that before. I have this note here; he said something that I thought was at the heart of what we are doing. He said (Brit read from a small piece of paper): *"It's as if you're helping me find something unforeseen, something I do not know anything about"* and then I just thought, I asked him if I could bring what he said to the meeting here today. He got a bit proud, I think. To listen with such welcoming kindness, so that it opens up for what he

himself did not even know he wanted talk to someone else about, that's a gift to get. Knowing this; it is not difficult to listen, because you are absolutely being filled with what is being told, and that is extremely exciting."

Ida is also talking about the unexpected, as an experience she has had from within the group process:

"I think this way of being together is about a way to be in the world, where the unexpected can happen, all the time, in a way. It represents a very hopeful perspective then. This is something we learn in theory, but in the group we experience it from within, in practice. It is a way of thinking and an attitude, which I think is useful for life as a whole, all the time."

Mia expresses the difference between a dialogic culture and that of a more monologic one:

"I am used to having my shoulders up, tensed, and at the same time leaning more forward, and it is all about doing the good reply. What characterizes the dialogue group, on the other hand is that we are sitting with lowered shoulders and that we listen more, without thinking about what to do next. We just take in what is being said, and then later on we might feel invited to respond into what is being expressed. It is very, very different."

Ida dwelled on how she had experienced meeting a group of collegues for our research conversation about dialogue groups. She continued after pausing for a moment.

"I could feel it, almost straight away, when we entered the room. I did't know that many of you, and you know, one usually feels a little apprehensive meeting a new group of people. But I didn't have that feeling today, meeting you guys. This feeling of trusting this way of being together. At work it is so different. When people meet we start to discuss, you know, going on and on like that. But here, now, today, we didn't need to talk about how to talk. We just started to talk and we listened to each other, not interupting. One at a time talked, using the time needed to be able to express ourselves and the rest listened carefully."

For Now…

My endeavor has become that of inviting group participants into relationships filled with playfulness, sensitivity, responsiveness, and creativity, and to demonstrate a willingness to dive into the uniqueness of every new encounter and every new movement, and be answerable inside that relationship.

What I have felt as most powerful when working with these dialogue groups has been that of experiencing the willingness and courage the group members show when they share their own insecurity and vulnerability, their beliefs and convictions. They have let themselves off the hook and dived into the emergence and unpredictable context of dialogue. The trust we all have worked towards anticipating that the process will embrace us and move us, not towards a goal but on an unforeseen journey that makes us more comfortable with the fluidity of movements. Over and over again we have learned to embrace spontaneity, ambiguity and intuition, and welcomed anxiety, risk-taking and improvisation in these groups. I have encouraged us to value coincidence, intuition, and embodied knowing, and I experience this attitude as contagious. I have confidence that participants in these groups not only tolerate uncertainty but also at times enjoy the unpredictability of life as it happens. Embodiment of a dialogical culture is about having the experience of dialogue as anticipated inner movements, which will affect the way we perceive and respond to a complex, fluid and unfinalized world. As Ingold puts it (in Bertelsen & Bøe, 2016) "...to convert certainty into a question, whose answer is to be found attending to what lies before us in the world, not by looking it up at the back of the book" (:378).

I believe a supervision context that creates an insistent dialogical culture, is practicing and emphasizing the skills Haley and Gehart underlined in the introductory quotes. Competent therapy work requires that we get outside our comfort zone and interact with clients in a flexible way and respond spontaneously. Improvisation moment to moment is an overall important professional posture to cherish.

References

Andersen, T. (1994). *Reflekterande Processer: samtale och samtal om samtalen*. Stocholm: Mareld.

Anderson, H. (1997) *Conversation, Language and Possibilities*. New York: Basic Books.

Anderson, H., & Goolishian, H. (1992). The client is the expert: A not-knowing approach to therapy. In S. McNamee & K. Gergen (Eds.), *Therapy as social construction*. Sage: London.

Bakhtin, M. (1981). *The dialogical imagination*. Austin: University of Texas Press.

Bakhtin, M. (1984). *Problems of Dostoevsky's poetics*. London: University of Minnesota Press.

Bakhtin, M. (1986). *Speech genres and other late essays*. Austin: University of Texas Press.

Bakhtin, M. (1993). *Toward a Philosophy of the Act*, with translation and notes by V. Lianpov, edited by M. Holquist. Austin, TX: University of Texas Press.

Bateson, G. (1972). *Steps to an ecology of mind*. New York, NY: Ballantine Books.

Bertelsen, B., & Bøe, T. D. (2016). He is quirky; he is the world's greatest psychologist. On the community of those who have nothing in common. *Australian and New Zealand Journal of Family Therapy, 37*, 367–380. https://doi.org/10.1002/anzf.1155.

Billig, M. (1996). *Arguing and thinking, a rhetorical approach to social psychology* (2nd ed.). Cambridge: Cambridge University Press.

Billig, M. (1999). *Freudian repression, conversations creating the unconscious*. Cambridge: Cambridge University Press.

de Peuter, J. (1998). The Dialogics of Narrativ Identity. In Bell, M. M. & Gardiner, M. (eds.), *Bakhtin and the Human Science*. London: Sage Publications.

Devlin, K. (1997). *Good Bye, Descartes. The End of logic and the Search for a New Cosmology of the Mind*. New York: John Wiley & Sons, Inc.

Dreyfus, H. (1979). *What Computers still can't do. A critique of Artificial Reason*. London: The MIT Press.

Gehart, D. (2016). *Theory and treatment planning in family therapy: A competency-based approach*. Northridge: Cengage Learning.

Haley, J. (1987). *Problem-solving therapy* (2nd. ed.). San Fransisco, CA: Jossey-Bass.

Holquist, M. (1990). *Dialogism, Bakhtin and his world*. London: Routledge.

Malloch, S., & Trevarthen, C. (2009). Musicality: Communicating the vitality and interest of life. In Malloch, S., & Trevarthen, C. (eds), Communicative Musicality, exploring the basis of human companionship. Oxford: Oxford University Press.

Mercier, P. (2008). *Night train to Lisbon*. London: Atlantic Books.

Moi, T. (2011). *Født sånn og blitt sånn*. Interview by Sandra Lillebø. In Klassekampen, 17.03.2011. Oslo.

Morson, S. M., & Emerson C. (1990). *Mikhail Bakhtin, creation of a Prosaics*. Standford: Stanford University Press.

Øfsti, A. K. S. (2010). *Parterapi. Kjærlighet, intimitet og samliv i en brytningstid*. Oslo: Universitetsforlaget.

Polanyi, M. (1966). [2009 reprint] *The Tacit Dimension*. Chicago: University of Chicago Press.

Shotter, J. (1993). *Conversational realities, constructing life through language*. London: Sage.

Shotter, J. (2010). *Social construction on the edge: Withness-thinking and embodiment*. Chagrin Falls, OH: Taos Institute Publications.

Stern, D. N. (2004). *The Present Moment In Psychotherapy and Everyday Life*. London: W. W. Norton & Company.

Vedeler, A. H. (2004). *Do you hear me?* MSc dissertation. Retrieved from http://www.taosinstitute.net/anne-hedvig-vedeler

Vedeler, A. H. (2011). Dialogical practices: Diving into the poetic movement exploring 'supervision' and 'therapy'. University of Bedfordshire. Retrieved from http://ethos.bl.uk/OrderDetails.do?uin=uk.bl.ethos.570935

Voloshinov, V. N. (1973). *Marxism and the philosophy of language*. Cambridge, MA: Harvard University Press.

Voloshinov V. N. (1987). *Freudianism: a Critical Sketch*. Indianapolis: Indiana University Press.

Vygotsky, L. (1986). *Thought and language*. London: The MIT Press.

Wittgenstein, L. (1953). *Philosophical investigations*. Oxford: Blackwell.

Chapter 8
The Supervisor's Power and Moments of Learning

Tone Grøver

There is a phenomenon I have noticed through many years as a supervisor and supervisee, which we will take a closer look at in this chapter.

Sequences of intense learning can arise in supervision. The sequences can be experienced as "breakthroughs," followed by statements such as: "I understood something new now," "This was a very important question to me, finally I was able to puncture it," "I got a new understanding of this now." Or it can be sensed by the atmosphere in the room, a particular participation and vitality, which arises through interaction in the group, and in the interaction between the supervisor and the group.

What we will take a look at in this chapter is:

Can we as supervisors apply the power and position which is attributed to the role in such a way that particular sequences of learning can originate?

Theoretical Anchoring and invitation to Criticalness

The theoretical traditions I know and utilize here are a selection in a sea of possibilities. They are not the "most important" ones—just important, the way I see it. The theories I rely on in particular are systemic and narrative, anchored in overarching approaches such as social constructionism and post-structuralism. Social constructionism and post-structuralism are in turn parts of a phenomenological philosophy of science. Phenomenology as a philosophical branch of science has a large undergrowth of theories, which can also be in reciprocal conflict with each other.

T. Grøver (✉)
Family Therapy Section, Faculty of Social Studies, VID Specialized University, Oslo, Norway
e-mail: tone.grover@vid.no

A. Vetere, J. Sheehan (eds.), *Supervision of Family Therapy and Systemic Practice*, Focused Issues in Family Therapy, https://doi.org/10.1007/978-3-319-68591-5_8

It is not always easy to understand the difference between the different theoretical traditions. Yet, they do have something in common. Holmgren notes:

> The philosophers Nietzsche, Heidegger, Wittgeinsein, Foucault, Deleuze, Derrida, Agamben, Bauman, Gergen, Shotter, Pearce, Cronen, Rotry, Dewey, James, Christie and the Danish philosopher Ole Fogh Kirkeby, are of the shared opinion that they are very critical towards the so-called naïve realistic understanding, that language represents or reflects the world. Despite the differences between them, they are of the mutual opinion that language does not represent the world, but it creates and produces the world we perceive and understand (Holmgren & Holmgren, 2015, p. 57).

The consequence of this statement is that to be a teacher, a supervisor, or the act of writing a text is to contribute to creating with others. And when we are to learn something with a teacher, a supervisor, or in a text, we will experience degrees of freedom or resistance in the process. The supervisor's, teacher's, or writer's way of applying their power will affect our response, and what and how we learn. Foucault's central point is that relationships without power relations do not exist. At the same time, he expresses a moral towards us, when trying to contribute to learning for others:

> "Relations of power are not something bad in themselves, from which one must free one's self. I don't believe there can be a society without relations of power, if you understand them as means by which individuals try to conduct, to determine the behaviour of others. The problem is not of trying to dissolve them in the utopia of a perfectly transparent communication, but to give one's self the *rules of law*, the techniques of management, and also the *ethics, ethos, the practice of self*, which would allow these games of power to be played with *a minimum of domination*" (Foucault, 1987, p. 129).

A minimum of dominance should also apply to a text. However, a minimum is not the same as nothing, as an absence of execution of power is impossible, according to Foucault. A central point in this chapter is to try to understand this application of power in relation to learning, and the text should live by the principles it promotes. Another central point is that the experience of resistance, freedom, annoyance, or inspiration you can get while reading says far more about what is important knowledge to you, than can any of the generalized ideas and points presented here.

The Archive of the Mind, Complex Libraries

When meeting the supervision group, we bring with us different abilities, different knowledge, different vulnerability, different expressions, and different humor. Going through life, we develop an experience of a "Self" (Bruner, 2004; Meares, 2000; White, 2009; White in Denborough, 2008)—which we bring with us into a group. Michael White calls this the archives of our minds: The identity conclusions we are all carrying, and which decides the significance we ascribe to the events that occur. White says: "All these conclusions, including those derived from types of internal acknowledgement, affect people's actions to a considerable extent: they shape life" (2009, pp. 99–100).

A central point in all systemic and narrative understanding is that conclusions we have about ourselves and our lives are interpretations, and interpretations are always mobile and malleable. In a supervision group, everyone is interpreting based on their own mind's archives, and what happens in the group will thus be perceived and interpreted differently by the participants. This acknowledgement constitutes the foundation in Maturana and Varela's (1992) theories about learning. Their theory of autopoiesis implies that processes of development of knowledge are self-referential. Individuals and social units use already established knowledge to determine what they see, and they use what they already know to choose what to look for in their surroundings. Everyone's interpretations are complex and multifaceted, created in the abundance of experiences we have gained throughout our lives, and shaped by the culture around us:

> The world is not given to us as a collection of well-defined objects and problems, but as an infinitely rich context for action. We do not discover the unambiguous truth of that context in knowledge but 'enact' a viable 'world' on the basis of our experience and culture.
>
> This is what human intelligence is all about, and it is quite different from representing a world, the outlines of which are clear in themselves (In Feenberg, 1991, p. 104).

These basic presumptions lead us to consider that in a supervision group, we need to make space for every individual's experience, it has to be revealed and be seen as significant knowledge, and at the same time create a shared universe of supervision. And supervisors experience this; in a group we are in between many minds' archives, and the group as a whole constitutes in combination a complex library, only without a library's internal structure and logic. What might be useful and new to one person might not be relevant to another. One might think that it is essential to talk loudly and a lot, while another might think that no one person should be able to dominate. One might feel easily hurt, another might want clarity. In this complexity, supervision is to take place.

The Subject, the Soul, and the Community's Significance for Learning

I believe most supervisors notice the heterogeneity in a group. Is there something we can do to create a fairly common universe which just about accommodates everyone, and which creates a possibility for learning for everyone, where they find themselves in their own experiences?

A couple of years ago I was with a group of leaders, we were going to be together for a whole week and have intensive supervision related to our jobs. I myself was a supervisee. The first day the supervisor asks us to present ourselves. One of the leaders—a top executive at a Danish large-scale enterprise—gets up, holds on to the back of her chair, and says with a clear, strong voice: "I want to tell you that I did not learn to read or write until I was 13 years old, because I was harshly bullied at school." She goes on recounting of loneliness, exclusion, but also of inclusion and significant moments, when she was shown confidence, and which became turning points in her life.

Elements in what she recounts, create resonance with everyone; the fear we once had and still carry with us, of wondering whether we were included, or whether we would be, whether we would be chosen, or not, whether we would be accepted, or not, whether we would be laughed at and seen as stupid—we were able to open the door to that recognition in life. And we offered this recognition to her.

Us offering, did not happen on its own. It happened because the supervisor demanded it from us. He asked us to write on small postcards what we recognized from our own lives and which came into play in our own stories, when listening to the leader. Afterwards, a few of us read aloud what we had written, others gave her their card so she could read it herself.

Why did the supervisor demand this from us? Because we were to learn, separately and as a community. And what did we learn? We learned to *practice* the understanding that we are created in relations, and how it happens, which we are concerned with from a social-constructivist and systemic perspective. Then it is not possible to stand on the outside of her, but we need to create the experience of a real community. What can be called a real community?

Skjervheim was preoccupied with this question when he, in Norway at the end of the 1950s, was much of the origin of the continuously alive positivism dispute. He wanted to show that to make an object of something or someone—the way the scientific ideal of verifiability requires—is to position oneself on the outside and thereby breaking contact. To illustrate this point, he uses, among others, the example of the psychologist who tells the young client that the client probably suffers from father fixation. The young boy answers the psychologist with the same warfare that objectification can bring at best:

> Good heavens, you seem to be suffering from an inferiority complex. Are you not just psychologizing the way you do, because this is a way for you to assert yourself, by making others small? Moreover, don't you have a strong urge to live in such a safe world, that you have built a wall around yourself, and then you psychologize away anything which might even come close to making a crack in your wall? And isn't this what in psychology is called "rigidity"? (Skjervheim, 1996, p. 76).

The young boy strikes back and wisely chooses a war as a reply to the objectification. It is worse when the objectification makes us lose our sense of self, makes us feel reduced, and lose our freedom to be ourselves.

Simone de Beauvoir thought along the same lines, when she in the book *The Second Sex* (De Beauvoir, 1970) broke through the prevailing view of women and pointed out that women were sacrificing their freedom in order to feel a minimum of security. Being an object was familiar, as the vassal to the feudal overlord. However, she said, if you are an object, you are not in a relation. The premise for a relation is that you meet in a subject–subject relation. Her existentialistic and feminist-philosophical reflections had freedom as the main purpose, and had and has been of great significance to our understanding of relations and freedom. Freedom can never be created in a subject–object relation.

In systemic and narrative approaches, these are such obvious points that saying this is like pushing at open doors. But it *was* not obvious, when our great source of inspiration and the father of communication theory, Gregory Bateson, in the 1950s made this the focal point of his communication theory. At that time, it was actually an eye-opener that communication did not revolve around sender and receiver. He saw all communication—not only human beings' communication, but the communication of every living thing—as ecology. The exchange where it is impossible to take the parts—objects—out of the whole, without at the same time harming both the parts and the whole (Bateson, 1972; Ulleberg, 2004).

However, theory is theory. Practically, we are all making objects of others, often with the best intentions. The word "client" originally means the person who responds when the master whistles (Christie, 2009, p. 24). We even speak of "my clients." If we take a hard look at the expression, we can truly have a wakeup call. To make an object of each other is ingrained in our language, in professions, and in institutions. We do it in everyday life, in places of work, in families, among friends, in supervision groups, and not least in parts of psychiatry and the treatment apparatus.

In the situation with the leader's story about bullying, the following could also be probable: We expressed that we truly felt for her, and that we admired what she had fought so hard for. We could have praised her for her courage, both here and now for sharing, and for back then when she was fighting for herself. And we could have omitted saying anything about our own recognition. We could have thought and also have said: I have never been bullied, but I really feel for you. We would then make her an object—again—the way she was an object when she was bullied. Now as an object of our empathy, but still fully an object. She could just as well—and rightly—reply with the same sharp irony which the boy used with the psychologist in Skjervheim's example. Because, who are we to give praise? What do we know about what she needs?

Our supervisor led us firmly into subject–subject relations. But more than that, he led us into what Foucault might call "soulful" encounters. And what the musician Peter Bastian would say is the same thing that music deals with; that one soul is contacting another soul (Bastian, 1987). It is an experience primarily in the body and the senses, and outside of the words, even though words usually are the instruments. By writing small postcards, something happened to the language. They started with "dear Nina" and continued in the same personal, narrative fashion of letters.

We can call the aim intimacy, as a contrast to alienation. It is not created by "language" or "relation," but by how the language is inside the relationship. This has become central to the narrative approach, not only to build insight through theory, but to the way in which we can be together, the way in which we can practice therapy or supervision. It is not as though the subject is free, while the object is unfree. It is not as though the subject *is*, while the object is *viewed*. One of Foucault's points, and a point which the narrative approach also rests upon, is that the subject is "ravaged" by the culture, the norms, and the modern power's discipline. In a way the subject does not exist, it is empty, but filled and pulled by culture and norms the way this takes place in a conglomerate of cultural power relations and norms. In Foucault's world, modern power is not visible nor apparent, in the way what he calls traditional power is. Modern power is the power which invades our thoughts, our understanding, and which makes us discipline ourselves.

When the leader stands up and narrates, she is not free—she is language and culture in these dimensions' power structure. When we are with her, we are the same. "He who is subjected to a field of visibility, and who knows it, assumes responsibility for the constraints of power; he makes them play spontaneously upon himself; he inscribes in himself the power relation in which he simultaneously plays both roles; he becomes the principle of his own subjection" (Foucault, 1977, pp. 202–203).

In supervision this means something. The subject cannot be free, if we stay with Foucault. It can only find a way to get a bit closer to its values gained through experience. Also here, we can be cocreators in supervision. To a freer space for thought, and to get in touch with that which means something to oneself. To let go a little bit.

Intimacy, Alienation, and the Nature of Language

Check. Can't we all feel language's dominance over us when we speak? Can't we all feel that we are more or less borrowing the language, and that it often does not quite fit? That language does something to us, and can in itself be inadequate or trap us a bit? Michael White pinpointed this at the narrative conference in Kristiansand in 2007. He asked the audience: Do any of you have any "personal strengths"? Many of us raised our hands. He retorted: no wonder, they already gained grounds in the 60s…

We need to tackle this when we are to get in touch with each other, always—and in supervision. And then it might mean just as much to understand the dimensions intimacy and alienation, as subject and object. This is not the same intimacy that we associate with lovers, but an intimacy in the *way* that the contact develops, and which agrees with ourselves.

Since we are various, we use and need multiple language-games, a range of conversational styles which lead to a sense of connectedness and which help to depict, and so bring into being, a personal reality (Meares, 2000, p. 31).

Meares conveys that connectedness is a condition in order to have one's own, inner world. And an own, inner world is fundamental to a sense of self and to learn. This is the point that the learning theorist Vygotsky also promotes, when he examines the relationship between language and learning. There is one language which is linear, and which we often use to adjust to something, for example learning new information. Meares refers to this as potentially alienating. Foucault might say, according to his complicated view of the modern person's soul, as mostly resembling our own private little discipline class—that it is the linear language which mostly feeds the soul's discipline of the body (1999, p. 30). Then there is another language, important to sense of self and to intimacy in relationships; the non-linear, which by nature is more like poetry. Meares writes about how Vygotsky explores this language the child has until it is 4 years old, and the babble has yet to move inside the child, but is spoken aloud. He found that, while the child is playing, a little story is told, with conceptions.

Many parents know this and have listened behind the door in fascination. We probably do not consider that what is happening within the child, is decisive to the child's sense of self. Meares states that what happens, among other things, is that the child makes the outer world his or her own (Meares, 2000, p. 25). To Meares, this is a part of his memory theory, and his theories of how our sense of self is created. To our purpose here it is especially important to understand how the language we encounter each other in, can bring a sensation of self, in supervision. Then, we do not only care whether it's a loving language, honest language, warm language, or whatever the ideal may be, but that the surroundings are possible for me to take in, that they are possible to make my own, that they coincide with what and who I am.

The little girl with her mother's purse, high heeled shoes and lipstick smudged on and around her mouth, is not just "playing." She is transforming the surroundings into her own world. If she cannot do this, she is a stranger in the world. Both discipline and freedom lie in this. And this continues throughout life. Everyone knows how alienated we can feel if we our intentions are misunderstood. If we for example are accused of wanting something bad, when we are trying to do good. How impossible this makes it to make our surroundings our own.

Meares states that freedom is the play's purpose to the child. "What is essential to the play (…) is freedom" (Meares, 2000, p. 24). To create the freest spaces possible to be oneself, think more freely, and to be in relationships as free as possible from restraint and marginalization are also the goals of post-structuralist and social-constructivist approaches, the way I see it. In this context, the systemic approach deals particularly with the *positions* we have in relation to one another and in interaction with each other, the same way the two philosophers we have included here, in a sea of possible philosophers and theorists, do. Meares and Vygotsky and the narrative approach are particularly concerned with *the character of language, the story, and the norms in the culture.*

How can we understand the significance this bears to learning? How do we learn in practice?

How Do We Learn? The Hole and the Darning Mushroom

When I was in supervision during my narrative psychotherapy education, my supervisor used a metaphor for learning. She used the image of a sock with a hole on its heel, which was going to be stitched. Nowadays, not many darn their socks, but most of us remember how it was done: We put the back of our hand or a darning mushroom into the hole, and started the darning from the edge of the hole where it was possible to attach the thread. Then we pulled the thread over to the other side, where it was also possible to attach the thread. There is no use to start sowing in the middle of the hole. My supervisor used this as an image of how our own holes in our knowledge can be filled; we need help to find out what we know about ourselves, our life or what we do for a living, and start from there. And there is always knowledge there already.

How can we find the edge where the knowledge is—where the supervisee is, with what she knows?

The learning theorist Vygotsky was preoccupied with this question. When we are in our own knowledge, on "the edge of the hole"—we can, through the process of learning, be brought to new knowledge. Vygotsky called this "the zone of proximal development." To be brought to the zone of proximal development does not happen by chance. One of Vygotsky's main points is that learning is always a social process. We learn by being in interaction with others (1978). How does it happen, specifically?

When Vygotsky studied children's learning, he discovered several things: First of all, the child *copies* knowledge. The child wants to know the name of things. If the child finds an apple, the child wants to learn the name of the apple. The child learns the name of what is in its surroundings: people, things, phenomena, feelings, as a prerequisite to be a part of the meaningful interaction.

Those close to the child will also discover that the child makes advances—it makes leaps which has nothing to do with copying. For example, the child has learned the name of many fruits, yet one day the child has also gained an overarching understanding of the concept "fruit." The child understands that the orange and the pear belong together, and that the carrot does not. The piece of Lego does not belong either, nor the teddy bear. The child has expanded its knowledge to the zone of proximal development. For those close to the child, this is magic. How has this happened? How can the child expand its knowledge and actually understand? How does this process happen?

Vygotsky uses the metaphor "developmental level." This is that which is attainable, but outside of where the child is at, and to get there, parents and others responsible are crucial. When parents for example understand that their child is very close to taking their first steps, the parents will intuitively get close to the child. Far away enough for the child to be able to take the first step on its own, yet close enough for it to be safe. It is in this gap of space that we make experiences, which make us learn. The child takes a step, and another step, and many steps, because someone is there in the right way:

> The distance between the actual developmental level as determined by independent problem solving and the level of potential development as determined through problem solving under adult guidance, or in collaboration with more capable peers (Vygotsky, 1978, p. 86).

The pedagogue Martin Nevers puts it this way:

> Vygotsky has been very significant to our way of thinking of education today. Very simplified, we can describe his theory as: we learn through activity, and new learning connects to what we already know. What I know with someone else today, I know alone tomorrow (Nevers in Holmgren & Nevers, 2012, p. 66).

The central point here, the way I see it, is the freedom in knowing something by yourself, and the importance of others in getting there.

Jerome Bruner (1999, 2004) and Michael White (2006, 2007) have developed Vygotsky's learning theory into a conversation methodology, given the metaphor "scaffolding." It involves building a scaffold in the conversation, so that movement can happen in the learning process. Conversation methodology has as a starting point already established knowledge about yourself or what preoccupies you, and from there creates movement to reflection about the more unknown. What can this insight mean to supervision?

First of all, it should appeal to criticalness. It is a part of our culture that it is desirable to be up, not down. The scaffold can easily entice, "oh, I can get up!" And there are subtle differences between helping someone get in touch with their own perspectives, own possibilities, own free spaces, and the present day's discourse of "realizing your potential," "seeing possibilities instead of limitations" and all the, at the end of the day, economic logic and be the master of your own happiness-reasoning, which this jargon is pervaded with.

Then, with criticalness as our companion, we can, in supervision, for example imagine the following scaffolding conversational structure in a group:

Questions to supervisee while the group listens in:

1. What is the problem at hand? What are you wondering about?
2. What do you know about this already? Which experiences do you have with this kind of problem?
3. How or in what way can these experiences possibly help you now? Which possibilities do you have based on your experiences—or about how you can understand the problem?
4. Given what you have now said: what do you think is possible to do? What do you think is the right thing to do?

Questions for the group:

1. Given what you have now heard: what preoccupies you considering your own experience?
2. When the group has shared where it has brought them, we go back to the supervisee, who says something about where it has brought him, when it comes to his own learning.

This is a very simplified presentation of a possible direction, and a variation of Vygotsky, Meares, Bruner, and White.

Yet, it is not this simple. All supervisors know this: It will not go the way the "recipe" predicts. And what disturbs, we can presume to be power.

Learning and Power

Surely, no one can look at history or the present time, and deny that power is in play in relationships: Between countries, people, religions, groups, cliques, in places of work, in families, and in couples. Those are the obvious plays of power. It can be more difficult to point out the more hidden ones, but they will be just as perceptible. I recently read an exam paper from a student. She is a public health nurse and described a story about little girls of 8 years old. They had been playing hospital. The nicest and shyest girl played the patient. The others were doctors and nurses. The patient did not want to play anymore, when the game took a turn she didn't like. But the playing continued anyway, just as the doctor decided. The public health nurse talked to them afterwards, and the girls' stories were completely different. The patients' did not resemble that of the doctors'. What was moving about the story was not that it was unusual, quite the opposite, it was normal in its recognizable simplicity. It was a typical story about 8-year-old girls, where power was in play. Not articulated, but *that* perceptible, power spins a web around the little girls' friendships. And we all remember this, from early on in life, that power was at play between friends. And it still is. Not out of malice, but because of different universes of understanding, and different intentions.

Foucault was preoccupied with this, when he more or less defines what this life is, in one sentence: "There only exists mutual relationships and the constant gaps between intentions in relation to one another" (paraphrasing Foucault in Heede, 2004, p. 14).

Another equally central point to Foucault is that power always creates something. He does not see power as something inherently negative or positive—but as productive. Whether power is to promote or hinder learning, constitutes more or less of a breaking point in the supervisor's exercise of his or her role. Whether power will contribute to more alienation or more freedom in the learning process, is a part of this break. It is the breaking point where power and power-play tips from being disruptive to learning and community, to furthering learning and community. Here we are talking about community in the way that we have made a basis for here, which makes intimacy and learning possible of that which is meaningful to each and every one.

I was a supervisor to a supervisor for about a year. She was supervising a group of therapists who worked in psychiatry, consisting of doctors, psychologists, and other therapists. For me to be relevant enough for her, she invited me as a participating observer while she was supervising the group.

For one, the following conversational sequence took place:

P1: I think we need to increase her medication. We are not getting anywhere with her compulsion, she is even more depressed now.

P2: I was out with her yesterday, and she managed to walk 4 km in the woods without any repetition.

P3: I think it's awful that we keep postponing her home visits all the time. We keep on not following up on this.

P1: I think we should start the increase now, and let it progress slowly over the next 14 days.

P4: I am the one who is her primary contact.

P1: Then we will see if it stabilizes at all, with regard to her compulsive acts.

Supervisor: You are talking about different things now. What is the most important here?
P1: Moreover, we need to focus on getting her to eat, and she should be following the nutritional program more closely.
Supervisor: Is it ok like this? Is this important?
Everyone: nods or keeps silent.

I experienced that the group's conversation was not coherent, but was leaping and bouncing depending on who was speaking. And I saw the supervisor keeping up to the best of her ability. Who decided where to leap? The supervisor, at least, was not in charge of that. This small sequence is a story about power. And it is a story about power in play. Who says the most important thing? Who says the most correct thing? Who has the position to dominate? Should the supervisor intervene, control, and in that case how and considering what?

She has to deal with this, if we are to be true to what we have said thus far. Because knowledge and learning are produced precisely because of the span between what we know, in interaction with the different knowledge positions we have in the group (Bruner 1999; Maturana & Varela, 1992; Vygotsky, 1978, 2001; White, 2006, 2007), and power-play is thus a potential source for learning, which we need for the supervisor to accommodate.

Let us have a closer look at this, because this might deal with some of the most important things for us to understand as supervisors.

Engagement Play and Responsibility

My experience from supervision groups is that power-play is tightly linked to engagement. What we know, we think is important. Consequently, we want that to be heard, understood, and to be of importance. We might even say that it is engagement which clashes in a group. And also responsibility. It can be just as correct to call it engagement play or responsibility play, when we are in supervision. I cannot keep my mouth shut about what I know, I have to say it, because I think it is important. My knowledge is different from yours. Our knowledge is different from theirs. And *there*, the moment when my knowledge is different from your knowledge—what we call power-play occurs, and *there* the supervisors should understand their role. Because in this perspective power-play carries the seed—to vitality, learning, motivation, and solidarity—to an intense learning experience, precisely because engagement is tied to knowing. No one would bother expressing their opinion, if engagement was not behind it. Therefore, power-play can be understood as engagement play or responsibility play. And we need the supervisor there so that someone's engagement and responsibility does not walk all over someone else's engagement and responsibility. No one wants to be the person who gradually quiets down on the chair, or undermines own knowledge. And we need the supervisor there so that the eager can be just that, without ending up in a dominating position. We need the supervisor, then, to manage the power so that what the group's participants know can be transformed into something coherent.

Foucault puts it this way:

> "It seems to me that power must be understood in the first instance as the multiplicity of force relations immanent in the sphere in which they operate and which constitute their own organization; as the process which, through ceaseless struggles and confrontations, transforms, strengthens, or reverses them; as the support which these force relations fin in one another, thus forming a chain or a system, or on the contrary, the disjunctions and contradictions which isolate them from one another" (Foucault, 1978, p. 92).

Foucault would probably say to supervisors that our assignment is therefore to "overturn the power relations," and once the power relations are "overturned," learning moments can occur. To "overturn" can mean that those who speak quietly are heard. That those who speak most, listen. That those with the "highest status" get out of the responsibility. All in all, that the power relations are changed and shifted.

Holmgren (2014) thematizes this, regarding leadership, and the importance of leaders listening to all the stories in an organization. I am of the opinion that this is just as relevant when it comes to supervision: *All* voices need to be heard, heard, and heard once more. Simply put: if all voices and stories in a group are heard, the group will learn in a freer space, because the productive force of power will have a freer space. Isn't this obvious? Yes and no. It might be obvious in theory, but as supervisors we know that this demands something from us, more or less all the time.

Illustration of the Importance of listening: Peacekeeping and a Sensation of Freedom

Throughout the year I was cooperating with the supervisor at the psychiatry department, she was practicing making listening more productive for learning in the community. She was aware of the power imbalances which took place. That some knowledge was seen as more meaningful or "heavyweight"—than other. She decided that everyone should be heard equally. She would start supervision with a round, where everyone got to say what preoccupied them at present—and what they wanted to bring to the supervision. Before anyone said anything, she wanted everyone to write down on a note what they were concerned with, to be able to stick to what they felt was important, and not what others thought was important. She knew that some would be very brief in a round like this. Then, she would ask many follow-up questions, show curiosity, and say: Maybe we should keep this problem and bring it back after the round? She also thoroughly wrote down what every person said. She used this to play off of what everyone had said, and to use this in the reflections throughout the supervision. As X said at the beginning today… As Y said earlier….

She kept doing this until she felt that all voices had been heard, and that everyone's knowledge was taken seriously. When we talked to each other again after a few months, she experienced the group as changed. Listening intently to everyone had made a difference. The ambiance was lighter. After a while the participants in the group naturally played more off of each other during the conversation. They were playing in the same band.

There could have been many different ways of doing this. She never thematized the power-plays, but *acted* with regard to them. She also could have thematized it in the group: I wonder if there is a difference in status among us? I wonder if the way we do this is just as ok for everyone? She also could have talked about expectations they could have of her as a supervisor, and what they would have wanted her to be/do more or less of. All of this could have worked well. What was important about her way of doing things is that she did not remove the intuitive from anyone by saying aloud what she was experiencing. She could have told the most active that they might stand back a bit. And they would have. We are talking about pleasant and agreeable people here. But would they then, to keep with Meares' insight into language, become more alienated and less intuitive?

She chose to use her supervisor power, her role, towards *making* a difference through linguistic action. By being conscious of the power-plays, she could speak in ways which changed them, without inhibiting anyone. In fiction we call this a rule of thumb: Show, don't tell.

What happens when power-plays are changed is, I think, an experience of freedom for everyone, the moment the remold is in the spoon. The responsibility—of being withdrawn or scholarly—shifts. And everyone can experience a new freedom of thought, action, and relation, when "… the game of incessant struggles and collisions which transforms, strengthens, or upheaves the power relations" (Foucault, 1995, p. 103) is in the melting pot.

We need to understand power-plays as something which has to be seen, understood, and dealt with all the time, if we are to see and learn something new. Then, new formations of power-plays are formed. It is always this way. However, we can see the potential in them; they are always carriers of opportunity.

To bring out this potential, we have the supervisor. His job is also to contribute to the conversion of power-plays. It might be an over the top expression, but processes of learning can be a type of "peacekeeping." This is the case in supervision, in leadership, in education, it is the case everywhere, where we are together to learn something.

Even more specifically we can say that when the power is unequal, it is most noticeable to those with least power. If someone is ascribed a higher significance, and represents the "most important" or the currently "most correct" professional standpoint, it might be experienced by others as inhibiting. Thus, listening to everyone does not necessarily involve listening "equally"—but rather resembles the conductor's way of calling forth different voices in different parts of the play, and moderating others.

Then the supervisor himself, as the conductor, needs to conquer power.

To Dare to Apply Supervisor Power: A Model for the Supervisor's Positions

There are no "answers" nor "true knowledge" about most of the subjects we supervise in. What is for example "good therapy"—this will probably always be an open question. This is illustrated in Hubble, Duncan, and Miller (2005). They wanted to clear up the bickering about what is most effective when it comes to what works in therapy. However, in the reports the researchers get from people with therapy experience, the descriptions of good therapy were filled by metaphors and non-definable concepts: "The critical or core conditions were conceptualized as accurate empathy, positive regard, non-possessive warmth, and congruence or genuineness" (2005, p. 33). Methods and techniques do not stand out as central, nor the therapist's professional background. It can be tempting to add that those answering the study are "hoaxing" the researchers. Because being "effective" has to be seen in relation to something. For example, in relation to being "healthy" or "normal." When we are in therapy, we would like to be our own intention, not the culture's, the economy's, or the effectiveness'.

It is not in such a way, either, that a supervisor will think that everything is just as right, as long as warmth and empathy is present. We bring our own ethics, in the span between our field and our personal values.

How can we do this, without stepping on any toes, yet at the same time not becoming obscure nor defying own values? How can we navigate in a large complexity, and at the same time making sure that the group gets the pleasure of learning together?

Personally I enjoy using a model which indicates fixed points to assume a position as supervisor. When I am teaching supervision for those who want to be supervisors, I use the model to create pegs for learning about power in the supervisor role. I have put together the model based on the understanding of power and communication derived from Foucault's understanding of power, Maturana and Varela's theory of autopoiesis, as well as Bruner, White, and Vygotsky's learning theories. Further, it is made with a starting point in, and with inspiration from, White's maps of conversations. If this model is helpful to anyone, it is because I have gotten every single thought from someone else. If the model is not very useful, it is my responsibility. I underline this because I do not wish for the narrative approach's position map to be caught in any undertow. Naturally, the model is very simplified, the way that models always are; however, it can be a navigation map for supervisors (Table 8.1).

In the centralized position the supervisor is in what he himself knows, while the decentralized deals with going over to the universe of the person/people you are supervising. When we are supervising, we are—based on the reasoning we have here—both in a centralized and decentralized position. And we can say that all the positions are necessary, and they are all important. If we are to observe a supervisor, we will probably see that he is moving between the position as if dancing. However, because power is in play between the participants, the supervisor should dare to take the reigns, and himself conquer power, if we are to keep up the rationale in this chapter.

Table 8.1 Navigation map for supervisors, in relation to power positions and the acts that might belong to each of them

	Centralized position	Decentralized position
Influential to learning	• Intervenes • Controls • Creates direction • Says yes and no • Prioritizes • Makes choices and decisions regarding process • Stops, interrupts • Gives advice based on own evaluation • Understands and employs linear and nonlinear language • Promotes and demands nonlinear language	• Promotes curious conversations which open up to the supervisee making decisions • Creates conversations from the" edge of the hole"—Builds scaffold • Conversations where the supervisee gets to know own knowledge and the supervisor learns • Direction which unites supervisees in recognition and subject–subject relations • Is in a language which develops subjectivity
Less influential to learning	• Boasts, commends, and gives acknowledgement • Is genuinely listening and warm • Supports and helps make decisions	• Listens to the problem and lets the supervisee reflect upon it • Asks the supervisee to let the question mature and food for thought take effect • Lets others' free reflections and initiatives be unleashed

Based on theory about how we in a combination of security and challenge can get from what we know, to new learning, we can say that the supervisor is most influential to learning in the two uppermost positions. It is in the two uppermost the supervisor is directing, and is using his role actively. The supervisor takes on a position of power, which *may* promote learning. If the supervisor were to avoid the upper-left position, he would avoid creating security, once the power would go its own way. He would fail to relate to the "power relations which are immanent in the field they are practiced" (Foucault, 1995, p. 103). The upper-left position is where the supervisor actively tries to lead a direction which includes everyone, and which hinders loneliness in the learning process. It is the position where the supervisor brings his own limits and own ethics. In the upper-right position, the learning questions are asked, and this is where the resonance between the supervisees is created, which unites them in a nonlinear language. This is where already established knowledge is brought forth (Maturana & Varela, 1992), which is not the supervisor's, but the group's participants'. This is where the supervisor can sow from the "edge of the hole." In the dance between the uppermost positions, the supervisor can use his power, to make the supervision as free as possible from the power's inhibiting force. It will never quite work out. Supervisees will have different "edges of the hole," be in different places, and no supervisor will ever be able to see, combine, and change power-plays at all times. What the supervisor sees is her interpretation, her story, her mind's card index, her way of being influenced by norms and culture in. The model is thus not meant to give other than pegs to build courage to supervise in ways in which you yourself can believe in and vouch for. And then you can also dare to take on a position of power.

The lower positions are also useful, in a certain time and place. Even though they might be less influential to learning, they are important enough. They are associated with creating a rhythm, a tempo, a warm atmosphere, breaks, and "letting the flowers bloom." Learning cannot be intense all the time—we also need excuses to slow down, praise, acknowledgement, lingering, slowness, etc. And sometimes all we need is understanding. To be met warmly. And also to be consoled. However, it can be argued that if we stay in the lowermost positions, the supervision easily loses its direction, intensity, nerve, or the experience of movement and learning. It can become what I call "drowsy." Vygotsky would probably say that we are not using our role to bring someone to the zone of proximal development. Or we can run the risk of fortifying a language play and intellectual or relational structures of power, and thus fail to promote moments of learning, and worst case, creating both constraint and loneliness.

In my personal experience, if we move mostly in the uppermost positions, the intense moments of learning can arise. However, there is a short distance between dominating too much as a supervisor, and daring to direct. Lastly, if we are to dare to make a ball park estimate of this balance, a rule of thumb might be that you should be 80% of the time in the upper-right corner of the model, 5% in the upper-left, and 10% in the two lowermost.

Conclusion

We have seen how we, anchored in phenomenology, can get help from theories in understanding what brings intense moments of learning. We have brought up theories which are central in traditions within philosophies of science, such as social constructionism and post-structuralism, including systemic and narrative approach. What might stand out most clearly is how meaningful it is for supervisors to understand the power pertaining to the role, and the power-plays which are always present in our midst. We point to the fact that it is the supervisor's role to make sure that the interaction in the group contributes to the freest learning possible, by way of the power-plays transforming, shifting, and changing.

The chapter seeks to encourage supervisors to use their position of power actively, to contribute to the freest learning possible. It might demand courage. However, the power which the supervisor possesses can appear to have a clearer ethical anchoring if it is applied actively, with the aim of letting all voices be heard with a sense of curiosity, that everyone can have their own starting point of knowledge, and that we meet in subject–subject relations, or in an atmosphere of intimacy as a contrast to alienation.

It is when the supervisor can accommodate this loving yet clear direction, it seems that these intense moments of learning can arise in supervision.

References

Bastian, P. (1987). *Ind i musikken*. København: Gyldendal.
Bateson, G. (1972). *Steps to an ecology of mind*. Chicago, IL: University of Chicago Press.
Bruner, J. (1999). *Mening I handling*. Aarhus: Klim.
Bruner, J. (2004). *At fortælle historier—I livet, juraen og litteraturen*. København: Alinea.
Christie, N. (2009). *Små ord for store spørsmål*. Oslo: Universitetsforlaget.
De Beauvoir, S. (1970). *Det annet kjønn*. Oslo: Pax Forlag.
Feenberg, A. (1991). *Critical theory of technology*. New York/Oxford: Oxford University Press.
Foucault, M. (1977). *Discipline and punish: The birth of the prison*. London: Allan Lane.
Foucault, M. (1978). *The will to knowledge. The history of sexuality* (Vol. 1). London: Penguin Books.
Foucault, M. (1987). *The ethic of care for the self as a practice of freedom*. Philosophy and Social Criticism special issue. The Final Foucault, 12 Summer, p. 129.
Foucault, M. (1995). *Seksualitetens historie I. Viljen til viten*. Oslo: Exil.
Foucault, M. (1999) *Overvåkning og straff: det moderne fengsels historie*, 3. utg. Gyldendal.
Heede, D. (2004). *Det tomme menneske. Introduksjon til Michel Foucault*. København: Museum Tusculanums Forlag.
Holmgren, A. (2014). *Fællesskab og fortællinger—Fordi det betaler sig*. Erhvervspsykologi nr 4.
Holmgren, A., & Holmgren, H. (red). (2015). *Narrativ supervision og vejledning*. DISPUK Forlag.
Holmgren, A., & Nevers, M. (red). (2012). *Narrativ praksis i skolen*. København: Hans Reitzels Forlag.
Hubble, M. A., Duncan, B. L., & Miller, S. D. (2005). *The heart & soul of change, what works in therapy*. Washington, DC: American Psychological Association.
Maturana, H. & Varela, F. (1992). *The tree of knowledge*. 2. utgave. København: Ask.
Meares, R. (2000). *Intimacy & alienation. Memory, trauma and personal being*. New York: Brunner-Routledge.
Skjervheim, H. (1996). *Deltakar og tilskodar og andre essays*. Oslo: Ascheoug & Co.
Ulleberg, I. (2004). *Kommunikasjon og Veiledning. En innføring i Gregory Batesons kommunikasjonsteori*.
Vygotsky, L. S. (1978). *Mind and society: The development of higher mental processes*. Cambridge, MA: Harvard University Press.
Vygotsky, L. (2001). *Tenkning og tale*. Oslo: Gyldendal.
White, M. (2006). *Narrativ teori*. København: Hans Reitzel Forlag.
White, M. (2007). *Maps of narrative practice*. New York: W W Norton & Company.
White, M. (2009). *Kart over narrative praksis*. Oslo: Pax Forlag.

Part III
Supervision in Special Contexts of Practice

Chapter 9
Supervision and Domestic Violence: Therapy with Individuals, Couples and Families

Arlene Vetere

This chapter explores the supervision of therapeutic work with individuals, couples, families and groups where violence is of concern, both past and present, and which includes neglect, physical, emotional, psychological and/or sexual violence and exposure to violence. The type of supervision considered here can be training, managerial and/or consultative, ranging from an educative function where the supervisor carries a clear managerial or normative role, to consultancy for experienced and qualified practitioners who hold responsibility for the therapeutic work they do with their clients. This always involves the development of skills, understanding and abilities, awareness of the emotional impact of doing this therapeutic work, and some functional and governance responsibility for the welfare of the clients and the supervisee. The supervision contract covers the five key areas of (a) practicalities, such as time, place, frequency, allowable interruptions; (b) boundaries, such as duty of care and confidentiality, and the relationship between therapy and supervision; (c) the working alliance in supervision, such as mutual expectations and the contract as a safety framework; (d) the format of the supervision session, such as style of working and preferred theoretical models; and (e) consideration of both the organisational and professional context within which the supervision takes place.

It is not assumed in this chapter that the supervisor and supervisee should always have the same type of training, or belong to the same discipline, because supervision in the context of interpersonal and family violence involves both formulation from different theoretical perspectives in order to understand, explain and prevent further violence, and is grounded in a safety methodology that is pan-theoretical (Cooper & Vetere, 2005; Vetere, 2012). In this chapter, I wish to reflect on how my supervision style changes in the context of domestic violence supervision, and on how we can create safe, trusting spaces for dealing with resonances in our

A. Vetere (✉)
Family Therapy Section, Faculty of Social Studies, VID Specialized University, Oslo, Norway
e-mail: drarlenevetere@hotmail.com

A. Vetere, J. Sheehan (eds.), *Supervision of Family Therapy and Systemic Practice*, Focused Issues in Family Therapy, https://doi.org/10.1007/978-3-319-68591-5_9

supervisees' lives, who may have experienced family violence in their past or who are experiencing this in their lives now (Hanks & Vetere, 2016).

A Safety Methodology for Safe Therapeutic Practice

As both a supervisor and a practitioner I work within a safety methodology developed over 20 years of co-directing the Reading Safer Families domestic violence intervention project in the UK (Cooper & Vetere, 2005; Vetere, 2011; Vetere & Cooper, 2008). This systemic approach to safety in couple and family relationships is designed to ascertain whether it is safe to undertake relational therapy where violence is of concern, or if another approach is warranted, such as a legal response, individual and/or group therapy and so on. The safety methodology has a number of features: (a) it includes a safety plan designed to help family members predict and prevent violent interactions; (b) it involves close liaison and co-operation with the family-professional network and creates a 'watching network' of concern; (c) it holds family members responsible for their safety, the safety of others and for their behaviour that harms others; (d) it develops a safety plan for both emotional and physical safety in family relationships; (e) it pays attention to the intergenerational and developmental legacies of violence in the family system, including both masked and overt trauma responses; and (f) it promotes healing and repair in relationships where possible. The contraindications for relationship therapy are clearly articulated within the methodology and are described at the end of this chapter. This approach is both the context and the driver for supervision. The main impact for me as a supervisor is in how it impacts on my level of activity with my supervisees and in the supervision relationship. I am more active and more directive in how I privilege safety for all concerned and how I both support and take action in this regard. For example, I might say it is time to discuss risk of future violence, the safety and well-being of family members and/or the supervisee. I would see this as my responsibility as a supervisor. Thus the supervision activity can be structured according to the level of known violence in the family system, such as our joint focus on safety for the family members and when to involve other professional practitioners in the work.

Our Preferred Ideas as Practitioners and Supervisors

When working therapeutically with interpersonal violence and in the context of its supervision, I have to constantly remind myself and seek to explore with supervisees our preferred and taken-for-granted ideas about emotional and physical safety in relationships, the risks of further violence, how we help people take responsibility for behaviour that harms others, and how we work equitably and collaboratively in asymmetrical power relationships. This self-reflexive emphasis is necessary because of the significant implications of these preferred ideas for both supervision and safe therapeutic practice.

Systemic practitioners will often organise exploration and enquiry around a process of self-reflexive questioning. Thus we might identify what theoretical ideas and practices we are firmly wedded to, those theoretical ideas and practices we sometimes draw on, and finally, those theoretical ideas and practices we are least attracted to, so that we might interrogate their implications for safe practice, in both supervision and therapeutic work. This forms the context for further exploration of how our relationship with particular schools of thought might constrain or enhance safe practice. Both supervisor and supervisee may need to challenge or experiment with their preferred theoretical ideas in order to develop their practice, and to further their understanding of themselves in relation to their preferred ideas. David Campbell once said that we do not want endless searching for new meaning, and no action (personal communication). Whilst we can acknowledge that there are many possible meanings in every interaction for both supervisor and supervisee, in the work we do to help family members stop the violence we need to take action, and we need to be seen to take action by all those in the family-professional network. This visible emphasis on safety and safe practice helps to reassure and settle the professional network, because anxiety in the professional system about whether we take safety seriously can lead to inadvertent and direct attempts to block therapeutic work. Thus we try to help supervisees maintain their manoeuvrability in their work with the family and in their professional relationships with their colleagues in the system of concern.

Anxiety, Authority and Organisational Defences

There are many sources of anxiety for those of us who work directly with violent interpersonal behaviour and intent. Anxiety can arise directly in our work with violent behaviour and vulnerable individuals, from a lack of support or a containing structure in the work organisation, from the team culture, and from wider systems constraints, such as underfunding and under-resourcing in our public sector services. When anxiety is experienced as overwhelming and both supervisors and practitioners feel pressure to act beyond their roles, there is a risk of dancing around the triangle of 'victim, rescuer and persecutor', with attendant feelings of resentment and disappointment and feeling punishing of others (Bryson, personal communication). For example, if anxiety is so high it constrains reflective thought, we might find people are more likely to blame themselves or others, for what is happening, or not happening. Then we can find ourselves both positioned by others, and positioning ourselves, and our action can become reactive because we see ourselves and others in 'fixed' roles of the 'victim', the 'persecutor' and/or the 'rescuer'. Such rigidity in the face of high anxiety quickly leads to disappointment and reluctance to engage and listen at one extreme, or to overwhelming emotional over-involvement with others, at the other extreme.

Thus, to repeat this, unmanageable levels of anxiety can lead to professional boundary violations, such as an emotional withdrawal and decreased engagement with the task and with family members, or at the other extreme, an over-involvement in the lives of family members. As systemic supervisors, when we discover such over-involvement, we always ask who else in the system might be stepping back. This is another example of how I become active as a supervisor. In my experience, it is always helpful to explore the organisational structure and arrangements for managing the difficult feelings arising in the work. An organisational focus allows us to acknowledge heightened anxiety whilst inviting a more reflective stance that views such difficulty more widely as a systemic issue, rather than as a failing of the supervisee. We underline and validate that good supervision (and supervision of supervision), clarity around our work role, a manageable workload and responsive organisational support for emotionally demanding work promote well-being for both supervisors and practitioners. Supervisors and practitioners need support in knowing their own limits in order to act effectively (Skovholt & Trotter-Mathison, 2011).

Dilemmas for Practitioners

> *'We are open to absorbing profound loss, hurt and mistrust from our clients but also to the stimulation of these human states, present in us all'.* (Berger, 2001, p. 189).

The psychological and social consequences for practitioners of working with violence in couple and family relationships, of hearing terrible stories and witnessing acute distress are well documented (Figley, 1995). Adverse consequences can be exacerbated by high case loads, with little or no supervision and no other organisational support for the work.

In supervision we ask about the most stressful aspects of our supervisee's work. We explore whether others in their team and in the wider professional system know what they are doing in their work, and whether these others have any idea of the impact of their work on their well-being? We are interested in how they pay attention to this, how their colleagues pay attention to it, and for each other, and then ask what would they like to do that they are not currently doing?

In our experience of supervising therapeutic work with family violence, stress in the work stems from the following:

(a) Hearing gruelling accounts of physical and emotional cruelty—this can range from repeated violent attacks to sadistic cruelty and intergenerational patterns of unremitting abuse and harm, and sometimes our supervisees are shocked by what they hear and what they feel in response, as they did not predict this for themselves—and for all of us as supervisors, we too are open to unexpected reactions of shock and disbelief;

(b) The feeling of disappointment when the violence continues despite the therapeutic and/or rehabilitation work—our supervisees may have worked long and hard to assist a family, and perhaps in the face of hostility from other colleagues who did not support their work, and so the disappointment can hit them hard;

(c) The risks of an inflated sense of responsibility around our work, particularly in the absence of support from a close colleague or line manager—supervisees can feel isolated and vulnerable at these times, so a strong and trusting supervision relationship can provide solace, relief and a space to reflect on whose responsibility is whose…; and
(d) The tensions around introducing emotional and relational ideas into a conservative legal system with little tradition of acknowledging the role of emotion or passion in people's thinking and behaviour—we support our supervisees to write reports for the family courts that acknowledge family members' intentions to do their best and to do things better for their partners and children than was done for them when they were children, even if the family cannot be a safe place for children to grow and adults to thrive—and of course, such positive comments are often met with hostility within a legal process that strives for certainty.

Some dilemmas are harder to resolve and some have to be lived with, so to say, but our experience teaches us that if we are able to speak calmly and directly about them, slowly and carefully, we can usually find a resolution that allows us to go on in the work. We see it as our responsibility to create calm moments for our supervisees, whatever their level of expertise and experience, to reflect on thought, feeling, intention and action—their own and others. Typical dilemmas we encounter in supervision include: (a) the practitioner getting overloaded with information about the family within the family-professional system without finding any clarity of purpose; (b) the tension of constantly being asked to judge risk and unpredictable behaviour, both for the therapist and the supervisor; (c) the practitioner losing sight of their own competence and abilities; (d) the practitioner seeking simplistic solutions and losing sight of the complexity when feeling overwhelmed; (e) practitioners becoming isolated by not sharing their concerns with their colleagues and managers and becoming preoccupied with the family and their situation; and (f) over-empathising with the victim of violence and/or repeating victim–rescuer–persecutor positions with resulting anger, frustration and resentment over agency responses and service or management decisions. In my experience as a supervisor these dilemmas are mostly the province of therapeutic practice and come to supervision for some attempt at resolution but it is important to say that supervisors too can feel overwhelmed in the face of their supervisees' difficulties. And, as a therapeutic practitioner myself, I find I can sometimes too easily 'stand in the emotional shoes' of my supervisees as I know too well what they might be experiencing!

What Are the Main Responsibilities of the Supervisor?

A supervisor's prime responsibility is to create a trusting relationship with the supervisee and develop an emotionally safe space in which indecision, doubt, reflexivity and action will be held in equal regard. The typical dilemmas and stresses that arise in the work with violence in couple and family relationships, as described above, are addressed in the supervision relationship—we clarify, explore, develop understanding and find ways in which to go on in the work. At the same time, we are looking for resources and signs of resilience, for both practitioners and family members. In the next section below, I shall describe an exercise or activity that can be conducted with both individual supervisees and supervision teams as a way of promoting co-operation and helping people hold the many different perspectives found in this work.

Supervisors and supervisees need to be clear with each other about their roles and their shared accountability and shared responsibility both within the supervision space and in the therapeutic work. This allows tensions and anxieties to be contained whilst still encouraging creative thinking and therapeutic risk taking. We believe it is always helpful for the supervisor to share with the supervisee some ideas about their supervisory style and their supervisory role. This leads onto a discussion about the acceptable and collaborative parameters for the supervision process. This is the context in which we tell our supervisees that we will always ask about their well-being and their personal safety. This is because it needs to be a natural part of the ebb and flow of the supervisory conversation. If we suddenly introduce a question or concern about the supervisee's safety in relation to a particular piece of therapeutic work for the first time, it can have the unhelpful effect of raising the supervisee's anxiety rather than acknowledging the safety and threat that runs through the work all the time. In particular we pay attention to the emotional well-being of our supervisees and the impact of doing the work on them. As supervisors, in our own supervision of supervision, we expect the same of our supervisors.

In work with family violence, there can always be unexpected moments when our own memories are triggered in ways that surprise us all. We support supervisees in making the covert overt, for example, working with family secrets, the tendencies to minimise the violence, both in the family and the professional system, and the implications for the self of the therapist. As supervisors we are clear that we will always be supportive around unexpected resonances in the work and it may be appropriate and agreed that we can explore and resolve it within the supervision relationship, and if not, we always offer advice and guidance for other referral. It is important to acknowledge that these boundaries are also the responsibility of the supervisor when their personal experiences and responses impact on their supervisory work. Thus we hold a commitment to trying to help our supervisees maintain a balance between not being emotionally overwhelmed by their work on the one hand, and not being underwhelmed (or frozen) and potentially unresponsive, on the other. We encourage supervisees to look for the detail in the signs of safety in family members' relationships, especially when other professional colleagues fear a recurrence of violent behaviour. Again, this has implications for us as supervisors in our supervision of supervision—to recognise when we are overwhelmed by the risks such that we too are overlooking what is going well. We recognise the potential for mirroring within the family-professional system and offer an opportunity to hold a meta-perspective on the work by developing systemic working hypotheses and promoting reflective practice (Vetere & Dallos, 2009).

Supervision: Creating a Conversation That Includes Safety, Doubt and Progress

In supervision with groups of practitioners, such as a mental health team, or child protection team, or with individual practitioners who are working therapeutically with couples and families where violence is of concern, we try to create emotionally safe and trusting spaces where colleagues can reflect on and engage positively with the uncertainties in their work. We need to set shorter and longer term goals for supervision in the face of unpredictability and the potential for further violence. The therapeutic work is never without risk of further violence. We know what we know and we know what we don't know, i.e. the other side of a story, the untold detail, and so on, and importantly, we don't know what we don't know—these are George Kelly's 'unknown unknowns'. We work from these three positions at any one time, and all the time, in both supervision and therapy. In supervision, we help colleagues to understand and manage the risks so that their clients can learn to predict, de-escalate and prevent violent interactions. This involves a recognition of the dialectical relationship between certainty and uncertainty, and thus how we can make it safe enough to address the doubts and uncertainties in calm and thoughtful ways. Thus the role of the supervisor can be crucial in helping to ground the practitioner and their team.

The following activity is designed to capture and hold the tensions between the desire for certainty in our work and the rather common experience of too much uncertainty! Thus, we often begin a supervision session by asking our supervisee to describe the referral and their work with the family from the different family members' points of view and from their agency's perspective. If we work with a team in supervision, it is helpful for one colleague to lead this description and for others to contribute as agreed. We always ask, if the family were here, what would they want us to pay attention to, and what would be their hopes from this consultation/supervision. We then widen the description and ask what other issues about and for the family do the team want us to know about? This widening of the context and system of significance is helpful in avoiding a problem focus that obscures the family's resources, strengths, successes and sources of support. We want to be sure to give the team and the family members credit for what is going well and what they are all doing right, especially with regard to safety. We then clarify the goals for the supervision session and possibly subsequent sessions if we shall continue to follow progress with a particular family. We ensure we have captured both the current and intergenerational history of violence in the family, and we ascertain what action, if any, has been taken. We take time to explore whether the supervisee and the team, and/or the agency and supervisor agree about the level of risk of further violence and on the action to be taken. We always end a supervision session by reflecting on what participants think the family members and other agency staff might say had they listened to our conversation.

Secondary Traumatisation: Protection and Growth

Supervision and supervision of supervision both validates and supports us as practitioners and helps us plan and use our personal and professional resources more effectively and satisfyingly (Vetere & Stratton, 2016). Knowing that we are not left alone to carry the difficulties and dilemmas in our work and that we can be helped to be proactive, rather than reactive, contributes to our sense of professional resilience. In a safe supervision space we can give and receive both content and process feedback on the impact of working with violence and harm, such as when our personal processes get in the way of hearing and seeing our clients and our supervisor/supervisee, the impact of being with our clients and supervisees during moments of high arousal, and learning to recognise our own somatic countertransference. Powerful feelings can be evoked in us all, such as intense compassion and feeling overwhelmed when dealing with children such that we intensify our efforts to be empathic. This can lead to reduced effectiveness and a sense of hopelessness. Sometimes we might experience post-traumatic symptoms, such as irritability, anxiety, hyper-vigilance, numbness, sleep difficulties and intrusive ideation (Figley, 2002, 2013).

So how can we anticipate and protect ourselves and support our colleagues in the best ways for all? Reflective supervision and consultation helps us become aware of any unexamined and unacknowledged feelings in relation to our work, to manage our emotional arousal and to set realistic expectations and goals whilst promoting self-care and supporting the development of confidence (Vetere & Dallos, 2009, 2016). Supervision can emphasise the role of social support and emotional balance in life. Attending conferences, reading the relevant literature and participating in teaching and training keeps us well informed and stimulated. Working alone in our view is unhelpful, so we encourage supervisees to develop alliances and co-working/co-consulting relationships wherever possible. This might take the form of a group of colleagues meeting every 4–6 weeks for discussion of how family violence shows up in their case work. Prevention work and collaboration with community groups widens our remit and provides support for persistence in the face of discouragement and when others are 'not listening'.

Contraindications for Relationship Therapy Where Violence Is of Concern

Therapists often bring their dilemmas, surprise and anxieties into supervision and of course, family violence is a working context where core values and ethical positioning are often at the forefront of supervision conversations. Therapists may have known of the violence before embarking on an intervention, or it may have been disclosed during other therapeutic work. Clearly we advocate working with no-violence contracts and making safety plans before proceeding with further therapeutic work that simply makes others emotionally vulnerable to interpersonal attack.

However, in supervision, we also carefully track the progress of the safety plan and interrogate the possibility that further relationship therapy may be contraindicated. The contraindications for relationship therapy are clustered around how someone can be helped and encouraged to take responsibility for their behaviour that harms others and to take responsibility for safety, for all the family members. If it is deemed unsafe to continue with relationship therapy, we support the therapists in helping family members find other solutions, such as individual and group therapy, safeguarding and social care support, a legal response and so on. This is where supervision takes a more active and directive focus in the work.

The contraindications for relationship therapy are not intended as a checklist, but more as an heuristic to guide decision-making about therapeutic safety for family relationships. In supervision, we ask therapists to look for signs that a perpetrator of violence can take responsibility for their actions. Initially this might be tentative, and our responsibility is to help others develop this capacity, but it does need to develop. If after six meetings of safety planning say, the perpetrator of violence is still blaming others and is not prepared to acknowledge that violence is a problem, such that their motivation to change is very low, we would not support therapists to carry on with couple or family therapy—we would help them look for another solution. Clients may struggle to make a commitment to the resolution of the problem of violence, be unwilling to consider the implications of violent behaviour for their significant relationships, may not want to reflect on past experience and be unwilling to listen to another point of view and/or empathise with the victim of violence. Clients may be challenged by experiences of unregulated and unhelpful physiological arousal within which anger and aggression is triggered and thus unwilling to seek help. Clients may not see other professionals as potentially helpful to them and their family, and could lack respect for social control of behaviour that harms others (Reder & Lucey, 1995). This might be paired with extreme macho and gender stereotypical values. If they have a substance use problem in the view of their therapist, and they are unwilling to seek help, we would consider that to be a strong contraindication for any relationship therapy given the high correlation between psychoactive substance use and physical and emotional violence. Finally we would encourage therapists to explore discrepancies between written reports about the violent behaviour in the family, such as police and social work reports, and verbal descriptions of the violence from family members. Discrepancies between written and verbal reports are not uncommon, but when marked discrepancies exist, in association with the factors described here, we would strongly urge caution before proceeding with relationship therapy (Cooper & Vetere, 2005; Vetere & Cooper, 2008).

Conclusion

In conclusion, we may find that our supervision relationships are much longer lived than our therapeutic relationships with our clients, and even perhaps longer than some of our professional and collegial relationships. For the practitioner, knowing and feeling that they have an emotionally safe and trusting relationship with their supervisor, who is both accessible and responsive around their doubts and concerns, acts as both a safe haven and a secure base, to use Bowlby's terms (1973). In my experience as a supervisor, the emotional containment offered within a relationship of trust promotes confidence, openness and curiosity, reflexivity and a more elaborated sense of our professional self. And this is what allows us to go on—to renew and refresh and continue to provide assistance to others, balanced with a compassionate approach to our own self-care.

References

Berger, H. (2001). Trauma and the therapist. In T. Spiers (Ed.), *Trauma: A practitioner's guide to counselling*. Hove: Brunner Routledge.

Bowlby, J. (1973). *Separation: Anxiety and anger*. New York: Basic Books.

Bryson, S. Personal communication.

Campbell, D. Personal communication.

Cooper, J., & Vetere, A. (2005). *Domestic violence and family safety: A systemic approach to working with violence in families*. Chichester: Wiley.

Figley, C. (1995). *Compassion fatigue: Coping with secondary traumatic stress disorder*. New York: Brunner Mazel.

Figley, C. (Ed.). (2002). *Treating compassion fatigue*. London: Routledge.

Figley, C. (2013). *Trauma and its wake*. London: Routledge.

Hanks, H., & Vetere, A. (2016). Working at the extremes: The influence on us of doing the work. In A. Vetere & P. Stratton (Eds.), *Interacting selves: Systemic solutions for personal and professional development in counselling and psychotherapy*. London: Routledge.

Reder, P., & Lucey, C. (Eds.). (1995). *Assessment of parenting: Psychiatric and psychological contributions*. London: Routledge.

Skovholt, T., & Trotter-Mathison, M. (2011). *The resilient practitioner: Burnout prevention and self-care strategies for counsellors, therapists, teachers and health professionals* (2nd ed.). New York: Routledge.

Vetere, A. (2011). Family violence and family safety: An approach to safe practices in our mental health services. *Partner Abuse, 2*, 246–256.

Vetere, A. (2012). Supervision and consultation practice with domestic violence. *Clinical Child Psychology and Psychiatry, 17*, 181–185.

Vetere, A., & Cooper, J. (2008). Supervision in domestic violence casework. In J. Hamel (Ed.), *Intimate partner and family abuse*. New York: Springer.

Vetere, A., & Dallos, R. (2009). Family mirrors: Reflective practice in systemic therapies. In J. Stedmon & R. Dallos (Eds.), *Reflective practice in psychotherapy and counselling*. Maidenhead, Berks: McGraw Hill.

Vetere, A., & Dallos, R. (2016). Supervision and attachment narratives: Using an attachment narrative approach in clinical supervision. In A. Vetere & P. Stratton (Eds.), *Interacting selves: Systemic solutions for personal and professional development in counselling and psychotherapy*. London: Routledge.

Vetere, A., & Stratton, P. (Eds.). (2016). *Interacting selves: Systemic solutions for personal and professional development in counselling and psychotherapy*. London: Routledge.

Chapter 10
Systemic Supervision with Groups in Child Protection Contexts

Randi Frieda Bagge

Introduction

This chapter will describe one way to supervise a group of professional practitioners in a social and child welfare therapeutic context. First, I shall describe some theoretical aspects about systemic supervision, the "not knowing position" (Anderson, 2003) and reflecting processes (Andersen, 2006). Then I will explore how to start a supervision group, and how to work together in a way that feels relevant and suits the supervisees. By using the "not knowing position" and reflecting processes, it will focus on how the supervisees can help each other to inform each other, identify, and catch new perspectives in their daily work. Then I shall follow the supervisees' own thoughts of the use of such supervision, and their reflections on how practice and theory are linked together. Finally, the strength of the dialectic relationship that arises in the interspace between inner dialogues, narratives, listening, and reflecting processes will be summed up.

Context

We are living in a diverse world, yet society is largely marked by a dominant culture, and dominant discourses concerning how people should live their lives, and how parents should care for their children. Child protection services is a public enterprise which is managed through legislation, rights, and responsibilities. This service is in place to make sure that all children and youth are guaranteed care, free from harm or exposed to risks by their own caretakers or society in general. Each

R.F. Bagge (✉)
Family Therapy Section, Faculty of Social Studies, VID Specialized University, Oslo, Norway
e-mail: randi.bagge@vid.no

A. Vetere, J. Sheehan (eds.), *Supervision of Family Therapy and Systemic Practice*, Focused Issues in Family Therapy, https://doi.org/10.1007/978-3-319-68591-5_10

individual child protection professional must handle cooperation with families in vulnerable situations, who are struggling with giving their children the care they need. Employees in child protection services are, as professionals, situated in this terrain, controlled by legislation and society's discourses. Child protection services can ask for help from expert teams to help families in difficult and distressing situations. The supervision group consists of family therapists who have taken on the assignment of giving help to families in their homes. The family therapists group is faced with great complexity in the families, as well as being pressed for time.

This chapter describes systemic supervision given to one of these teams, in the following called "supervision group."

Before I describe the supervision process, I want to bring forward some essential dilemmas we find in a child protection service context. The main function of the family therapists is, as said, to provide help to multiproblem families. This is going to happen in cooperation with and on the instructions of the referring instance, the child protection service. Is it possible for family therapists to provide help in such a context of control? Is it possible for parents to receive help from therapists that at the same time cooperate with the controlling instance? Will it be possible to develop alliance and cooperation between family therapists and families in such a context? The parents can be in the situation where they have asked for help voluntary and have a high level of motivation to parents that have a long carrier with unsuccessful attempts to solve the family problems, and where the child protection service have told the parents that this remedial action will be the last attempt to help the parents to keep the children in the family. Is it possible to develop change only when parents ask for it, voluntary? Is it possible that pressure into a changing process will be turned back into a constructive cooperation with openness and clarity, considered as basis for all cooperation? What does the therapists do with the worries that come forward during the cooperation at the same time, as they have to be recourse oriented? As reader, you can observe there are many dilemmas that the therapists are meeting in their work, and that they bring into the supervision group. Before I describe the supervision process, I also want to bring forward essential elements in systemic supervision.

Essential Elements in Systemic Supervision

Systemic supervision can be defined as a cooperation which aims to be a learning process for everyone involved (Andersen, 2011). An objective can be the individual's increasing awareness of their own professional scope of action, through a combination of professional theory, knowledge, methods, and their own background, experiences and personal lives. The systemic supervisor's starting point is in the supervisee's experiences and concerns at present. Another point of departure for supervision is that the supervisee is a part of the therapeutic system in which he/she is working, in the same way that the supervisor is a part of the supervision system. This means that the supervision content several positions and perspectives at the same time. It deals with (a) the issue at hand, the issue's context and participants; (b) the supervisee's relation to the issue and to the supervisor; and (c) the supervisor's relation to the issue and to the supervisee.

All phenomena gain their meaning in a given context. Consequently, exploring the supervisee's context is vital. Here, context is understood as the supervisee's total frame of reference, from own background, education, and experience, to the underlying structures for scope of action and the current situation. In other words, it refers to the supervisee's frames of reference, both the structural and the psychological. It also deals with what the supervisee brings with him/her in the encounter with the other(s), and how the supervisee responds to this encounter. The supervisor is more concerned with the supervision participants' ability to explore the patterns which form with the interaction, than with cause-effect. This entails both patterns *within* the issue which the supervisee brings to supervision, as well as patterns in the relation *between* the supervisee and the issue. The systemic supervisor employs circular processes in the supervision: in the supervision group and in the individual supervisee's context, and also between supervisor and supervisee(s). The systemic supervisor seeks to understand how certain sides to an issue or a relationship gain precedence over others, and how this can be understood circularly; how different relationships mutually affect each other. More than simply being concerned with phenomena as such, the systemic supervisor is concerned with exploring the relations between the phenomena, the effect of these relationships, and how the different contributions lead to preservation and/or change. The supervisor seeks to contribute to the supervisee's increased awareness of the distribution and limitation of responsibility. This concerns the distribution of responsibility within a field, responsibility for processes, and responsibility for own reactions. This means that the supervision process is unpredictable, in that both supervisor and supervisee are participating in a joint research process of the supervisee's affairs, with the intention of bringing to light more perspectives through which the supervisee may discover other, or new, solutions. It also means helping supervisees in developing a sensitivity when it comes to the influence of own preconceptions, which we all have, and becoming conscious of one's role as a member in an observing system, as well as creating space for each person's conception of reality.

The supervisor is positioned in the group in a so-called "*not-knowing position*," which in short entails that one "*does not know, in advance, nor assume anything about the other's lifeworld before having asked and listened*." Not-knowing position refers to an attitude and a belief that the supervisor does not have access to privileged information, cannot understand another person completely, and will always need to learn more about what has been said or what has not been said. Not-knowing means that the supervisor is not sure of what he/she knows. Not-knowing involves respectful listening—listening in an active and responsive way. The supervisor listens in a way which shows the supervisee that they have something worth listening to. Showing receptiveness and involvement towards the other's story is significant for dialogue to take place. Not-knowing position does *not* mean that the supervisor does not know anything, nor that he/she should discard, or not put to use, the knowledge he/she possesses. It does not mean that the supervisor is laid-back, does nothing, and cannot express their opinion. Not-knowing does not signify that preconceptions are bad, something we should not have. Everyone has preconceptions, and we need to be aware of how to put them to good use. All this means that the supervisor contributes with knowledge, whether being questions, opinions, speculations, or suggestions. The supervisor asks for permission to share, and this is presented through a wondering attitude, which shows respect for, and openness towards, the other(s)'s perspective, and towards possible new perspectives created in the group (Anderson, 2005).

Throughout the supervision process, *reflective processes* will be put to use in different ways. The most central idea in reflective processes is that when listening to something another is saying, one is moved by what is being expressed. What happens within the listener when he/she is moved, can be returned to the narrator, by way of for example a question or a feeling. *The story moves the listener and the listener returns what happened to him or her.* This can cause movements to arise in people's encounters. This presupposes that the conversation is organized in a way which guarantees that the person talking will be able to do so without interruption, and that the listener can be, undisturbedly, occupied with their internal dialogue. This is what separates *listening* and *talking*. These processes are improved and clarified through context and instruction (Andersen, 2011; Lund-Jacobsen & Wermer, 2001). By structuring the supervision, so that one is talking and another is listening, in combination with time for breaks and thoughts along the way, makes room for internal dialogues. Each person in supervision can have internal dialogues which can move, without being disturbed by having to have an opinion at any given time. In this conversation process, where roles and positions are interchangeable, opportunities for multiverse and polyphony are created. The idea is that those reflecting out loud should bring forth thoughts and ideas they have encountered while listening to the story, with the narrator's story as a starting point. The person reflecting should try to express themselves in a light and acknowledging manner: Acknowledging of the articulated problem. Attempt to see the problem from another perspective and from other points of view. Can play with ideas, turn around understanding, see the other side of the coin. Linguistic juggling with mounds of ideas and versions. Attempt to put into words how it can be understandable and meaningful that everyone involved do what they do and think as they think. Attempt to understand the logic and complexity of the system. Express different hypothesis, unusual or surprising ideas. Formulate dilemmas, contrasting relations, resources, and possibilities. Illustrate and consider possible consequences of different understandings, attitudes, and actions (Lund-Jacobsen & Wermer, 2001).

This abundance and variety can give the supervisee the opportunity to apply those versions or ideas which seem meaningful to the supervisee.

An Example of a Supervision Process

As a supervisor, I am concerned with how I can meet each individual supervisee, and at the same time meet them as a group. This as a foundation for creating an alliance and mutual trust, which is fundamental in all cooperation. The first meeting always consists of different ideas about what the collaboration can encompass, and how the supervisees should interact. Firstly, creating context for dialogue and exchanging expectations is emphasized.

In the following it will be described a supervision process with a group of family therapists who have taken on the assignment of giving help to families from the child protection service. The example is put together from different experiences and anonymized. At first I will describe the two first meetings with the group. Then I will describe a supervision meeting later in the process in the same group:

> "In the first meeting the supervisees were asked to express their expectations out loud, and share this with each other, as I took down what was being said. For the second supervision meeting, I as the supervisor shared with the group, in writing, what was said of expectations, including all supervisees' contributions represented word by word. In the following this text is presented, which was read aloud together:
>
> *'I wish to be here and now, and starting with an issue or topic, when something has come to a full halt or a particular concern I have. I want to develop, keep the focus on my process with the issue, how I am, what I think, how I do things, and what it is that makes me think and do as I do. I am preoccupied with how we can make each other great, us together and in a collaboration. I wish for reflection, how to change directions, be affected in my chosen route, to make space for feedback and adjustments. Explore the balance between pushing, supporting, and challenging. Suggest creative elements, sensations, variations, and nuances. I would like a supervisor which guides the process and holds the reigns, makes sure that misunderstandings do not arise, is acknowledging of all, and who creates an atmosphere of openness. I would like a good place to be, where there is room for everyone, and I can leave with an uplifting feeling.'*
>
> The supervisees experienced response and recognition. Additionally, we agreed upon simple and necessary rules for the supervision process."

This beginning of the supervision process can be seen both as creating an alliance, and at the same time the supervisees experience an acknowledging attitude from the supervisor. They also see that there are many dilemmas in common, and something they had not previously considered, which will be interesting to explore further. In the following it is described how a supervision meeting later in the same supervision process took place:

> "We started the meeting off by going the rounds, where everyone could reveal thoughts they have had since the last time we met. Subsequently, there was another round to see if anyone had a topic or a concern. We had an open conversation about topics presented, and selected an issue to focus on. The choice of issue was the topic which the majority of the group would like to prioritize. This might as well be a particular issue or topic which one of the other supervisees had presented. I then asked how the supervisee would like the supervision to proceed. The supervisee first wanted to be interviewed by the supervisor, he would like for me to draw on the chalkboard, so that we could have a picture to look at and reflect around. He would like for the other supervisees to listen to the story, and take on different positions concerning what was being presented.
>
> Before the actual interview, I asked the supervisee what made him want to talk about this particular situation. The supervisee responded that it was because he was stick, it was a known dilemma, it was an important topic for the supervisee. Subsequently, I asked which expectations and wishes the supervisee had in bringing up the issue here today. Was there a particular question he wanted answered, was there a topic he would like to discuss, was there new ideas for further work, was this related to an increased understanding of the family's problems and the like. When the supervisee had answered these questions, the rest of the supervisees were divided into listening positions. They could each choose to take on a

position, meaning that they took on the perspective of one of the participants in the story, as they heard and saw how the story was playing out in front of them. After that, I interviewed the supervisee.

The supervisee and I placed ourselves outside of the supervision group, who now became observers and listeners to our exploration. After this, I asked the supervisee who the participants in the story were. The supervisee told me who the participants in the matter were, and I could start drawing on the chalkboard. I draw using a genogram structure. Subsequently, I asked the supervisee to share what he thought was important for the rest of us to know about the situation, considering that we should have the necessary and relevant information in relation to the supervisee's expectation of the supervision. This dealt with examples of situations, relations, tried and tested solutions, participation, understanding, opinions, commentary, clarifying roles and positions, what the supervisee had been doing, and thoughts about what had been tried out, as well as wonderings and challenges et cetera. In the example shown in the drawing (see illustration), the mother had contacted child protection services and asked for help with her two sons. The mother was pregnant, and very tired. The sons were 16 and 10 years old, respectively, and were very angry boys, and the mother could not handle their attacks, both psychologically and physically. She had a new partner which both boys were very aggressive towards as well. The mother wanted help, while the new partner felt they could handle the situation themselves. Child protective services had asked the therapist/supervisee to get into position to collaborate with the whole family, and to give the family the help they need so that the care situation with both boys changed for the better. As the story progresses, a map of the people, relations, opinions, and problems they were struggling with was drawn, as well as resources which came to light (Fig. 10.1).

When the map was finished with the information the supervisee held, the situation was turned around, and the colleagues in the supervision group studied the picture which had been drawn. The supervisee now sat down on the side in a listening position. The colleagues were asked to include as many different perspectives as possible in relation to what the

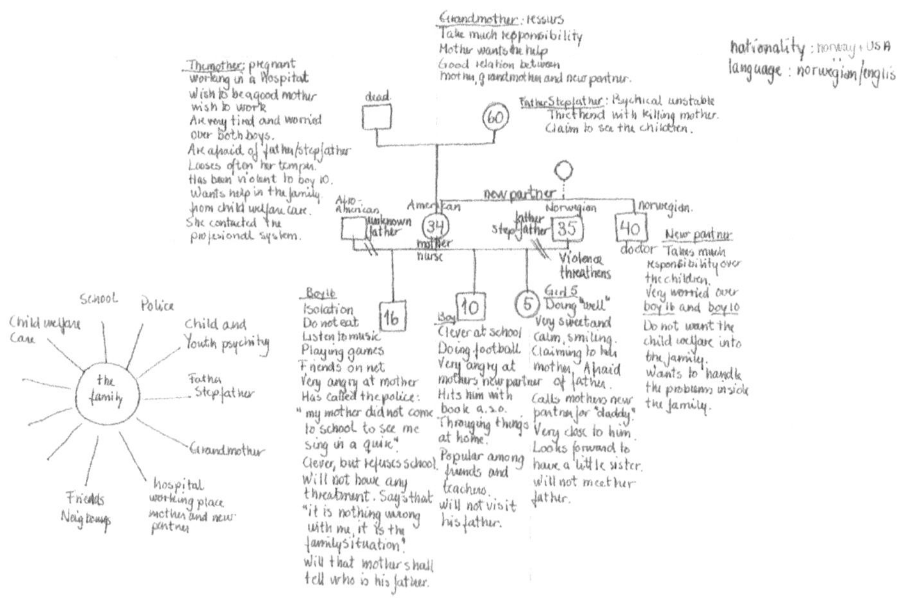

Fig. 10.1 Map of the people, relations, opinions, and problems in the story

supervisee expected from the supervision. I also asked them to take on the perspective of the different actors, and speak from the point of view of this 'I' position. The supervisee and I listened. The supervisee was free to simply listen, he did not keep eye contact with the 'reflectors,' so that he was free to let his internal dialogues move with what he was hearing, and he could take in what he found suitable and relevant to himself. This unattached/free position made it possible for the supervisee to have access to as much as possible of the reflective conversations, without being halted by thoughts such as 'I have already tried this,' 'this will not work in this family,' 'I should have thought of that,' et cetera. I also asked the supervisee to listen taking on the position of one of the other family members' 'I' position, being the 'mother,' 'boy 16,' et cetera.

When the reflection was over, we took a break. This was so that the supervisee could have time for internal dialogues, afterthought, and reflection considering what he had heard. Afterwards we again turned the situation around, and I had a conversation with the supervisee about his experience of the reflections. I made space for the supervisee, so that he could reply in the way he preferred to talk about it. I asked him if anything that he had heard appealed to him. Subsequently, I asked for permission to ask a few questions about something which triggered my interest, or to share some ideas I have had while listening to the reflections. We were not looking for solutions in this context. The supervisee took the reflections with him, and considers afterwards how he would like to deal with the issue in the continuation.

We ended with an open dialogue about the experience of the process we had just been through. Not a discussion about the content of the supervisee's story, not as questioning the practice itself."

The intention of drawing the map, constructing a picture, is to position what it deals with outside of the supervisee and the colleagues, so that they can see a whole picture. This process opens up to the possibility of discovering new patterns, other connections and relations, which previously has not been explored. The complexity of a problem description can be overwhelming when the story is inside the body and head. This visualization becomes an externalization where the problems can be seen as from the outside, which in turn can open up to new perspectives. The colleagues can reflect around what they have heard, and thoughts they have had related to what the supervisee has asked for, from the standpoint of the position they have taken on.

To place the supervisee in a free position without eye contact, together with taking the different family members' perspectives can contribute to open up sensitivity towards each individual family member, who all have individual perspectives. This process can increase the possibility to understand the complexity and there through new possibilities.

At the end of the session it is vital to avoid the situation where the other participants in the supervision become experts who wish to discuss the content, or wish to suggest solutions, and instruct the supervisee. Those participants who are too eager to help are suggested to write down their input or suggestions, ask if the supervisee want them, and then give them to the supervisee after the supervision has ended. At this point in time it is essential to keep from disturbing the supervisee's new internal dialogue about what has happened in the supervision.

This type of supervision opens for the possibility of both internal and external dialogues with oneself and with each other, and the reflection space increases when the supervisee moves between being a narrator and in a listening position. Essential elements can be summarized:

1. The narrating supervisee can choose what she wants to tell and how she wants to tell it, and has a protected space without restrictions where it can be told.
2. A drawing is made of the story, which is guided by the supervisee, which all the participants share an understanding of, and which functions as the focal point in the supervision that we are all focused on. The story can be seen as a "story ball" (Anderson, 2003), a ball which is placed on the table, containing a story, and the supervisee holds his hand atop it and guides it around. The supervisor's hand is also on the ball, but will throughout be able to ask questions from their own perspective, which will always be different from the supervisee's perspective.
3. There is room for polyphony. Everyone listens to all the voices, and no one's voice is concealed from the supervisee.
4. The supervisee chooses what prompts interest and curiosity in the reflections, and what she would like to think about further/talk about more, and take with her.

The therapists were asked how they experience this type of supervision. What can be understood from their answers is that they largely experience benefit from concretizing and putting the stories related to their practice "out there." Being listened to, and at the same time being able to participate in different reflective processes from different positions, seems to give the supervisees a feeling of something understandable and manageable in the complexity that is family work, instead of something which overpowers them and makes them paralyzed. This process of trying to grasp and comprehend, combined with how meaningful it is for them to contribute to creating movement in deadlocked and complex family problems, can help them see that there are different ways of helping a family. These processes give experiences of coping which the supervisees can generalize to basic knowledge through the supervision, which can be used in the different situations they face. They experience a "*feeling of connection*" in their professional practice which forms a foundation for grasping and handling what they are faced with, in a way which makes sense (Antonovsky, 1995; Cederblad & Hansson, 2012; Eriksson & Lindström, 2015).

In the Following, Prominent Perspectives in Systemic Supervision

Uninterrupted speaking. The person speaking is given the opportunity to talk about what he/she prefers, rather than what the listener thinks is important. Questions such as "what would you like for us to know about" help to keep this distinction. The narrator can narrate without being interrupted in their story.

Ordered listening. The ordered listening position allows the participants to listen in a different way than they would have done if they were involved in speaking and responding. It is difficult to keep complete focus on another's story, if you at the same time are supposed to ask questions, commentary, share ideas, and propose suggestions. By being in such an ordered position, the listener is given the opportunity to experience the difference between listening to what they want to listen to, and what they think they should listen to, versus what the supervisee wants them to listen to. The participants can experience how a premature understanding, understanding too soon, can close the opportunity to see the diversity/abundance in the other's experiences. The listening gives time and space to, after a while, forming internal dialogues in external speech.

Polyphony. There is room for polyphony, and many perspectives, both in narrating—listening, and in reflection. The participants experience that there are many ways to tell a story, and just as many ways of listening. The participants also get the opportunity to experience the abundance in the different voices, and that every voice can hold polyphony at the same time, and even contradicting perspectives. This invitation of polyphony decreases the possibility of certain voices' dominance.

Public disclosure as a way of opening up. The participants experience the value in making private thoughts visible (Anderson, 2008). The colleagues' voices are throughout a few voices among many possible, which are put on the table, and the supervisee can choose what she wants to see, and what she wants to address. Both the supervisee and the colleagues experience that they are capable of talking about everything they want to talk about related to an "issue," and all questions are possible. There is no censorship, and no one knows in advance what is helpful to the supervisee. What is vital is the way, the tone of voice, the attitude, and the intention with how things are said, because this is what affects how words are heard and received.

Process without solutions. The participants experience that they do not need to strive for a final product, nor a solution. They are part of an ongoing process, where possibilities such as new meaning, new perspectives, actions, feelings, thoughts about the future, etcetera, can develop in the external or internal dialogues.

Relational innovation. When the supervisee listens to the colleagues' voices, and all participants listen to each other's reflections, they experience that their own ideas change. They also experience that ideas are not given to others as finished ideas, but can be changed "*en route*" from the sender to the receiver, in the space between. Everyone responds to, and interacts in relation to, everyone else's contribution, and is shaped along the way. The new part comes to life because of the "fluid condition" and the "back and forth" communication which happens in the process between telling and listening (Anderson, 2008).

Dilemmas in This Context and Possibilities with Systemic Supervision

In the supervision it is regarded as significantly to clarify dilemmas about assistance and control, and how power and control is divided between the referring instance, the family therapists and the parents. It is of a great importance to help the therapists to develop approaches that reduces tension and increases the opportunities for cooperation. This is done by showing transparency and clarity about the client's and the therapist's position in relation to the family. Essentially conveys child protection service control aspect, while therapists to help the family in the process of change take the role of helper.

Family therapists need to get in position to families. Then it is of great importance how therapists and parents deconstruct and reconstruct the assignment so that they gain a common understanding of the nature of the cooperation. Parents must see that it is their project to be implemented and not the child protection service. Basic to this process is to create a relationship based on transparency, clarity, and proximity between the helpers and family members. Finally, I mention how reversal of the concern overflowing from something hidden and dangerous into something open and less dangerous it will be made with, creating constructive cooperation on issues. Therapists and parents collaborate on understanding of the issues and how they can jointly find solutions. Recognition together with transparency of attitudes, ideas, knowledge, and methods creates curiosity and innovation of ways to collaborate, which helps to give family members control over their own development. The same can be said about the counseling process, the supervisees develop control over their own professional development.

The strength of this approach in supervision is the provision of a polyphonic diversity of thought and unspoken voices. The supervisor encourages and invites openness, and at the same time respect for being closed off, prejudice, and moral. Feelings which are listened to and understood are encouraged, as well as unheard and misunderstood feelings. Experiences can be reaped with the abundance in different and contradicting feelings, as well as experiencing what is lost when only the voices of the experts are heard, and when voices move towards consensus. It is important that the supervisee has the possibility to experience "being in the middle of it," a way of experiencing which is different from technique. The supervisor and supervisees can experience the emergence of unexpected news, endless possibilities, not a solution for the problem. The problem can even dissolve, or be perceived as something possible to understand and handle.

Not-Knowing Position and Reflective Processes

To assume a not-knowing position concerns everyone in the room. It deals with what each person thinks he/she knows and what he/she does not know. It concerns attitude, intention, and the way we position ourselves when we introduce what we bring to the supervision, whether being knowledge, preconceptions, discourses, or life experience. This process is *mutual*.

No one knows exactly who the others are, what they meet, and how they are affected in the meeting. This operates in us all, in thoughts, feelings, and body, and affects our reactions in relation to each other.

By asking for and giving permission to share knowledge, either through stories, questions, comments, suggestions, and reflections, it is a way of participating in a creative conversation which leads to something new and other possibilities for the people in question. This sharing is considered food for the conversation, or as Tom Andersen said, "to help people to talk to themselves and each other in a way which they have not done before" (Anderson, 2008).

As a supervisor, I can never know anything about the others, I do not have access to what happens in others' bodies and thoughts and feelings. At the same time, I am influenced by preconceptions which are continually affecting me, and trick me into thinking that I do know. Another side of the surprise which supervisees experience when they are met with a not-knowing attitude. We are all used to meeting others who try to understand, and often have an opinion of what we bring to the conversation. Curiosity is provoked when I, as a supervisee, met with a supervisor and colleagues who ask repeatedly what I am thinking, what my opinions are, and what things mean to me. I do not have to be concerned with whether the other understands or not. No one is censoring me. I experience the freedom of getting to know unknown and new sides to myself. I am brought into a "not-knowing position" in relation to myself, and to my own thoughts about what I do.

Self-Reflection

This type of supervisor position requires knowing oneself well, reflection about own intentions when it comes to what I, as a systemic supervisor, take with me into the supervision, as well as how I handle this in the encounter with the supervisees. This is an ongoing process which demands continuous self-reflection. It deals with *movement*, not necessarily expecting that the supervisees will accept or agree with what I propose. It requires for me as a supervisor to be *curious* and *open* to being challenged, because my knowledge will always be uncertain. I aspire to be spontaneously responsive, and therefore I have no control over what will come of it. I am open to surprises which can originate at any time during the supervision.

Conclusion

By striving for a not-knowing position, the supervisor takes on a position where she conveys that she is not an expert, but a collaborator who talks <u>with</u> and not <u>to</u> (Anderson, 2003). The supervisor and the supervisee are experts in their own fields. The supervisor is an expert at preparing the context for open dialogues and process, while the supervisees are experts at the content of what is brought to light in the supervision. Reflective processes encourage, and lay the groundwork for, polyphony, and a liberation from rigid ideas and actions. The supervisor and the supervisees meet here and now, because the supervisees have a concern. Through showing movement, openness, and curiosity towards each other, everyone shows that they are not subjects who are necessarily trapped by, and locked in, preconceptions, methods, and techniques, which might objectify us in relation to each other.

Supervision in a child protection services context takes place in a context, as previously said, which might have a high to a low degree of voluntariness for its users and therapists, but always has a high degree of normative regulations through legislation, the society's culture, and dominant discourses. My experience as a supervisor is that the smaller this normative room for practice, experience exchange, and opportunity is, and the more complex the supervisee's context is, the more important it is for the supervision to follow the described attitudes and positions. Trust is shown, which is important in creating a mutual trust, so that we can explore difficulties together. We make room for each other, share understanding, and together find directions and possible ways forward.

References

Andersen, T. (2006) Reflekterende samtaler, min versjon. I *Reflekterende prosesser i praksis* Redigert av Helge Eliassen og Jaakko Seikkula. Oslo: Universitetsforlaget. Chap. 2.

Andersen, T. (2011) Et samarbeid av noen kalt veiledning. I *Veiledning i psykoterapeutisk arbeid* Redigert av M.H. Rønnestad, S. Reichelt. Oslo: Universitetsforlaget. Chap. 6.

Anderson, H. (2003) *Samtale, sprog og terapi*. København: Hans Reitzels Forlag. Chapter 3 og Chap. 7.

Anderson, H. (2005). Myths about "not knowing". *Family Process, 44*, 497–504.

Anderson, H. (2008) Om å skape rom for et fruktbart fellesskap. I *Inspirasjon* redigert av Harlene Anderson og Per Jensen. Oslo: Gyldendal Akademisk. Chap. 3.

Antonovsky, A. (1995). *Hälsans mysterium*. Stockholm: Natur och Kultur.

Cederblad, M., & Hansson, K. (2012). Salutogen familjeterapi. *Fokus på Familien, 3*, 244–264.

Eriksson, M., & Lindström, B. (2015). *Haikerense guide til Salutogenese*. Oslo: Gyldendal akademisk.

Lund-Jacobsen, D., & Wermer, A. (2001). Invitation til nysgerrighet: En systemisk tilgang til supervision. *Fokus på familien, 1*, 36–49.

Chapter 11
An Approach to Supervision Practice with Therapists Who Work with Pregnant Substance-Abusing Women in Voluntary and Compulsory Treatment Settings

Siv Merete Myra

Introduction

This chapter is written for supervisors and psychotherapists who work with pregnant substance-abusing women in the Specialist Health Service in Norway. This chapter describes an approach to supervision, which arises as a result of the findings from a research study conducted with therapist working with pregnant substance-abusing women. The study was conducted in Norway, and I am confident that the reflections on the supervision offered in this chapter can be relevant for therapist in different part of the globe working with the same population.

Therapeutic work is demanding, and the therapist encounters different dilemmas. The background for women with substance abuse problems is that substance abuse during pregnancy has become a significant problem and has led to accelerated attempts to develop specific treatments, both voluntarily and compulsorily. I wanted to investigate through supervision how practitioners in the family-oriented substance abuse services understood their mission, and the aim of this chapter is to investigate how the professionals who work with both voluntarily and compulsorily admitted substance-abusing pregnant women describe their work.

S.M. Myra (✉)
Family Therapy Section, Faculty of Social Studies, VID Specialized University, Oslo, Norway
e-mail: siv.merete.myra@vid.no

A. Vetere, J. Sheehan (eds.), *Supervision of Family Therapy and Systemic Practice*, Focused Issues in Family Therapy, https://doi.org/10.1007/978-3-319-68591-5_11

Research and Legislative Context of Treatment

International research shows that substance-abusing pregnant women have limited resources, little social support, are less educated and their pregnancies are most often unplanned (Grella, Joshi, & Hser, 2000; Mayes & Truman, 2002; Pajulo, 2001; Suchman, McMahon, Slade, & Luthar, 2005). Substance abuse creates major challenges for motherhood. Becoming a mother is a major responsibility for any woman. Women with substance abuse have often had different childhood experiences that challenge the role of motherhood (Myra, Ravndal, Wie Torsteinson, & Wiig, 2016). They also frequently have partners with substance abuse problems. Most intensive treatment interventions for women who are pregnant are primarily aimed at protecting the unborn child. These pregnancies are often unplanned, and the mother's guilt is often reinforced by societal stigmatization of addicted mothers. Their pregnancies can also be a period of fear, anxiety, and guilt regarding the health of the child (Pajulo, Suchman, Kalland, & Mayes, 2006).

In Norway, the use of involuntary treatment for pregnant drug-dependent women was legalized in 1996. The core of the law is that pregnant substance-dependent women can be retained in inpatient treatment without consent if the abuse makes it reasonably likely that the fetus can be harmed, and if voluntary health measures are insufficient. The health of the unborn child in this context is favored by lawmakers against the woman's right to liberty (Søvig, 2004). Norway is the only country in Europe with such a law for pregnant substance-dependent women (Leppo, 2009).

The background for this legislation is that there is a growing literature showing the adverse effects of intrauterine substance exposure (Helmbrecht & Thiagarajah, 2008; Topley, Windsor, & Williams, 2008; Vucinovic et al., 2008). In Europe, an estimated 30,000 children are born every year to mothers with opiate abuse problems (Gyarmathy, Giraudon, Hedrich, & Wiessing, 2009). For children of mothers with drug abuse, there is a lack of statistics for the numbers born each year with Neonatal Abstinence Syndrome (NAS). The clinical picture of children born with NAS is hypersensitivity to stimuli, motoric unrest, and persistent crying with varying degrees of fever, vomiting, and tremor (Elgen, Bruarøy, & Lægreid, 2007). Internationally, it is estimated that there are between one and four children per two thousand live births who may have Fetal Alcohol Spectrum Disorder (FASD) while in Norway it is estimated that 600 children with FASD are born annually (Alvik, 2007). FASD is presumed to have a prevalence that is ten times higher than Fetal Alcohol syndrome (FAS) alone (Alvik, 2007).

Substance abuse clinics in Norway have established family wards with the twin goals of preventing harm to the fetus when women are pregnant and preventing the development of substance abuse problems in the next generation. The treatment has focused on the parent's internal working models of parenting, how they understand the process of becoming a mother and their potential for the development of attachment to their unborn child (Kristiansen, 2015).

One of the aims in both voluntary and compulsory treatment is to support the mothers in becoming drug-free. While working closely together with the expectant mother, the focus is to ensure an in-utero environment as developmentally optimal as possible for the unborn child. The women are often in a situation in which they must make several great changes in their lives and need support to make room for the expected child both psychologically and practically (Pajulo et al., 2006).

Supervisions Goals and Dilemmas

The women need guidance and help from professional therapists regarding psychological issues as well as in dealing with practical and social perspective.

The focus in supervision with this group of professionals is to explore therapists' experiences regarding pregnant women both in voluntary and compulsory inpatient treatment. The study was also interested in the particular challenges these therapists brought with them into supervision.

Eight therapists working with both voluntarily and compulsorily admitted women participated in group supervision as a part of the project. The therapists had a median age of 45 years (range: 29–61 years), and all worked at inpatient treatment facilities. The team consisted of nurses, midwives, family therapists, child protection workers (educators), and psychologists. Important aims in the supervision were to be open to what the therapists were concerned about, and to explore how they described their understanding and their work with the pregnant substance-abusing women. Which discourses did the therapists draw on in describing pregnant substance-abusing women's experiences of pregnancy? How did they present the necessary preconditions that had to be present in the women and in the women's contexts for them to be able to undergo a pregnancy and to become good enough mothers? In addition, were there any differences between those voluntarily and compulsorily hospitalized as seen from the therapist perspective?

The supervision meetings were based on open questions that emphasized therapists' understandings of how developmental and attachment processes play a role in the treatment processes and how treating the women affected them as therapists and human beings (Willig, 2013).

One key dilemma issue that emerged for the therapist supervisees was whether to work with attachment themes or substance abuse. The following extracts give some sense of the different ways this dilemma was experienced by the therapist supervisees.

> *"If the mother gets to keep the baby or not, attachment is really important for the child and gives what the child needs to become secure around people. So, everything one does from the beginning of life is part of providing the foundation that carries one further through life, whether the child remains with the mother or with others." (Anna, Voluntary staff)*

Attachment—establishing a relation to the child—is important independent of the mother's challenges with substance abuse.

> *"Attachment begins when the fetus is in the womb, the psychological and emotional attachment starts the moment the woman becomes pregnant."*

(Karen, Voluntary staff)

"We see that if they come in early in the pregnancy, the better the odds are for mother and the unborn child." (Elisabeth, Coercive staff)

"It takes a whole village to raise a child" (Anna, Voluntary staff).

"We work quite purposefully to promote the attachment if we think that it can be difficult to achieve, either because you have lost a child before, but there can of course be many reasons that you hold back, we work very purposefully with finding out what it is that's blocking". (Elisabeth, Coercive Staff).

"We are like, raised so that we're happy to give birth to a child" (Ellen, Voluntary staff).

"Everyone has a heavy drug career behind them independent of whether they're admitted coercively or voluntarily, we don't see any difference in that". (Hannah, Coercive staff)

"We see that they struggle to develop an attachment to the expected child. They express that it's difficult because they're afraid that they won't get to take the baby home with them from the hospital. Not in relation to coercive admittance or voluntary, and not if they have lost a child before, they're afraid that the child will be taken from them in the hospital. We see this most clearly in those who've been admitted by force, but all show a fear of it." (Hannah, Coercive staff)

The therapists describe experiencing the women admitted coercively as especially vulnerable and that coercion as a context increases the fear of losing custody of the child. It then becomes especially important to work with attachment. Myra et al. (2016) explored whether coercion as a context influenced attachment to the unborn child from the perspectives of the women. The main finding was how involuntary detention enabled safety for and connection with the unborn child. Those same findings also show that the most significant barrier for their ability to bond with the expected child was the women's own relational experiences and developmental histories. This shows some of the complexity and challenges therapists face. This study showed that women experienced being admitted coercively and in this way to offering security, were able to position themselves to create a relation to the expected child. This speaks against the discourse that coercion as context is more challenging for women in relation to developing an attachment to the unborn child.

The main aim in supervision is to reflect on why we do this work, what meanings our work holds for us, and what power words can have. Supervision offers an opportunity to reaffirm and clarify supervisees' experiences of the meaning of language and power. This means the limits of their own and others power and influence. Both supervisor and supervisee need to interrogate implied and specific ideas and prevalent discourses about what is good practice in supervision and therapy and recognize the limits of our own and others' power and influence.

The supervision of this group shows that the key dilemma therapists experience is between a focus on attachment to the unborn child and work with substance dependency, regardless of whether women are coercively or voluntarily admitted. This issue is complex and must be into the context of supervision, along with the content and structuring of treatment. The focus on women's own relational experiences is not worked with systematically enough. Therapists are most concerned with achieving an attachment relation between the mother and child as they have the idea that this provides the best prognosis for mother and child following the birth.

With regard to the understanding of the relation between mother and child, the therapist drew upon two different attachment-related discourses. The first of these discourses linked attachment to its roots in biological development, while the second considered attachment as a learned pattern, grounded within a psychodynamic understanding. The following extract exemplifies the first type of attachment-related discourse

> *"Attachment is something that begins when the fetus is in the womb, the psychological and emotional attachment starts in the moment the woman becomes pregnant." (Karen, Voluntary staff)*

This illustrates attachment as biological and as a matter of course, something that happens completely by itself. Within this discourse, motherhood and attachment are cultivated as something that simply occurs.

The second type of discourse, that which considers attachment as a learned pattern, can be seen supporting the speaker in this extract:

> *"It's about understanding the seriousness of becoming parents, what they haven't understood themselves they can't pass on, it's OK of course, as long as it's a doll." (Anna, voluntary staff)*

Here a discourse is spoken forth based in the psychodynamic understanding that says something about the relational experience of the individual. What you have not received (experienced) you cannot pass on, and reflect ideas about generational transference of experience (Bowlby, 1998). Even though therapists describe the understanding of generational transference of experiences, this is not included in their descriptions of how they intervene.

In line with this understanding, working with prenatal attachment and psychological mothering as well as parenthood are the most important perspectives of the therapists. This includes working with the reflective capacity of the mothers to give them an opportunity to see their child as a person in his or her own right. The mother–child relationship from pregnancy on is underlined by the following supervisee extract:

> *"Substance abuse wins out over 'the mothering process', but we put the most into what concerns the focus on the child, we have to make space for the child, but also talk about the craving for the high, they show a strong grief over loss of the high, but the focus on the expected child comes first." (Ellen, voluntary staff)*

When they talked about working with substance abuse and abstinence, therapists encountered a dilemma, and they showed how they focused on the women's attachment and relational experiences in the belief that these were the most important issues for preparation for life outside.

Liberating Different Styles in Systemic Supervision: Narrative/Dialogic Perspectives

This writer found significant advantages in using narrative and dialogical perspectives in the supervision of this group of therapist working with this population of substance-abusing pregnant mothers. However, in the effort to open new perspectives for the supervisees on their practice understandings and interventions it was necessary to draw upon particular ideas within the narrative therapy tradition that focused upon the different ways that supervisees can tell the story of their practice activity. Such a perspective on the narrational styles of supervisees draws attention to narrative considered as a process in contrast with its conception as a completed product (Sheehan, 1999).

Sheehan (1999) claims that the problem for the systemic therapist or supervisor utilizing a narrative perspective comes from at least two sources: the first concerns the use of metaphors such as "authorship" in a way that tie it too closely to fictional narrative and risks fostering an illusion of control for narrators in therapy and supervision that remains the preserve of the fictional author; the second source of difficulty comes from an approach to narration that limits its meaning to that of a contributory function to narrative as a completed product at the expense of a focus on narrative as process, which seems to permit more attention to be given to the indeterminacies and freedom attaching to narrated events whatever their context. Safeguarding freedom within therapeutic or supervisory dialogue requires a de-emphasis on narrative as product in favor of narrative as process. Sheehan (1999) pointed out that resources for approaching this challenge could be found in certain concepts from literary theory. Elements from Bakthin (1991) and Morson (1994) are here used to illustrate some of these ideas raised by Sheehan (1999) primarily in the context of systemic therapy and developed in this chapter for the context of supervision.

By using Bakthin's (1981) frame of multi-voices, the therapist/supervisee can share their different voices and, in this way, create new understandings from multiple perspectives. In this way, the supervision can create possibilities that open a space in which different voices can be heard. By allowing the team to share their thoughts and ideas, one opens to a further level of multi-voicedness that provides the opportunity to view a dilemma from several sides and to view other alternatives.

This multi-voicedness can respond positively to the complexity therapist's face and can open up a greater range of choice and thereby freedom, in the context of relatively fixed intervention strategies that may block new opportunities and perspectives. The opportunity to tell and retell, as well hearing different perspectives of others on the team, gives the supervisee freedom to develop their understanding of practice events and to speak about them in a new way. Providing space for a multi-voiced dialogue with accounts of the golden moments creates space for several voices and several stories being released and heard. Such a listening space creates the atmosphere in which none of the many voices have the last word, but all have an opportunity to be heard, expressed, commented upon, confirmed, deconstructed, reconstructed, and put into context.

Morson (1994) described the different ways that fictional authors have of telling about events in time. His concern was with the way these different approaches either expanded or contracted the sense of freedom, possibility and contingency available to the actors within the events being told. He used the concept of "shadows" to illuminate the way different narrational approaches affected these variables. "Foreshadowing" and "back shadowing" were two literary devices used by narrators which conferred upon time a sense of closure. In the first of these two concepts, events in the present are being bound to occur in the way they do because of events to come. Sheehan (1999) explains that foreshadowing involves a type of backward causation in which a future event already exists in some sense, and casts a sign back in a causative way on the present and makes it happen (p. 60). In contrast, "back shadowing" is a kind of foreshadowing after the fact. In backshadowing, the past is treated as if it inevitably had to lead to the present we now know. Both foreshadowing and backshadowing reveal types of narrational style which close down time, give a sense of time moving in an entirely linear way at the same time as reducing any sense of the contingency attaching to narrated events. Morson uses the term "sideshadowing" to describe those narrational devices that contribute strongly to the sense of openness, contingency, and freedom. When events are narrated using this literary device, Morson tells us that the telling, "casts a shadow from the side", that is, from the other possibilities (p. 118). In sideshadowing, he suggests, two or more alternative presents, the actual and the possible, are made simultaneously visible. In other words, within this type of narrational style we construct around each actualized past a haze of others possibilities, other things that could have happened or been done, each with their own potential. In the following paragraphs, I will look at how the supervisor can ask certain kinds of questions in supervision, questions "that cast a shadow from the side" (Sheehan, 1999, p. 63), in the interest of expanding possibilities for supervisees in the context of their practice with this vulnerable group of substance-abusing pregnant mothers. The reader will note the use of the words "other", "might," and "different" in the questions used as indicators of contingency and possibility.

Questions that can be asked that have the possibility of freeing a therapist from the grip of a single perspective and a single intervention strategy: What other intervention could have been possible, apart from the one you chose? Focusing on attachment to the unborn child versus working with substance dependence? Questions about the golden moments: What might have happened if you had had a conversation with the women about their own relational experiences? Questions about the future: What different kinds of things do you think you can talk about next time you meet Amanda? Theoretical consequences of applying thinking around multi-voicedness and dialogue can contribute to overthrowing the strict dividing lines between different theories and discourses and give opportunities to reopen dialogue between professionals with different perspectives who belong to different disciplines. Bakthin (1981) claims that the core of this approach is that it opens for and increases accessibility to the sides of a person's life that would not have emerged in the same way in a monological position. Through telling our stories, we can become conscious of the role of culture in creating the advice given, and can see dominant discourses. Consciousness around how one's own cultural context produces preferences in relation to our choice of one view over another, as something more actual than something else, and so forth.

How to Create Space That Opens

How the stories are told can lead to closing or opening. When a therapist in supervision tells his or her story, the desire is often to be understood; one tries to speak in a way that suggests reason and possibly to legitimate what one has done and thought. This structure can lead to the closing of the story. Things have been legitimated and do not require any other perspectives. What kinds of experiences could such an organization of supervision have? It could introduce and underline the deterministic challenge that establishes the unavoidable fact that the intervention/event had to be the way it was, there was no way to do it otherwise, it had to be like this. The meaning of what happened is communicated, and the story establishes a meaning for the storyteller. We always look for meaning/what things mean. It is in this understanding of meaning that we must understand that one and the same event can be accounted for in different ways, strengthened by different values and characteristics that give meaning and which become meaning-bearing for us. It further presents us with a picture of time as relatively closed. The account with the actual event told in a logical order is an account constructed in an open picture dominated by events/activities set logically into connection and spread out in time (Sheehan, 1999). By observing narrational styles, we can focus on whether an account closes too early, the nuances and eventualities, freedoms, and choices. Accounts that open connect to past–present and future as revealing greater freedom and choice options that exceed the deterministic accounting form that closes out new and different perspectives, and this is a useful perspective to take along for the one who supervises.

Opening for multi-voicedness in supervision of therapists within different disciplines is about establishing the dialogical character of all account-making, and the creativity connected to an account/narrative considered as part of a dialogical process rather than a completed product. In Dostojevsky's novels (Bakthin, 1984), life is composed of several independent and unblended voices and consciousness, with the same rights, each with its own reality, bound together (without being mixed) through events within a whole. In as far as life is structured, it is structured through dialogues rather than through monologues. Creativity is found in the multi-voiced dialogue. The co-creation of accounts has a processual character, that is to say that it goes on in the form of a process that invites us to emphasize the account as a process in itself that can be viewed as supporting possibilities for alternatives and redefinition (Bakthin, 1984).

In this way, this approach offers a way to reflect upon why we do this work, the meanings our work holds for us and how these meanings may have changed over time. The supervision group may be the only context where there is the time and the safety for these reflections. Through this approach, we can reaffirm and clarify supervisees' experiences in therapy.

> "*The high wins out over the mothering process, but we put the most into this about focusing on the child, we have to give space for the child, but also talk about cravings, they show a strong grief over loss of the high. However, focus on the unborn child comes first.*" (*Ellen, voluntary staff*)

Having a focus on attachment processes makes problems surrounding substance dependence fall into the background. Therapists describe the dilemma between helping women to attach themselves to the expected child and focusing on the substance dependence. The supervisees show that work with attachment to the unborn child "wins" in therapists' belief that this will provide the best prognosis for mother and child in the long run. Discourses therapists speak illustrate the idea that, if the pregnant woman establishes an attachment to the unborn child, the prognosis for mother and child following birth is good (Bowlby, 1988).

The major dilemma the supervisees experienced was one between focus on attachment to the unborn child and work with substance dependency. This issue is complex and must be taken into supervision. Working with prenatal attachment and psychological mothering as well as parenthood is the focus. Other important foci, such as working with the substance abuse came in the shadow of working with attachment processes, such as the experience of substance craving as stronger than motherhood.

Conclusion

This chapter has tried to highlight and draw attention to certain challenges that the therapist encounters when working with pregnant substance-abusing women in voluntary and compulsory treatment, and to how supervision can assist with these. The therapists' dilemmas are illustrated by their different voices of concern in their work with pregnant substance abusers. The chapter has attempted to offer different perspectives on the dilemmas therapists meet. By using Bakthin (1981) frame of multi-voices, the supervisee has an opportunity to listen to different approaches. In this way, the supervision can create possibilities that open for a space in which different voices can be heard. This can take away some of the responsibility that each therapist feels and relieve them of the feeling of having to choose between the focus on attachment processes or working with substance abuse problems. The awareness of being able to focus on both issues and more, and to how talking together about how and when, could be an important opening that creates new understanding and that opens new opportunities in therapeutic work with pregnant substance abusers.

References

Alvik, A. (2007). *Alcohol use before, during and after pregnancy: A population based study in Oslo, Norway*. Doctoral dissertation, University of Oslo.

Bakthin, M.M. (1981). *The dialogic imagination* (M. Holquist & C. Emerson, Trans.). Austin, TX: University of Texas Press.

Bakthin, M. (1984). Problems of Dostojuvskys poetics, ed. and trans C. Emerson. Minneapolis, M.N: University of Minnesota Press.

Bakthin, M. (1991). Dostojuvskijs poetick. Stockholm: Anthropos.

Bowlby, J. (1998). *A secure base. Parent–child attachment and healthy human development*. London: Routledge.

Bowlby, J. (1988). A secure base: clinical applications of attachment theory. London: Routledge.

Elgen, I., Bruarøy, S., & Lægreid, L. M. (2007). Lack of recognition and complexity of foetal alcohol neuroimpairments.*ActaPaediatrica, 96*,1–5.https://doi.org/10.1111/j.1651-2227.2007.00026-x.

Gyarmathy, V. A., Giraudon, I., Hedrich, D., & Wiessing, L. (2009). Drug use and pregnancy—Challenges for public health. *Euro Surveillance, 14*, 33–36.

Grella, C. E., Joshi, V., & Hser, Y. I. (2000). Program variation in treatment outcomes among women in residential drug treatment. *Evaluation Review, 24*(4), 364–383. PubMed. https://doi.org/10.1177/0193841x000 2400 402.

Helmbrecht, G. D. & Thigarajah, S. (2008). Management of addiction disorders in pregnancy. *Journal of addiction medicine, 2*, 1–16.

Kristiansen, R. (2015) *Gravide innlagt på Borgestadklinikken*—Norway. ISBN 978-82-999733-4-2.

Leppo, A. (2009). Illusionen om enkla lösninger [The illusion of simple solutions]. *Nordic Studies on Alcohol and Drugs, 26*, 314–317.

Mayes, L., & Truman, S. (2002). *Substance abuse and parenting*. In M. Bornstein (Ed.), *Handbook of parenting, Vol 4. Social conditions and applied parenting* (Vol. 2, pp. 329–359). Mahwah, NJ: Lawrence Erlbaum Associates.

Myra, S. M., Ravndal, E., Wie Torsteinson, V., & Wiig, E. M. (2016). Pregnant substance-abusing women in involuntary treatment: Attachment experiences with the unborn child. *Nordic Studies on Alcohol and Drugs, 33*(3). doi:https://doi.org/10.1515/nsad-2016-0023.

Morson, G. S. (1994). *Narrative and freedom; The shadows of time*. New Haven, CT: Yale University Press.

Pajulo, M. (2001). Early Motherhood at Risk: mothers with substance dependency. Turun Yliopiston Julka Isuja. Sarja D, ISSN 0355-9483. Medica- Odontologica.

Pajulo, M., Suchman, N., Kalland, M., & Mayes, L. (2006). Enhancing the effectiveness of residential treatment for substance abusing pregnant and parenting women: Focus on maternal reflective functioning and mother-child relationship. *Infant Mental Health Journal, 27*(5), 448. https://doi.org/10.1002/imhj.20100.

Sheehan, J. (1999). Liberating narrational styles in systemic practice. *Journal of Systemic Therapies, 18*(3), 1999.

Suchman, N. E., McMahon, T. J., Slade, A., & Luthar, S. S. (2005). How early bonding, depression, illicit drug use and perceived support work together to influence drug dependent mothers caregiving. *American Journal of Orthopsychiatry, 75*(3), 431–445. PMC free article PubMed. https://doi.org/10.1037/0002-9432.75.3.431.

Søvig, K. H. (2004). *Tvang overfor rusmiddelavhengige: Sosialtjenesteloven§§ 6-2 til 6-3* [Coercion against pregnant women with substance addiction]. Bergen: Fagbokforlaget.

Topley, J., Windsor, D., & Williams, R. (2008). Behavioral, developmental *and* child protection outcomes following exposure to Class A Drugs in pregnancy. *Child: Care, Health and Development, 34*, 71–76. https://doi.org/10.1111/j.1365-2214.2007.00768.x.

Vucinovic, M., Roje, D., Vucinovic, Z., Capkun, V., Bucat, M. & Banovic, I. (2008). Maternal and neonatal effects of substance abuse during pregnancy: over ten-years experience. *Yonsei Medical Journal, 49*, 705–713.

Willig, C. (2013). *Introducing qualitative research in psychology*. New York: McGraw-Hill.

Chapter 12
Group Supervision with Couple Therapists Located in Rural Areas in Norway: Exploring Memories, Bodily Sensations and the Richness of a Non-linear Language

Anne Kyong Sook Øfsti

Introduction

In this chapter, I will share some experiences from supervising couple therapists living in "rural areas". My aim is to describe supervision processes, which hopefully might inspire supervisors and therapists to explorethe potentials of connecting various forms of knowledge —to become a wiser wise. It is not remarkable. It is just about travelling, moving, being an explorer. It is about listening, to oneself and to the others, the team, and bringing in some alternative perspectives. It is like making food together or playing music. The richness is in the ingredients, the voices, the instruments, the accords available, and the time invested.

Traveling with the Early Morning Train

I often travel by train. It is a truly blissful moment, these early mornings, when it is still quite dark, and I am drinking my first sip of coffee. The window seat is available and the train compartment is like a warm, safe cottage, smelling of people's early morning preparations.

These past 10 years, I have had the privilege of visiting several family therapy guidance centres, with the more open and exploratory tasks of "We need to get inspired. Make us wiser and more sensitive as couples therapists". I hold these three

A.K.S. Øfsti (✉)
Family Therapy Section, Faculty of Social Studies, VID Specialized University, Oslo, Norway
e-mail: annekyoungsook.ofsti@vid.no

A. Vetere, J. Sheehan (eds.), *Supervision of Family Therapy and Systemic Practice*, Focused Issues in Family Therapy, https://doi.org/10.1007/978-3-319-68591-5_12

concepts in mind: *inspired, wiser and sensitive,* and this is the reason why I continue travelling. I am humble and proud and of course a bit timid at being invited since these concepts touch a nerve for me. They have high stakes, as I recognise them for myself as a true nourishment for my own practice as a therapist, teacher, writer and supervisor.

The family therapy offices, in which I have offered supervision, have in common that they are located in rural areas. The physical space of the Family Therapy Guidance centre is commonly placed beside the Church, the School, the Administration and the Hospital. Some of them are old-fashioned houses built in timber with cute cotton curtains and fireplaces, while others are modern styled with fancy interiors in steel, which convey a minimalistic impression of influence.

The train has left Oslo. When I am looking out of the window I enjoy waiting for daylight to come. This is Norway. The nature and the landscape changes. I am always excited by the varied scenery. The richness in the Norwegian environment is special. Sometimes I arrive at villages lying by the open sea, with the slight salt smell of ocean and seaweed in the air. Other times it is open fields with green acres and pinewood. I have even been at small places up in the mountains, where it is nearly impossible to arrive by train or bus, and the leader in the Family Therapy Office must pick me up in his or her private car.

Truly, I am interested in this question; how does nature, and the varied landscape impact, form or even suppress people's lives differently? Will the deep, dark forest shape your mind set, your emotions and practices differently than the wide, wild sea? Moreover, how does living in rural areas form relationships, families and intimacy?

Several myths about life in rural districts exist, in folklores, literature, in the media, and among people. One of them is that people care about each other in small communities. Life is transparent: everyone knows each other and one is supposed to live a healthy life in close connection with nature. Another one is that living in small communities is and must be, experienced as too constricting: there is little room for being otherwise, and if you diverge from the valid norms, it can lead to isolation and discrimination. Still, one thing might be clear; Norwegians are nostalgic, their collective soul longs for narratives about the authentic life out in the rural district. The idea about the Man in the forest, self-supported, by the growth from the soil, and fishing from the surrounding coastline, is alive.

The Rural Therapist

As the caffeine drifts in the body and the train is approaching the destination, I start preparing by tuning myself into the process. How is the preparation process different and similar from teaching, and from doing couple therapy? Teaching offers subjects, such as Discursive Couple Therapy, Emotion Focused Therapy, models and thinking in Attachment Adult Therapy, among others. The preparation process when teaching expects me to update myself on research and literature. When doing couple therapy, I usually have some timeout to start an inner dialogue. When it is to be the first time I meet a couple, I try to imagine how it might be for them to come. I am gearing up my curiosity, how it is to be them, what has happened now since they have decided to come. What are their values and sorrows? When I have already met the couple, I reflect upon what has happened since our last meeting, how are they, each person and together. What kind of new dialogues, intimacies or hostilities have they experienced?

When supervising, I am more open, more playful and attentive to the group that I shall meet. What do I know about being a therapist in the countryside? How do I connect with the experiences of living in rural districts? The therapists often have a kind of communal continuity, they or their partner might have parents or close relatives near by, or they might have moved out of cities for the values of family and child raising. As the community is more transparent, the couple therapist often knows the couple beforehand and even perhaps the couple's families and relatives. What is more, the clients can turn out to be their neighbours, their GPs, and the man who works in the groceries shop. Even if the therapists deal with these networks as best they can, by avoiding taking acquaintances on as clients, they might have the experience that their new hairdresser or the teacher of their children has been a former client.

These thoughts work as a backscreen when I tune myself into the supervision waiting ahead.

Approaching the Building

Especially on the cold, pale winter days, it is a relief to enter the Family Therapy Guidance Centre. The smell of coffee, and the sound of chatting from the meeting room sounds familiar. It is a quarter to nine and the therapists mingle and drink hot drinks.

I find a comfortable chair and a cup of black coffee. As I am sitting and listening to the therapists, and their colleagues who work in the office, before the supervision starts, I remember when I worked on a daily basis as a therapist. I often wondered: How does the night before, the quality of sleep, and the dreams affect and influence our meeting with the couples. And even more thought-provoking, how have the early morning hours, alone or with family members, a lover or children impact on the therapists? When meeting couples and families, the therapist has already experienced the beginning of a day, as bodily sensations, as uneasiness, stress and sadness, or with joy, playfulness, happiness, and self-confidence. Do we listen, do we pay attention to the therapist's intimate, everyday environment? How does a marital quarrel influence the therapist when meeting a couple? Do they experience a possible vulnerability? Or will a playful time with a child, in the morning, shed light in particular ways into the therapy room?

Hosting Themes

In my Doctorate, "Some Call it Love" (Øfsti, 2008), initially I was interested in Norwegian couple therapists' love images. What kinds of archetypical images were they bearing in my mind when couples asked them, *what is love? How do we know that this is love—or what do we do, when one feels love has gone?* The research process led me from a phenomenological approach to a more discursive one as I ended up looking at different discourses at play in therapy. One of my main findings was that the therapist's significant implicit knowledge sources stem from movies, novels and their own life experiences such as memories. Another finding was that existential and ethical questions and knowledge engaged the couple and the therapist. These questions were more at stake, such as, *Can a person continue in a relationship when one feels love has gone* or … and the textbook and curriculum does not necessarily theorise that. So I came to an important insight that within the field of couple therapy there is a lot attention paid to the knowledge borrowed from the language of poetics and memories, and media and discourses, besides the models and theories of psychology.

Having these discoveries in mind, the supervision has been more about exploring the couple therapist's *self*, their connection to each other as a team, and their individual and common knowledge sources. A reservoir of inspiration, along with the commitment to practice and the exercise of transparency, enlarge and enrich narratives about the issues and blurred borders between issues in couple therapy and themes in everyday life.

An Open Window, Setting the Tune, Offering a Voice and a Listening Position

The Beginning of the Day

It has evolved as a tradition: for 1 h, I have the privilege to speak freely for 60 min about issues that I am interested in, *for the time being*. Sometimes (and especially when I was new to the group) those 60 min took the form of a teaching session about a concrete theme, for example, *"What is discursive couple therapy"*? or *"How to work systemically with gender issues, and/or sexual problems in couple therapy"*?

After a while I began to explore and investigate issues which were not clearly methodological, i.e. in pointing to ways of doing things in more "linear" skill-based ways. Rather, I started to talk like an outsider, a guest, invited to share some thoughts, reflections, questions, myths and enigmas and in a more existential approach. I am freely picking from not yet finished thoughts and questions that interest me, at the present time. I do not prepare these 60 min by writing a text beforehand. Rather, the tuning-in process happens on the train, it takes its shape while traveling along, away from my ordinary duties and tasks. The distance and the movement releases and activates thoughts that have been slumbering. And we must not forget the privilege of someone waiting for your thoughts, and appreciating the *philosophical small talk* in the early morning. I get ideas which I play out in this hour of open talk. The thinking behind this is to look for relevant meanings and ideas in the traces that are not so clear, or in the random sidewalks.

Sometimes I read some lines from a novel, or I play a clip from a movie, from You Tube, or I play a piece of music. Or I might pop questions and issues like:

How do we cope with uncertainty?

What have we learned about alternative processes of healing, what we might call unnatural?

How do we nourish ourselves as couple and family therapists?

Growing Together as a Team, Exploring a Non-linear Language

Since the team size varies from 3 and up to a maximum of 15 , it is an opportunity to hold the group with all present, including the leader and sometimes also the people who work in the administration. Professional and personal growth is only possible in a safe space. For me as an outsider, I am aware of the different and possible vulnerable inequalities. First of all, if there are some conflicts in the team, we need to have a talk about the process of supervision. Where, when and how will the conflicts be taken care of? And, what needs to be said about the conflict, so the supervision can be fruitful and inspiring? This is because personal and professional growth is difficult to realise in a threating and hostile atmosphere.

Secondly, we negotiate the contract: all the structures and exercises, are in an open, un-demanding, and non-evaluating format. This means that each member of the group is free in what they want to share, and how. I am clear that the supervision processes are not some covert modus of "adjusting" the therapists to be and act in certain ways. I do not accept hidden agendas from leaders: *Please make him or her, more prepared to self-disclose, or get this particular therapist to finally talk openly about her Achilles' heel.*

After the morning "speech" ends, the team works together, often picking up, and weaving in threads and themes from what I have already hosted. After listening, the therapists are eager to connect to their own experience, impulses and thoughts. The team reflections are rich, personal, intuitive and often come with the relief of a tone of "irreverence". Continuing in the spirit of exploring implicit knowledge, the therapists are invited to bring with them issues from their recent meetings with couples. Often, therapists express acute need: *What can I do with them, what should I do with him, since he is so angry at her. I am getting lost. It is such a difficult couple, and so on...* I attempt to resist the impulse to rush in as a first aid person, to assist the therapist with solutions, or pedagogical questions, and to help the therapist to cope. Rather I, invite the team into the mood and thinking, how can the team, possibly develop a wider and extended understanding, using the case as a challenge, more like an existential and relational enigma. Sometimes we work like we play "detectives", inspired from the crime, where the crime, is life itself, when it seems to be demanding and unfair:

Nina and Paul. A married couple, been together since they were 20 and now they both were in their early 50s. They have two children. Nina has had breast cancer, and Paul has been supportive, and solid as a rock, through her recovering process. Now Nina wants a divorce.

Around the table, the team members are invited to share their gut feelings. Each therapist is free to explore and to get responses to questions—just so we enrichen our non-linear language and our linguistic repertoire.

Turns Around the Table

What is recognisable? What is to be understood? What do they want to share from a witness position (and not from an expert position)?
How do we approach ideas we already think we are familiar with, to widen up the known?
What kinds of questions are not asked, yet?
What can we say to clients, to express an alliance with the nonaddressable, the unclear and the ambiguous.
What kind of formulations offer safeness, trust and support, without taking (stealing) the uneasiness and conflicts from the clients?

Growing Together as a Team: Working with Life Scripts

Often, clients ask: *is this normal?* Is this a normal, reaction, emotion and/or practice?

In exploring implicit knowledge and making it explicit, we make our expectations, norms and values transparent. The notion of normal stays in relation to abnormal or marginal. What informs us about normal are the cultural and familiar discourses and life scripts. A life script is a time-line that prescribes what a person should do, and when. For instance, a heteronormative life script can be described as certain bus stops, which a well-functioning individual should stop by, in her lifeway. For instance, a woman is expected to get a partner of the opposite gender in the midst of her 20s, marry at 30, give children (2, 3) between 30 and 40, administrate the task of carrier, for the children's needs and care, till the children move out, and then waiting for the grandchildren to come.

In Norway, and perhaps, particularly in rural areas, this is a distinct yielding script.

Drawing lifetime scripts for themselves helps make the therapists aware of expectations and their own positioning regarding processes of normal and margin, for example, *How come that my timeline is so normal—or how is it to realises that I am not following the track?*

We have had fruitful dialogues about whether the expectations are different for people living in the rural areas rather than in the capital or big cities, where you can to a certain degree hide from being observed. And, we work with genograms and family myths—and have dialogues that look at how each therapist's family myths, influence how the therapist's sense and reflect on values, ideas and terms when they meet the various forms of being couples and families in therapy.

Growing Together as a Team: Working with Memories to Explore Implicit Tactile Knowledge

Another pleasure in supervising the rural therapists with this common understanding of the joy of exploratory approaches is that I have had possibilities to introduce and do Memory Work. The memory workshops, mainly inspired from Frigga Haug, are a source in which to grasp implicit, personal and cultural knowledge and make it available as a therapeutic repertoire. Originally these workshops were designed for feminist research, and when I read about them, I wanted to employ the models and thinking within supervision. Memory work is text work beyond conventional narrative analysis (Crawford, Kippax, Onyx, Gault, & Benton, 1992). A theoretical prerequisite for the work with memory is the assumption that we know much more about ourselves than we normally assume. Many things have been censored out of our self-image because we deem them not essential, too painful, or too chaotic.

The Memory Workshop Process

Memory work needs a memory: I present a theme, in a common language to which everyone can relate, such as; *A time when I was afraid; A Christmas Eve I never forget; When I heard my parents quarrel; and My first school day.*

As a trigger point (helping the memory to wake up) I play something from You Tube (The opening scene from the Hour) or I play music (Fairest Lord Jesus) or I read a text.

The Remembered Scene

Then, the memory will be written down by the therapists, following a structure, inspired by a discursive, narrative model which again stems from feministic memory work. In memory work participants are advised to use the third-person form of narration, since the choice of third-person narration both distancing the narrator and contextualises the narrative as historical—which is then useful for the discussion afterwards. It is important that it is a memory of an experience, an event, or a scene that may be written. Sequences or biographical stories should be avoided. During the writing, some therapists prefer to sit in group, writing down their individual memories, and sometimes they choose to sit by themselves in their offices and write down the memory. For practical reasons, they are asked to write no more than one to two pages.

The Collective as a Process

It is such an atmosphere of concentration when the group is gathered and the therapists are reading aloud, each of their memories. It is like being read to when we were children, and being introduced to a magnificent world. After reading aloud, the procedure of memory work starts with deciding which memory (one or two, dependent on time available)—will be the "research" material. The chosen memories are copied, distributed and are analysed as text.

We use a whiteboard as we often use that when working with exploring meaning. Several questions are posed and explored very much like a discourse analysis. For example, what is the meaning that the "author" wishes to convey? By picking and writing this memory, the author might say something *about being in the world, about being vulnerable.*

Further we look for "common sense" statements, for example, like women should avoid meeting strangers in the dark? Or, you must know that you can be punished as a child by grown-ups if you do something you know is wrong. Then we analyse elements in the language: we look at verbs, we write up every verb on the whiteboard and look at activity, passivity and how many times the different verbs occur. It gives information about the engaged person, their emotions and values. We look for how emotions are expressed by linguistic peculiarities. In addition, we write up the absence and presence of others in the memory (where is the father in the Christmas Eve memory?), and vacuum, contradictions and constructions of I, and constructions and of others in the text. Then we talk about how all these linguistic elements are drawing on social, cultural discourses, as well as therapeutic knowledge. Sometimes, we rewrite the memory, after a collective analysis, and that is quite interesting.

The memory work is all about understanding the construction of meaning and it is a process which becomes emotional, fun and interesting, and after the workshop, the feedback is that the group learns to know each other and themselves in more depth, and the resources which exist in the group, are more visible and accessible.

The Train, the Trip Back and a Resonance

Going back, in the evening, after 1 or 2 days in the countryside, I get on the train and I am tired. It keeps surprising me, the strange feeling I recognise: my body is satisfied like after a long run, my mind is exhausted, as if I have been at the airport, with lots of different languages. The paradox is that when I am left Oslo two days ago, my mind is as quiet as a silent wood landscape, and when returning my mind is full of sounds. But I am also fulfilled. The gift, or the privilege which lies in the possibility to create a meeting, to facilitate processes with no explicit aims of an outspoken efficacy or preformed value standard, is so valuable. Living in a time where therapy and couple therapy too often may be restricted to reporting in forms of quantity statistics (how many couples do you meet through a day) and due to evidence-based research methods, some therapists experience fatigue. They ask themselves, what happened with my unique longing to be trained as a therapist and working with issues and questions that really matter. So, as I am heading back, I am full of impressions. It is like I have been wandering in my inner landscape, searching for meaning.

The train is approaching Oslo. A couple is sitting in front of me. I cannot avoid listening.

He*: I don't like you going out, drinking some beers with this new guy at your office. I know you, something is going on.*

She*: I am so sick and tired of you controlling me. Can't you trust me? If I say we are only friends, why don't you believe me? Is it not allowed in our relationship to get new acquaintances?*

And I open my mobile and write down: Next Supervision: *How do we understand jealousy and what repertoires are available to explore it?* And then I am getting off the train, and in my head I am planning what to make for dinner.

References

Crawford, J., Kippax, S., Onyx, J., Gault, U., & Benton, P. (1992). *Emotion and gender: Constructing meaning from memory*. London: Sage.

Øfsti, A. K. S. (2008). *Some call it love: Exploring Norwegian systemic couple therapists' discourses of love, intimacy and sexuality*. London: University of East London.

Chapter 13
Research Supervision

Arlene Vetere and Jim Sheehan

Doing research can be life changing. It can shift our world view, open up opportunities, promote new significant relationships and sometimes even contribute to them ending. Our relationship with our research supervisor is often one of the most significant and formative relationships in our professional life. This chapter is concerned with postgraduate research supervision at Masters, Professional Doctorate and Ph.D. level. In our experience, the quality of the research process and of our research dissertation can hinge on the presence, or otherwise, of a trusting and well-grounded relationship with our research supervisor. We echo Bell's (2005) conviction of the importance for the student researcher of establishing a good working relationship with their research supervisor. The researcher, experienced or inexperienced, who 'goes it alone' and succeeds in producing quality research is the exception rather than the rule. This is why it puzzles us that there is relatively little written about the research supervision relationship. Is it that the role, relationship and activity of research supervision is somehow taken for granted? Is it because the relationship is often housed in an institution of higher education that the wisdom from supervision in the helping professions does not penetrate or even seem relevant? Or is it that the supervision process underpinning a postgraduate research project becomes overshadowed by the student achievement of their individual award? Both of us have supervised higher education practitioner research for many years, alongside our supervision practice with trainee and experienced psychotherapists. It seems clear to us that there are many overlaps between the two domains of supervision and that both need a secure base of trust for effective problem solving within the context of ongoing professional development.

A. Vetere (✉) • J. Sheehan
Family Therapy Section, Faculty of Social Studies, VID Specialized University, Oslo, Norway
e-mail: drarlenevetere@hotmail.com; jimssheehan@outlook.com

A. Vetere, J. Sheehan (eds.), *Supervision of Family Therapy and Systemic Practice*, Focused Issues in Family Therapy, https://doi.org/10.1007/978-3-319-68591-5_13

Triangular Relationships

In systemic theory, the basic relationship is understood as a triangle, i.e. when any two people get together, their relationship is influenced by their separate relationships with a common third person (Dallos & Vetere, 2012). There are multiple interlocking triangles at play during the research process: our relationship with our research question and with our main supervisor; our relationship with our research participants, especially during the intensity of qualitative interviewing, and our research supervisor; our relationship with our main supervisor and our university of registration; our relationship with our research and our close family members; our relationship with our research and the research of our postgraduate colleagues; and so on. For example, in university-based research supervision at doctoral level there is now a requirement for at least two supervisors, so the research student is working in an actual triangle, and the common wish is that this functions as a stable triangle. We have probably all had experience in an unstable triangle, where one of us is caught in a loyalty bind with the other two, i.e. if you please one, you displease the other; or where we form a stable alliance with one against the other, and so on. The presence of such unstable triangles within the research process creates a ground of anxiety on which student research projects must be completed. The research community can sometimes be competitive, and the responsibility of the institution that registers the Ph.D. student is to require that the student does not get caught up in conflicts between the supervisors. If this should happen, the student is not always sufficiently empowered to seek external advice and help, and to seek alternative supervision arrangements. For this reason, the department or faculty needs to monitor the supervision arrangements and the wellbeing of both the student and the supervisor within those arrangements. In our experience, where such monitoring of supervision arrangements by senior faculty are routinely built in to the research supervisory process there is a greater likelihood that difficulties in the supervisory relationship can be identified and addressed at the earliest possible opportunity. Such 'servicing' of the supervisory relationship can be the best guarantor of supervisory continuity for both the student and their project.

We do not wish to suggest that research supervision arrangements are often problematic, because in our experience, they are mostly supportive and creative, with an enduring impact on our adult development. Conflict though is unavoidable, in the sense that difference will always exist. For the most part these differences are growth enhancing and in an environment of trust, we are encouraged to be curious and to explore difference and newness, and importantly to take intellectual risks. However, at Masters level, there may well be only one supervisor. This can create an intensity at times that is difficult for both supervisees and supervisors to manage. Where there might be disagreement or conflict, the triangle of support needs to be actualised. The third perspective in the triangle may be taken up by a colleague through formal consultation, or by other students in informal and peer arrangements. We always both create and encourage opportunities for students to participate in learning groups organised around a shared research methodology or topic, and where they give and receive feedback, mutual support, share resources and audit each others' research analyses.

One way of moderating the intensity of the supervisory relationship at Masters level occurs through the provision of a clear set of guidelines for the conduct of the relationship. These guidelines might cover such matters as the frequency and number of supervisory meetings, how supervisory meetings may be called, how communication should take place outside of such meetings, the timing of supervisor feedback on a trainee's dissertation chapter drafts, whether there should be a short written summary of the main points arising from each supervisory meeting, and so on. Such guidelines often provide a little safety for student and supervisor as they set off on what is essentially a two-person voyage. They are not meant to 'strait-jacket' the relationship. For the most part we find that once a student and supervisor have engaged well with each other and with the unique project being undertaken guidelines fade into the background and the relationship finds its own inner regulation based upon a shared commitment, albeit from different perspectives, to the successful completion of the project. And, we should add, the relationship often becomes energised through a shared enjoyment of the work!

Our Relationship to Research

A Masters level student may have joined the programme straight from an undergraduate degree, with a view to engaging in practitioner training afterwards. Here though we wish to write about working with Masters level students who are currently practitioner trained, perhaps at diploma or undergraduate level, who undertake a further professional training that requires Masters level academic work and a research dissertation. There may be some in the training group who have been away from academic study for many years, and/or who may have had very little research experience. Also, as postgraduate family therapy training programs broaden the number and variety of entry routes through which training can be approached, it is likely that any cohort of trainees will contain within it professionals with greatly varying prior relationships to research. For some students, it may be their first experience of undertaking a research project. Others may have done a research project within their prior discipline-of-origin training but such projects may have been very different from that required by their current Masters level training in family and couple therapy. No matter what the student's prior research experience is they will need to know about the standard required of projects being undertaken within their specific program. Indeed, one of the more important functions performed by the research supervisor within the supervisory relationship is that of a gatekeeper of standards.

We begin the process of research engagement for students with reflective activities that invite consideration of their previous experiences with research, their own and/or others (Dallos & Vetere, 2005). Some might have participated in colleagues' research endeavours, for example. The barriers to clinicians' involvement in research are well known, to include: too little time, long waiting lists and other pressures of working life, and concern that the research question has little applied and practical relevance to their client communities (Sandberg, Johnson, Robia, & Miller, 2002). We continue the activity by exploring their beliefs and prejudices, both positive and negative, about research, and what role they think research has in systemic therapeutic practice. We ask them to think of some research that has had a personal impact on them, and why, for example, physical health and/or nutrition research, smoking cessation, and so on. Finally, we ask the students to discuss what criteria they use to judge the usefulness of the research they mentioned. We find that this activity clears the way to speak openly about any worries or fears in relation to research performance and for us to offer reassurance and make clear that the research journey is not intended to be a lonely one!

While the Ph.D. or Doctoral level research project can, as we note in the following section, occupy a time period between 4 and 6 years, the Masters level project usually occupies a much shorter time period which can be anything from 9 to 18 months. Depending upon the way that a particular Masters level program is constructed students may be completing other elements of their Masters program at the same time as undertaking and completing their research project. Hence the Masters level research supervisor is usually working in a highly pressured context where students, who are usually in employment and often making a reasonable effort to maintain some presence as a parent and partner in the context of their family life, are chasing different deadlines concurrently. The stressful nature of the bubble students find themselves in can be increased by the timing of promotional opportunities in the workplace where they may be required to have achieved an award in order to be an eligible applicant for more senior positions.

The Masters level research supervisor, then, can expect to work within contexts that are often, but not always, marked by pressure, stress and anxiety. By comparison with Doctoral level research supervision the exercise can often feel more like a long sprint rather than a marathon. This means that there is a shorter period of time in which things can go right or wrong and shorter windows of time to correct things should they go wrong. In some universities the missing of submission dates can mean students incurring additional fees prior to program completion. In the midst of these stressful contexts, it is still our experience that most supervisory relationships at Masters level work satisfactorily for both students and supervisors. Notwithstanding this experience there are two particular student styles of engagement at Masters level that supervisors need to take careful account of. The first is the student style which is overly demanding of supervisory assistance while the second presents as avoidant of the supervisory relationship and supervisor assistance. High levels of student anxiety can underpin both of these styles.

When supervising the student with a very demanding style the challenge for the supervisor, once the pattern is noticed, is to name what appears to be happening—for example, that the student seems to be seeking assistance with a great many things to do with the research that they are capable of working through for themselves—and to have a meta dialogue about the supervisory relationship itself. While the supervisory relationship in research is, and should be, a learning relationship, this does not mean that the relationship should be allowed to become an extended question and answer session in which the student asks an extensive array of smaller and larger questions and feels entitled to the supervisor's 'answers' as a way of going forward with their research. Whether fuelled by anxiety or a little laziness, or both, the supervisor must respond to this style by encouraging the student to work out as much as possible for themselves, albeit with the support of the supervisor who shows confidence in their abilities. Far from giving the answers to a series of student questions and dilemmas, the supervisor can meet their responsibilities in these contexts by engaging the student in a reflective dialogue about the dilemmas and choices they face at different stages of planning, conducting and writing up their project.

When working with a student with the second style mentioned above, the supervisor faces a different kind of challenge. The supervisor with the supervision-avoidant student is often met with responses such as 'thanks very much for the offer of supervision appointment but I think it (the project) seems to be developing really well and its great to know that I can call for help should I need it'. When such students are invited to submit to the supervisor some of their early chapter drafts, the student will sometimes send them their 'findings' chapter first before they have had any supervisory discussion about the methodology being used in the study and how they might approach the analysis of their data. If you are a supervisor who has had a number of cancellations of supervision appointments by a student and who has not had any of the student's work in progress submitted to you, it is time for an appropriate level of worry. We need to remind ourselves that we are supervising a Masters level student who may not ever have completed a project like this before. We also need to remind ourselves that we are doing the student no service at all by colluding with the belief that they can bring their project to successful completion with little or no supervisory assistance. For many supervisors the worst nightmare of all can be the receipt of a full project draft from the trainee a couple of days prior to the submission deadline where they have little or no time to work on the many problems in their research that might have been avoided had they engaged at a reasonable level with their supervisor. Where the supervisor gets a sense of such a process at work in the student it is critical that a proactive stance is taken and the student advised of the risks involved in not engaging in a timely way with the supervisory process. The challenge here for us as supervisors is not to mirror the student's avoidance of supervisory contact by avoiding our own supervisory responsibilities.

Research Gets in Your Blood

Postgraduate research usually requires a long-term commitment to research engagement. For example, while a Masters level project may take 12–18 months from conception to completion, a part-time Ph.D. registration can last for 6 years. That is a long time in any busy adult life. And as we become absorbed in our research and especially in the early confusion of data analysis around handling large data sets, we become preoccupied: we start to breathe our research, to sleep it, to dream it; to eat it, and so on, and as we do, we can become even more preoccupied, absorbed, and thus potentially less available to others around us. As supervisors, when we enter a new research supervision relationship, that can expect to last between 4 and 6 years, we tend to give a general 'public health warning' and anticipate some of this preoccupation for our supervisees—not to scare them off, as such, but to recognise that research gets in your blood, when it goes well, and when it goes not so well! We often find that our new supervisees have not fully discussed their new commitment with their nearest and dearest—again, not for their permission, as such, but for them to be informed about the amount of time and mental energy involved, as it varies from Masters, to professional doctorate to Ph.D. This new commitment can have an impact on availability for household duties, child care arrangements, social life, and so on. For some trainees/students, who are already juggling careers with family life, a thoughtful discussion at this stage often helps future planning and preparation, and at the very least, lets the student know we understand the multiple demands on their time and energy.

Research Reflexivity

We supervise mixed methods research and qualitative research, popular amongst practitioners in health and social care fields, because these methods enable them to take a deeper look at personal meaning and experience in a small 'local' sample. The questions that arise in clinical practice lend themselves to the qualitative methodologies, and that imposes a direct expectation on the researcher that they make explicit their 'speaking position' or interpretative framework. In qualitative research, the researcher is the research instrument so to say and they have an ethical responsibility to deconstruct their position and make themselves visible through the data collection process and data analysis. This expectation involves an ongoing commitment to reflection—in supervision with us, with peers, in a regular research diary, and in a self-reflexive interview. Some of our supervisees have a background in quantitative research and experience some discomfort at the thought of self-disclosure. We suggest they engage in at least two self-reflexive interviews, with a trusted peer, near the beginning of the research process when they are honing their research question, and again, near the end of the data analysis. We suggest they do this with a peer, in a dialogue, rather than as an internal thought process only. This is because our peers can push our thinking further during interaction with us than we can often do for ourselves. We suggest they pose these questions: Why am I interested in this topic? What motivates me? What is my experience with it? What do I expect to find? What might surprise me? What are my prejudices, both positive and negative? What might I miss, or not see in the data? What sensitivity might lead me to over focus in one area? And so on. Thus when this interview is repeated near the end of the research process, we not only have a basis of comparison between the two interviews, but we can see the development of the researcher and what aspects of the researcher's interpretative framework has influenced the research process and the research outcome. We suggest that both interviews be subjected to a theme analysis and appear in the self-reflective parts of the methodology and discussion sections of the thesis (Dallos & Vetere, 2005).

When we work with a supervision group, we introduce aspects of the above self-reflexive interviews as brief activities. This provides an introduction or 'taster' for those group members not used to reflective practice. We might invite them to reflect quietly on the thoughts and feelings they have had over the last few moments in relation to a topic we have been discussing, or a paper we have read, and the way in which it was presented. Then we invite them to turn to their neighbour and wonder about how these responses can 'get into' research activity, for example, how we meet participants, shaping the questions we ask, how we ask them, and so on. We then seek process feedback, i.e. what did they notice in that activity, what surprised them, and how did their 'position' takes shape, and so on.

We encourage our students to open their thesis with an orientation that both states their position statement in relation to their research question, supported by their personal reflections, and that outlines why they think their area of research is important. Clearly this has to be supported by the empirical literature and extant theory, but because the outcome of the research analysis represents a dynamic interaction between the researcher, their participants and the data, including the researcher's interpretative framework, we encourage curiosity and an early engagement with this important issue. Throughout the supervision process we revisit the following questions: What did you bring to the analysis? What personal investment do you have in the topic? How might this have shaped the way you interpreted the data? How are you reflecting on your emotional responses to the data and to accounts from individual participants? How have you been affected by doing the research? If they are involved with a research group we ask them to reflect on the group analytic process. This is a dynamic, iterative activity that in turn strengthens the supervision bond and develops the confidence of the qualitative student researcher in their analytic competence.

Step Changes: From Masters to Ph.D.

In our experience, many successful Masters students cannot appreciate the step changes required to advance their work to doctoral standard. Stepping up can involve a lengthier and more critical engagement with a literature review (Hart, 2002); a more detailed and elaborated appreciation of the differences between research methodologies; a more extensive and reflexive understanding of the underpinning research philosophy; a more thorough going examination of our own reflexive positioning; an exhaustive consideration of ethical dilemmas raised by the research process, such as, research as intervention into research participants lives; more detailed and intellectually demanding data analytic methods; and a more robust examination of the social utility of the findings. In our experience there is more scope for teaching and learning in the research supervision relationship, for all parties, when we step beyond Masters level. However, we have found that one of the more common misunderstandings within intending Doctoral or Ph.D. level students is to interpret this step change as one solely related to size—for example, a larger project with more research participants—rather than a step up with respect to quality and depth of analysis and the other dimensions mentioned above.

Many research supervisors express a preference for Ph.D. and doctorate level research because of the learning opportunities it affords, but also because publication of the research is a requirement now, during the Ph.D. process. Many colleagues have complained to us over the years of interesting research they have supervised that does not reach publication. Sometimes we find that professional doctorate candidates do the research component almost begrudgingly because they only want to be psychotherapeutic practitioners. For this reason, we make clear that we require a contractual understanding of how the research will reach publication if the student does not want to be actively involved following graduation.

Emotional Support and Wellbeing

As we say above, research engagement can be long lasting and preoccupying. The process of doing research can be predicted to have its ups and downs: the moments of surprise, and of despair; the moments of deep satisfaction and of confusion; and the many moments of worry and anxiety, especially when research recruitment is not going well, or when the research ethics committee seems intent on misunderstanding our purposes! It seems to be always helpful that as research supervisors we can always remember our own Ph.D. research journey. We know all too well the sleepless nights, the complaints from family members about our whereabouts (even when we are in the same room!) and the stress of trying to juggle career, research and family commitments. But we also remember that the journey is indeed a process and that we do emerge from the long tunnel. The emergence is sometimes slow, but a thoughtful and grounded research supervisor can guide us and comfort us with the knowledge that we will get there! Knowing that our research supervisors have been through a similar process enables us to manage the uncertainty, confusion and indecision that inevitably occurs, and to learn to see it as part of the journey of learning. So rather than research being an unpleasant rites de passage to career development, the supervision relationship provides the space in which we can reflect, experiment, take risks and appreciate our personal and professional growth (Delamont, Atkinson, & Odette, 2004).

Some practitioner research addresses special and poignant topics, such as working with death and dying, involvement in terrible and violent acts and events, trauma experience, loss and betrayal and so on (Harper & Thompson, 2012). Not only can the witnessing of these experiences during an in-depth research interview stimulate an empathic response in the researcher, but they can also stimulate a resonance of these states for the researcher and often too, for the research supervisor. Stimulation of these states, present in all of us, when it occurs, needs timely and gentle opportunities for discussion and emotional processing. Albeit rarely, the processing and resolution of these states may need additional psychotherapeutic support. So the supervisor needs to know how to support such a referral in their responsibility for their supervisee, and in their own self care in their supervision of their supervision. This is not to find the supervisee inadequate in some sense, which is what they may fear, but to ensure the continuing robust development of their resilience as practitioner researchers. Here, of course, we are referring to more or less experienced practitioners who are learning their craft of postgraduate research—so they bring many resources to this task, as we often emphasise. But we wish to note that during the often long and extensive process of part-time Ph.D. research, for example, life happens! And sometimes, we simply have too much on our plate! In addition, we often find research supervisors have not established a supervision of supervision arrangement for themselves, more likely relying on an informal network of support, that is sometimes not always adequate for the task of processing and resolution at hand. We always encourage research supervisors to seek regular supervision for their supervision practice. So our commitment here is to establish, without prying, that our supervisees have a responsive and adequate network of support to sustain them on this long and sometimes very emotionally intense journey.

Therapy as Research: When Therapy Skills Can Be Research Skills

The supervision of Masters students in practitioner programmes brings its own set of challenges. The beginning Masters student may have been a long time away from academic study. Some of the students want to be practitioners only and are afraid of what research means, and the challenges it poses them, as we discussed above. We address these fears in an activity where we invite the students to reflect on their practitioner skills, and imagine how these skills will help them to do research, and to be researchers. For example, we think about hypothesising skills in therapy practice; the positioning of therapy as enquiry and the practitioner as curious; we think about practitioner observation skills; their collaborative practice skills; we think about practitioner engagement skills and especially their skills in interviewing around sensitive topics, and of course, their heightened ethical awareness and lengthy engagement with codes of practice. We recognise practitioner's understanding of organisations and their structures and functions, and their long experience of working with organisational affordances and constraints, and their developed ability to navigate and negotiate organisational obstacles. These skills are enormously helpful in negotiating access to sensitive groups for research purposes and for conducting research with such groups on a basis of reciprocity. In particular when researchers explore culturally sensitive areas of practice, their practitioner experience of working with difference and diversity helps them make the research enquiry a mutually beneficial process for all. It is never acceptable in our view, for researchers to 'take' data from participants and not to 'give' something back. As we reflect further on these areas of overlap between therapeutic practice and research process, many students come to realise that their therapeutic activity is a form of research enquiry. One of the best ways we have found of ensuring the development of student reflection on the connection between practice skills and research skills is by having research modules present within Masters level programs from the very beginning. Correspondingly, one of the least helpful approaches is to leave all research teaching and practice to the final year of a program which inevitably constructs a view of research for the student as something 'additional' and 'different'.

Giving and Receiving Feedback

We live in a world of feedback—some of which we offer, some of which we receive, and some of which we ignore. We all bring a history of a varied relationship to this business of being in feedback loops. That history is often emotionally laden and sometimes emotionally labile when triggered by further feedback. The process of feedback often becomes more salient and intense during the honing of the research question. Our experience with practitioner-based research teaches us that the research question needs to be applied and applicable and ultimately to be do-able. Most of us start out wanting to win the Nobel Prize and the process of scaling down a grand question into a do-able question can be uncomfortable and a little disappointing at times. Particularly at Masters level it can be important to convey the idea that 'small is beautiful' when it comes to settling on a research question and the student can be reminded that a great deal of learning can emerge for them from a carefully limited project.

Where a research supervisor is not part of a program's project approval process, special challenges are set for the feedback processes within academic faculty. This can mean that a supervisor commences the supervisory relationship with a student around their project after the research question and project plan has been approved by others. In our view, it is important that the proposed supervisor also feels that both the research question and project plan make sense and that they can visualise the project being brought to successful conclusion. It is the faculty's responsibility to see that all questions and doubts in the mind of a proposed supervisor about feasibility have been ironed out before commencing the research supervision relationship.

A further important aspect of this process of giving and receiving feedback is that it is the vehicle through which the student becomes concretely aware of the standards required for the successful completion of the research project. For this reason, it is critical that the supervisor's feedback on chapter drafts submitted is specific and clear. Supervisory dialogue needs to address the question of whether the feedback is understood well enough by the student. Comparing approaches with other research supervisor colleagues about the challenges of giving clear and helpful feedback can be an important way of developing skills in this area. This must mean more than just having a conversation together about how you each approach the issue and should include showing each other concrete examples of what you have said and written to students in specific research circumstances.

A dilemma that we occasionally face, and that colleagues bring to us for consultation, is when the supervisor is suggesting to a doctoral student that further elaboration of a theory or the introduction of a new theory, to help explain research findings, meets some resistance from the student. This is more likely to occur at the writing up stage, when the student is 'fed up' and wants simply to complete. Yet as supervisors, we know that the addition of the theory will further strengthen the thesis and make it less likely they will be asked to make corrections at viva. These are the kinds of quandaries that rely on the secure base of supervision to speak openly and clearly about our views and opinions, and how we resolve differences. Sometimes supervisors can become 'fed up' too and appear to want to 'give up' in the face of this kind of disappointment, i.e. when the student appears not to want the feedback. Yet our responsibility is to ensure the work is 'good enough' for viva, and our experience teaches us it is always better to put these issues on the table, between us all, for discussion. This careful empathic recognition and exploration of difference, and why the student is so 'fed up', goes a long way to helping the student take the feedback that will help them graduate.

Ethical Dilemmas

Participation in research is an intervention—an intervention into someone's life. This is particularly poignant for qualitative research where the purpose is to invite exploration and illumination of the meaning and lived experience of often very sensitive moments and events in our development. Research ethics scrutiny requires that our research proposals and research designs are collaborative, in that we seek consultation with potential participants or their representatives before we develop and hone the research question. At this stage we seek consent for participation, but it is not informed consent until the research participant actually experiences the research procedures. Thus we are required to create safety nets for our participants in case the research enquiry is unhelpfully arousing, for example, sign posting to counselling services, and so on, and making very clear that participants can withdraw at any time without any consequence, for example, for their treatment if they are users of mental health services and so on. Very often the research student does not have access to these resources of support and rely on their supervisors to navigate the network of support on their behalf. This places a joint onus on the student and the supervisor to collaborate actively around the wellbeing of the research participants, and of course, of the researcher, who may be similarly impacted by participation in the research, as we describe above. These complex and dynamic processes need a watchful eye at all times.

Common Pitfalls

In conclusion, we shall mention some common pitfalls we encounter in the written research thesis. Conducting research is complex and often involves the student in learning new skills and adapting existing skills, as we say above. In addition to this, learning to write up a Masters level or Doctorate research study is almost like having to learn a new language. The secure base in supervision provides both the framework and containment for the emergence of competence in the student, and the development of a respectful and reciprocal relationship between the supervisor and the student. Postgraduate research supervisors are aware of the many intellectual and methodological pitfalls that await their students. For example, thin descriptions in the data analysis, limited critique of the methodology and extant literature, making unsupported assertions and writing with certainty, limited social utility in the findings, under-developed self-reflexive positioning, and so on. For these reasons, it is essential that feedback can be offered and exchanged by both supervisor and student in such a way that strengthens the final draft of the dissertation.

Alongside our supervision responsibilities, we also both act as external examiners for academic institutions within the UK and Ireland, and the rest of Europe. These activities offer a perspective from outside the research supervision relationship, so to say. The more robust theses that we examine show evidence of the research training, both in the 'fit' between the research question and the design, and in the thoughtful application of the findings to practice and policy. Our engagement and resonance with the research thesis, as examiners and scholar practitioners in our own right, is found in the student's ability to persuade us with their cogent argumentation and their reflections on how the research design could be improved—in short, that they have learned something of benefit to their development and for the good of others.

References

Bell, J. (2005). *Doing your research project: A guide for first-time researchers in education, health and social science*. New York: Open University Press.

Dallos, R., & Vetere, A. (2005). *Researching psychotherapy and counselling: Exploring outcome, process and theory*. Milton Keynes: McGraw Hill and Open University Press.

Dallos, R., & Vetere, A. (2012). Triangles and triangulation: A possible bridge between systemic theory and attachment theory. *Journal of Family Therapy, 34*, 117–137.

Delamont, S., Atkinson, P., & Odette, P. (2004). *Supervising the PhD: A guide to success*. Maidenhead: OU Press.

Harper, D., & Thompson, A. (Eds.). (2012). *Qualitative research methods in mental health and psychotherapy*. Chichester: Wiley.

Hart, C. (2002). *Doing a literature review: Releasing the social science research imagination*. London: Sage.

Sandberg, J., Johnson, L., Robia, M., & Miller, R. (2002). Clinician identified barriers to clinical research. *Journal of Marital and Family Therapy, 28*, 61–67.

Part IV
Looking after Ourselves as Supervisors and Supervisees

Chapter 14
An Attachment Narrative Approach to Systemically Informed Supervision Practice

Arlene Vetere

Introduction

This chapter is written primarily for supervisors of qualified counsellors and psychotherapists, and also has relevance for the supervision of pre-qualification practice. The focus in this chapter is emotional safety and the co-construction of safe places for reflection and for the understanding, containment and exploration of doubt, anxiety and uncertainty in our therapeutic work. The framework outlined here for the promotion of emotional safety and relational resilience is an integration of three major schools of thought: modern attachment theory with narrative theory and systemic theory and practice (Dallos & Vetere, 2009; Vetere, 2017; Vetere & Dallos, 2016). The focus in modern attachment theory on interactive emotion regulation processes and non-conscious relational responding will be linked with the focus in narrative theory on coherent narrating as skill development. Thus we are concerned with understanding the conditions of emotional safety that enable us as children and young people as we grow into adulthood to use all our memory resources of thought, feeling, action and intention to integrate experience, to reflect on experience, our own and others, and to communicate it in a way that others can understand and respond as appropriate. The triangular nature of supervision relationships, i.e. therapist–client; supervisor–supervisee; and supervisor–supervisee–client/s will form the context in this chapter for systemic thinking in supervision and practice.

A. Vetere (✉)
Family Therapy Section, Faculty of Social Studies, VID Specialized University, Oslo, Norway
e-mail: drarlenevetere@hotmail.com

A. Vetere, J. Sheehan (eds.), *Supervision of Family Therapy and Systemic Practice*,
Focused Issues in Family Therapy, https://doi.org/10.1007/978-3-319-68591-5_14

Ordinary Therapy and Ordinary Supervision

> *"Lest we forget, it is the therapist who makes psychotherapy, and other helping professions, effective. Accumulating research demonstrates that in practice, as well as in clinical trials, much of the variability in outcomes is attributable to the therapist, regardless of the treatment being delivered."* Wampold, 2011, *p. 1*

Therapeutic work is emotionally demanding. Over time, its effects can show in many ways, such as somatic counter-transference, enhanced empathic responding, or under-responsiveness, if not sometimes a lack of enthusiasm for the work and even our relationships at work and at home (Hanks & Vetere, 2016; Skovholt & Trotter-Mathison, 2011). In no other professional grouping do we find such a tension between our own self-care and the care of others. We are trained to look after others and this training becomes honed with the passing years. The risk is that we may overlook or even neglect our own self-care. A trusting supervision relationship is a unique space within which we can be fully seen, heard and cared for—the focus is on us and what we need in the moment. When our supervisor is fully present with us, and we feel deeply heard, we are able to calm and soothe, find some clarity of thought and turn our attention to necessary action. It is in these aspects of the supervision process that we find one of the well springs of personal and professional resilience.

There is a good research literature on the impact on us as practitioners of working at the sharp end of professional practice, such as with identified trauma victims in specialist working contexts, such as natural disasters, sexual abuse and domestic violence (Berger, 2001; Figley, 1995, 2002, 2013; Hanks & Vetere, 2016) (and, for example, see Chaps. 10–12 in this book). However, there is less research and less written about the impact of doing 'ordinary' therapeutic work over the life span of a professional career. In my experience, all our therapeutic work is infused with loss, grief, distress, despair and trauma responses—this is not specific to specialist therapeutic services. However, it is of interest to me that the joys, surprises and satisfactions of our work that both sustain and enthuse us are less well researched (Norcross & Guy, 2007; Skovholt, 2008). So, how do we understand this apparent lack of interest for the demanding and growth-promoting impact of our 'ordinary' work as it would seem to be such a taken-for-granted aspect of professional life? I would like to clarify at this point that I believe this 'ordinary' work to be extraordinary as we maintain our energy in the continuous flow of our work, and make ourselves readily available, present and connected with those who seek our help. In supervision, we can reflect on why we do this work, why we continue to do this work, what meanings our work holds for us and how these meanings may have evolved and changed over time. The supervision relationship may indeed be the only context where there is the time and the emotional safety for these reflections. In supervision we can reaffirm and clarify supervisee's experiences in the therapy, we can listen intently and slow down the supervision session to allow a supervisee to process and integrate difficult and complex material, including somatic counter-transference responses, and offer understanding and comfort in response to powerful and shared human experiences. As Diana Fosha writes, the roots of resilience are to be found in the sense of being understood by and existing in the mind and heart of a loving, attuned and self-possessed other (the supervisor!) (2009).

Supervision, Power and the Arousal of Anxiety

The contexts for supervision practice are various, for example, hierarchical arrangements in organisations, line management and case management, developmental and growth oriented supervision, peer supervision, group supervision, and so on. Whatever the context, we need to pay attention to power and control in the supervision relationships and in the wider working contexts. In supervision, our therapeutic work is subject to scrutiny and to the gaze of others. When we disclose, expose and explore our doubts and uncertainties, such as our mistakes and prejudices, we make ourselves vulnerable to others' gaze. Surveillance of our work might be part of the contract, for example, with training, and line management. The supervisor's task is to hold indecision, reflexivity and action in equal regard. This can involve differentiating personal and structural power. Exploration of the relationship between felt and actual power and powerlessness involves acknowledging both wider system constraints on action and potential on the one hand, and acknowledging both the supervisor and the supervisee's position in the system on the other hand. This means that both supervisor and supervisee need to interrogate implied and specific ideas and prevalent discourses about what is 'good' practice in supervision and therapy and recognise the limits of our own and others' power and influence. In so doing, it is helpful to critique our preferred ideas and ways of working, and to compare them with our less preferred ideas and ways of working for their implications and impact on our well being and collaborative practices, for all concerned.

Attachment Narratives in Supervision and Consultation

May I begin this section with a self-reflective pause for you, the reader: Think of a time in your early training and professional practice when emotional risk-taking in the supervision relationship was crucial for you as a supervisee. What word or phrase captures an aspect of that experience? Can you identify a specific memory that illuminates the experience? Consider what you have learned from this for your own practice as a supervisor and for what you seek from supervision. How has this shaped how you both define and approach emotional risk-taking in supervision—for both yourself and your supervisees? What do you hope your supervisees will learn from your experience that they can take forward into the future of their practice as supervisors in their turn?

The above activity exemplifies the inter-generational nature of learning in professional practice and the continuing influence of emotionally significant events. The activity draws on modern attachment theory and the research on representational systems or 'dispositional representations', as Damasio calls them (2008). This section will now review research on dispositional representations and strategies of attachment that has relevance for supervision practice, and in particular, the supervision relationship.

A key challenge for both supervisors and supervisees is how to work with what is communicated that may not be symbolised with words, both in the therapy and supervision relationships. We need energy, commitment and safety to manage our arousal as we bring these processes into awareness and take our bodily reactions seriously. Trust is essential for a felt sense of emotional safety in the supervision relationship. Accessibility and responsiveness in the other are the key building blocks of trust in all significant relationships (Gottman, 2011). It is that combination of empathy, perceptual flexibility, tolerance of uncertainty and ambiguity, and emotional sensitivity that promotes compassionate and collaborative ways of working and being together. Felt security in significant relationships correlates positively with more balanced affect regulation, greater likelihood to seek help and support from others, a more open, reflexive and curious approach to information seeking and processing, a more disclosing, empathic and assertive approach to communication, and finally a more elaborated and positive sense of self (Mikulincer & Goodman, 2006).

Modern attachment theory posits the central role of non-conscious interactive regulation in establishing attachment relationships (Schore & Schore, 2008). The regulatory processes of affect synchrony and implicit non-verbal communication co-create a growth-enhancing context that promotes interactive repair and modulates states of unhelpful arousal. Extrapolating to the supervision relationship and the supervision of the therapeutic relationship focuses our attention on learned strategies for the management of arousal and on how relationships are represented or held in mind. When we are upset, unhelpfully aroused and physiologically flooded our ability to reflect on what is happening is constrained—it is harder to reflect, our information processing for negatively laden events slows down, we are more reactive and preoccupied with our own arousal, our ability to read relationship cues suffers, and we may have a tendency to rely on 'fall back' positions of coping, i.e. our self-protective strategies of attachment and arousal regulation. We are not often upset in supervision, but it happens, perhaps in a rupture in the supervision relationship (see Chap. 15 Hans Christian Michaelsen and Gudmund Fossli) or in reliving a difficult moment in the therapy or in experiencing an unexpected and powerful resonance, perhaps with an unprocessed trauma memory for either the therapist or the supervisor. Clearly supervisors and supervisees have different responsibilities in the supervision process but nonetheless, a frank appreciation and possible prediction of the activation of a preferred 'fall back' position when upset enables both to work quickly to find a resolution.

A robust and trusting supervision relationship contextualises the supervisor as a work-related attachment figure with attachment significance for the supervisee. Damasio (2008) suggests that dispositional representations of attachment are neurological patterns of activity that arise from all our interactions with our attachment figures. These patterns of activity include thoughts, feelings, intentions and actions. Damasio goes on to suggest that these representations are reworked every time we think of our attachment figures. These representations are considered to be dispositional because they dispose us to act in particular ways to maintain our connections to our environment and relationships, along with our expectations of the outcome. Distortions can occur as a result of self-protective processes, such as exaggerating or minimising the probability of attachment-related dangers or threats. These can be fears, such as fear of rejection, fear of failure, or fear of being a disappointment to others. A fear that is commonly expressed to me by those in psychotherapy training is a fear of being discovered to be a 'fraud', i.e. having no right to be on the training programme where it is only a matter of time before they are 'found out' and rejected in a shower of shame! Such fears, if left unexpressed, and unprocessed, might lead a trainee to cover up a difficulty for too long and not seek help sufficiently early to prevent an escalation of any problem. Sadly, I sometimes find that these earlier unprocessed fears can cast a shadow into supervisees' post-qualification practice that are hard to shake off.

Our mental representations of our relationships with our significant attachment figures are thought to be multi-layered and to include our thoughts and beliefs, our feelings and sensations, and our intentions and actions as understood by current memory research: procedural, sensory, semantic, episodic and integrative memory systems (Crittenden & Landini, 2011; Tulving, 1993). Procedural memory represents what we do and how we do it in our significant relationships, for example, how we look after each other, listen to each other, and so on. Sensory memory holds emotion and sensation, for example, a felt experience of safety, the look of a smile, the feel of a reassuring hug, and so on. Semantic memory pertains to our thoughts, ideas and attitudes, for example, expectations of supervision, ideas of good enough therapy, and so on. Episodic or narrative memory holds the stories we tell about our experiences, for example, a helpful supervision session, or an unhelpful one. In narrative theory, a coherent narrative has a structure that the listener can follow, and combines action, feeling, thought and intention (Bruner, 1990). Both the form and the content of our narratives express and also construct our attachment relationships. Finally, integrative memory is our capacity to reflect on what is happening, for example, on why and what we might be thinking, feeling, acting, and intending, with sufficient calm to enable effective problem solving. For example, episodic memory and the telling of the story can be reactive when we are upset and preoccupied with our arousal, and thus not at all reflective in that moment. Reflection can be challenging as it involves awareness of contradictions in what we say, feel and do, for example, and of inconsistencies both within and between our representational memory systems. Our ability to reflect and integrate requires a secure emotional base; and it is our capacity for reflection and reflexive thought that we are trying to promote and sustain, especially in the face of heavy work-related demands.

Self-Protective Strategies

Thus the supervisor and/or the supervisee might have preferred self-protective strategies when they are upset or feel threatened with rejection or criticism, and so on. Examples of self-protective strategies include strategies of arousal down-regulation, becoming overwhelmed with unhelpful arousal, and balanced strategies where both elements are present. A down-regulating or dismissing strategy tends to down play or deactivate emotional responding, accompanied by an attempt to persuade ourselves 'we are feeling fine', when perhaps we are not. This approach emphasises cognition and semantic memory, as feelings are not considered a good guide to action. A dismissing or deactivating approach can break down if too much is demanded of the person (for example, a heavy case load, professional isolation, other worries and concerns, organisational stresses, and so on) such that an emotional response can break through, almost like a trauma intrusion, and surprise everyone, including the person concerned. Sometimes this can become a source of shame, for example, crying at work, or running from a meeting in a distressed state, shouting at a colleague, and so on. At the other extreme of coping, we find a preoccupied strategy, where the person is preoccupied with the struggle to manage and regulate their arousal when they perceive themselves to be under attachment threat, i.e. fearing rejection, not being seen as good enough, and so on. All of this could be accompanied by defensiveness as part of a self-protective strategy. And of course, if and when we behave defensively, the other may not be able to see through the strategy to the fear, sadness or shame that might lie behind it. And so begins a cycle of unhelpful escalation, unless it is possible to stay sufficiently calm to overview and reflect on what is happening in the relationship. For many of us we balance our self-protective responses with a mix of de-activation and occasionally feeling overwhelmed. In a trusting relationship it becomes possible to explore what we perceive as an attachment threat, our preferred coping positions and how they might have developed over time. This forms the basis for exploring how these self-protective processes might become activated during therapeutic work, in both expected and unexpected ways, and what enables us to stay calm, thoughtful and reflective in the face of loss, despair, hopelessness, criticism and contempt.

Conversely, when I find myself as a supervisor becoming irritated and stressed in the supervision work, I tend to become more directive and less curious. As much as I am capable of over responding in these moments, I may also be capable of under responding. I take this observation of my action, my felt experience and my preliminary thoughts to the supervision of my supervision and seek help with deconstructing what might have been happening in that moment that triggered my reactivity. Re-organisation of our attachment relationships and our attachment strategies requires reflection and integration of our different representational systems. Part of this process of deconstruction involves exploring what the supervisee and our relationship represents for me, and where an unhelpful resonance might lie. My actions and state of mind may have caused a rupture in the supervision relationship and certainly needs acknowledgement and apology.

In my supervision practice, I always ask my supervisees about their well-being every time I meet them. They come to know this about me, and come to expect it. Sometimes they tell me they think about my enquiry in advance on their way to meet me, and wonder what might they say today….? Sometimes, they tell me, they realise they do not know how they are, or what they might tell me. This helps them realise they have been too busy or too preoccupied to consider their own state of mind and their own self-care and thus that we need to focus on this in the supervision. In a context of trust, we can internalise the sense of safety we feel with the other and take it with us as we go about our lives. Sometimes in the course of our therapeutic and organisation work, there are times of trouble and concern. It is at these times we can draw on our 'internalised other' and imagine what they might say to us, or how they might look at us, or the sound of their voice, and so on. The internalised representation of our supervisor and our shared relationship is a resource that we can call on when we need help to calm and soothe, and importantly, to think! Knowing that we are held in mind by someone who cares for us lessens our sense of isolation and helps us regulate our unhelpful arousal. In relation to this, I have been influenced by the supervision work of Barbara Kohnstamm (Kohnstamm & Vetere, 2016). She has helped me develop an emotion focus in my supervision practice. For example, when I meet a new supervisee, part of our contract is to explore resonance in their therapeutic work, and in our supervision work. I ask them if there is something in their own attachment history that they want me to know about and understand, so that if they become 'stuck' in their therapeutic work, we can quickly zoom in to the resonance, throw light on the current therapeutic dilemma, and then zoom out. Clearly if this process of illumination indicates a need for further therapeutic support, I will help my supervisee find this at their request.

Conclusion

Therapy and supervision require both co-presence and inter-subjectivity in order to show our connections with each other, to understand processes of mirroring, to seek to stand in the emotional shoes of the other and to jointly explore preferred and subjugated narratives from an emotionally safe base. Transformational learning in supervision involves helping supervisees to organise different aspects of their experience of their therapeutic work into a more integrated whole, i.e. a coherent narrative. Reflection and integration across our representational systems requires emotional safety, both in therapy and in supervision. This is effective dependency in action and with repeated experience we are more likely to seek assistance when we need it. In the face of difficulty and hard to resolve dilemmas, the co-construction of the secure base assists us in knowing how to go on, and to go from excursions to expeditions.

References

Berger, H. (2001). Trauma and the therapist. In T. Spiers (Ed.), *Trauma: A practitioner's guide to counselling*. Hove: Brunner Routledge.

Bruner, J. (1990). *Acts of meaning*. Cambridge, MA: Harvard University Press.

Crittenden, P., & Landini, A. (2011). *Assessing adult attachment: A dynamic-maturational approach to discourse analysis*. New York: Norton.

Dallos, R., & Vetere, A. (2009). *Systemic therapy and attachment narratives: Applications across a range of clinical settings*. London: Routledge.

Damasio, A. (2008). *Descartes' error: Emotion, reason and the human brain*. New York: Random House.

Figley, C. (1995). *Compassion fatigue: Coping with secondary traumatic stress disorder*. New York: Brunner Mazel.

Figley, C. (Ed.). (2002). *Treating compassion fatigue*. London: Routledge.

Figley, C. (2013). *Trauma and its wake*. London: Routledge.

Fosha, D. (2009). *The healing power of emotion: Affective neuroscience, development and clinical practice*. New York: Norton.

Gottman, J. (2011). *The science of trust: Emotional attunement in couples*. New York: Norton.

Hanks, H., & Vetere, A. (2016). Working at the extremes: The influence on us of doing the work. In A. Vetere & P. Stratton (Eds.), *Interacting selves: Systemic solutions for personal and professional development in counselling and psychotherapy*. London: Routledge.

Kohnstamm, B., & Vetere, A. (2016). A supervisor's progression: From personal and professional development training in group settings to the inclusion of the self of the therapist in supervision. In A. Vetere & P. Stratton (Eds.), *Interacting selves: Systemic solutions for personal and professional development in counselling and psychotherapy*. London: Routledge.

Mikulincer, M., & Goodman, G. (2006). *The dynamics of romantic love: Attachment, caregiving and sex*. New York: Guilford.

Norcross, J., & Guy, J. (2007). *Learning to leave it at the office: A guide to therapist self-care*. New York: Norton.

Schore, J., & Schore, A. (2008). Modern attachment theory: The central role of affect regulation in development and treatment. *Clinical Social Work Journal, 36*, 9–20.

Skovholt, T. (2008). Two versions of erosion in the helping professions: Caring burnout and meaning burnout. *New Therapist, 52*, 28–29.

Skovholt, T., & Trotter-Mathison, M. (2011). *The resilient practitioner: Burnout prevention and self-care strategies for counsellors, therapists, teachers and health professionals* (2nd ed.). New York: Routledge.

Tulving, E. (1993). *Elements of episodic memory*. Oxford: Oxford University Press.

Vetere, A. (2017). Systemic theory and narratives of attachment: Integration, formulation and development over time. In P. Stratton & M. Borcsa (Eds.), *Origins and originality in family therapy and systemic practice. EFTA Book Series Volume I*. Berlin: Springer.

Vetere, A., & Dallos, R. (2016). Supervision and attachment narratives: Using an attachment narrative approach in clinical supervision. In A. Vetere & P. Stratton (Eds.), *Interacting selves: Systemic solutions for personal and professional development in counselling and psychotherapy*. London: Routledge.

Wampold, B. (2011). Qualities and actions of effective therapists. *Continuing education in psychology*. Washington, DC: Education Directorate, American Psychological Association.

Chapter 15
When the Supervision Process Falters and Breaks Down: Pathways to Repair

Gudmund Fossli and Hans Christian Michaelsen

No one likes to fail. It feels so much better to succeed. However, to define what is success and what is failure in the supervision process is not the easiest task.

> *Some of us feel you are discriminating against us when you focus your attention. You always seem to favour the topics of certain participants in this supervision group. Although you say that all voices are equally interesting, it seems clear to us that your attention is drawn towards the higher educated ones in the group.*

Have I as a supervisor failed to be sensitive to everyone in the group? Or are some of the participants oversensitive to differences in the level of education in the group? How can I discuss this intervention made by the group in a way that does not lock the differences even more?

> *We think we have reached a point where we need another type of supervisor. You seem to go in circles, both with the structures you suggest, and with your ideas and references. We feel we move in repetitious ways, and have sort of expected you to get us out of them. Isn't that what you as a supervisor from the outside is supposed to contribute with – to inspire us to thinking and doing in new ways?*

Indeed, I have also felt this. I have become desperate to be able to be creative, and tired when I can't manage. Before every session I have felt I am up to an exam, not in knowledge, but in personality almost. Will I be able to think creatively enough, to be sensitive enough, to be bold enough and even to listen well enough? Will they like me today?

G. Fossli (✉) • H.C. Michaelsen
Family Therapy Section, Faculty of Social Studies, VID Specialized University, Oslo, Norway
e-mail: gudmund.fossli@gmail.com; hans.christian.michaelsen@vid.no

A. Vetere, J. Sheehan (eds.), *Supervision of Family Therapy and Systemic Practice*, Focused Issues in Family Therapy, https://doi.org/10.1007/978-3-319-68591-5_15

In these two instances, the conflict or disappointment was addressed and verbalized by the group. In many cases, nothing is expressed about such matters. The supervisor may only be sensing it, not being able to pin-point anything particular, but an uneasy feeling may be growing in her body. Or even worse, she doesn't sense it all. One day it will explode, and how will she then go on? Will repair, healing and even growth be a possible outcome at all?

In our own experience, we have noticed that we like to consider and reconsider incidents of breakdowns as potential learning experiences for everyone involved. And maybe they are! Likewise, eager to always pursue growth and development and to expect visible signs of it, we have not always recognized the success in silent, slow and not so expressive development in supervisees. In such instances, we have felt that something is wrong. We may have blamed ourselves, we may have blamed the supervisees, or we may have blamed someone else. But since we don't want to be in the blaming business, we thought: let's try to analyse some of these situations instead, and see what we find. Maybe there are some phenomena and factors that are recognizable to others, maybe we don't have to feel so alone in experiencing failures, and more importantly, maybe we can be able to act more constructively in the somewhat foggy landscape between failure and success.

Consequently, we wish to share some experiences from supervision when the process breaks down for various reasons and also some of our attempts to move forward. Sometimes the attempts did not succeed, and we will share them as well. In addition, we will describe some situations where breakdown might have happened, and how they were managed and avoided.

The experiences that we share are primarily related to group supervision, and one individual supervision, in various professions and work contexts in the public and private sectors within health and social services, family counselling, child welfare and educational institutions.

Introduction

An Attempt to Describe Success in Supervision

Supervision has been described as a learning process, where the aim is that the supervisees will act more in accordance with the theories and methods of their profession, and thereby exercising their work in a more competent manner (Teslo, del 1). If this is happening and the supervisees are experiencing growth and are making new discoveries about themselves and about the process between themselves and their clients, we may say that the supervision succeeds. The process should address two levels, a greater and deeper understanding of both the professional approaches and of the clients they serve. The supervision may then, in its outermost consequence, have led to client(s) experiencing better help. In supervision there may be both pain and pleasure. Both can nurture learning and processes of development.

An Attempt to Describe Breakdown in Supervision

Breakdowns (BD) may be complex and various—which is our aim to elucidate in this chapter. One of the effects of BD may be the emergence of a lack of confidence in the supervision project. The supervisees may experience being in conflict both within the supervision group and/or with the supervisor. This may initially seem to hamper the learning project. The supervisor and the group may become rigid, and sometimes a hostile atmosphere may occur, which in turn can cause members to leave supervision, to just drop out or they become passive with nothing to share in the group. Bad experiences in supervision have had traumatic effects. On the other hand, breakdown *may* be the seeds of a greater learning and growing process, but it presupposes that the situation is being handled by the supervisor and the group in a non-judgmental way, and that the supervisor takes the initiative to talk about it in an inquisitive and respectful manner. BD can in turn lead to a greater growth than if it had not happened at all.

Why Are We Interested in this Topic?

We tried to find literature and research dealing with the topic of breach in supervision processes, but found little (Burck & Daniel, 2010). Although a bit puzzled by this, we could see that dealing with the subject from a supervisor's point of view could be challenging. The process of looking closely at our own experiences with what we called 'failed supervision incidents' has been demanding emotionally. We have easily been thinking, "*It's me there's something wrong with; I'm not competent enough, not experienced enough, not brave enough. That's why this supervision got screwed up*".

This causal reaction makes it is easy to end up in a one-dimensional explanation which becomes entrenched and gives little learning. Our attitude and experience is a contrary one. It leads us to believe that there is a lot of learning in looking at the various factors and processes that unfold in a breakdown. Sometimes we have also been tempted to think, "*It's the others, it's their fault, there's something wrong with their attitude, their motivation, their understanding. Or they too easily feel offended*".

Furthermore it can be tempting at times to resort to explanations about the supervisees showing resistance, they are making transference projections and even experiencing personality disorders when there is a break in the alliance. Neither these explanations are particularly constructive or learning, but they may in the short term help keep our own feelings of shame away. On the other hand one should not reject such explanations completely, as it sometimes may occur that such factors come into play. Our hope is that our experiences may give others and ourselves some food for more reflections, and maybe some insight and wisdom in dealing with unforeseen setbacks. Breakdowns are sometimes inevitable and even necessary. We would like to believe that our competence may be increased by dealing with failures, since we have seen they are in a very limited degree being discussed both in literature and among colleagues. The mainstream discourse seems to be that we are telling ourselves to be strong, competent and coping in every situation.

A Map of our Discussion in This Chapter

We will describe and reflect on some phenomena and areas that might be risky for the supervisory relationship and process. They may lead to conflict and even breakdown. These descriptions are of course not exhaustive or static, and they are largely based on our own experiences. Consequently, they must not be considered as areas or topics one should or must avoid. The relationships between supervisors and supervisees are obviously complex, and we will therefore never be able to describe what was "really" going on. But we shall offer some punctuations (Watzlawick, Weakland, Fisch, & Erickson, 1974) which hopefully can be of benefit to others as well. We do not wish to explain breakdowns in a linear, causal way, but rather try to reflect on possible factors that influence. Paradoxically risk factors may contribute to build and strengthen the relationship if the supervisor and the group manage to deal with them in a systemic and a reflexive way.

In section "Some Risk Factors", we will present some risk factors through ten phenomena which serve as case examples. They are all anonymized and in some cases approved by the supervisees. These are our stories as supervisors about what we experienced happening in the supervision groups. The supervisees will most probably have quite other stories about what happened.

The first 5 of the 11 phenomena will be structured by an introduction of the phenomenon, followed by a case *example*. An extract of the *inner dialogue* of the supervisor, which was not verbalized, is included before a *discussion* of the case. Finally, the presentation is rounded up by a short reflection called "*In the golden light of hindsight*". The last five of the phenomena will be presented without examples in the above-mentioned structure.

Of course, each example may contain more than the one risk factor that is described. However, we have chosen for more simplicity and clarification to deal with only one risk factor connected to each example.

In section "Some Pathways to Repair and Healing" we will discuss some pathways to repair and healing, looking at what we have learned and what some of the literature says about repair. This is obviously not an exhaustive list, but rather a few suggestions.

Our Own Maps of Understanding

We have a systemic and a social constructionist perspective to dialogical help in general and to supervision in this context. As supervisors we are also participants who influence and are influenced, who affect and are affected, professionally and personally. Relations are created, and relations create. When we attempt to think something or say something about another person, it is not so much about the person herself/himself, but to a much larger extent about the relationship to the other.

We believe in the importance of co-creating frames and structures with the supervisee(s). Context creates meaning, and structures will frame and liberate creation of meaning.

Furthermore, we think that we cannot change another person, we can only change ourselves to some extent. However, we may help the other to get input from others which may lead to a changing process. In other words, we are more inclined to think that something *may be*, rather than that something *is*.

In the first session, before supervision actually begins, we usually give an introductory presentation on how we understand supervision in this particular context, and what kind of processes we suggest to emphasize. We review some supervision theory and some models for learning and development. We then give an opportunity to each participant to share what expectations, need, wishes and goals he or she has for this series of supervision meetings. We also explore what experience and expectations they have for the group dynamics, and on this basis try to establish some guidelines for communication and processes. We discuss how to deal with uneasiness that may occur, reminding about the responsibility each participant is expected to have for taking care of herself/himself with regards to reactions, positions and roles.

To provide structures that invite and enable each supervisee to participate and be heard is the responsibility of the supervisor. The aim is to give room to all voices, none any more or any less than others (see Chap. 8 this volume). We emphasize ongoing feedback about the supervision process, both in the beginning and the end of each session. This kind of introductory preparation applies to all the examples in this chapter. More discussion of our principles of understanding is presented in section "Some Pathways to Repair and Healing" of this chapter.

Some Risk Factors

We will present 11 selected factors that may create risks. They may separately or together constitute a risk for faltering or for breakdown in supervision.

Phenomenon 1: Lack of Trust and Confidence

Trust and confidence is one of the most important premises in a supervision process, as it is in most interpersonal interactions and in other forms of dialogical help, also in therapy.

For the supervision process to be useful and fruitful, trust between group members and between the group and the supervisor is essential. Trust is not a constant factor and it is individual. The boundaries of trust will vary. Sometimes one person's mistrust may infect the others, and vice versa, some may infect the others with confidence. One of the moves that may create trust and confidence is when the supervisor is transparent with his thoughts and dispositions, ensures that everyone in the group is heard and seen, and reminds everyone of the right to experience and see things in their own way, the right to one's own version of reality.

The example: *"We have decided that we do not want to have you as a supervisor any more."*

One supervision group expressed in the very beginning that they were all very experienced and that they wanted an equivalently experienced supervisor. Another important prerequisite was that supervisor had been working with the same target groups and the same kinds of assignments. For these reasons they had confidence that I knew how demanding their job was and they chose to hire me. In the fifth session I asked in the beginning how they had experienced the previous session. The supervisee who had had focus time last time was wondering if I was in alliance with the management, and she was not the only one with this impression. The group had been talking about it, and several of them were wondering about the same thing. When she talked about this, she was looking at the others, and they seemed to give her confirming reactions. I was quite unprepared for this feedback, and they asked if I wanted to hear it blunt and to the point. Yes, that is what I want, I responded.

The story went like this: In the last session she felt that I had been so offensive. She had presented a problem where she was referring to a situation where she didn't feel met by her leader. When I had asked her what she thought her leader had meant or thought or intended with what he had said about it, my supervisee experienced very little understanding and recognition from me. When I even had asked if the manager may be interpreted and understood in a different way or in an additional way, the supervisee started to think that I had some bond with the manager. This became even more likely by the fact that it was the manager who had hired me and I knew him from before. The supervisee said that what she needed was an emotional embrace and no challenges.

I responded to this by assuring that I in no way whatsoever had any bonds to the manager, nor had I had any conversation with him about the supervisee. Another member of the group then said that she after this incident did not have any trust in me any more and that she was very unsure if she could ever get it back. I said I was very sorry for this and that I regretted deeply and sincerely that I had asked these questions in the last session, and that I had not quite understood how hard this encounter with her leader had been for the supervisee.

I had the impression that the following conversation in the group developed into a healing process, and that trust and confidence could be restored. The relation to the supervisee and to the rest of the group—with an exception for the one who doubted if she could ever trust me again—seemed to improve in a safe way. When I asked the supervisee in a very explicit way if she thought that trust and confidence in me could be restored, she confirmed, "All relationships need to be worked with".

The Supervisor's Inner Dialogue

> "Oh—now I've screwed up. How could I possibly make such a stupid mistake? On the other hand, is she completely without the ability to reflect on this matter? Am I supposed to *only* stroke her, and not give her any challenges? She has said that they are experienced, no? Besides, I'm afraid that this supervision may develop into complaints against the leader, something I have very bad experience with. I know that this will take a lot of hard work if confidence shall be restored again. I'll try to do my best for it to succeed. I just need to lie down flat and take it on the chin, but can I do it? This is painful for me, and I can feel the shame of having messed up and made it difficult for others. At the same time I can feel a duality between shame and despair or resignation with regard to both myself and the others in the group".

The Example Continues

In a later supervision session, she presented a clinical case, and she got a lot of feedback from the group and from me. I collected all the ideas on a flip chart, and at the end I gave a reflection on the proposals and said that I did not believe that all the ideas should be implemented, but the list could be perceived more as a "bank" for suggestions. On the next supervision she said that this was completely unnecessary for me to say, and that I in this way had communicated that I had no confidence in her judgments. She said that the group had agreed that they would not want me to be their supervisor any longer. The others in the group who were present supported her statement. Since they had decided that they would end the supervision with me, I asked if we could talk about what went wrong. That was quite okay with them. They told me that they had given me a second chance—but I had not seized it and, moreover, they had had individual supervision before which they experienced as better. They needed more of an "emotional embrace" than what I gave them and as such they lost confidence. In individual supervision they got more of that "emotional embrace".

When I asked if there had been anything at all that they had experienced as useful in our supervision sessions, they reached the conclusion that there were some times they had been able to make some use of it, which also was my experience. One of them said she had received some kind of help she needed. Another said she had received help in a case where she struggled, but she missed that I had challenged her more about what the case did to her. Yet another said she did not experience this supervision much more different than the professional, academic discussions they had internally at the workplace, and as such they did not need an external supervisor since I didn't add something more. Supervision was terminated in a polite and respectful manner by all, but with a clearly expressed message that they did not have confidence in me as a supervisor.

The Supervisor's Inner Dialogue

So they are sitting there every session considering me, evaluating me if I'm good enough—it's as if I'm up for the exam in each session. I cannot bear to "emotionally embrace" especially the one who is complaining and moans the most. She is too demanding for me. I wonder if these are persons with personal problems that are more in need of therapy than supervision. One is burned out and will fortunately retire. Another is new and is being overrun by the others with regard to what she should think. There is tension between them, and they put it out on me. I'm glad this supervision came to an end. They make me feel small and incompetent. I do not fit as a supervisor. Maybe I should find something else to do? I'm being accused of not being sensitive. I think this is the first time I hear this. I see myself as very sensitive, listening, receptive and accepting. I really need to tell myself that this is not my fault—but I do understand that I've had my contributions that have not made it easy for them. Me oh my, what a mess.

Discussion

When I tried to initiate reflection in the group, it was perceived as criticism and lack of confidence. In this case, it would probably have been best to just give space and accommodate the other's feelings. To challenge, or to initiate reflection did not fit there and then. When someone is very overwhelmed by something, it is often not possible to reflect. I did not quite capture this. My intention was in good faith to help them reflect on the case from several angles, for the supervisee to get a freer relation to the case. I needed to make the necessary distinction between two facts: they are very experienced, and they are vulnerable at the same time. The person in focus was probably much more precautionary and vulnerable than I realized. In simplified terms, one may say that there are at least two ways to meet another person; on a cognitive level and on an emotional level. Obviously, a third way is a combination. In this case, the supervisee was met on a cognitive level—while she, at least in the first place, needed to be met on an emotional level. "I had needed to be emotionally embraced", she said.

Watzlawick claimed, that we punctuate always on several levels simultaneously, analogue and digital. I punctuated mostly digitally. In other words, I was mostly concerned with her words and not so much with her analogue message, and therefore I didn't notice it or pay attention to it. Her analogue message was more about emotions attached to not feeling seen and understood by her leader. And this was even repeated in her interaction with me going through the case. In psychodynamic thinking parallel processes are important to be aware of. Some of what happened between her and the manager happened also between her and me.

After the first breach in this supervision, I became afraid of hurting and of doing anything wrong. The group probably also reacted in becoming hesitant of exposing dilemmas out of fear of not being met at what they needed. In this way, this supervision developed into something like "pretended supervision" and therefore naturally also became less rewarding for the group. I became very cautious in moving forward. It was for me like being caught. I was afraid of being interpreted as blaming if I expressed how I felt, and therefore I thought that this was my problem. During the supervision, after the first breakdown, I tried to be transparent with my own reactions and feelings, and what consequences it might have on the group.

The needs of the group also seemed to go in different directions, ranging from those who only wanted confirmation, to those who wanted to have distinct challenges. It became difficult for me to give each and every one what they needed, so I was forced into a sort of a middle way, that was not good or satisfactory for any of them. I also feared that the supervision might develop into a lot of complaints with the management. I wanted to avoid that since I recently had seen in another context how splitting and destructive such activity can be to a group. I tried indirectly to avoid it, rather than addressing the matter directly.

I could have met the group more humbly and with more questioning. The group was probably right in that I was seen as somewhat blaming, and possibly I had a vague distrust of the work they did. When they were referring to conversations with clients, I caught myself thinking that I would not have carried it out in that manner, since from my perspective it seemed somewhat insulting. As such, I probably came into opposition to them, and the questions I asked must have been coloured by this. I therefore became less affirmative. In this perspective, we might say that the lack of confidence became mutual. Perhaps from my side there was even a lack of a genuine interest in them, both as individuals and as a group. Under the section "Some Pathways to Repair and Healing" we will discuss the concept of love and how it may be relevant and linked to this example.

"In the Golden Light of Hindsight"

Even the most experienced supervisees and supervisors are vulnerable. One should never underestimate the importance of genuine confirmation, or of emotional embraces.

Phenomenon 2: When Supervision Is Compulsory and Not Wanted by All

Supervision is by its nature a voluntary process into which we enter to learn and develop. Mandatory supervision assigned by the management represents challenges on several levels. It may cause tension in individuals and between individuals in the group, between those who want supervision and those who feel forced to participate. From a management perspective there may be good reasons for having mandatory supervision. Qualitative management often requires supervision in the workplace. New and more experienced colleagues need to exchange values, ideas and competence. But there may be resistance of many kinds. Previous experiences from supervision may be unsuccessful or non-existent. Heavy burdens of work-load may draw the interest away from spending time on a meta-level. Anxiety or feelings of burn-out may also prevent a positive or active participation. The supervisor may find herself in the position of having to "sell in" the concept of supervision to create an interest in this type of self-development and self-awareness. There is also the ethical question of doing supervision with someone who does not demand it? An equally legitimate question is to ask if there is an obligation for the individual to seek developmental challenges in order to be of better help for the clients?

An example from mandatory supervision with an individual, where the supervisor also has a lower professional status.

This may be a very challenging situation. A supervisor with a lower educational degree and status will be supervising a colleague on a compulsory basis. The difference in status may lead to the supervisee taking on a higher position, and the supervisor a one-under-position. The supervisor may try to compensate by claiming that both of them are in the same situation, both being in the supervision context on a mandatory, not voluntary basis, and thus try to avoid the one-under position. In this manner he may rather position himself as equal or even one-up.

Such a supervision situation increases the risk of a break-down if the supervisor and the supervisee are not able negotiate a common ground. Wisdom and flexibility is demanded of both.

The example: *Does our manager think I don't have enough competence since you are supervising me?*

He was in the middle of his career and had long experience with substance addiction. He was a specialist within his professional group. I had less experience in this field. My experience was mainly with a family therapy perspective into different subjects and areas of professional work. For this reason our leader had decided that I would do supervision with this supervisee, who was new at the workplace, about the family therapy perspective. He seemed surprised at the idea of having to have supervision. After having recovered from this little shock, he asked, "Does our leader really think that I know nothing about family therapy? I mean, it was actually part of my specialist training! And it was only passing in the hallway I was told that I was to have supervision with you."

We had a conversation about what it was like for both him and me to enter into this supervision relationship on these particular grounds. He said that this wasn't easy for him and that he frankly did not have much faith in the project at all. He didn't think he would get much out of it. I tried to invite him to reflect on what topics or areas he actually might be interested in for supervision. He had nothing much to say about it. In my eagerness to make this compulsory supervision something he would find a bit exciting, that could give him some food for thought and practice, I suggested that we might talk about some different schools and approaches in family therapy. I was rather experienced in this from teaching and training, and rather successful at it too, so I thought this might give him some clues along the way to find some areas that could be useful for him to explore further. He was quite polite in agreeing to this invitation.

After a short while it seemed as if the supervisee was totally uninterested. He looked demotivated and without strength. I stopped my presentation and mentioned what I observed.

He totally agreed with my impression. He could absolutely not find any interesting novelty in this, and furthermore, he did not have anything to share or discuss that would interest him.

The next three sessions continued in much the same way. One of the sessions was postponed, but then" forgotten" by the supervisee.

The Supervisor's Inner Dialogue

I feel trapped. The leader has ordered me to do supervision with someone who has been ordered to have it. How am I to move in a trapped situation like this? How are we to find our way, he and I? I really like the supervisee, and I think he likes me, so maybe there is some hope in that? I would really like to make this happen, it would mean a lot to me. Even if this has been a terrible and not moving start, I still have some kind of faith somewhere that there must be an opening to find a way to go on, and a rewarding one too. I would really like to show my leader that I am capable of becoming a good supervisor for this colleague. But I feel inferior to him, since he has a higher status and position in my eyes, and he has so far not given me any hints or suggestions about anything that might be of interest to him to focus on. It turns out that I have become the engine in this alone, which is a very unhealthy and not fruitful way of supervision.

The Example Continues

In the fourth session the supervisee said that he saw no point in continuing. I had rather good contact with him between sessions, and I felt that we had established a fairly good relationship. So I asked him if we in that case just could talk about what had happened and about how it was for both him and me to find ourselves in such a situation. He agreed to that, and said that he felt it quite humiliating to be ordered to supervision, as if the leader had not even bothered to read his CV to find out that he in fact was qualified with a high degree of competence in family therapy. He pointed out that it had not so much to do with my person, but more with the situation. It had affected his self confidence. It was important to him to be seen as competent, especially now that he was new in the workplace. Having to go in supervision with me, was experienced as a confirmation of lacking competence on his part. When talking about this, there were tears in his eyes.

I just listened and felt open to all he said, receiving it the best as I could, and even I had tears in my eyes, because it touched me in a profound way to see how this had affected him. When he finished his story, I asked him if he would like to hear my story, and what it had been like for me trying to make this supervision work. He would like that. I said something about how I desperately had tried to make this interesting for him, and how I felt that I had failed.

In the fifth session, he said; "Thank you for not being scared by me and that you can endure me – I think we may find a way together over the next months we are placed to be with each other. I think you have just the right degree of softness and strength, and that suits me very well."

The Supervisor's Inner Dialogue

How good it feels that a break-down was avoided, and that we managed this together! I am so proud of both him and myself. What a relief! Everything here is not solved, but there is quite another true and honest dialogue between us now. I'm sure this has not been easy for him at all. It is only me who has been preoccupied with his and my professional status. That doesn't seem to bother him at all, I don't even think he has thought about it. It seems to have been my problem only.

Discussion

When the supervisor has a lower status, and supervision is mandatory, risk is at hand. The supervisor may easily feel the pressure to establish his credibility, both through competence, knowledge, in practice and in how to meet and talk with the supervisee. In this case a break-down was close. We both felt like giving up. Maybe it was to my advantage that I was so intensely aware of his higher status, that it made me even more humble and eager to do my very best for the supervisee to experience something meaningful. One of the openings that made it possible for this supervision to seem more useful for the supervisee, was that we both managed to give space to each other. This opened up the opportunity for a real and true relationship between us. The supervisee got recognition for what it was like for him to have compulsory supervision, and that he was recognized for his competence. We also were able to acknowledge each other's vulnerability, which generated some sort of warmth, compassion and understanding for our mutual situation, which none of us had asked for. It was as if we realized that we were in this together. Our situation and relationship became more important than the supervision project.

One might suggest that I could have encouraged the supervisee to talk with our common leader about the premises for his supervision. If we look to de Shazer and Berg and solution focused therapy, we may recognize the supervisee as a "guest" more than a "customer", and he might have turned into a "complainer". With a "guest" it is hard to move into a real learning, growing and developing supervision process. To find that area, where the "guest" may move to become a "customer", is a mutual exploration that probably requires sensitivity, humbleness, curiosity and patience.

"In the Golden Light of Hindsight"

"To sell sand in the Sahara desert"—it is not an easy task. We may find ourselves trying to do exactly that sometimes in supervision. But if we try too hard, we will probably find that the supervision dries out too.

Phenomenon 3: When the Team Leader Is a Participant in the Supervision Group Without Everyone's Approval/When Someone in the Group Gets a Different Position—A Leader Position

Many colleagues recommend that the team leader not join the supervision group. There may be good reasons for this. The team leader's presence might put a damper on the participants' candidness and sense of security. They might hesitate to uncover their own weaknesses and vulnerability, they might be concerned about having work assignments taken away from them, and feel insecure about the consequences for their professional careers. Nevertheless, we have experiences with this working well in certain cases. Yet some important presuppositions need to be present. Advantages and disadvantages have to be discussed beforehand and without the team leader being in attendance. First of all, all the participants need to want the team leader to join. Further, the team leader has to have the same work assignments as the others and participate correspondingly. The team leader has to be a supervisee like the others, and not participate while taking on the role as team leader. If this is possible, that the team leader is not positioned as an observer or perceived as such, it can be an asset to the group. Then it can be experienced as favourable that the team leader is involved, and can share what he or she is struggling with on the same level. The team leader can be perceived as being "one of us".

If this is not discussed beforehand and actively considered, but instead just ends up that way, it may lead to a breakdown. In these cases it is necessary to openly speak about these different functions, the team leader has to accept the consequence of this and step out of the group. Then the relationships can be healed again.

<u>The example</u>: *When the group process is hindered*

A supervision group had existed for a long time. One of the members got a team leader position, but kept going to the group. It was discussed whether he should step out of the group, but no one wanted this, quite the opposite, it was expressed that he was a part of the group. After a while the supervision became very slow-going. Few had anything they wanted to bring up. They asked the supervisor for more teaching, and the discussions were very general. The one who had become a team leader took on a more observing role and shared little about his challenges. On one occasion when he was not in supervision, someone dared to say that they no longer felt secure in the group and that they therefore could not share their vulnerability and challenges. The insecurity had to do with them feeling observed and assessed by the team leader, both in the supervision group and otherwise. Most people in the group felt that there were advantages and disadvantages in having the team leader present, while one thought it was a clear advantage because then the processes were open and everyone was included. One of them felt that it was very unfortunate that the team leader joined. She said she neither would nor could share how she felt, because she was scared that the team leader would view her as weaker than how she perceived herself, and that the team leader would not give her the confidence she wished for. Most of them agreed that the supervision process had become less rewarding and many had "good" reasons to be absent from the supervision. Some said that the supervision was wasted when the team leader was present. The life of the supervision was at stake. The group could potentially become divided and break down.

The Supervisor's Inner Dialogue

I perceive the group as divided. There are strong voices both pro and con. Some have a confidence in the team leader and think it is nice that he is there. Others experience being inhibited. Is it possible to create a framework which everyone can accept? Can it be secure enough with the team leader present? Can I put my inner dialogue out there and just see what happens? Can I trust that the solution lies within the system in this case? I do want to support everyone's opinions, but I also feel that if only one of them perceives it as insecure with the team leader present, then he should step out. Should I also say that it should be the team leader's own decision, since he has hired me as supervisor?

The Example Continues

The supervisee's inner dialogue was presented to the group, without the team leader present. Everyone decided that they should respect that it was difficult for some, and they wanted me as supervisor to covey this to the team leader. I did this, and the team leader respected this and chose to notify everyone that he would no longer be joining the supervision. The supervision continued. The openness increased and some of the security returned.

Discussion

The group managed to put into words how the individual experienced that a former colleague—now a team leader, was present in the supervision, without him participating actively on the same level as the others. If he had shared his challenges, the group would probably have experienced it differently. Some felt observed and assessed, which made it feel unsafe to them. It was an advantage that they were able to articulate this. As a group they were able to find a unified path. In this way, they recreated the group security so that they could continue. It could have resulted in a breakdown in supervision if they hadn't been able to understand how this was experienced by the individual—both those wanting the team leader present and those who did not.

"In the Golden Light of Hindsight"

When someone in the group has a new role, the contract has to be renegotiated without the new team leader present. This must be done transparently. If the team leader insists on participating in the group and a number of people are against it, I need to consider whether I can continue as supervisor.

Phenomenon 4: When There Are Internal Conflicts in the Workplace

When there are internal conflicts in the workplace, it will often become apparent in some way in supervision. It could be that someone is unsure of some else, or that someone has a greater power to define. The conflict can lead to insecurity, which in turn can hinder the individual from being open. Some co-workers can be highly disliked by others. For example, some might think that others evade their duties.

The example: We do not want you as supervisor any longer and you are blamed for it (but there are inner conflicts which makes us not want to continue).

A local municipality asked me to supervise three groups of five to seven participants in each group. This place of work was within care services. They had to wait approximately half a year before I could start, but they thought this was worth it, considering they had had such good experience with me from earlier work, years ago. The management expressed that most of them were very motivated. We agreed that I was to have three groups in a day, once a month, with sessions lasting one and a half hours per group. The agreement with the management was that I would conduct six gatherings in the first 6 months. After that they would consider whether I should continue or not, however, they did indicate that this would last a considerable amount of time.

What the management had commissioned was that the employees wanted supervision regarding themselves as professionals, and how they could handle difficult situations and develop into becoming more secure and steady. They expressed that they did not want case supervision, but process supervision. I utilized the first meeting with every group to find out which expectations each person had to the supervision, to the group, and to me. I also said something about what my understanding of supervision was. It seemed to me that there was mixed interest in the supervision. The management had decided that everyone had to attend. With three groups in a day, and short breaks in between, the supervision became quite challenging to me. It was agreed upon that everyone in the groups would have focus time, one each time. After the third gathering, some people in every group could not attend. They had more important appointments, was the message I got. Few showed any interest in me when I arrived in the mornings, and during the lunch breaks I was sitting alone. My experience was that they were fully preoccupied with themselves. In the supervision I experienced that in two of the groups, the participants were very taciturn, and they seemed insecure. I was particular about evaluating after each gathering, and everyone expressed then that the supervision was useful and educational.

After the fourth gathering I tried to get hold of the management to hear what they were thinking about going forward, but I did not succeed in doing so. I talked to a deputy director who had been involved, but he was very evasive and ambiguous. I thus sent an e-mail to the director and said that I needed a clarification of whether I would continue with the supervision or not. A long time passed before I received a reply. Right before the last scheduled gathering, I received this e-mail:

> "Hi
>
> We have now had a review of the supervision demand in the group. The feedback is that they do not want this sort of supervision going forward. They would like more supervision internally regarding cases and those who work in the same supervision. Therefore, we will not be renewing our contract with you after the summer. Many are very pleased with what they have gotten in the supervision and will take this with them going forward, however, the group has decided that they want something different. We can talk the next time you are here."

I read this e-mail right before I was going to a meeting to discuss another supervision job. During the whole meeting the e-mail was whizzing around my head and my inner dialogue was:

What have I done here, and not understood? I thought we were going down the right path and that they were benefiting quite a bit from the supervision. Indeed, I have been evaluating regularly, and none of this emerged then. I also feel that the atmosphere has been quite good, however, there have been some who have been reluctant to share. Have all the participants in the three groups been overrun by a few strong opinions? I feel completely exhausted, down, and am insecure of whether I am suited to be a supervisor, even though I have experienced succeeding a lot through 25 years of activity.

This feedback stunned me, as mentioned—at the same time as it confirmed some of what I had experienced. Therefore, in the last gathering I spent time trying to understand what hadn't worked or what they wished would have been different. Some said they wanted more of this type of supervision, while others said that they rather wanted something which could unite them. I tried to understand what they meant, but I was struggling a great deal, and expressed that I experienced this as being dropped as a coach for a football team before being able to complete the job.

Three years later I received an e-mail from the same director:

> "Could you take on being a supervisor for us again?"

In the mean time I had run into a few participants from the supervision group in other contexts, and they said that the reason why the supervision had not been extended was that there were a few strong participants who defined the supervision as "not good" and that the others did not dare contradict them. Some also claimed that they did not feel secure around some colleagues, and therefore little was being said. They were afraid that what surfaced in the supervision, would not stay there. One also said that she was forced to be in a group she absolutely did not want to be a part of, and that she consequently did not want to be open about how she felt.

I replied to the director that I could do it, but on other terms than last time. Everyone who was to participate had to want it themselves, it had to be voluntary, and they had to participate in a group in which they felt safe enough. I wanted to have two groups per day and more time per session. These conditions were accepted by the director. Some had quit since the last time and were replaced by others. The first session in each group I asked what had made them want supervision with me specifically, since a majority had not wanted to continue with me 3 years ago. Many said that the supervision had been useful and that it didn't have anything to do with me, but more about tensions among themselves, and that the supervision was mandatory. The new people had heard about me or had been in supervision with me in other jobs earlier on, and had good experiences and thus were very positive about getting started. The supervision has been in progress for a year's time now, and everyone has eventually chosen to join a group. It seems as if they get a lot out of the supervision and they talk about it to others as very useful, educational, and reassuring to the group. As a supervisor I feel freer and more creative. There is a lot of humour, tears, and laughter. They are very open with each other.

Discussion

After a 3-year break, and maybe a necessary breakdown, the supervision was restarted. Some of what lead to the breakdown was probably linked to inner conflicts and that a few voices became dominant and the basis for the premises. Those who got a lot out of the supervision in the first round, did not quite communicate this, and it was difficult for me to take in these nuances and expose them. Sound frameworks are also crucial. It is necessary to have enough time for each group and solid breaks in between. The supervision also has to be voluntary and desired. Conflicts and insecurities in the group which are not shed a light on, are destructive. My confidence was profoundly shaken after the first round. The temptation to say that "I do not want anything more to do with you, as you have caused me such discomfort", was something I experienced. However, I am happy and proud that I was able to enter into this again so that it ended up being a good experience both for them and for myself. Breakdown and repair deals with human processes, but also with how frameworks can create and influence.

"In the Golden Light of Hindsight"

Everything does not have to do with me, but *some things* are about me. In this case it was smart not to sulk.

Phenomenon 5: When the Supervisor Has Roles and Positions for the Supervisees Beyond Being Supervisor

When the supervisor is also the team leader for the same people, it can present challenges. Other roles can be a close, personal friend of someone in the group, or a spouse. In other words, relationships can tie you up. Leadership has a different goal than supervision does. Leadership can be to contribute to the service reaching specific goals, while supervision to a larger extent deals with the individual reaching their developmental goals. If the supervisor is also the team leader, the goals of the enterprise can be mixed into it, other interests can play a part, and the supervisees might end up feeling inhibited. If a supervisor who is also a team leader is to succeed, it requires that these possible conflicts in roles are discussed, that everyone in the group acknowledges both the person and the roles. If for example the same people experience that decisions are being made outside of the supervision sessions which go against their wishes, it can be difficult to have a good relationship in supervision.

The example: *I don't want anything more to do with you*

At one workplace I was both team leader and supervisor. I made an unwise decision as team leader towards a person who was a part of a supervision group I was leading. In the supervision sessions after this episode, this person was very critical towards me as a supervisor, and would interpret me in ways which I did not recognize. I tried in every way possible to build a good relationship with this person again, but did not succeed. After about half a year, the person in question quit their job. The group continued, and it was discussed how things were now that this person had resigned and left the group. I said it had been a very demanding process for me—something the others had seen and recognized. I could not share everything I had done as team leader with regard to this person, nor how I had tried to repair it, because it belonged in another context and was a confidential employee issue. They felt it was good that I said this, because then at least it had been talked about to some extent, which made it easier. I was not able to fix the relationship with the person in question, neither as a team leader nor supervisor. This person also expressed clearly in supervision that the leadership (including myself) were not to be trusted, and uttered statements such as: "At this point, the leadership has to take action and not just let things take its own course. This is a demand we must push for".

The supervisor's inner dialogue (from one of the last supervision sessions the person in question joined): "This person is out to get me. I need to sit quietly in the boat and just take it. I am the supervisor now, not the team leader. Perhaps if I'm not on the defence, it might help rebuild the relationship again. Any attempt at explaining or adding nuance, the person in question will clamp down on – even though what the person says is completely different from what the leadership has thought and said. I hate being in this double-role now. I know that the person in question is not right, yet I have to tolerate it. I have to think and act as if I were an outside supervisor. I will try to be approving, exploring, and curious. This is demanding. I am feeling both anger, frustration, and sadness that it has turned out this way. If only the person in question could forgive me. I have done what the person asked of me to make things alright again, yet this person is still "digging" at me. How will this turn out?"

Discussion

To be team leader and at the same time be a supervisor, turned out very badly here. Nevertheless, I do have good experiences with being able to tend to both roles at the same time. This time it did not succeed, and much of the explanation concerns a fatally bad decision I made as team leader, and which had consequences for the person in question. The breakdown and the insufficient repair cannot be explained by my behaviour alone and the roles I had. However, in this case I was perceived more as a team leader by this person, and being able to enter a good position of supervision, was far too demanding both for the person in question and for me. If these different roles are to work, it is important that the supervision group has experienced that what emerges in supervision, will not be used against them in other contexts, and the other way around. In this case, the rupture happened in the leader position. I tried to repair it as team leader, but did not succeed. I then became quite impeded as supervisor, because I noticed how difficult it was for this person to be a part of the group as well. Thankfully, the group managed to handle the person in question quitting without placing the blame only on me as supervisor for what had happened. This was probably because I had a very good relationship with them, and through nuances and reflections together, it turned out well for them without the difficult process with the person in question dragging the others into a breakdown. If I had not been this person's team leader, or if I hadn't made the poor decision as team leader, this situation would probably not have arisen. This shows that the two roles have built-in pitfalls, and demands a high degree of consciousness, openness, and continuous evaluation to avoid a breakdown and to attain development.

"In the Golden Light of Hindsight"

Empty what is full, fill what is empty, and scratch that itch.

To ride two horses at once demands a great art of equilibrium.

In other words, if you have done something unwise as team leader or supervisor, try to repair it as soon as possible, seek help from the others, and if this does not work, you should accept it and live with it. Wisdom exists in all breakdowns, if you have the energy to search for it.

Other Risk Factors

We mention and discuss here a few more risk factors without giving extensive examples. However, these factors can also lead to breakdowns if the situations are not handled wisely enough both by supervisor and supervisees.

Phenomenon 6: When There Is an Imbalance Between Confirming and Challenging/Moving

If the individual gets too much or too little of something, it can lead to a breakdown. As supervisor it is necessary to always move between these two dimensions, compare the example in phenomenon 1. Confirmation deals largely with the individual feeling seen, heard, and understood. However, confirmation without movement rarely creates new insight or new skills. The supervisor's role is also to create a disruption from the outside. Another way of seeing things, a new question, a different perspective, different glasses can lead to discoveries which can make a difference. Sometimes the supervisee simply needs a confirmation of what it is like to be oneself. Other times one might want more of a challenge and movement to grow and develop. Many say: I need a good dose of both things. The Aristotelian happy medium is a good compass for the supervisor to navigate to the difference which is just right.

Phenomenon 7: When There Are Conflicts Between Management and Employees

If supervision is used to complain about difficulties and conflicts in the workplace, it can lead to the group finding strategies to try and change the situation to the better. Unfortunately, it can also lead to bigger problems and difficulties because the group is talking behind others' backs and can become adamant about their perception of how impossible others are or the leadership is. The supervisor should encourage a conversation about ethical ground rules, for example, talking about someone who is not present, and how this possibly should be done, or not at all. Should the focus be on "the impossible leader" or on one's own contribution to the conflict and what they can do about it, for example.

In one group they talked a lot about how difficult it was for them when leaders either made poor decisions or didn't make decisions at all. To me it seemed like quite an unhealthy work environment. I therefore encouraged them to bring this up with the leader. The group agreed and designated two people to do this. This was the start of a lengthy personnel conflict which ended in several people taking sick leaves. One of the employees resigned after experiencing considerable pressure from the senior management. This also led to the management suggesting that they couldn't have this kind of supervisor who encouraged the employees to stir up trouble, in other words a supervisor who had messed up.

At times I have suggested that if conflicts exist with the management, this needs to be handled in other ways, such as by means of a safety delegate, union representatives, conflict resolution work, team building, organizational development, or directly with the management. Other times someone can be so "filled" with strong emotions and frustration that they have "leaked" no matter how I have tried to say that this needs to be tackled in other contexts. Being displeased with or complaining about the leader is a repetitive phenomenon. If it is not communicated clearly enough, and the premises for how it should be dealt with in supervision are not agreed upon, it can lead to a breakdown. The supervisees might say: "Can't you understand how difficult this is for us", or they can say "how can you allow someone in the group to speak in a derogatory manner about someone who is not present. We cannot have you as our supervisor". This can be perceived as a "double bind" because what might be the solution to some (to talk about the leader), can be the problem to others (that they are talking about someone who is not present). Again it is clear that explicit discussions and clarifications about the premises for the supervision before beginning is decisive both to prevent unproductive conflicts and as a reference in evaluations.

Phenomenon 8: When the Contract Is Unclear, Vicarious or Not Clarified Enough

Occasionally one is asked for professional supervision when the need is, for example, conflict resolution, team development, or to get rid of "troublesome" co-workers. If the framework for supervision is not perfectly clear and explicit both to the supervisor and the supervisees, a complicated supervision relationship can arise.

A leader who had commissioned supervision for a group, told me when we had been proceeding for about half a year: "I hope you will tell A how hopeless she is as a therapist so that she understands that she should quit". This is obviously not a supervision task, but a leader's responsibility, was my answer. When I discovered that this was not only the group's leader's wish, but also that of several others in the group, it became clear to me why the supervision was so slow-going. They said that they were waiting for me to tell A some home truths. (see Chap. 2 this book.)

Phenomenon 9: When Supervision Has Blurred Boundaries About How Much and What Is to Be Shared of a Private and Personal Nature

What is shared first and foremost in supervision, are experiences from the professional scene. Social worker and lecturer Ken Heap (Heap, 1988) said that the personal and private can be brought up when it affects the professional practice. This means exploring how private and personal experiences can affect you as a professional and how this manifests itself in therapeutic practice. The idea is not to go in-depth into the personal and private, but to see how it affects you. A further exploration of how these private experiences have transpired and how it has shaped you, belongs to therapy.

In a supervision group with highly experienced therapists, two of the participants shared vulnerable parts of their private lives. I myself as supervisor let them recount without stopping them, because I thought that this was relevant to how it affected them as therapists. To some of the others this sharing was too private, and the existence of the group was at stake. We spent a part of the successive supervision sessions to share how the individual had been influenced by these stories. The two who had shared, showed great understanding of that it might have been too much for some of the others and apologized for going too far. My contribution to this which was difficult for some, was perhaps that I had neglected to check with the group if it was alright to keep going with the personal perspective and how this could be productive. Later on we discussed the framework for supervision, and everyone in the group stayed on. To some, a breakdown was very close. The group had suffered a crisis, but had pulled through. Possible contributions to this was that we as a group had been able to talk about it openly, and that those who had experienced it as uncomfortable, related how it affected them without pointing fingers. Those who had shared the private matters, showed understanding of how this could be difficult to others.

Phenomenon 10: When Some Voices Get a Too Dominant Position

When someone with authority claims something, it can be difficult for others to have another opinion. They might even think that it is "not allowed" to experience it differently. This can be expressed by strong voices being perceived as defining the supervision, either through evaluations in the group or outside. This definition can make things "constricted" both to the supervisor and the other supervisees, compare phenomenon 4 above. As supervisor it is thus important to invite everyone's voice in. In this way breakdowns can be prevented. I often try to say that it is permissible to have completely different opinions here in this group, because the supervision can be experienced very differently. How you are feeling on any given day, the context, which processes you are in, private affairs and the like will colour how you feel, think and what you say. If I get the sense that there are voices who do not dare come forward, it can be useful with a meta-question such as: "If someone thought something different from this, would that be allowed to be said in this group?".

Phenomenon 11: When the Energy of the Supervision "Dies"

When the supervision has been underway for a long time, both the supervisor and the supervisees might lose some of the initial curiosity about each other. Most everything seems predictable and conventional. The energy drops, and often the supervision is being given a lower priority by the participants, other tasks become more important. The supervisor might feel more and more that the responsibility to make the sessions interesting and innovative rests largely on her. It becomes difficult for everyone. In this case, a breakdown of the supervision is more the result of wear and tear, exhaustion, and lacking energy, than lacking a need for supervision. A good piece of advice is that the supervisor not only treads water and keeps it going by doing more of the same thing, but rather introduces a meta-perspective by asking: What is happening? Supervision does not have to be about the supervision in itself, but also about how supervision is created. When the supervision dies, the supervisor should invite a discussion around the need for supervision, the structure of supervision, and what gives every individual participant energy or feeling of powerlessness. In some cases, it might become clear that the time has come to end the supervision with this supervisor, and a process towards rounding off can begin. Such a process can often uncover new personal goals which can be worked on in another context.

Some Pathways to Repair and Healing

What can be reparative is naturally very complicated to know, and it is especially difficult to predict whether a repair can be transferred to other situations. What works as a good approach in one situation, might have little or, in the worst case, a bad effect in another. It is our experience that it doesn't take much before the attempt at a solution makes the problem in question even worse. We have chosen to call it "repair", however we do not imply that it is something mechanical or instrumental. We use this concept because it is often utilized in psychotherapy, and we find that there are many parallels. From newer research on therapy it is claimed that the relationship between client and therapist is highly significant for people's ability to develop (Goldsmith, 2014; Nissen-Lie, 2012; Wampold & Imel, 2015).

Terje Tilden (2015), the assistant research leader at Modum Bad, Norway, has summarized what he believes several researches disseminate about what seems to work in therapy. Most agree that there needs to be a therapeutic alliance, and in this alliance three factors seem to be significant; consensus regarding goals, consensus about tasks, and experiencing emotional bonds. When a breakdown happens in supervision it can be useful to think through and evaluate whether one or more of these factors were weak or missing.

There are many relationships in a supervision group, both to each other and to the supervisor. In other words, there are many relationships which need attention and to be tended to, for there to be a safe and good atmosphere for learning and development. We have decided not to discuss breakdowns in light of a psychodynamic understanding in this context, but will mention briefly that one possible way of understanding a breakdown, is that there is a transmission and a counter-transmission between the supervisee and the supervisor. We do not discount these processes, because they can give meaning to a way of understanding breakdowns and a language many will recognize in the exploration when a breakdown has happened. An example could be that a supervisee has certain reactions towards the supervisor, because the supervisor reminds this person of another person with power, with which there had been conflicts. With this understanding the supervisor can choose not to take these reactions as personal attacks, but become more concerned with how the supervisee can become more conscious of different factors which might appear in the interaction the person in question is a part of. Other explanation methods in a psychodynamic understanding can be to regard breakdowns as a type of resistance and consequently a solution for the supervisee to avoid uncomfortable topics. It can be interesting to many to understand processes and breakdowns in supervision groups with background in theories about transmission, counter-transmission, resistance and parallel processes (Bang, 2007; Rønnestad & Reichelt, 2011). In this chapter we mostly try to emphasize a basic systemic understanding, however, we naturally acknowledge other theories and explanations. We certainly discover that we might be "infected" by these other ways of understanding, when we in the following summarize some of what we have found which might be reparative. If one is to become wiser, we believe that it is useful to view these processes from several points of view (and different traditions).

Participant

It is easy to think "them" and "me", rather than that we are constructing each other together. We can think: "They have misunderstood now, shown resistance, or one or more of them have personal problems which resemble a personality disorder. I have done things to the best of my ability, and they have turned out not to be "supervisable". Or perhaps it's me who is not competent enough to handle these processes?".

We have found it to be more useful to think that we are all participants in a supervision process, including in a possible breakdown happening. The breakdown can sometimes seem understandable and recognizable, other times incomprehensible and barely recognizable.

We consider such an attitude and way of thinking as an expression of us instead of thinking "them" and "me", we try to think "we". What do "we" co-create? In this co-creation we are many participants (see Chap. 7 this volume) (Nissen-Lie, 2012). Every individual person participates, however encompassing frameworks can also contribute to creating what is. How the room is furnished, the air, the temperature, outside disturbances, furniture and the staging of the room, if we are in a busy workplace or in a place which creates calm and good experiences—all these context markers, contribute to creating conditions and processes.

In recent years we also notice how technology and social media contribute to co-creation. How does the supervision group create their culture? For example, is it acceptable to keep your phone in front of you and be available at all times to children coming home early from school etc.? How are these cultures established and perchance changed? There are innumerable factors which create and affect the supervision relations. As supervisor I am responsible for my own contribution to what becomes "we". I am in a leading position and am a role model. It can be useful to think that as a supervisor I am not *more* or *something else* than the others, but I am in another *position*. This gives me, first and foremost, freedom, and an important focus is to preserve this freedom. My initiatives are thus meaningful when it comes to attempts at repair. We believe that it is important to initiate the wording of what happens in a genuine, open, and honest way. To preserve one's freedom, it is beneficial to dare to be unafraid and to make a personal effort. One can become insecure and afraid of course, but to dare means to take a chance on openness. As a role model, this is actually one of the tasks the supervisor has. One cannot expect the participants to dare more than oneself. To be able to show one's vulnerability can give the participants the assurance to show their insecurity, and that it is okay not to have command of everything and all situations. In this way, the supervisor's position becomes a starting point for the idea that we create each other in co-creation (see Chap. 8 this volume).

Everyone Is Right

When a breakdown has happened, it is important that each individual gets acceptance and acknowledgement of their experience, and that no thoughts, opinions, feelings, and reactions are "wrong". To repair is not about someone being right, but about encountering the other with curiosity. It is usually not productive to hunt The Possible Cause, but rather to expand the possibilities for many different ways of understanding the situation. If one, instead of reflection, invites discussion, one might win the discussion, but lose the relationship.

Love

This can be a confusing concept to utilize in a professional context, because it evokes associations of a relationship or condition between two people of intimate nature. In a religious and Christian context, it might mean that a person does everything for the other person to be happy, and that one is not seeking one's own happiness. It also indicates that one should love a person because he or she *exists* and not because he or she *acts*. Hilde Maria Thrana (2016) points out that the concept of love disappeared with the professionalization of health care professions. From having been the responsibility of the extended family and women's charity work, health care became a public affair in Norway during the 1900s. "Love" was replaced by other concepts in professional work. Thrana (2013) suggests love as a core expertise in child- and social professional work, and discusses the concept of love from two perspectives. One perspective is the love of one's neighbour as a moral requirement where others are met with respect, care, and compassion. The other is love as a type of acknowledgement, based on Axel Honneth's theory (2008). Love as acknowledgement is considered to be a treatment approach which establishes trust and confidence. The Norwegian psychiatrist Svein Haugsgjerd (2005) also asserts that love is a main subject in treatment; the fight to experience love, share love, maintain love. It is a driving force for everything which has lasting value, in being together, relationships, and creative endeavours.

According to the Chilean biologist Humberto Maturana, an individual's learning and development requires that three fundamental conditions are present. These are *love*, a *disruption or impulse* from outside, and *time* for reflection (Maturana & Varela, 1987). *Love* is according to Maturana a fundamental force for all development. He describes it as being seen and heard by a person or environment which wants the best for you. The love of ourselves and of others is a condition for all social life.

When we use the concept of love here, it concerns an attitude of wishing others well, where one does not judge or dislike the other. This is in line with Honneth's utilization of the concept of love as respect, acknowledgement, and equality. When we choose to use the concept of love, it is because we think it sharpens and illustrates the opposite, when we do not have this unconditional attitude towards others. Psychology specialist Svein Øverland writes in a chronicle that "Therapy is love", continuing "It is as a mature affair where two lovers not only complement each other, but expand each other" (Øverland, 2014).

When we look back on some of the supervision relationships which have gone down a not very constructive path, and where it has not been possible to rectify, we recognize that we have probably been coloured by insufficient love and that this has probably been communicated. It has not been sufficient to "make the right methodological moves" when the participants haven't felt good enough or accepted and respected for who they are. We therefore aspire to, to an even higher extent, try to like and "love" those we are to supervise. In a framework where both supervisor and supervisees experience this love, creativity seems to get more space, and the fear of not being good enough diminishes. Virginia Satir once said (loosely translated): "Everything we do is an expression of: Do you love me?". In a supervision group with experienced therapists someone once said: "Do you love me as much as the others, since you forgot that it was my turn to get focus time?".

Humbleness and Openness

A humble attitude by the supervisor towards what might have been going in the group both concerning processes and content, can be of help in becoming wiser, both to the supervisor and the supervisees. Humility involves being willing to give away one's definition of power about what has been going on, and together with the group try to understand and make connections by sharing experiences in a non-judgemental, non-conclusive manner. All research and exploration starts with humility. Here the supervisor has an important task in encouraging the participants in "expanding the opening hours" of understanding, in other words to not understand too quickly.

Example: A supervision group with experienced therapists was "slow-going". Some individuals in the group expressed practically a distrust towards me, and thought I had too much structure, while others thought I shouldn't let myself be managed by those who wanted less structure. I wanted to share with them how these two contradictory messages affected me (see the section about meta-communication). I expressed that it is important to me that everyone in a supervision group experiences being seen and heard, that all voices are equally as important and that I have a wish for the supervision to be perceived as useful. The contradictions which had arisen were challenging to me because they touched the sore point called "wanting to please everyone". I emphasized not blaming anyone. At the end of the supervision course the group seemed to enter a mode in which both I and the supervisees managed to reach each other and meet each other in a more sensitive and respectful way. During evaluation they asked me how this group and supervision has been for me. I felt a sense of joy and confidence because they asked me this. I tried to the best of my ability to articulate which feelings, dilemmas, thoughts, and choices I have been concerned with, as openly and humbly as I could.

The group received this in a very empathetic and sensitive way. More than one of them said: "It would have been nice to continue the supervision now".

Meta-Communication

Meta-communication is to communicate about communication. These conversations are often useful, both as routine elements and as interventions when for example discomfort is felt, but difficult to word. It can help the supervisor and the group to move on from a deadlocked situation. The meta-conversation can resemble evaluation, yet it is on another level. Evaluation is more of an all-round assessment and reflection of how the supervision has worked and which benefits the participants have had.

In a meta-conversation we have found the following questions opening and useful:

- What is happening between us now? What is happening in the group? Do you experience what we are talking about as useful to you or would you rather focus on something else? How is your experience when talking with us about this? How is security and openness experienced in this conversation? In what way are we listening to each other? And how are the responses? Is there anything about my or our way of communicating which makes it difficult?

This type of conversation about the conversation often results in an increased sense of security, increased experience of meaning, and often a new vitalization of the supervision process. Supervisees often find inspiration to practice this themselves, both professionally and privately.

To Sort Out

What is mine in what is happening? What is each of the other's?

We are talking about having an ownership of one's own affairs, and being able to sort out what I can and have to take responsibility for, and what I cannot control. What should I put my energy into and what should I let go? Self-help groups all over the world have used the sentences which the American theologian Reinhold Niebuhr formulated as 'The Serenity Prayer' in the beginning of the 1900s, as a help to analyse and sort out everyday life's small and large dilemmas of this kind:

> *God, Grant me the serenity to accept the things I cannot change; courage to change the things I can; and wisdom to know the difference.*

I quickly think that "it's my fault". However sometimes it isn't my fault, but factors I can't control which have triggered the situation. The supervisor (and the supervisees) will benefit from asking themselves: What is my contribution to a breakdown, and what might be my contribution to a repair? It might be, for example, that I am not good at dealing with situations where people are complaining a lot or that they do not take responsibility for their own situation. Instead of thinking linearly and looking for causes outside of myself, the 'sorting-out-work' should be started. What is it in me which is challenged by this? Which of my own sources have been touched, my own contribution? The discomfort seems to be coming from the outside, and that might be the case, but if I am handling this poorly, do my reactions have to do with my own thoughts, feelings, and sore spots? What are they? One of Socrates' first sources of wisdom was: "Know thyself". When putting into words one's reactions in the group, a part of this 'sorting-out-work' is to clarify who is the subject, who owns the thoughts, feelings, and reactions. You should talk from the perspective of yourself, and not from 'one', 'people', 'you', or 'we'. I am the one who has an opinion, I experience, I think, I feel, and I believe. The I-message shows ownership, which prevents blurriness and the insecurity which is created when something is up in the air, by 'someone thinking that…'. A clearly sorted out communication leaves less room for guessing and obscureness, and makes it easier and more open to relay what each individual experiences.

Take Responsibility and Take Measures

As supervisor it is my responsibility to try to get learning and development out of conflicts, whether it is a conflict between the group members or between them and the supervisor. As supervisor I should thus ask and perhaps express what I think is happening and explore how it is experienced by the individual. I should be one step ahead and be open about my own impressions. They might be unfounded, they might indicate what many are experiencing. In any case, it is a part of the supervisor's position to be a sensitive catalyst when necessary. Avoidance is usually not a useful strategy, but something which might in the short-term make things less uncomfortable, especially when dealing with tensions between people. When you as a supervisor initiate trying to put into words uncomfortable processes, you are also a role model for how uncomfortable things can be talked about. When supervisees see that I as a supervisor dare to, it can create a security which might start repairing processes. "He can be trusted, he is doing something about it".

Apologize (Profusely)

When a breakdown occurs and the supervisees experience that the supervisor has messed up, and it feels recognizable to me as supervisor, it is necessary to apologize profusely and in an empathetic and credible way. When we have done this, it can be useful to ask whether the apology can be accepted. This last part is easily ignored, because we are used to thinking that when an apology has been uttered, forgiveness is automatically given. To ask whether it can be accepted, opens up a further elaboration of that which created the conflict.

Transparency

We believe that it is enlightening and ethically right to strive for an openness both about the process and the content in a supervision. The supervisor is no closed sphinx who is pushing secret buttons. What you are thinking, why you are asking as you do, what the thought is behind the direction and structures you are suggesting, should be promoted as suggestions and be explained openly. Even when one has this intention, we believe it to be naïve to think that we succeed in doing this at all times. Even though we might not succeed in doing this at all times and consistently, the attitude is important, as is the will to do it. Openness kills many fantasies. Openness is often easier for the supervisees to respond to, than unclear and hidden intentions and motives on the supervisor's part.

Give Space for the Emotions

In a conflict, strong feelings usually arise, such as fear, anger, shame, guilt, disgust, discouragement, and frustration. These feelings and conditions I should, as supervisor, try to recognize and help the participants to put into words. If I am able to handle and hold these reactions, I am showing that these feelings and conditions aren't dangerous, but natural, and can further the process. Feelings aren't just reactions, but also important information sources. What are these/this feeling

(s) trying to tell you and us? Which resources can you hold? All behaviour is communication (Watzlawick et al., 1974), not least feelings and body language. The supervisor should see these expressions and know how to use it as information in a respectful way.

Humour

Humour can be a door-opener, a bridge-builder, and a liberator. Humour in the group is often a good sign of a well-functioning group. Where the conflict level is high, there is usually no room for humour, the perspective is too narrow for it to get through. Humour can also be a wall, something which conceals and covers uncomfortable topics to avoid conflicts. The supervisor can hold a position which opens up to, or closes down to, humour. To find humour's legend and energy-giving powers, and to uncover its concealing function, should be part of the supervisor's clinical judgement and improvisational ability. Humour cannot be planned, but needs to occur spontaneously (Dahl, 2013).

Externalize

When we do not succeed, or experience it that way, we might think that we are inadequate, when it comes to ourselves or others. It is human to consider the people or the relationships as the problem. Another perspective might be to see the threat of a breakdown as the problem in itself. What is this problem (the breakdown) capable of making us do? With this perspective one might be able to view more freely what happens or has happened, and how it affects each individual. It does require, however, that the supervisor has created an understanding of this way of talking about it. Otherwise objections might arise indicating that you are trying to evade the problem or disavow the responsibility. However, an externalizing approach emphasizes to a large extent that you take responsibility for how you deal with the problem and what you can do about it (White & Epston, 1992).

In a supervision group where two supervisees were about to get into a vehement discussion and argument which might have led to a breakdown, the supervisor intervened and asked whether there was a 'performance-ghost' in the room who wanted to ruin the relationships and the group? She had noticed that there were many in the group who had very high standards and were self-critical. This made it difficult for some of the participants to accept good feedback. The supervisor's reflection and suggestion to call this the 'performance-ghost' resonated with many and made it easier to talk about. The class ended with the supervisor opening the door and chasing away the 'performance-ghost' and locking the door. A lot of laughter ensued, and the atmosphere became lighter.

Personal Skills

Therapy research (Tilden, 2015; Wampold & Imel, 2015) has shown that the therapist's personal qualities are what end up being of significance to the patient, even more than methods and theoretical foundations. To a large extent, this probably applies to supervision as well. Therefore it is useful to be conscious of which personal qualities one has which can be of use in a repair process. In feedback informed supervision, where one asks for feedback systematically, it is possible to get to know even better how supervisees experience one's strengths and weaknesses. Through our own supervision it is also possible to develop one's consciousness about how a person functions and interacts with others. A personal characteristic could be that a person is unafraid and straightforward, or has a friendly and trusting expression. This can be decisive in a repair process where the supervisee(s) is invited to share how they have experienced something which was difficult.

"To Be in Place"

If one is to try to repair relationships, it is a strength that you know yourself, as mentioned previously. As supervisor, you should consider: How does this feel to me? Which feelings are activated? How do I react to my own emotions? Which thought-patterns do I enter into? If I for example keep a narrative about myself as an empathetic and sensitive person, this story can be threatened when I hear other stories about myself, which do not support my own. Am I not empathetic and sensitive after all? Is it just something I am imagining? As supervisor it is an advantage to know oneself and one's reactions well, and being able to handle them. Most of us do not like being rejected, but we need to tolerate it as supervisors, and be able to see the nuance between what we do and who we are. As supervisors we get the opportunity to practise holding onto our own self-perception, all the while moving and changing. It is therefore meaningful that we are able to develop a self-compassion, which is different from self-pity. It is simply to have empathy with yourself and treat yourself in a respectful and loving way. A very experienced supervisor once said: "If I were to treat and speak of others the same way I do to myself – I would probably be punished". In other words, it is a demanding task to show self-compassion, because many of us are prone to listening more to the strict judge within. Therapy research (Wampold, 2014) shows that therapists who aren't perfect, but who have their own struggles, often get the best relationships with their patients. They do not come off as 'superhumans', but as someone the patients can easily identify with. We presume that the same can be applicable in supervision relationships. To show one's weaknesses and incompleteness can be freeing to the supervision group. In other words, in this case to lead the way as a "bad example". We believe that there is a lot of wisdom in what *doesn't* succeed, as Leonard Cohen puts it in *"Anthem"*:

"Forget your perfect offering
There is a crack in everything
That's how the light gets in".

Experiences (Issues) from the Previous Supervision Session

Supervision sessions should start by seeing if anyone has something to bring up from the last supervision session. This might be something which can be elaborated, corrected, or appreciated. It can also be loose ends, something up in the air, something which turned out badly, something someone wants to say to another, or something which has popped into your head. Joy and gratefulness can also be expressed, or something one has managed or accomplished since last time. Many a time this round has helped them put into words something they experienced as pent-up or unfinished. In this way, these situations can be dealt with quickly, before they are able to grow larger.

It might be that I, as supervisor, experienced the last session as good and successful. In the evaluation the supervisees spoke of benefits and learning. Yet in retrospect it can be experienced differently, and that is why it is important to ask the question of whether something needs to be said from the last session. At times they might wonder why I said and did as I did, and then this yields a possibility to explain and clarify. This is often a good preventative measure to strengthen and develop the relationship so that it becomes sustainable. It should make room for trials and errors both on the supervisor's and supervisees' parts, and consequently for clarifications and reconciliations. In addition, these questions and the round ties the supervision sessions together.

Final Reflections

We have presented examples of when the supervision has broken down without the possibility for repair. We have also presented cases which have been repaired, as well as some which could have led to breakdowns, but which didn't. We have not suggested any clear recipe of how it should have been repaired in the examples, because there are many possible paths which could be used. Therefore we decided to present a few elements which we have experienced to be efficient in an attempt at repairing. It has struck us how emotionally demanding it has been to contemplate these events. Some experiences we have wanted to forget, or we wish that they had never happened. However, by conveying them in this chapter, we have had the chance to look at them again, and with you the readers in mind, it has helped us process them. Perhaps we have become slightly better supervisors both because of the experiences and by telling about them. By trying to understand again what has happened, and by asking the individual supervisees who were there about how things looked from their point of view, we have gained valuable new insights. As Virginia Satir has said: "It is difficult to change one's point of view. It is less difficult to change the point from which you view".

One can question whether it is possible to proceed with supervision where the relationship has broken down. Relationships need to be built over time. But after a breakdown, and when it has been possible to repair, the relationship usually feels even safer, and more mistakes are tolerated on the supervisor's part because the supervisees feel appreciated and seen. This is also described in therapy as "tears and repairs". Finally, we would like to say that in most supervisions we do not experience breakdowns, but we have learned to consider breakdowns and the danger of breakdowns more and more as an opportunity to learn, develop and grow—although still in a very demanding way. If one does not manage to go through a breakdown, it might not be advisable to take on the supervision task, because supervision can be a risky project. Without risks it might not be a place of learning, because supervision is a relational cooperation project where all the participants, including the supervisor, encounter each other with their own vulnerabilities and strengths.

References

Bang, S. (2007). *Rørt, rammet og rystet, faglig vekst gjennom veiledning*. Oslo: Gyldendal Akademiske forlag.

Burck, C., & Daniel, G. (2010). *Mirrors and reflections: Process of systemic supervision*. London: Karnac.

Dahl, I. (2013). *Humor som terapeutisk praksis*. Master's thesis, Diakonhjemmet Høgskole, Oslo, Norway.

Goldsmith, J. (2014). *Why is alliance in psychotherapy crucial?* Lecture: Kildehuset Modum Bad, Viksersund, Norway.

Haugsgjerd, S. (2005). *Kjærlighetens kraftlinjer*. Oslo: Pax Forlag.

Heap, K. (1988). Personal communication.

Honneth, A. (2008). *Kamp om anerkjennelse: om de sosiale konfliktenes moralske grammatikk*. Oslo: Pax Forlag.

Maturana, H. R., & Varela, F. J. (1987). *The tree of knowledge*. Boston: New Science Library.

Nissen-Lie, H. (2012). Hva kjennetegner gode og mindre gode psykoterapeuter? "Mellanrummet" nordisk tidskrift för barn- och ungdomspsykoterapi. *Nordic Journal of Child and Adolescent Psychotherapy*. Oslo no. 26, 2012.

Øverland, S. (2014). Tidsskrift for Norsk psykologforening. *Terapi er kjærlighet* (*Therapy Is Love*), *51*(5), 406–407.

Rønnestad, M. H., & Reichelt, S. (2011). *Psykoterapiveiledning*. Oslo: Tano Aschehoug.

Satir, V. (n.d.). https://satirglobal.org/about-virginia-satir/

Teslo, A. (2016). *Mangfold i faglig veiledning for helse- og sosialarbeidere*. Oslo: Oslo Universitetsforlaget.

Thrana, H. M. (2013). Kjærlighet: en kjernekompetanse i profesjonelt barnevernsarbeid? Tidsskriftet Norges Barnevern, 90(1), 4–17.
Thrana, H. M. (2016). Kjærlighetens inntreden i barnevernet - en utfordring for den profesjonelle relasjon? Tidsskriftet Norges barnevern 02/2016. Volum 93.
Tilden, T. (2015). Personal communication.
Wampold, B. (2014). Personal communication.
Wampold, B., & Imel, Z. E. (2015). *The great psychotherapy debate*. New York: Norton.
Watzlawick, P., Weakland, J., Fisch, R., & Erickson, M. D. (1974). *Change: Principles of problem formation and problem resolution*. New York: W. W. Norton & Company.
White, M., & Epston, D. (1992). *Experience, contradiction, narrative and imagination: Selected papers & 1989-1991*. Adelaide, South Australia: Dulwich Centre Publications.

Chapter 16
The Supervision of Supervision: A Thematic Analysis of Family Therapy Supervisors' Experiences of a Group Supervision Structure in a Training Context

Jim Sheehan

Introduction

While there is a growing body of literature and research on systemic supervision there has been no comparable engagement in the systemic literature with 'the supervision of supervision' within the field of systemic couple and family therapy. In the most comprehensive works on systemic supervision thus far (Burck & Daniel, 2010; Todd & Storm, 2014), the topic is mentioned only a handful of times (Abela & Sammut Scerri, 2010; Haber et al., 2009; Prouty & Storm, 2014; Reiner, 2014) and always in the context of other supervision-related themes. For this writer such a gap left something of a mystery with respect to how systemic supervisors meet their need for reflection on their systemic supervision practice. I wondered whether contemporary systemic supervisors simply include this part of their professional practice in what they bring to their regular professional supervision. I wondered also whether or not systemic supervisors think of this sphere of their systemic practice as requiring any dedicated space for exploration and reflection. Some postgraduate training programs clearly have mentoring opportunities available for novice systemic supervisors (Prouty & Storm, 2014) within that domain. However, in the absence of program accreditation requirements relating to the supervision of systemic supervision, it remains unclear whether postgraduate family therapy training programs put formal systems in place for the ongoing support and development of their systemic supervisors. Where such formal systems are in place it is not clear how they are perceived and experienced by those participating in them. The occasion for this current study arose through the identification of a program where such a formal system for the support and supervision of systemic supervisors was in

J. Sheehan (✉)
Family Therapy Section, Faculty of Social Studies, VID Specialized University, Oslo, Norway
e-mail: jimssheehan@outlook.com

A. Vetere, J. Sheehan (eds.), *Supervision of Family Therapy and Systemic Practice*, Focused Issues in Family Therapy, https://doi.org/10.1007/978-3-319-68591-5_16

place for a significant period of time. While it is acknowledged that qualifying training programs are just one of the many contexts in which systemic supervision takes place, such training programs have an important function for the profession of couple and family therapy as gateways into professional practice and they are very often the context in which systemic supervisors first 'cut their teeth'.

This chapter aims to address elements of this gap in understanding through reporting the findings of a qualitative study of systemic supervisors' experiences and reflections on their participation in an ongoing group-based 'supervision of supervision' event. The context of the eight participants' systemic supervision practice was a 4-year postgraduate, Masters, program in couple and family therapy. The program-based systemic supervision in which they were engaged was a combination of group and individual supervision of trainee clinical work (both live and retrospective) with couples and families. The program in which they supervise is based in a European city and its graduates meet the criteria for registration with the European Family Therapy Association (EFTA). All of the eight systemic supervisors interviewed for the study were fluent English speakers and the interviews were conducted in English. Their group-based supervision of supervision event happened for one and a half hours each month, had been in operation since the year 2008, and was continuing to function in its ninth year at the completion of this study in the middle of 2017. The group was referred to by its participating supervisors as a 'supervision forum'. The eight participants in the study comprised the total cohort of systemic supervisors currently supervising within this program.

The Research Questions

The research found its focus through the following two questions: how do the participants experience their participation in this group-based 'supervision of supervision' event? And, secondly, what connections do they make, if any, between this participation and their systemic supervision practice. When, as researcher, I initially framed these questions for the study I was thinking primarily of the connections the participants might make between their participation in the group supervision of supervision event and their program-based supervision of the clinical work of students in training. As the interviewing of the participants gathered momentum it became clear that the relevant connections for them were not limited to their program-based supervision but encompassed the broad range of systemic supervision practices in which most of them were engaged. An additional interest in the research was how these supervisors experienced the 'group' character of the supervision of supervision they were engaged in.

Hopes for the Study

At the planning stages my hope for the study was that it could throw some light on the elements that might be relevant and important for systemic supervisors in the context of the supervision of their supervision practice. What did they hope for within the experience? What kind of impact on their supervision practice did they perceive as arising from their participation in the 'supervision of supervision' group? In what ways might they have felt that it contributed to the quality of their systemic supervision practice? Might there be different ways in which supervisors approached their participation and, if so, what might these differences be? Such questions reflect some of the additional points of interest behind the two primary research questions mentioned above.

Organisation of the Chapter

As a research report, the chapter will commence with a brief literature review focusing on the way certain elements within the literature and research on the supervision of supervision provide a background and context for this specific study. The chapter will continue with a description of the methods used in the generation of data for the study, the professional and supervisory profiles for the eight participants in the study, an outline of the approach to thematic analysis being deployed in the study, as well as an account of the ethical considerations to which the study gave rise. This section of the report will also make explicit the theoretical and other assumptions guiding the research through its different stages. In particular, this section will describe the researcher's own relationship to the theme of the study. This section of the chapter will close with an account of the sequential steps taken in the analysis of the data as the process through which the study arrived at its own particular findings.

The next section of the chapter will present the findings of the study in the form of a thematic map denoting the key themes and accompanying sub-themes arising from the analytic work. In addition I will note any contradictions or other points of interest arising within the process of analysis. The chapter will conclude with a discussion of the study's findings in the light of existing literature and research as well as considering some of the implications arising from the study for the practice of systemic supervision and its own systemic supervision.

The Supervision of Supervision: A Developing Tradition Within Psychotherapy

As a prelude to exploring the literature on the topic a search was conducted using the search engines of a local university library. The search was conducted under the terms 'supervision of supervision' and 'the supervision of psychotherapy supervision'.

In contrast to the idea of supervision the concept of the supervision of supervision appears to be of relatively recent origin within the psychotherapy tradition. However, Power (2013) reminds us that the actuality of supervision of supervision may be just as old as the practice of supervision which gives rise to it. The developing story of the supervision of supervision in psychotherapy appears to reflect a movement from informal, ad hoc, collegial types of dialogue to more formal, structured arrangements in which professional bodies are set to take such activities under their wing. Yerushalmi (1999), writing from within a psychoanalytic/psychodynamic tradition, notes that despite a long-standing assumption evident within that branch of psychotherapy literature that experienced clinicians with extensive supervisory and therapeutic experience do not need assistance with the supervisory process, experience suggests that psychotherapy supervisors often 'turn to colleagues, hold informal meetings, or even convene regularly to resolve troubling supervisory issues and discuss their experiences as supervisors' (p. 427). A certain scepticism regarding the need for the supervision of supervision is also present in the broader field of psychotherapy (Jacobs, 2000; Leader, 2010). This scepticism moves towards an aversion to the activity in some writers (Mander, 2002) where the supervision of supervision is seen as promoting 'an unnecessary and unwieldy proliferation of watchdogs *ad infinitum*' (p. 132). Notwithstanding this scepticism along the way the United Kingdom Council for Psychotherapy produced a policy document on supervision 5 years ago which stipulates that: 'Supervisors must receive appropriate supervision of their supervision from a supervisor who meets the criteria as set out in this document' (2012, p. 8a).

Within the arena of systemic psychodynamic supervision, Reiner (2014) describes movements in the direction of the supervision of supervision. Psychodynamic supervisors are reported as counting among their responsibilities that of 'reflecting upon and assessing their own functioning as systemic supervisors and for arranging periodic evaluation of their supervision (e.g., obtaining supervision-of-supervision)' (p. 177).

Two important research studies conducted at the turn of the century, one in North America and the other in the UK, threw some light on the phenomena of supervisor countertransference and the prevalence of supervision of supervision respectively. In their qualitative study of supervisor countertransference, Ladany, Constantine, Miller, Erickson, and Muse-Burke found that supervisors managed their countertransference by talking with colleagues. The authors of the study suggested, however, that such informal approaches could not be recommended as they seemed to leave too much to chance. Instead they proposed that supervisors might need 'a scheduled activity' in order to offset the risk of supervisor countertransferences going unchecked (2000, p. 111). It seemed as though this advice was already being followed in the UK where Wheeler and King's (2001) survey of accredited supervisors within the British Association of Counselling and Psychotherapy found that 90% of respondents reported availing of supervision of supervision. They also found that the three areas they were most likely to discuss within their supervision of supervision were ethical issues, boundaries and the competence of their supervisees.

Yerushalmi (1999), writing from the context of the supervision of trainee psychoanalytic psychotherapists, recommends the use of group supervision of supervision for senior professionals engaged in the regular supervision of trainees. Despite the challenges arising both internally and externally from the group character of such supervision, Yerushalmi suggests that among the great advantages of the supervision group are its capacities to promote feelings of security and containment in supervisors, to validate their perceptions of reality and to reduce their potential feelings of vulnerability.

The training of psychologists as supervisors is another arena in which a group approach to the supervision of supervision has been found beneficial. DiMino and Risler (2012) report on the training of two small cohorts of doctoral level psychologists as supervisors. They endorse the group approach to the training of supervisors once the supervisors of supervision pay adequate attention to group processes, relational themes and to the boundary maintenance issues that inevitably arise from the multiple relationships that characterise the larger training context in which supervision training occurs.

While Power (2013) generally endorses the use of supervision of supervision, which she sometimes refers to as 'supervision consultancy', she cautions such consultants to focus predominantly on the relationships happening in the supervision room and to a lesser extent on what is happening in the therapy room. Given that so much supervision happens in groups it is seen as important for both supervisors and supervision consultants 'to have some understanding of group dynamics and an alertness to the kinds of defensive processes which may impact on exploration and understanding' (2013, p. 392).

Within the systemic psychotherapy tradition, Haug and Storm (2014) place the practice of supervision of supervision firmly within the framework of supervisors' ethical responsibilities. They underline the importance of supervisors practicing and modelling what they regularly preach to their supervisees, namely, a commitment to lifelong learning and continuous peer supervision. They tell us that: 'Periodic consultation on the supervision supervisors provide, so-called supervision mentoring, is the primary vehicle for supervisors to become aware of their own blind spots and to continually expand their competencies' (p. 20). Prouty and Storm (2014) elaborate their perspective on the concept of mentoring in supervision by indicating that they see it 'as a form of peer mentorship done by experienced colleagues' (p. 399). From the perspective of these authors the supervisor mentor carries two functions. The first of these is concerned with assisting novice supervisors in getting established in their role. The second function is the provision of advanced training to experienced supervisors. They explain that the pathway into becoming a mentor is an experiential learning process and that in the North American context there is no formal training for mentors who rely on peer consultation and participation in continuing education in supervision as the chief ways to develop their mentoring capacities.

Systemic supervision is often a context in which multiple relationships arise. Some members of a supervision group or the members of a supervisory dyad may have had longstanding professional relationships of different kinds. Abela and Sammut Scerri (2010) suggest that the complexities arising from multiple relationships within systemic supervision can be a challenge not only for supervisors in small communities but also for those practising in large cities. They note, in particular, the potential helpfulness of 'a safe supervision-of-supervision relationship' in the context of supervisors managing certain aspects of their relationship with supervisees. In particular, they point to the importance of this supervision of supervision relationship for supervisors when sexual attraction begins to emerge within the supervisor-supervisee relationship. Recent years have also seen a growing interest in systemic supervision as a place where the cultural sensitivity of psychotherapists can and should be promoted (Hardy & Bobes, 2017). Interestingly, supervisory challenges relating to gender and culture featured minimally in the findings of the current study.

The supervision of supervision, as the foregoing literature suggests, is gradually revealing itself as a developing field of supervisory endeavour. It has a presence not only within psychotherapy training institutions of different kinds but also in a range of service areas where psychotherapy is practised. However, in the movement from an informal to a more formally structured approach to its practice there remains little focused study of the topic. The current qualitative study aims to address one aspect of this gap. It will examine the experiences and reflections of a group of supervisors who have been engaged in a group-based supervision of supervision event over a long period of time. While much of the existing literature in the area provides very rich descriptions by experienced supervisors/mentors in the psychotherapy field of the processes and challenges involved in the provision of supervision of supervision such descriptions needs to be complemented by careful attention to the reflections of those supervisors immersed in the experience themselves and hoping to gain something from it for their own supervision practice. It is these reflections that form the heart of the current study of the topic within the field of systemic supervision.

Methods and Methodology Used in the Study

The chapter will now describe, in turn, the data collection methods used for the study, the professional profiles of the eight participants, thematic analysis as used in the study, the ethical underpinnings of the study, the theoretical and other assumptions guiding the study as well as a description of the steps undertaken in the analysis that led to the study's findings.

Study Methods

In the context of a qualitative study focusing on systemic supervisors' experiences of, and reflections upon, their own group supervision event, the face-to-face, semi-structured interview with individual supervisors was chosen as an appropriate method of generating data for the study. When guided by a semi-structured interview schedule the face-to-face interview gives participants an opportunity to express themselves freely and fully on the topic at the same time as allowing the researcher opportunity to clarify in the moment any aspect of what is being said. The possibility of utilising a mixture of focus groups alongside individual interviews was also explored with potential participants but the logistics of co-ordinating focus groups with a number of very busy systemic practitioner/supervisors proved too challenging. While a focus group might well have generated a different quality of data at the same time as bringing variety into the contexts through which data was gathered, feasibility determined the choice of data collection method in the end. The result was that all of the eight supervisors attached to this postgraduate training program in systemic family therapy consented to participation in the study and met with the researcher for individual interviews at a time that was suitable for them. Their contribution to the study was marked by a spirit of generosity throughout. Seven of the eight interviews were conducted face-to-face at the program's family therapy training centre while the final interview was conducted on the telephone due to the logistical challenges of meeting face-to-face.

Following a meeting about the study with the leader of the identified family therapy training program the researcher met with most of the participants together about 2 months in advance of the commencement of the study to talk with them about the proposed study and to ask them to give some consideration to their possible participation. As the individual supervisors consented to participation they were provided with a copy of the interview schedule a week in advance of their interview. Interviews lasted between 40 min and 1 h. The transcription of the recorded interviews was undertaken directly by the researcher and it was these eight transcripts that became the central data for analytic endeavour.

Professional and Supervisory Profiles of the Participants

At the commencement of each interview information was collected from the participants concerning their professional disciplines-of-origin, the length of time since completion of their own family therapy training, the length of time since completion of their own training as systemic supervisors, the range of practice contexts in which they have offered systemic supervision to supervisees, as well as the number of years in which they had participated in the group supervision of family therapy supervision known locally as 'the supervision forum'. The table below summarises information on these five variables for each of the eight participants.

Professional profiles for participating supervisors

Systemic supervisor (SS) (M/F)	Discipline of origin	No. of years qualified as family therapist	No. of years since training as systemic supervisor	Range of practice contexts of their supervisees	No. of years participating in supervision forum
SS1(F)	Psychology	21	14	Domestic violence; Child and adolescent mental health; Adult mental health; Institutional abuse	9
SS2(M)	Social work	21	15	Child protection; Child and adolescent mental health; Private practice; Adult mental health	9

(continued)

Professional profiles for participating supervisors					
Systemic supervisor (SS) (M/F)	Discipline of origin	No. of years qualified as family therapist	No. of years since training as systemic supervisor	Range of practice contexts of their supervisees	No. of years participating in supervision forum
SS3(F)	Nursing	12	6	Child sexual abuse; Child and adolescent mental health; Family therapy training	5
SS4(F)	Psychology	16	11	Addiction; Sexual abuse; Forensic psychology; Adult mental health; Youth justice disability; CAMHS	4
SS5(F)	Psychology	22	11	Adult mental health; Psychology students; Training family therapists	9
SS6(F)	Nursing	27	11	Addiction treatment; Agency family therapy; Adult mental health; Separating parents	5
SS7(F)	Social work	27	20	Child and adolescent mental health; Training programme; Adolescent counselling; Agency supervision	9
SS8(F)	Nursing	26	9	Adult mental health; Social work; Intellectual disability; Private practice	6

Profile of participants' qualifications and experience, supervision practices, and supervision-of-supervision experience

As can be seen from the table, the participants included three psychologists, three nurses and two social workers. All of the eight participants had completed either a 1 or 2-year, part-time training in systemic teaching and supervision and the range of their post-qualification years as systemic supervisors spanned from 6 to 20 years. This group of supervisors offered systemic supervision in many different formats and contexts outside of the program supervision that was at the heart of this study. Their systemic supervision experiences included group and individual supervision, agency-based as well as privately-contracted supervision. The practice contexts in which they supervised included the fields of addiction treatment, adult and child mental health, child protection, child sexual abuse investigation and treatment, disability services, youth justice, child and adolescent mental health and couple and family therapy. The length of time of their participation in the supervision of family therapy supervision group varied from 4 to 9 years. It should be noted that participation in the supervision of supervision group was not always continuous for each of the participants as some dropped out of the experience for a year or two if they were not supervising a trainee group in those particular years. All of the participants were also practicing systemic psychotherapists, to different degrees, during the period of time they were participants in the group-based supervision of supervision event.

Thematic Analysis Used in the Study

Thematic analysis (Boyatzis, 1998; Braun & Clarke, 2006) was chosen as the approach to guide the analysis. Thematic analysis has been described as 'a method for identifying, analysing and reporting patterns themes) within data' (Braun & Clarke, 2006). Its basic purpose is to facilitate the organisation and description of a data set in rich detail. While it always provides a richly descriptive component as the first level of analysis it regularly goes beyond this to offer, at a second level, an interpretative component with respect to the topic being studied (Boyatzis, 1998). As a method of qualitative research two of its key proponents (Braun & Clarke, 2006) see it as a flexible method that is not inextricably linked to any pre-existing theoretical framework. They show how the method can be used within a realist approach (which simply reports the experiences, meanings and realities of research participants), within a constructionist approach (where the realities, meanings and experiences of participants are seen to be the effects of both wider societal discourses as well as the outcome of more local social exchange) or within a 'contextualist' approach which reflects elements of the two poles of realism and constructionism (where there is an appreciation of both the way individuals make meaning of their experience, as well as of the ways the broader social context impacts and gives shape to those meanings, without surrendering a perspective on the way reality, particularly in its material aspects, sets limits on those twin processes). This very flexibility, however, imposes a responsibility on a researcher using thematic analysis to be clear about the theoretical positions presiding over their study and the interpretation of its findings.

Theoretical Perspective Underpinning the Study

This study fits theoretically within a constructionist framework (Gergen, 1985; 1994; 2009; Gergen, 1985; McNamee & Gergen, 1992; Shotter, 1993). From the moment the central research questions were shaped, through the interviewing of participants, the transcription of audio-tapes, to the process of analysis which resulted in the construction of a thematic map, and the eventual writing of this report, the researcher has had an active engagement with the participants, their audio-taped interviews and the resulting transcripts. Notwithstanding the presence of the researcher's interpretative hand at every stage of the study, the research process, particularly in its analytic phase, has endeavoured to remain faithful to the total set of meanings and perspectives conveyed by the participants during their interviews. Such aspiration of fidelity to the utterances of participants has meant that the analytic process has remained data-driven throughout. As such, it represents an inductive, or 'bottom up', type of thematic analysis as opposed to a deductive, or 'top down', type of thematic analysis where the analytic endeavour is more theory-driven. It will only be in the concluding 'discussion' section of the chapter that the commentary will break from its moorings to participant utterances and engage in a deeper reflection on the meaning of the study's findings, conceived in more abstract terms, in the light of existing literature and research. However, not even at this stage of the study will the commentary surrender its goal of fidelity to participants' meanings. On the contrary, it will aim to realise the significance of these meanings more fully as they are brought into contact with perspectives arising from the literature, contemporary discourses on systemic supervision and the researcher's own experience of the topic.

In the construction of the thematic map at the heart of the study's findings two criteria have guided the choice of what are presented as the central themes and accompanying sub-themes in the study. The first criterion is that they are significantly reflective of patterns of meaning occurring throughout the entire data set. The narrative account of these central themes and accompanying sub-themes will give the reader an idea of their prevalence within the set of data items (the eight participant interviews) without actually recording in the text the extent of their prevalence across the entire data set. The second criterion guiding the choice of central themes concerns whether or not the theme has something relevant to say with respect to the research questions underpinning the study.

Ethical Considerations

In October 2016, the study received exemption from full ethical review from the Human Research Ethics Committee in the University where the supervisors are engaged and from where their family therapy trainees receive their awards. All the participants signed consent forms which indicated they understood the nature of the study, had opportunities to ask the researcher questions about the study, and understood that their participation was voluntary and that they had the right to withdraw from the study at any stage without giving reason. Their consent also underlined that neither they nor their trainees, either individually or as a group, would be identified in any future publication of the study and its findings.

Researcher Relationship to the Study Topic

The researcher undertaking the study qualified as a family therapist 34 years ago and has been a systemic supervisor for the last 33 years. He has been involved in the development of systemic supervisor training in two European countries and has contributed to the training of systemic supervisors in a number of other countries. He was director of a masters' level program in family and couple therapy for 25 years. He is known to the participants in this study through his role within Europe as a systemic practitioner, supervisor, consultant and trainer.

Stages in the Thematic Analysis of the Data

The analytic process within the study followed the six-stage stage model proposed by Braun and Clarke (2006). The first of these stages involved *familiarisation with the study's data*. In this particular study, the work at this stage included listening a number of times to the audio-taped interviews as part of the process of transcription in advance of reading and re-reading the interview transcripts and further checking them against the audio-taped interviews. The second stage in this study involved *setting up initial codes across the entire data set* at the same time as holding together pieces of data belonging to each code. The third stage was focused on *the search for potential themes* arising from the researcher's combination of different codes. The fourth stage involved the *checking of candidate themes* in relation to coded extracts as well as against the entire data set. The finishing point of this stage was the construction of a thematic map for the analysis as a whole. The fifth stage of analysis concerns itself with *the naming of themes* in such a way that they are clearly distinguishable from each other and that each of their sub-themes hang together sufficiently well 'under' their key theme. The sixth stage in the analysis was *the production of the research report* which involved the final selection of extracts, consideration of the overall story about the topic being researched that was generated at the previous stage, as well as the relating back of the findings to both the literature and the research questions.

The Study Findings

Following engagement with the complete data set through the stages of the analytic process described above, the following four key themes, with their accompanying sub-themes, seemed to best encompass the broad set of meanings found in the study. The four themes are: The Group as a Valued Space; Positive Functions of the Group; Limitations of the Group; and, Impact on Supervision. These themes and their accompanying sub-themes are represented in the thematic map displayed in the figure below.

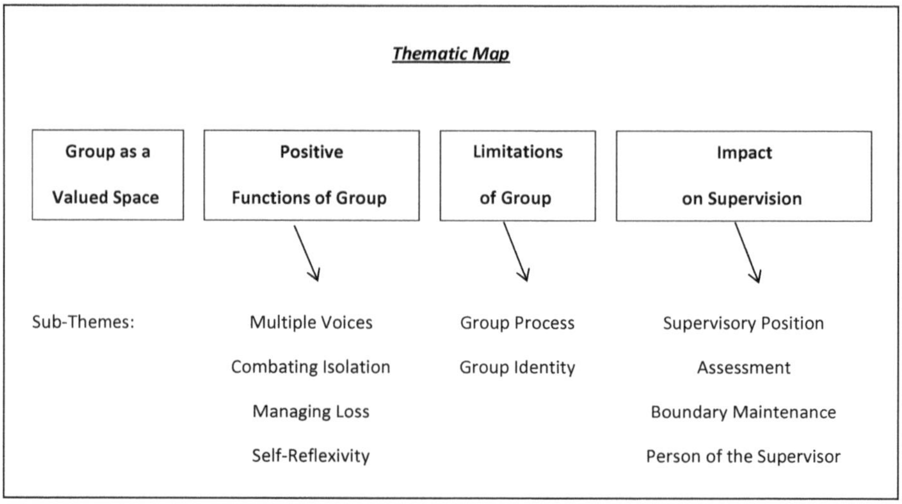

Thematic map of supervisors' experiences of supervision-of-supervision

The Group as a Valued Space

The essence of this theme lies in the appreciation of supervision of supervision as a valued and necessary space and activity. There was no sense in any of the participants' interviews that the activity was an 'optional extra' added on to an already onerous supervisory task. This perspective becomes relevant in the context of some previous contributions in the area (Jacobs, 2000; Leader, 2010) where considerable doubt was expressed about the activity as a professional requirement, and in the context of others (Mander, 2002) where risks and possible dangers attaching to the activity were noted. All eight participants in this study expressed very positive feelings about the supervision forum and their experiences of participation within it. However, they valued the group in different ways and for different reasons. Two participants' comments valued the forum's role in facilitating *connection* between supervisors:

'It is something that I came to value very highly and I wouldn't miss it....and it does take a lot of effort for me to be there...I find it great. I think without this we would be very disconnected'. (SS8)

'I am not part of the faculty so it's been a really important connection for me with the other supervisors......hugely important because it's the only time I meet them'. (SS4)

Another participant valued the opportunity to *share experiences* with other supervisors in a space apart from the students:

'...the overall thing for me was that it was a space apart from the students to talk, and to hear, yourself and to hear other people's experiences'. (SS7)

The supervision forum as a coming together of *peers and colleagues* was emphasised by another:

'...when the supervision of supervisors came along I was delighted....because I was sitting with my peers and sitting with my colleagues, working together, and that for me was very attractive'. (SS2)

The *support* derived from hearing the experiences of other supervisors was the basis of positive valuation of the group in another participant:

'...the group was very supportive.....to hear some of the reflections and the struggles that the other supervisors were raising and how they matched some of my struggles....that was quite supportive'.(SS6)

A fifth participant valued the forum as a *safe* place to share:

'...for me it was a safe place.....it certainly was....it just felt safe and comfortable....it never felt like a space where you would feel uncomfortable to share something'. (SS5)

Collegiality, connection, safety, support, and the potential for sharing experience were all experienced by these participants as bases for their strong valuation of the supervision of supervision vehicle. This theme is also clearly linked to a sub-theme of the next-mentioned theme in this description of findings—namely, the combating of what is often experienced as an isolation attaching to the supervisory role with students in training.

Positive Functions of the Group

This theme draws attention to the several positive functions which together created a richness arising from the group character of this supervision of supervision event. The group appeared to provide for the individual supervisors a sense of togetherness in the face of the potential for isolation, a multiplicity of different voices and perspectives against which to form their own position on matters relevant to their task, a holding environment in the context of intense and unanticipated grief, and support for the exercise of a reflexive supervision practice. The supervision forum was experienced by the research participants as having this broad range of important, positive functions not just for themselves as individual supervisors but also for the program as a whole. The four sub-themes that best reflect the range of these positive functions identified by the participants are as follows: Multiple Voices; Combating Isolation; Coping with Loss; and, Self-Reflexivity.

Multiple Voices

Seven of the eight participants spoke of the positive impact for them of being exposed to the voices of multiple others in the group. Each of them, however, identified the way particular aspects of this 'multi-voice' character of the group worked well for them. One participant commented on how this feature of the group assisted her:

> *'...there is a mutual influence......one idea comes up but there might be six different voices about it but that's the richness of it...and it is then finding your own position.'* (SS3)

A second participant emphasised the value for her of this dimension in relation to reflecting on particular students and their progress. She noted that the group:

> *'creates spaces where different viewpoints can be heard about a student.....but in terms of a group think I think there can be a general agreement that a student is struggling or maybe not as strong as other students.....or even that some groups are not as strong as other groups......a group group think!.....but it's interesting listening to that too as it sort of helps when somebody says something about somebody and your experience is something different......actually I think they have changed or moved on...it creates those spaces where different viewpoints can be shared.'* (SS5)

A third participant focused on the challenge to their thinking arising from hearing the experiences of other supervisors:

> *'I think I was challenged in it from hearing other people talk about their experiences.....I am thinking of one or two examples where maybe I would have a student and got on good and thought they were doing really well.....and then moved into another group....there would be lots of different aspects of them that would be highlighted and did I miss them and how was my experience so different.....that bit...there was an enrichment in that..'*. (SS7)

Another participant appreciated the continuity between this experience of multiple voices in the group and a perspective used in program teaching:

> *'...but to have multiple voices....it's very like what we are trying to teach.....that people feel things in different ways...and they impact on people.....I find that to be a very valuable aspect of it'*. (SS8)

Combating Isolation

Four of the participants commented in different ways about the role that the supervision forum played in combating their sense of isolation or aloneness that often accompanied the activity of supervising a group of family therapy trainees or performing a particular role within the training task. One participant appreciated the discovery within the group that he was not alone:

'...finding that I wasn't on my own because quite often when you are a supervisor, you know, you are on your own' (SS2)

A second participant responded to a clarifying question I put to her about what she specifically got from the group that helped her as an individual supervisor:

'Support, ideas, listen to your complaints....because it can be quite isolating....there is a sense in the group of us being in it together and that's really important for me'. (SS4)

A third participant, who was also the program leader, referred to one of the important functions the group had for her in the context of the seniority of her institutional role:

'It's one of the places I still feel equal despite being moved up the pole....because I do feel quite alone in this post'. (SS1)

Coping with Loss

This research study was done just 2 years after the unexpected death of one of the training program's most experienced supervisors. One of the most important functions of the supervision forum for all eight participants during this time of sadness, shock and loss was the containing and holding part the group played, directly, for each of its members, and indirectly, for the program students and the program itself. In the face of this sudden death of this supervisor colleague one participant described what the group was for him:

'I used the supervision forum to actually come and support each other....to share our ideas.....that metaphor of holding each other physically....we held each other....I think that came from a depth....I'm not sure we could have done that if we had not had the supervision forum.....somebody says 'we are going to meet now'....how would we support our colleagues and how we would support the trainees.' (SS2)

Another very experienced participant also noted the holding character of the group immediately following the death:

'The group piece was very holding around times like that.' (SS5)

The same metaphor was used by the most experienced participant who described the unfolding process of holding that joined individual supervisors, the program students and the program itself:

'I think each of us were struggling in ourselves...hugely....so the group held it in some way I think....and we held it for the students....the faculty and the supervision group had to hold it for the students....while getting on with the course'. (SS7)

One of the participants who had more recently joined the supervision forum, but who had been part of the group at the time of her senior colleague's death, described the way that the group itself, in responding to the loss of one of their members, had been transformed by the event:

'...that definitely had a profound influence on the group....as to what influence.....I think there is a holding of respect for what was lost, sharing of that intense experience...and a

need to continue to honour it by moving forward in terms of the work, in terms of practice, in terms of supervision....there is something there that it does thread through.....it threads the past and the future in some way for the group....it gave the connectedness a depth..... another dimension.......another level of meaning'. (SS3)

There are clear connections between this sub-theme and that of 'boundary maintenance' attaching to the final theme which addresses the 'impact on supervision'. Coping with loss can be thought of as a kind of boundary maintenance function that protects individuals from being emotionally overwhelmed. Both sub-themes have a relevance for the topic of supervisor burn-out and its prevention which will be discussed in the next and final section of the chapter which reflects further on these findings.

Self-Reflexivity

Six of the eight participants explicitly named self-reflexivity as an important, positive and necessary function of the supervision forum. Those who didn't mention it explicitly demonstrated it in the different ways they spoke about their experiences of the group. In speaking about some of the functions the supervision forum had for him one participant spoke of:

'..transference...brought in here...into the forum.....when I'm frustrated with someone.... when somebody for whatever reason I just don't get on with them.....and the opportunity to come in here and to listen and to share and to engage.....so I have used it for that'. (SS2)

And later the same participant returned to the importance of this theme for him in the context of the group process:

'...it's always trying to not only have some theory of reflexivity but to actually practice reflexivity in a context'. (SS2)

Another participant spoke about a number of different ways in which the supervision forum both engaged her in self-reflective practice within the group itself as well as encouraging her to take the relational risk of engaging in a type of relational reflexivity with her own student training group. In the first of the following two extracts she describes how the group facilitated in her a reflection on how she was engaging in the process of student assessment:

'It was really important to hear the voices of the forum in helping me think about how I was judging their practice, how I was thinking about how they were presenting, how was I experiencing them being reflective or not...'. (SS3)

In this second extract she describes how her participation in the supervision forum had encouraged her to take a type of relational risk with her students:

'to ask for feedback from the students.....to ask them as to how our relationship....is assisting your learning or not....I don't think I would have been brave enough to do that with anyone....without the support of that supervision'. (SS3)

Self-reflexivity has steadily grown to be seen as at the heart of what makes both therapeutic (Jensen, 2016) and supervisory (Burnham, 1993) practice systemic. These participants have pointed to the facilitative role of the group in achieving a self-reflexive practice in both of these domains.

Limitations of the Group

Notwithstanding the positive valuation of the supervision of supervision group that was evident within the whole group of eight participant supervisors, there were also a range of shortcomings or limitations experienced by some participants concerning the functioning of the group. What this theme essentially points towards are some potential challenges for group members arising from either the internal organisation of the group or an uncertainty relating to the identity of the group. Hence, the two sub-themes attaching to this theme are: Group Process; and, Group Identity.

Group Process

Three of the participants made some reflections about how the group process may have inhibited certain explorations or expressions. One participant felt that:

> *'...there may have been some avoidance on occasion.....as I hear myself talk to you....God, was it too comfortable?'* (SS5)

The same participant later elaborated a little more on the same reservation:

> *'Maybe we didn't develop it into a lot of personal resonances because probably there wasn't enough time for that....there could have been a lot more space for us to develop.... and look at ourselves, at how we were managing as a group.'* (SS5)

There is an interesting contrast here between the two extracts where 'time', with its impersonal character, is seen as the limiting factor in the second extract while 'avoidance', which implies a type of agency, accounts for limitations in the first.

A second participant also commented on what she experienced as missing within the group process:

> *'...we are always so positive as systemic psychotherapists and that's what we try to do but actually some groups can be incredibly destructive and I remember this whole idea of the anti-group.....I think what we don't do in the forum is the idea of group reflexivity.....but I wouldn't feel comfortable to have that conversation.........I think.............it's about the culture'.* (SS4)

The same participant expanded on how the group process as she experienced it inhibited certain kinds of expression:

> *'I could never imagine getting upset in this context...I'm not sure I would let myself....I'm not sure if that's part of the rules of this group.....I'm not sure if that's the culture.....it's very professional.....there haven't been conversations where people have got upset'.* (SS4)

A third participant tried to express something else that was experienced as challenging, and perhaps limiting, about the group process underpinning the supervision of supervision event:

> '*...at times I experienced a certain......no actually I was going to say competitiveness but I don't think I experienced that....generally I think people have been generous.....there's a generosity of...you know....and a shared idea of us struggling to give the best to these students..... what I mean competitiveness I think I was more thinking about was like a caution sometimes to appear like you didn't know what you were......you know maybe a professional pride maybe.......so I sometimes do wonder are we as kind of open as you would be in a private... sometimes I wonder about that..*' (SS1)

This participant, towards the end of the extract, seems to be contrasting some of the challenges experienced in the group supervision context—namely, the complexities of having to position yourself in some way in front of your colleagues and peers—with the freedom to be more 'open' in the private context of individual supervision.

This sub-theme may well have an intimate connection with the following sub-theme of 'group identity'. Such connection will be explored in the 'discussion of findings' section of this chapter.

Group Identity

It was clear from the participant interviews that the supervision forum convened about once per month for a period of either one hour or one and a half hours. The group is now in its ninth year of operation and functions without any defined leader or facilitator. Some participants expressed reservations relating to what they experienced as an uncertainty regarding the kind of group the supervision forum is while others expressed some reservations about the internal organisation of the group. Yet others had an appreciation for the benefits of what had evolved over time.

With regard to the character and *identity of the group* one participant commented about her early experiences in the group:

> '*I think initially it was difficult for me to understand what it was....I wasn't really sure how it worked....there was a sense that everyone knew each other and I didn't know anybody.*' (SS4)

Later the same participant commented further on what she experienced as the uncertain nature of the group:

> '*...it's not an unstructured process group, it's not a structured business group....I don't think it knows where it fits on that.....management meeting* versus *a group......it doesn't know where on that polarity it is.*' (SS4)

A second participant expressed a range of contrasting feelings about this uncertainty concerning the nature of the group and how they experienced the impact of this on the development of their *sense of safety* in the group:

> '*I think I was ok with that uncertainty and I suppose some of the silence* (their own) *would have been part of that.......and then there's also something about the safety.....you know everybody in the group and I don't.....you have to wait to be sure it's safe before....those*

safety aspects in the beginning.......that they are not an issue but you just have to be clear.... what's ok to be said, not said, what's talked about.......if there was limits'.(SS6)

A third participant expressed something about her beginning experience in the group related to this uncertainty:

'I found it a bit daunting in the beginning....I was a newbie...and I didn't quite know what I was supposed to be at'. (SS8)

This uncertainty about the identity of the group was further reflected in the comments of two other participants about the current name of the group. One of these participants reflected:

'I often wonder do we need to look at the title....supervision has got so many connotations attached to it.....do we need to think of a name that responds to what the group is about differently.....it is about supervision, but.......how supervision is used in other contexts and it can have a negative type of context......something about the importance of creating a space where people can come together and reflect.' (SS6)

The second of these two supervisors reflected on the connection of the name of the group to her experience of what the group was for:

'What is the group really for? Is it about supervision of supervision? ......it is not.....that's not where that comes.....I call it peer supervision in my diary.....I see it as supervision of me as a trainer rather than supervision of me as a live supervisor'. (SS4)

Participants' comments clearly indicated that the *internal organisation* of the group had moved from being a more structured group in its earlier years to a less structured and more open experience in recent years. Five of the participants offered comments which indicated different degrees of reservation about this transition. One participant seemed to indicate that something may have been lost but also gained in the transition from more to less structure within the group's own internal operations:

'...the group has moved from quite a structured peer group to maybe a less......there's pros and cons in that....I like structure and focus so when the group was structured that way where there was a very definite issue that somebody wanted to bring in.....that particular time was given......and then reflection.....I did get a lot from that. But when it moved to a more open-ended......and just seeing what somebody might bring....there was a fluidity in that.......sometimes touching on something that quite a few people might have felt strongly about.......so a bit of both......that works best.......there is an edge in your listening to one person'. (SS7)

A second participant contrasted the internal organisation of the group in its early years with how it had evolved in more recent years:

'..there was always a structure.....around having a particular theme or one person would identify an issue and that one of the team would have facilitated conversation around that......that gave someone the space to talk and the rest of us would listen, engage, reflect....I liked that structure so again it was an opportunity to listen and learn......that has evolved over time with the change of group composition......it has got a lot less structure.....more driven by the agenda on the day.......when you have got a structure you have got a facilitator ......it gives a sense of focus or a sense of direction.....in supervision it would be very easy to keep a very thin conversation for the duration.' (SS2)

Two other participants took a different focus on the transition within the group's operating procedures and did not share the reservations expressed by participants in the preceding two extracts. One of these participants noted that:

> *'...in the early sessions there was kind of very distinctly a reflective space and it still is...... When you know people very well sometimes you can get into things very quickly rather than maybe setting the space out.'* (SS5)

The second supervisor saw the transitions in internal organisation as giving rise to something very positive for her:

> *'I think the group has maybe shifted, changed in how we organise ourselves......sometimes it started in a more.......where we possibly would have interviewed each other and reflected back and did a lot more of that......and somehow there's more of a shared experience now..... and the trust has been established and it is easier for the group to challenge or reflect without needing to use that structure.'* (SS3)

As can be seen from the above extracts not all participants experienced deficits arising from the structure of the group as it has evolved over time. This variation in experience provides a challenge to analysis that will be taken up in the next section of the chapter.

Impact on Supervision

The final theme constructed from the data concerns the impact on their supervision practice that was experienced by the research participants as arising from their participation in the supervision of supervision group. This theme was chosen because of its relationship to one of the central research questions which explored the connections that participants made between their participation in the supervision of supervision group and their supervision practice. Hence, what this theme is centrally concerned with is the connections the participants made between their participation experiences in the supervision forum and their supervisory practice as they have seen it unfold. The following are the four sub-themes attaching to this theme: Supervisory Position; Assessment; Boundary Maintenance; and, Person of the Supervisor.

Supervisory Position

A number of participants spoke about the way the group helped them to maintain their position as supervisor within their supervision of a training group. Referring to the impact of the group one supervisor noted:

> *'..it puts me back in the supervision, the supervisor's position, and takes me away from the therapist's position....when I get into that struggle I become the frustrated therapist behind the screen.....I feel I can let it go and maybe the forum has helped me to do that a little bit more.'* (SS1)

A second participant spoke of the way the group was experienced as helping with this 'letting go':

> '..*the letting go of your therapist's hat and being able to talk about that....sometimes I think that struggle is over but it comes back again and again...being able to talk about that...... even getting to know you are not the only one who feels it at times.*' (SS8)

Another participant commented upon a different way of experiencing this struggle:

> '*What has been really useful in being part of this was the idea of ....the frustrated therapist....how to manage that piece of leaving the students to grow and develop........that's what I saw the space as...that bit of myself, becoming aware of that bit....of wanting to control, and letting go of that*'. (SS6)

The same participant noted how the group helped with a double kind of movement. On the one hand, they needed to take a certain control on occasions within a supervision group because of the supervisor's ethical responsibility for client welfare, and, on the other hand, to let go of that control. She spoke of:

> '*....moving from the frustrated therapist with a different style to actually knowing there's a space here I have to step into.....and then to step back from that*'. (SS6)

Assessment

Six of the eight participants reflected on the impact their participation in the supervision of supervision group had on their engagement in the process of student assessment. One participant described the group's impact on her decision-making process regarding the relative strengths of a student in a clinical practice module:

> '*A lot of the ways in which I have found it helpful is when you are struggling with a student and what I found helpful is deciding whether it's because the student is a weak student or is it because of the style clashing.....that your style clashes with their style....is it something you are missing.....that you are not seeing the full picture because you are too close to it, or whatever, so I found it very helpful that way to allow me to stand back and, you know, kind of in a sort of more objective way*'. (SS1)

A second participant emphasised the role of the supervision forum in assisting their process of self-reflexivity around the supervisory task of judging a student's therapeutic practice:

> '*It was really important to have the voices of the forum in helping me think about how I was judging their practice, how I was thinking about how they were presenting, how was I experiencing them being reflective or not...*' (SS3)

Another participant underlined the group's role in helping her think about the fairness of her assessments:

> '*...it is also helpful in terms of helping me reflect on the part of being a gatekeeper...thinking, are you being fair?*' (SS5)

One of the most experienced participants described the group as helping her to position herself within a changing field as she addressed the task of student assessment:

> *'...sometimes when I would come to assessing students and doing the assessment part of it that I did express concerns at times........one of the ways it helped is actually for me to realise that things don't stay the same...that programs do move on........that I also need to move on.'* (SS7)

It is unsurprising in the context of a postgraduate training program in family therapy that supervisors would look to their supervision of supervision experience as a resource in managing the challenges of the assessment task. What is of real interest, however, is the different ways that supervisors conceptualise that task as well as the different ways they experience the group as supporting them in the same task.

Boundary Maintenance

Different kinds of threats to boundary maintenance within student supervision were noted by three of the eight participants. One supervisor appreciated the boundary maintaining function of the supervision forum in the face of all that a supervisor might be called upon to give within the supervisory role:

> *'...we give a huge amount of energy, time, care and consideration........sometimes in the process we can get very tired ourselves or stressed a bit.....it puts a boundary around it..... this is what supervision is.'* (SS7)

Another participant pointed to a similar impact the group had for them in the context of her support of a supervisee in personal crisis:

> *'...they were going through personal struggles....but I took on too much....I brought it to the group and by that time I was very distressed....I was held by the group.....people weren't judging me negatively...'.* (SS8)

Person of the Supervisor

Half of the participants spoke of their experience of the supervision forum as facilitating them to come into the space of supervision as their personal selves rather than simply presenting a professional persona. One participant reported that:

> *'...some of the supervision forum helped me with going in as myself into the clinical group and really paying attention to how do I relate to each of the students..'.* (SS7)

A second participant emphasised how the group had helped with:

> *'bringing me, Danya, into the work....it's a more personal space.'* (SS3)

Another participant referred to both his presence in his clinical supervision group and in the supervision forum:

> *'I am coming in here as Alexander....and that is who I am in this forum'.* (SS2)

A fourth participant spoke about how she perceived the supervision forum as facilitating the bringing of herself into her supervision group with students:

> *'..and that you have to bring yourself with all strengths and the things that are different to us....it did that and I think a lot of that was through other people in the peer group....their openness and their struggle and their frustration at times and their questions....it was a shared space in that and really important I think.....Look after the parents!'* (SS7)

This sub-theme seems closely connected to the sub-theme of self-reflexivity mentioned earlier under the theme of 'positive functions of the group'. It may be that the exposure to a range of differences of different kinds (multiple voices, multiple perspectives) in the supervision forum creates a context for the greater appreciation by each supervisor of the uniqueness of their own experiences and of their own life. This appreciation may well bring with it a desire to be more fully themselves in the supervisory context at the same time as feeling an imperative for that self to be a reflective self in the context of their supervisory role.

Discussion of Findings

This qualitative study invited eight participant supervisors to share their experiences of, and reflections upon, participation in an ongoing peer supervision of supervision group attached to the postgraduate family and couple therapy training program where they were engaged as supervisors. The findings of this study suggest that the supervision of supervision group is a highly valued space for all eight supervisors for a variety of different reasons which include its provision of a sense of support, experiences of connection and collegiality, and a space for sharing experiences apart from trainees. The study also found that this group supervision of supervision vehicle held four key positive functions for the participants as well as two main limiting factors. The group offered, on the positive side, a context of multiple voices against which supervisors worked out their own positions on matters of concern, was an antidote to feelings of isolation attaching to the supervisory role, provided a holding and containing function in the face of losses of different kinds and promoted attention to self-reflexive processes within supervisory functions. Limitations of the group were felt to be bound up with a lack of attention to group process and an uncertainty with regard to the identity and precise nature of the group. Finally, the study found four key areas in which supervisors felt that participation in the supervision of supervision group impacted their supervision practice. These areas were the maintenance of a supervisory position with supervisees, the assessment of supervisee competencies, boundary maintenance within the supervisory relationship and the facilitation of the ongoing presence of the person-of-the-supervisor in the performance of the supervisory task.

The findings in this study concerning the positive functions of this group supervision of supervision vehicle resonate strongly with the reflections of Yerushalmi

(1999) on the same type of structure within the psychoanalytic/psychodynamic training context. He notes the emotional containment function that a group of professional peers can provide for each other in the face of the many potentially overwhelming experiences and responsibilities that can arise in supervision. Such containment allows supervisors an opportunity to relax and regress for some moments from the deep emotional tensions associated with supervisory responsibilities on the way to reorganising themselves emotionally and practically as they address complex tasks once more. One of the participant supervisors (SS7) spoke of the way the group assisted them in 'relaxing into' the supervisory role 'a bit more' and in carrying the responsibilities of the supervision without anxiety.

Yerushalmi also noted the function of such groups in helping their members cope with narcissistic vulnerabilities of different kinds. While supervisees must regularly cope with the narcissistic vulnerability of being in the position of novice therapists, supervisors in psychotherapy are, for the most part, in either the midlife or later life stage of their development (Yerushalmi, 1993). As such they are challenged to cope with what Segal (1981) refers to as 'the indignities of life' that attach to their developmental stage. Supervisors must cope with various personal losses which can include some loss of physical appearance and function, the loss of children through growing up or moving away, as well as the loss of loved ones through death or separation. While the participants in this study only made indirect allusions to their life stage (retirement from employment, impending professional retirement) the greatest reported vulnerability they experienced was the unanticipated loss through death of one of their colleagues who was part of their group. However, many of the participants also noted the function of the group in holding and containing them in the face of other losses such as children leaving home, the loss of other loved ones through death as well as impending losses associated with institutional changes.

A further vulnerability alluded to just once in the study by one participant, but seen as critical by Yerushalmi (1999), arises from the similar professional status of the supervisor members of the group. He reminds us that apart from 'the support, holding, and sense of similarity that the members of the group provide for each of the participants, there is also competition for recognition, admiration of one's professional methods, and power' (p. 436). He perceives it as important for 'the inner strength and greater cohesiveness of the supervisors' professional personality' (p. 436) that the supervision of supervision group satisfies these two conflicting sets of needs simultaneously. In the study reported here there was little recognition by participants of possible competition between professionals of equal status and just as little mention of the theme of professional power. One participant (SS1) mentioned the possibility of competitiveness in the group but immediately replaced it, initially, with the idea of generosity and the idea of a shared struggle to give of their best to the students. This idea of competition was later transformed by the same participant into the idea of caution. They wondered whether a kind of professional pride in front of one's colleagues and peers might have produced a caution in group members in terms of being as open as one might have been in the more private context of individual supervision. Another participant (SS2) made the only reference in the study to the issue of power which clearly related to the use of power in the supervision group rather than the supervision of supervision group. How can we understand the relative absence of reports of these themes of competition and power in the relationship between group members in the context of this current study of systemic supervisor experiences of a supervision of supervision group? In the following paragraphs a possible explanation is offered concerning this relative absence. The exploration and explanation are connected to the character of the group as a leaderless group of peers as well as to certain contemporary discourses that define systemic psychotherapy.

The idea of equality was an important feature of group relationships for the participants in the study. Throughout its 9-year history the group had never operated with a designated supervisor or supervisor consultant. This is in contrast to other supervision of supervision groups already described in the literature (e.g. DiMino & Risler, 2012; Power, 2013; Yerushalmi, 1999). The group may have moved over time from exhibiting a more structured internal operating framework to a less structured, more open and fluent style of mutual engagement but it was always a group of peers. The terms 'collaborative' and 'dialogical' were used on many occasions by the participants to describe approaches to their supervision practice as well as to their own relationships within the supervision forum. Indeed, these terms seemed to characterise the culture of the supervision group as a peer supervision group. Such a culture seemed to maximise certain 'peer' aspects of the group such as connection, collegiality, sharing experience and support. At the same time, it may have set some challenges with respect to the 'supervision' character of the group. One voice within the participants noted the asymmetry between the supervision operating in trainee clinical supervision groups and processes at work within the supervision forum. Another voice was significantly attuned to the negative, surveillance-type meanings that often attach to the term 'supervision'. Such perspective has already been noted in Mander (2002). Fine and Turner (2014) comment upon the many complex challenges facing collaborative systemic supervisors as they take care of issues of power in supervisory relationships. While not explicitly naming assessment activity as an exercise of power, it was central to the culture of this group of supervisors to achieve as much fairness and balance as possible in their evaluation of student clinical performance. When it came to the performance of their own relationships within the supervision forum the hierarchy which was present within their own supervision training groups was formally dispensed with. In this 'turning away' from hierarchy it may be that power relations and the hierarchy on which they were based continued to be practised in an oblique way.

It may be that one root of the reported absence of attempts to address group process within the supervision forum stem from ambivalences within the discourses surrounding collaborative systemic supervision concerning the exercise of power. It may be that addressing these issues would involve, in the minds of participants, the exercise of a certain kind of leadership and power that could threaten the ongoing supply of the 'peer' fruits of the group experience. Alternatively, Gediman and Wolkenfeld (1980) suggest that such limitations may be a necessary part of peer arrangements whose usefulness can be undermined by defensive collusion. Power (2013) acknowledges that peer groups will clearly differ between themselves with regard to their capacity to deal with their own group process and suggests periodic external consultation as one way of safeguarding 'against the tendency amongst colleagues to keep things comfortable' (p. 396).

While this was an ongoing, open supervision of supervision group of peers who shared the same professional status as systemic supervisors, there were obvious, but unnamed, hierarchies within it. As can be seen from the profiles of participants, they differed amongst themselves, sometimes quite considerably, with respect to their experience as systemic supervisors and to their length of participation in the supervision forum. The apparent lack of introduction of new members to the kind of group it was intended to be created a working hierarchy in which new members seemed to have to take a 'wait and see' approach as they learned the operating rules of the group from the longer-standing group members. It is notable, however, that the newer members did not feel that a more explicit introduction to the group, its functions and its rules would have assisted them to any great degree in more speedily acquiring a sense of safety about their participation.

The group of impacts on supervision practice noted in this study and experienced as connected to participation in the supervision forum share some similarities with previous studies and also exemplify some differences. Wheeler and King (2001), in their 17 year old study of the supervision of supervision, found that the areas supervisors most often brought to the supervision of their supervision were ethical issues, boundaries and competence in supervisees. The current study, set within a systemic training context, found that two of the four key impacts on supervision practice were boundary maintenance and assessment. The issue of boundary maintenance speaks both to the emotional intensity of the learning environment for both supervisees and supervisors and to the multiple and varied demands that supervisors face in the training context. In the context of this study the withstanding of the challenges to boundary maintenance seemed to be achieved through the holding (Bion, 1961) and containing (Winnicott, 1958) functions of the supervision of supervision group. While Hanks and Vetere (2016) have drawn attention to the need to pay attention within supervision to burn-out prevention for both systemic psychotherapists and their supervisors this finding concerning boundary maintenance shows the importance for supervisors of the supervision of supervision in the prevention of their own burn-out.

It is unsurprising that in the current study, set in a systemic training context, one of the key areas of impact on supervision practice experienced as arising from participation in group-based supervision of supervision was the assessment of supervisee competencies. However, what is important in this study is the way this impact was achieved through the promotion of the self-reflexive dimension in each supervisor's performance of this supervisory function. For many systemic supervisors this dimension is the cornerstone of an ethical therapeutic or supervisory practice (Burnham, 1993; Jensen, 2016; Kohnstamm & Vetere, 2016).

Perhaps the first of the four sub-themes relating to impacts on supervision practice arising in the study's findings, namely, the maintenance of a supervisory position, is uniquely felt within systemic supervision. While potentially challenging in any type of psychotherapy supervision this supervisory skill is most severely tested in the live-supervision context. The live supervision of supervisee's practice remains a hallmark of systemic supervision training. In this context the supervisor is directly exposed to their supervisee's practice and its immediate impact on client welfare. It is here that the containment of therapeutic impulses in the supervisor and the maintenance of their supervisory position become pivotal in the learning and development of supervisees. The findings of this study clearly suggest the contribution of the supervision of supervision group to the performance of this skill in the concrete moments of the supervisory relationship.

Conclusion

The limits of the current study are bound up with its focus on a single supervision of supervision group within a single context of systemic supervision, namely, that of systemic psychotherapy training. Its sample of participants was consequently limited to the full cohort of systemic supervisors engaged with this group. The study's data collection methods were limited to a series of eight individual, semi-structured interviews. Hence, the study did not benefit from the enriched quality of data that might have emerged from a mixture of focus groups and individual interviews. A further limitation of the study lay in the gender balance (seven females, one male) of the participants. Notwithstanding these limitations, the study allowed for the examination in rich detail of the experiences of eight supervisors of their participation in the same supervision of supervision group over a relatively long period of time. The findings of the study clearly endorse the value of a group supervision of supervision vehicle for systemic supervisors in the training context. The study raises interesting questions concerning the way in which a systemic supervision of supervision group without formal facilitation or leadership may enhance the peer-related benefits of group participation such as a sense of support, collegiality and connection at the expense of supervisory benefits arising from an examination of group process that would require the more explicit use of power by members of the group. The discussion of findings suggested that such a 'trade-off' may be related to the way the local, supervisory culture is impacted by ambivalences within wider contemporary discourses in systemic psychotherapy concerning the use of power.

Acknowledgement My thanks to Professor Per Jensen who supervised this research study.

References

Abela, A., & Sammut Scerri, C. (2010). Managing multiple relationships in supervision: Dealing with complexity. In C. Burck & G. Daniel (Eds.), *Mirrors and reflections: Processes of systemic supervision* (pp. 289–308). London: Karnac.

Bion, W. R. (1961). *Experiences in groups*. London: Tavistock.

Boyatzis, R. E. (1998). *Transforming qualitative information: Thematic analysis and code development*. London: Sage.
Braun, V., & Clarke, V. (2006). Using thematic analysis in psychology. *Qualitative Research in Psychology, 3*, 77–101.
Burck, C., & Daniel, G. (2010). *Mirrors and reflections: Processes of systemic supervision*. London: Karnac.
Burnham, J. (1993). Systemic supervision: The evolution of reflexivity in the context of the supervisory relationship. *Human Systems: Journal of Systemic Consultation and Management, 4*(3–4), 349–381.
DiMino, J. L., & Risler, R. (2012). Group supervision of supervision: A relational approach for training supervisors. *Journal of College Student Psychotherapy, 26*, 61–72.
Fine, M., & Turner, J. (2014). Minding the power in collaborative systemic supervision. In T. C. Todd & C. L. Storm (Eds.), *The complete systemic supervisor* (pp. 297–313). London: Wiley.
Gediman, H., & Wolkenfeld, F. (1980). The parallelism phenomenon in psychoanalysis and supervision: Its reconsideration as a triadic system. *Psychoanalytic Quarterly, 49*, 234–255.
Gergen, K. J. (1985). The social constructionist movement in modern psychology. *American Psychologist, 40*, 266–75.
Gergen, K. J. (1994). *Realities and relationships: Soundings in social construction*. Cambridge, MA: Harvard University Press.
Gergen, K. J. (2009). *An invitation to social construction* (2nd ed.). Los Angeles: Sage.
Haber, R., Marshall, D., Cowan, K., Vanlandingham, A., Gerson, M., & Fitch, J. C. (2009). Live supervision of supervision: Perpendicular interventions in parallel processes. *The Clinical Supervisor, 28*, 72–90.
Hanks, H., & Vetere, A. (2016). Working at the extremes: The impact on us of doing the work. In A. Vetere & P. Stratton (Eds.), *Interacting selves: Systemic solutions for personal and professional development* (pp. 65–84). London: Routledge.
Hardy, K. V., & Bobes, T. (2017). *Promoting cultural sensitivity in supervision: A manual for practitioners*. London: Routledge.
Haug, I. E., & Storm, C. L. (2014). Drawing the line in ethical issues in systemic supervision. In T. C. Todd & C. L. Storm (Eds.), *The complete systemic supervisor* (pp. 19–42). London: Wiley.
Jacobs, M. (2000). A roundtable of views. In B. Lawton & C. Feltham (Eds.), *Taking supervision forward* (pp. 201–210). London: Sage.
Jensen, P. (2016). Mind the map: Circular processes between the therapist, the client and the therapist's personal life. In A. Vetere & P. Stratton (Eds.), *Interacting selves: Systemic solutions for personal and professional development* (pp. 33–50). London: Routledge.
Kohnstamm, B., & Vetere, A. (2016). A supervisor's progression: From personal and professional development in group settings to the inclusion of the self of the therapist in supervision. In A. Vetere & P. Stratton (Eds.), *Interacting selves: Systemic solutions for personal and professional development* (pp. 85–98). London: Routledge.
Ladany, N., Constantine, M., Miller, K., Erickson, C., & Muse-Burke, J. (2000). Supervisor countertransference: A qualitative investigation into its identification and description. *Journal of Counselling Psychology, 47*(1), 102–115.
Leader, D. (2010). Some thoughts on supervision. *British Journal of Psychotherapy, 26*(2), 228–241.
Mander, G. (2002). Supervision of supervision: Specialism or new profession? In C. Driver & E. Martin (Eds.), *Supervising psychotherapy* (pp. 132–139). London: Sage.
McNamee, S., & Gergen, K. J. (Eds.). (1992). *Therapy as social construction*. New York: Macmillan.
Power, A. (2013). Supervision of supervision: How many mirrors do we need? *British Journal of Psychotherapy, 29*(3), 389–404.
Prouty, A. M., & Storm, C. L. (2014). Training the next generation of systemic supervisors. In T. C. Todd & C. L. Storm (Eds.), *The complete systemic supervisor* (pp. 399–416). London: Wiley.

Reiner, P. A. (2014). Systemic psychodynamic supervision. In T. C. Todd & C. L. Storm (Eds.), *The complete systemic supervisor* (pp. 166–185). London: Wiley.
Segal, N. P. (1981). Narcissism and adaptation to indignity. *International Journal of Psychoanalysis, 62*, 465–476.
Shotter, J. (1993). *Conversational realities*. London: Sage.
Todd, T. C., & Storm, C. L. (Eds.). (2014). *The complete systemic supervisor: Context, philosophy and pragmatics* (2nd ed.). London: Wiley.
Wheeler, S., & King, D. (2001). Do counselling supervisors want or need to have their supervision supervised? An exploratory study. *British Journal of Guidance and Counselling, 28*(2), 279–290.
Winnicott, D. W. (1958). *The maturational processes and the facilitating environment*. London: Hogarth Press.
Yerushalmi, H. (1993). Stagnation in supervision as a result of developmental problems in the middle-aged supervisor. *The Clinical Supervisor, 11*, 63–81.
Yerushalmi, H. (1999). The roles of group supervision of supervision. *Psychoanalytic Psychology, 16*(3), 426–447.

Index

A. Vetere, J. Sheehan (eds.), *Supervision of Family Therapy and Systemic Practice*, Focused Issues in Family Therapy, https://doi.org/10.1007/978-3-319-68591-5

www.ingramcontent.com/pod-product-compliance
Ingram Content Group UK Ltd.
Pitfield, Milton Keynes, MK11 3LW, UK
UKHW020242290926
15470UKWH00002B/689
9783319685908